Housing the Aged
DESIGN DIRECTIVES
AND POLICY CONSIDERATIONS

Housing

the Aged

DESIGN DIRECTIVES AND POLICY CONSIDERATIONS

EDITED BY **Victor Regnier, A.I.A.**

Associate Professor
Schools of Architecture and Gerontology
Andrus Gerontology Center
University of Southern California
Los Angeles, California

AND **Jon Pynoos, Ph.D.**

United Parcel Service Associate Professor
of Gerontology and Urban Planning
Leonard Davis School of Gerontology
Director, Program in Policy and Services Research
Andrus Gerontology Center
University of Southern California
Los Angeles, California

ELSEVIER

NEW YORK • AMSTERDAM • LONDON

Elsevier Science Publishing Co., Inc.
52 Vanderbilt Avenue, New York, New York 10017

Sole distributors outside the United States and Canada:
Elsevier Science Publishers B.V.
P.O. Box 211, 1000 AE Amsterdam, the Netherlands

Library of Congress Cataloging in Publication Data

Housing the aged.

    Bibliography: p.
    Includes index.
    1. Aged—Dwellings.   I. Regnier, Victor, 1947–
II. Pynoos, Jon.
HD7287.9.H7   1987   363.5'9   87-5253
ISBN 0-444-01012-2

Current printing (last digit):
10 9 8 7 6 5 4 3 2 1

Manufactured in the United States of America

CONTENTS

FOREWORD

This book's unique contribution is summarized well in the subtitle: *Design Directives and Policy Considerations*. There has been a steady stream of published research on housing for the elderly over the past two decades. While much of it had, to be sure, clear design and policy implications, these implications all too frequently had to be made explicit by the reader. To a great extent this lack of explication by researchers had resulted from their hesitancy to develop directives for decision making from empirical data they may consider too fragmented, methods that may be called into question, and the difficulties of isolating specific design or policy variables from broader contexts. However, it is clear that the continuing need for improved environments for older persons will not await the completion of all requisite research. What is needed is an approach, concurrent with on-going research, that sensitizes sponsors, designers, planners, developers, and managers to the characteristics and needs of this specialized user group and then applies general principals to improve the quality of the environment. This book goes a long way in relieving the burden of interpreting esoteric research findings into meaningful language and practical judgments that can be applied to problem situations.

This book both summarizes most of the important research of this period and provides the explicit links between the research findings and their applied significance. The editors have achieved a most unusual degree of coherence among the chapters by adopting a common framework that highlights the relationship between research and practice.

The content of the book is presented from the perspective of a variety of disciplines and covers housing environments for the well/active, moderately impaired, and frail elderly. While the contributions of architects and planners are prominent, the mix is enriched by expertise from the fields of psychology, sociology, industrial design, and economics. Their combined message thus makes the important point that the needs of the older user are the concern of many disciplines. Only through the continued collaboration of such problem solvers can the communication barrier that blocks design and policy-relevant knowledge from implementation be diminished.

M. Powell Lawton

Philadelphia, Pennsylvania

PREFACE

This edited book evolved out of our desire to assemble materials that could be of use to architects, planners, developers, and other decision makers involved in the design, planning, construction, and production of housing for older people.

The housing types discussed cover a broad spectrum, from individual dwelling units to institutions. The book is organized into three sections: planned housing that primarily serves the well, active elderly; supportive housing that serves moderately impaired older persons; and housing environments for frail or handicapped older persons. The boundaries of these categories are, of course, permeable, and authors often cross over them in their discussions, treating housing as a continuum. Nevertheless, for purposes of organization, we feel the partitioning will be helpful.

As architects and urban planners, we have been frustrated by the lack of specific information that has resulted from much of the policy and design research conducted over the last 10 to 15 years. For this reason, each chapter in this book includes a section on design directives and policy considerations, which we have jointly authored with each contributor. These sections "translate" the research described in each chapter for the reader. In doing this we have been careful to maintain high standards in framing our conclusions, using the authors to provide guidance and perspective on their own work. The result, we believe, is a collection of carefully worded statements that take the most important and salient aspects of the research and describe it in simple "action" language. In making these translations we have been careful to avoid simple-minded applications of the research findings. We believe that these directives and policy concerns are detailed enough to stretch the application of the research to its practical limit while not over-generalizing the work. We hope this publication will not only provide practical information to design professionals but will also provide researchers with a model that allows the further refinement of research issues for future investigation.

The chapters have been structured within an identical format that allows the reader to make comparisons between chapters or to focus on salient issues developed in each chapter. Topic sentence subheads have been used to facilitate skimming, and illustrations with descriptive captions are located strategically to support chapter discussion and reiterate important findings.

We recognize there is an inevitable interaction between design and policy. The settings in which older people live constitute only one element of a larger system encompassing environmental, social, organizational, and political components. The environment as older persons experience it is a function of the interactions of these subsystems. For example, the provision of space for health services or recreational activities in an elderly housing development often will be maximally effective only if staff and management encourage their use.

Similarly, such facilities are more likely to be used if residents have a voice in their programming. Furthermore, in some cases the existence of such facilities is dependent upon government approval of funds for their inclusion. Thus, while design directives and policy considerations are treated independently in this volume for the sake of clarity, they remain interrelated.

One frustration in assembling this book has been that the research projects available for translation into design directives and policy considerations did not comprehensively cover all important housing concerns. However, the fundamental topics that impact the design and organization of housing activities are addressed by this collection of work. In this regard, the two introductory chapters on design directives and policy considerations review twelve thematic design and policy issues defined by the work collected in this book.

Together the themes and their discussion provide a fresh conceptualization of the research ideas explored in this volume as well as providing a context for further understanding the collective impact of the work. The two introductory chapters also identify future research topics that deserve closer scrutiny and more careful attention.

ACKNOWLEDGMENTS

In constructing this book, patience and cooperation has been essential. Perhaps the most patient have been the contributors, who have provided us with much information during the six-year gestation period of the publication. Almost every chapter was extensively rewritten, sometimes two or three times, in order to simplify the language and focus the research on issues of practical import. All of the contributors have been helpful in pursuing this final format and in identifying the most practical and helpful insights from their own work.

In addition, secretarial and support staffs from the University of Illinois and the University of Southern California were involved in the refining of the manuscripts and patiently helped to assemble the final product. Partial support for this publication was provided by the UCLA/USC Long Term Care Gerontology Center, funded through the Administration on Aging.

Last, but not least, we both owe a deep debt of gratitude to our respective spouses, Judy and Elyse, who contributed intellectual insights as well as encouragement during this period, and to our children Jennifer, Heather, Jessica, Rebecca, and Joshua who lost their daddies to this project on numerous weekends and evenings.

Victor Regnier and Jon Pynoos

Los Angeles, California

CONTRIBUTORS

Sharmalee Bernhardt, M.S.G.-M.P.A.
Administrator, Easton-Lincoln Nursing Home, North Easton, Massachusetts

Dorothy Butterfield, M.L.A.
Assistant Professor, School of Landscape Architecture, College of Design, Louisiana State University, Baton Rouge, Louisiana

Frances Carp, Ph.D.
Research Psychologist, Wright Institute, Berkeley, California

David Christensen, Ph.D.
Associate Planner, Golden Gate Bridge Highway and Transportation District, San Rafael, California

Evelyn Cohen, M.A.
Gerontological Design Consultant, Evelyn Cohen and Associates, Santa Monica, California

Galen Cranz, Ph.D.
Associate Professor, Department of Architecture, University of California at Berkeley, Berkeley, California

Thomas G. David, Ph.D.
Coordinator of Clinical Research, Division of Adolescent Medicine, Teenage Health Center, Childrens Hospital of Los Angeles, Los Angeles, California

Linda J. Davis, M.P.H., Ph.D., OTR
Director, Pacific Geriatric Educational Center, Assistant Professor of
Clinical Psychiatry and Adjunct Assistant Professor of Gerontology,
University of Southern California, Los Angeles, California

Chester Hartman, Ph.D.
Fellow, Institute for Policy Studies, Washington, D.C.

Robert Herman, A.I.A.
Principal, Robert Herman Associates, San Francisco, California

Leonard F. Heumann, Ph.D.
Professor, Department of Urban and Regional Planning, Housing
Research and Development Program, University of Illinois at Urbana-
Champaign, Urbana, Illinois

Lorraine G. Hiatt, Ph.D.
Consultant, Environment Design and Aging, New York, New York

Jerry Horovitz
Urban Planning Consultant, San Francisco, California

Michael E. Hunt, Arch.D.
Assistant Professor, Department of Environment, Textiles, and Design,
School of Family Resources and Consumer Sciences, University of
Wisconsin-Madison, Madison, Wisconsin

Joseph A. Koncelik, B.A., M.A.
Professor and Chairman, Department of Industrial Design, The Ohio
State University, Columbus, Ohio

Sonne Lemke, Ph.D.
Psychologist Research Associate, Social Ecology Laboratory and
Geriatric Research, Education and Clinical Center, Veterans
Administration Medical Center, Palo Alto, California

Rudolf H. Moos, Ph.D.
Professor, Social Ecology Laboratory, Stanford University Medical
Center, Stanford, California

Arvid E. Osterburg, Arch.D.
Associate Professor, Department of Architecture, Iowa State University,
Ames, Iowa

Leon A. Pastalan, Ph.D.
Director, The National Center for Housing and Living Arrangements for
Older Americans; Professor of Architecture, University of Michigan,
Ann Arbor, Michigan

Jon Pynoos, Ph.D.
United Parcel Service Associate Professor of Gerontology and Urban
Planning, Leonard Davis School of Gerontology; Director, Program in
Policy and Services Research, Andrus Gerontology Center, University
of Southern California, Los Angeles, California

Victor Regnier, A.I.A.
Associate Professor, Schools of Architecture and Gerontology, Andrus Gerontology Center, University of Southern California, Los Angeles, California

Edward Steinfeld, Arch.D.
Professor, Department of Architecture, State University of New York at Buffalo, Buffalo, New York

Raymond J. Struyk, Ph.D.
Director, International Activities Center, The Urban Institute, Washington, D.C.

Gerald D. Weisman, Ph.D.
Associate Professor, School of Architecture and Urban Planning, University of Wisconsin-Milwaukee, Milwaukee, Wisconsin

Susan Weidemann, Ph.D.
Professor, Department of Landscape Architecture, Housing Research and Development Program, University of Illinois at Urbana-Champaign, Urbana, Illinois

DESIGN DIRECTIVES AND POLICY CONSIDERATIONS
AN OVERVIEW

1

DESIGN DIRECTIVES
Current Knowledge and Future Needs

Victor Regnier

E nvironmental design research in the area of "environments and aging" has focused on the goal of understanding the interactions, interdependencies, and effects between the environment and the aging person. The work in this
area has been carried out primarily by social scientists and by architects with training in social science methods.

Social Science–Based Research is Often Theory Driven

The general criticism of social science–based research is that it is
theory driven and that the results are not in a form that allows
them to be useful to design and policy decision makers. Design-
based research, on the other hand, is sometimes myopic, focusing
on a single example. It has therefore been criticized as lacking the
theoretical foundation necessary for generalizing the results to
other situations and settings.

The happy medium between the theory and practice approach
has been described by Michael Brill as the "squishy middle." It
constitutes an area where little work has taken place but where
more productive and careful attention should be focused in future
research.

Translating Research into Design Decisions is the Critical Problem

Social scientists and environmental designers are responsible for
a large amount of high-quality research in the area of aging and
the environment. However, the difficulties with application, men-

tioned above, have limited the amount of data available to design decision makers. A number of special efforts organized by the Gerontological Society of America and the American Institute of Architects have wrestled with the problem of communicating and translating research findings. These efforts have met with only limited success.

This introductory chapter on design directives and the introductory chapter on policy concerns that follows identify common themes that arise from the research reviewed in this book and identify important topics for further exploration. These themes have special relevance because many chapters respond to them in part or in whole and because they represent a collective synthesis of the research ideas explored. Of further interest are the important research topics that the contributors to this book do not directly acknowledge or address. The final portion of this chapter is devoted to defining and describing some of these important future research issues.

Design Concepts and Environmental Issues

Six design related concepts and issues were identified as cross-cutting themes. Each of these themes has been explicitly or implicitly acknowledged as important by several contributors. Table 1.1 is a matrix that illustrates author by theme. The six themes include:

- Resident satisfaction
- Social interaction
- Management
- Sensory aspects
- Physiological constraints
- Way-finding

In the table, the plus symbol indicates a substantive, empirical, or theoretical focus on the issue, while the zero symbol signifies a less substantive acknowledgment and/or discussion of the theme. Table 1.1 reveals two major clusters of activity and emphasis. Those projects that represent post-occupancy evaluations generally deal with the resident satisfaction, social interaction, and management themes. In contrast, the sensory aspects, physiological constraints, and way-finding themes are tied to more general research explorations, which do not focus on the success or failure of one particular building or a specific collection of buildings.

The following reviews the meaning and relevance of these six themes. The discussion of each theme reveals how each has been defined by the research, why it is important, and what progress

TABLE 1.1 Design Themes Strongly Addressed or Recognized by Authors

Authors	Resident Satisfaction	Social Interaction	Management	Sensory Aspects	Physiological Constraints	Way-Finding
Carp	+	+	+			
Cranz	0	+	0			
Christensen	0	+	+			
Butterfield	+	0	+			
Hartman	0		0			
Moos	+	+	+			
Regnier	0	+	+			
Heumann	0	0	+			
Struyk					+	
Pynoos		0		0	+	
Steinfeld				0	+	
Hiatt	0			+	0	0
Koncelik			0	+	+	+
Osterberg			0	0	0	+
Hunt					0	+
Weisman				0	0	+

Key + = theme strongly addressed
     0 = theme recognized but not strongly addressed

(if any) has been made toward understanding the implications of that theme for design application.

Resident Satisfaction

The identification of general measures of resident satisfaction or the selection of a cluster of attributes that contribute to satisfaction with the environment has been the objective of several contributors. The most sophisticated statistical explorations have sought to identify the specific factors associated with the housing environment that contribute to an overall level of satisfaction or dissatisfaction with the environment.

Management, Maintenance, and Aesthetics Affect Resident Satisfaction: Generally in independent elderly housing, attributes such as maintenance, management, safety, aesthetics, and the unit design are the most influential and powerful factors that influence resident satisfaction. In congregate housing where social, health, and supportive services are provided, management style and management policies take on greater importance.

Regression analyses using satisfaction with the residential environment as the major dependent variable have helped to subdivide the complex gestalt of the housing environment into manageable components. Theoretically, improvements in the most influential components (such as maintenance, management, or aesthetics) have the greatest impact on increasing residential satisfaction.

Resident Satisfaction Research Tends to Be Too Abstract: Criticisms of this research frequently center on the abstract nature of the concepts that are identified. For example, aesthetics may be considered a powerful force in influencing residential satisfaction, but without further elaboration and detailed definition the finding leads to little that can be considered meaningful to designers and policy decision makers. Future research must begin to specify tangible attributes of the physical environment to enable this work to result in effective change.

Longitudinal research with the elderly has also focused on the use of health data, rates of institutional transfers, and even mortality to measure the ultimate effects of "life satisfaction" (Lawton and Cohen, 1974; Carp, 1975b). Because an older population generally declines in overall health status with time, measures that focus on how the environment has supplemented losses, provided support, and mitigated problem circumstances to maximize independence can be particularly useful to design decision makers.

Social Interaction/Social Exchange

One of the primary purposes behind the development of age-segregated housing for the elderly has been the desire to increase opportunities for social interaction and formation of friendships. Implicit in the research that addresses this topic is the assumption that the environment can increase the opportunity to control one's social activity level, which in turn can combat depression and lead to a higher level of life satisfaction. However, there is a general lack of experimental or even quasi-experimental research that has carefully tested this assumption.

Much of the research in this area has come from post-occupancy evaluations, which, through behavior observation and tenant interviews, have sought to identify environmental features and physical configurations that support or encourage socializing (Howell, 1980a; Regnier, 1985b). Spaces intended to promote social interaction—such as community rooms, entry areas, and lounges—are closely scrutinized in these evaluations. Patterns of spatial use from behavioral mapping research combined with attitudinal data from tenants and management can help resolve evaluation questions related to intended or preferred use.

Careful Space Planning Can Lead to a "Friendly" Building: In general, the research has been quite adept at revealing factors associated with successfully designed social spaces. Linking social areas with heavily trafficked circulation routes has been shown to affect the potential for use (Zeisel, Welch, Epp, and Demos, 1983; Howell, 1980a). Similarly, making the space visible before entering (previewing) has been shown to affect the motivation for use (Fig. 1.1). Problems have included the under-utilization of decentralized

FIGURE 1.1   The Captain Clarence Eldridge Congregate House in Hyannis, Massachusetts, contains a "Preview Landing" which overlooks the dining room and lounge space below. This landing allows residents to view the activity below and decide whether or not to participate before they formally enter the space.

lounge spaces and the identification of territorial conflicts that can occur when community and resident populations are accommodated in the same area. These problems have cautioned designers to think carefully about how they intend social spaces to be activated, controlled, and managed.

Designing housing for the elderly to promote friendship formation and sociability is a goal that all designers should embrace. An emphasis on promoting socialization, however, should be coupled with an understanding of privacy and the need to control, manage, and sometimes avoid social interaction. More research is needed to understand how furniture, partial partitions and screens, various amenities and activities, and the ecological composition of the resident population interact and mediate the social success of purpose-built projects.

Management and Design

Some researchers have theorized that the success of any elderly housing project is dependent on three factors: the quality of the neighborhood (the site selected), the skill and careful thought reflected in the design of the building, and the influence of management and management policies (Fig. 1.2). Managers are frequently faced with a job that requires technical understanding of building equipment, accounting skills for rent collection, a social outgoing presence to stimulate group activities, and counseling skills for solving personal problems or tenant conflicts.

FIGURE 1.2   A tripod analogy illustrates the dependence of resident satisfaction on location, unit/building design, and management. A shortcoming in one "leg" can be compensated by an increase in another of the two legs, but this compensatory ability is limited.

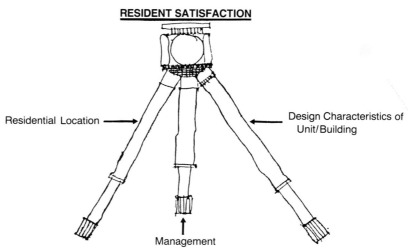

RESIDENT SATISFACTION

Residential Location ⟶   ⟵ Design Characteristics of
                                    Unit/Building

↑
Management

Much of the work in the area of management has focused on how management policies have encouraged or discouraged the use of various activities, spaces, and settings. Management can influence the overall success of a building design by interpreting spaces as opportunities to facilitate resident activities or by establishing rules and policies that discourage or openly forbid certain behaviors, activities, or uses (Lawton, 1975).

Managers and Administrators are Often Unaware of Design Intentions: A lack of attention characterizes the instructions provided to management about how to manipulate this extraordinarily complex environment. Environmental programmers frequently quip about the detailed owner's manuals provided for relatively simple appliances that describe in detail how to "troubleshoot" and solve problems when the equipment malfunctions. Yet rarely are managers provided any guidance whatsoever about how activities can be accommodated on the grounds or within rooms that have been set aside for social purposes.

There is a need to understand how spaces are used and how they could be improved for social purposes. Dialogue with management or a design/management guidebook (developed from the architectural program) can detail how spaces are intended to function. Management should be aware of how various spaces have been designed to accommodate programs and desired activities. Better definition of how spaces are intended to function from a management perspective will frequently lead to more thoughtful and careful design attention.

Sensory Aspects of Design

Changes associated with normal aging frequently affect the acuity, accuracy, and general functioning of sensory organs. Taste, touch, sight, and hearing can all experience normal decremental losses as an organism ages. In some cases, these losses can be profound and need to be fully understood so that design practices and decisions will not exacerbate them.

The most common and perhaps architecturally demanding sensory loss is that of sight (Fig. 1.3). Low light levels and poor figure-to-ground contrast in signs, labels, and graphics can make it difficult and sometimes painful to read important messages (Pastalan, 1979). One of the strategies available for dealing with problems of visual loss is to create a high level of diffused light on critical surfaces (Hiatt, 1980b).

The Treatment of Light is a Major Issue: The addition of more light can cause major problems by introducing glare. To mitigate this, single light sources and major contrasts in light levels should be avoided. Design solutions should strive to utilize indirect light

A

B

FIGURE 1.3 The "Emphatic Model" developed by Leon Pastalan allows younger people to experience the normal age-related vision losses that affect each older person differently. A demonstrates unimpaired vision. In B, the stove controls and burners viewed through the "emphatic lens" demonstrate the effects of glare, decreases in visual acuity, and difficulties in discerning color intensities.

sources because they minimize glare. Food preparation counters in the kitchen, areas around the toilet and bathtub, and corridor spaces where an older person can trip and fall are a few of the critical settings where careful attention to lighting can increase safety.

Hearing loss can also be a critical sensory issue. Increasing the absorption of unwanted sound in spaces where conversations take place and minimizing reverberation and background noise are common strategies in responding to hearing problems.

Redundant Cueing Relies on Several Sensory Messages: Since sensory loss varies by individual, it is important for designers to fully utilize compensation devices. Redundant cueing is a concept that involves a combination of light, sound, and surface texture in alerting the older person of an upcoming event or problem. Redundant cueing is particularly helpful with older people who may be suffering a severe loss of one or more sensory modalities. One of the most common examples of redundant cueing is the simultaneous use of a lighted button and a synchronized tone in an elevator to alert the rider when the appropriate floor has been reached. Also becoming popular are street signals coupled with a two-tone sonic alarm to alert the blind when to safely cross streets.

Physiological Constraints

One of the most critical yet overlooked aspects of the physical environment is the matching of equipment, furnishings, and design details to the special physiological needs of the older person. The most obvious and embarrassing of design errors are those that reflect an ignorance of basic physiological requirements. Windows that are impossible for the arthritic hand to manipulate, kitchen storage that requires backbreaking bending or a reaching device to access, doorknobs that are difficult to turn, controls that are impossible to read, and furniture that is difficult to enter or exit are a few of the most frequently cited design mistakes (Fig. 1.4) (Koncelik, 1979).

FIGURE 1.4 Lever door handles of sturdy and handsome design are an obvious improvement over the standard round door handles which are difficult to grip and twist.

Better Communication of Research Findings is Needed: The results of numerous post-occupancy evaluations and the growing experience and sensitivity of manufacturers to the "graying" profile of the American consumer have had some influence on product development. However, it is still relatively easy to find new elderly housing projects without lever door handles or congregate housing projects that specify bathtubs without grab bars. Some problems in this area do not require more research but rather better communication of research findings and good practice habits for design decision makers.

Older consumers who have been sensitized to these issues now frequently insist that safety features and "considerate" design so-

lutions be employed. Some solutions, however, appear so institutional as to make them clearly unacceptable because of the associations they have with disability or nursing home environments. The consumer's insistence that more attractive, less institutional solutions to these physiological problems be included in market-rate housing have sensitized developers and designers to specify these features.

Good Environmental Solutions to Physiological Problems are Attractive and Free of Stereotype Associations: In this regard, some of the best solutions to physiological impairments have been those focused on improving the appearance of stereotyped items. Perhaps the best example is the handrail. Innovative solutions to this problem have often sought to make the handrail a larger element that appears to resemble a chair rail or a wainscot trim. Some solutions have included lighting fixtures that are mounted under the rail and direct light to the floor surface, where it is needed (Koncelik, 1976).

The work of product designers in developing better, safer appliances for the elderly and handicapped has also improved the functional aspects of some kitchen and bathroom designs. These two spaces have generally been considered critical because mistakes in the kitchen or bathroom can potentially threaten safety or endanger life.

Much work needs to be done in understanding how inexpensive adjustments to single-family housing can enhance safety and independence. Because approximately 70 percent of those over age 65 live in independent, single-family, owner-occupied dwellings, solutions that retrofit these environments in ways that support the older person's independence can have great influence.

Another area of concern involves the design of adaptable fixtures and cabinetry that can be adjusted to meet new physiological needs as a resident ages. The architect or designer who is unaware of the physiological changes associated with aging can create problems by specifying design solutions that limit the independence of the older resident.

Way-Finding

One design feature that affects a person's self-confidence as well as his level of anxiety when using a new building is the degree to which he can orient himself and move from one area of a building to another without getting lost. The disorientation that results is both disturbing and frustrating. The ability to find one's way in the environment is so fundamental a concept that it may even account for misdiagnosed confusion in some older people. Complex and poorly organized buildings that provide very few orienting cues can easily confuse the user (Fig. 1.5).

A

FIGURE 1.5 Greenhouse style windows (A) open the double-loaded corridor in the Villa Marin, a San Rafael, California, elderly housing project, to (B) views of the surrounding countryside. This provides an effective orienting device while pleasantly daylighting the corridor.

B

Relocation Trauma is Related to Way-Finding Research: The importance of useful graphic information and design cues to aid navigation within a familiar environment, as well as techniques to understand a novel environment, make this line of research intriguing to those interested in relocation. For example, some theorists contend that having a difficult time orienting oneself to a new environment may contribute significantly to the relocation trauma many nursing home patients experience when transferred from one setting to another (Weisman, 1981).

Future research in this area should attempt to link more effectively the cognitive processes with the types of environmental cues that aid orientation and navigation. This will further outfit designers with ideas, images, and design techniques to simplify complex environments.

In addition to its importance in cases of relocation, being able to find one's way in the environment is particularly salient to those suffering from a cognitive loss that reduces their spatial ability. Older people living in long-term care facilities frequently suffer from this problem. Partially in response to this deficit, way-finding research has been actively pursued in the aging-environment literature. Research in this area has focused on using building forms, maps, and graphics to provide users with orienting information and cues.

Future Research Topics

Introduction

A careful examination of environmental issues frequently leads to a better understanding of related phenomena and a better sense of how design can clarify, facilitate, and improve the environment for the user. However, further speculation and identification of more complex and far-reaching considerations is also an expected by-product of any research endeavor.

The following 11 topics, cited by many of our contributors, represent interesting and fruitful avenues for further research exploration:

- Application of high technology to housing
- Cohort/generational housing preference changes
- Supportive housing for the frail
- Housing forms that support age integration
- Environments that promote social interaction
- Environments that encourage the development of social/helping networks
- Environments that facilitate house sharing
- Housing and services that are oriented to the neighborhood

- Housing design that conserves and manages energy
- Design of outdoor/site spaces
- Adaptive environments that extend independence

This list is by no means exhaustive, but it includes problems that designers and policy makers frequently raise when discussing important current and future concerns.

Application of High Technology to Housing

Advances in communication technology have brought about major changes in how we store information and communicate with others. New technological advances have found their way into the security and management control systems of new housing projects for the elderly. Many of these new congregate developments have computer systems that manage the accounting, order the food, monitor smoke and fire safety, control energy needs, monitor emergency call systems, and secure the building. In the future, advanced technological devices will likely monitor individual health status and even provide individual self-diagnoses.

High Technology Applications to Housing Could Help Older Residents to Maintain Independence More Easily: Some of the most advanced technological devices currently being developed are designed for the handicapped and for older users. This group has been selected by researchers because it is assumed that they will profit a great deal from the household management help that these devices provide. However, very little research or projective forecasting has been done in anticipation of how these advanced technological devices will affect housing form and the lifestyle of older people in the future.

Although attempting to forecast future problems is not normally the type of research that environmental designers pursue, some careful thinking and speculation is needed about how future housing forms should be developed to liberate and emancipate the older person from environmental dependence. Focused in this way, research can be helpful in developing systems that place the older person in control of the environment, rather than systems that control the older person.

Cohort/Generational Housing Preference Changes

One interesting trend reflected in the current housing demands and preferences of middle- to higher-income older persons is the differing expectations they entertain regarding retirement housing compared to retirees who preceded them in the 1970s. For example, evidence gathered by Laventhol and Horwath (1983) in longitudinal and cross-sectional analyses of Continuing Care Retirement

Communities (CCRC) shows an increase in the popularity of larger size units. While the studio or one-bedroom unit has been the most popular unit choice in the last 10 years, two-bedroom and even three-bedroom units are becoming increasingly popular for affluent retirees over the age of 75.

Upcoming Cohorts of Elderly Have More Elaborate Expectations for Housing: Sociologists and political scientists have written about cohort differences which characterize pre-Depression and post-Depression generations (Cutler, 1983). Housing expectations and preferences tied to this cohort phenomena will demand revisions in the way we think about retirement housing. This may radically affect the common spaces and the activities programmed into new facilities. Recent preferences for exercise and wellness programs and a move toward greater self-governance are trends characteristic of this phenomenon.

Research dealing with the differing expectations of pre-retirees will help anticipate the activities, services, and unit features that an increasingly sophisticated and well-educated older population will desire.

Supportive Housing for the Frail

One of the most startling demographic trends projected by the U.S. Census Bureau's projections to the years 2000 and 2025 is the enormous growth of the oldest age cohorts. The population over the age of 85 will increase at a rate that is more than twice as great as the overall increase of individuals 65 and over (Brotman, 1981).

Congregate Housing Programs Should Encourage Self-Expression: New housing forms that provide free choice, maximize independence, pursue self-governance, stimulate the creative and self-expressive needs of individuals, and optimize control over the environment are strongly needed for this more dependent age group.

FIGURE 1.6 This congregate housing project, planned for a site in Beverly Hills by a group of older people working with a design team, demonstrates the epitome of choice with seven different options for taking a meal. *Source:* Regnier, 1985a.

Many existing congregate facilities share an operating philosophy similar to that of long-term care settings (Fig. 1.6). Thus, they have contributed little to the understanding of how this housing form for the frail can increase the quality of life.

Research is sorely needed that clarifies the role that housing form, design features, and management policies play in the development of a stimulating and rewarding social experience for residents. An ever-increasing older, frail population will require special housing. Hopefully new congregate housing settings will increase resident choice and maximize resident control over the environment.

Housing Forms That Support Age-Integration

Increasing the volume of housing research for the elderly may likely increase the preference for age-segregated arrangements as a solution to the problem of housing older people. Further understanding of age-segregated arrangements often serves to underscore the potential problems in mixing older and younger families. In age-segregated arrangements, older residents are not exposed to younger families in a direct or natural way. Conversely,

FIGURE 1.7 One major issue that requires more careful future analysis and research is the design of housing that stimulates inter-generational exchange.

younger families are removed from the opportunity of having an older neighbor.

Few Good Age-Integrated Housing Success Stories are Available for Scrutiny and Replication: Many social activists, like Maggie Kuhn, are adamantly opposed to age-segregated housing, in part because they believe it furthers the societal rift between generations. Unfortunately, age-integrated housing either in its naturally occurring form or as intentionally designed in newly constructed housing has not been carefully scrutinized with regard to the issue of inter-generational exchange. More careful scrutiny of successful age-integrated projects is needed in order to understand how mechanisms that bring together younger and older people can develop (Fig. 1.7). Understanding how spaces and activities successfully mix generations will allow us to develop, encourage, or engineer settings where this type of interaction can take place.

In their efforts to scrutinize and understand age-segregated housing, researchers have all but abandoned the issue of stimulating intergenerational exchange through innovative age-integrated housing. More careful research is needed to understand how the goal of age-integration can be met through the development of new housing prototypes.

Environments That Promote Social Interaction

The design and layout of social lounges and activity areas can have profound impacts on the amount of usage they receive. Past research has shown that even minor changes in the relationship of common spaces to circulation pathways can affect the amount of use a space receives (Howell, 1980b). More careful, in-depth examination of these relationships will lead to a better understanding of how lounge and lobby areas, recreation and educational spaces, and activity spaces can be related to one another. Understanding these underlying relationships will lead to schemes that promote the use of those spaces (Fig. 1.8).

How Can Housing Design Encourage Social Interaction While Maximizing Resident Control? Research that clarifies the interaction effects of circulation and adjacency relationships on use can also be helpful in avoiding awkward or ineffective common space layouts. The microcharacteristics of environments (such as furniture, screens, or half walls) that support social interaction and social exchange also need to be more carefully scrutinized. Are single-loaded corridors more socially effective than double-loaded corridors? Do glass window walls that visually link activity spaces with circulation pathways pique the curiosity and satisfy the anxiety of individuals who may be too shy to enter a space or pursue an activity without a better understanding of that setting?

FIGURE 1.8   This double-hung window provides an unusual visual connection between the manager's office and the entry lobby of the Captain Clarence Eldridge Congregate House in Hyannis, Massachusetts.

Environments That Encourage the Development of Social/Helping Networks

One major benefit of age-segregated housing is that it provides an environment within which residents can easily develop friendships. It is not well understood how the environment aids, supports, or encourages friendships that lead to informal mutual helping networks.

Architects frequently speak about designing clusters of units in housing to simulate a small "neighborhood." The notion that underlies this romantic interpretation is that a certain number of individuals, a certain corridor configuration, and a particular tenant mix will promote sociability that leads to an informal helping network.

Informal Helping Networks Can Provide Needed Support: Neither the social variables nor the physical variables that promote these networks have been well defined. However, we continue to see demonstrations that these mutual support systems flourish under

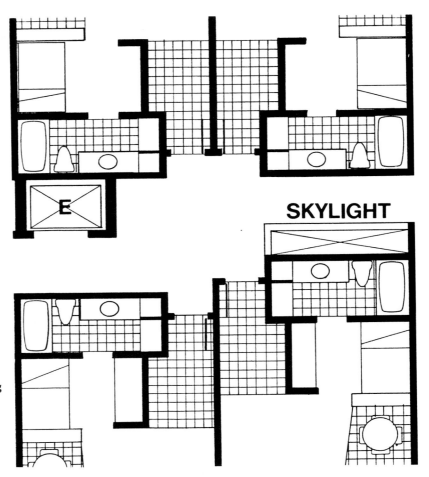

SKYLIGHT

FIGURE 1.9 Clustering four unit entries in an alcove recessed from the corridor is an architectural response that formally defines this subgroup of units.

the right set of circumstances. When these networks work well, they provide reciprocal, peripatetic help at critical times. They can even be so powerful as to forestall premature institutionalization. Research into the physical and social aspects that promote these mutual helping networks can outfit the designer with concepts and ideas that lead to a physical setting that better supports these activities (Fig. 1.9).

Environments That Facilitate House Sharing

Future projections that plot population distributions of retirees in suburban housing demonstrate the logistical problems that may occur with a larger aged population located in low-density suburban settings where social, health, and supportive services are difficult to deliver. Many of these older people will live alone in "underutilized stock" (more than three rooms per person) and may be able to gain security and some extra income by renting out a portion of their dwelling which they are not using.

Privacy, Territoriality, and Sharing Need to Be Considered in Research: Various strategies for shared housing are likely to become an even more important part of the housing policy picture in the future. Preliminary research evaluating matching successes and failures has shown that the way privacy and sharing of facilities is handled can contribute to the success of a match.

Remodeling designs that increase privacy and reinforce autonomy for both the sharer and sharee are needed in order to make this housing choice a more fruitful and productive option in the future. Likewise, housing research that addresses the shared housing prototype and suggests how to resolve the physical problems that may lead to unsuccessful attempts at sharing will increase the viability of this policy choice in the future.

Housing and Services Oriented to the Neighborhood

Senior citizen centers and neighborhood-based facilities oriented to the social, health, and service needs of older community residents will become more popular in the future as greater numbers reach retirement age. European neighborhood-based service centers are frequently located adjacent to or within elderly housing projects and are designed to provide services to neighborhood residents as well as to elderly housing residents.

New Publicly Subsidized Housing Developments Must Also Meet the Service Needs of Community Residents: When this approach has been taken in the United States, the design of the community spaces and their relationship to the neighborhood has sometimes caused territorial problems that discourage community residents from freely utilizing the activities and resources available at these settings. More research is needed to understand how the massing and configuration of housing with supportive services can be designed to serve the purpose of supporting the needs of both older people in the neighborhood and residents of adjacent housing.

In the future it is likely that publicly supported age-segregated housing will be expected to serve the needs of surrounding neighborhood residents. In order to effectively combine housing with service centers we need to understand how physical design variables can be used to avoid territorial "turf" problems. Effective solutions to this problem will lead to housing/service prototypes that support the needs of elderly housing residents as well as the social, political, educational, recreational, and health needs of community residents.

Housing Design That Conserves and Manages Energy

As a person ages his physiological response to heat and cold can sometimes become more of a problem. Accidental hypothermia frequently affects older people and children more than those in other age groups. Hyperthermia has been shown to be a major problem among older low-income community residents who frequently perish during hot and humid summer months because they are afraid to open windows at night to ventilate poorly insulated housing units. The 1980 Harris poll, which outlined the "very serious" problems of a national sample of older people, identified the cost of energy as the single greatest "very serious" problem facing people over the age of 65 (National Council on the Aging, 1981).

Temperature and Ventilation Control Must Be Individualized: Increasingly more sophisticated, centralized control systems are being pursued in order to manage effectively the energy needs of large buildings. It is important to recognize that the heating and cooling needs of older residents may vary and that flexible systems need to be designed with individual controls. More careful research in the area of energy management and more post-occupancy evaluation research on solar heated, super-insulated, and other energy conserving residential designs should be pursued from a behavioral perspective so as to identify problems that might uniquely affect the older resident.

Design of Outdoor Site Spaces

The design and programming of elderly housing is frequently viewed as an exercise in developing interior spaces that support the lifestyle and social needs of residents (Fig. 1.10). The larger context within which the building is placed—that is, the site and the neighborhood—is often overlooked. Community spaces that are intended to encourage social interaction and community activities inside the building are often developed with little thought toward how outdoor seating and outdoor activities can contribute to the social and recreational needs of residents.

The interaction between the architect and the landscape architect along with the choice of building type can establish the parameters within which outdoor space opportunities are pursued with diligence or ignored through negligence. More research is needed to understand the complexities of designing successful outdoor spaces that meet social and recreational needs while stretching the potential for new therapeutic and aesthetic experiences.

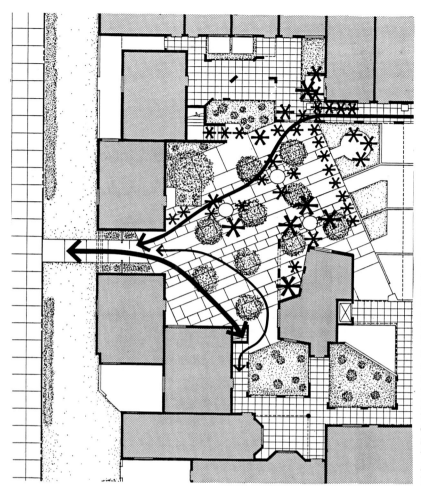

FIGURE 1.10 This outdoor courtyard is a popular place for elderly residents to gather. The pedestrian circulation pathways that lead through the courtyard to stairs, elevators, and parking activate the space. This makes it interesting for residents, who frequently sit on the edge of the space in movable chairs and "people watch." *Source:* Regnier, 1985b.

Adaptative Environments That Extend Independence

The growing number of people over age 65 will continue to fuel interest in the development of housing appliances and household products that take into consideration the sensory losses and manipulation problems of older users. Stoves with automatic shutoff features and large dials for easy manipulation, as well as building products that minimize the effort required to open a door or clean the kitchen, will make life easier and more manageable, particularly for the older, frail user.

Adaptive aids that allow an impaired older person to overcome barriers in the environment will become increasingly more common as greater numbers of older, higher-income individuals pursue an independent lifestyle in their own single-family house. One sign of this trend is the increased visibility of aids that promote continuing independence in mail order catalogs and in medical rental outlets.

Accommodating Environments Must Be Researched and Demonstrated: More research is needed to understand how the architecture of the housing unit can be adapted to these changes in sensory acuity, physical strength, and competency. Adaptive aids typically are designed only to facilitate a particular task and not to solve larger problems. By designing for changing contingencies in the very beginning, an architectural solution can result which is flexible and adaptive. More careful thinking is needed to sort out the relationship between architectural design, graphic design, and product design.

Conclusions

Although research in the area of environments and aging needs to expand to pursue the changing policy and environmental design preferences of future older cohorts, it is important to underscore the need for "translatable" results that can inform decision making in the future. The research conclusions gleaned from the highest quality work will have very little impact if those conclusions are not translated into a form that makes them meaningful to design and policy decision-makers.

2

HOUSING THE AGED
Public Policy at the Crossroads

Jon Pynoos

H ousing policy for the elderly is in the throes of major change. Federal production programs such as public housing and Section 202, once in the vanguard, have lost much of their political support (Pynoos, 1984). At the moment, it is unclear what, if anything, will take their place, particularly since there is a de-emphasis on housing assistance programs as a national priority. At such a juncture it is important to establish objectives by which housing policies, programs, and projects for the elderly can be judged.

Such objectives, which will be presented later in this chapter, provide the context for debate about housing for the elderly. In this regard, it is important to note that no housing program will be able to meet all the objectives. In fact, a major theme that emerges from the articles in this book is the need for a more balanced housing approach than has been used in the past. Nevertheless, such objectives should help us to evaluate proposed programs and to set new directions for housing policy.

The Definition of Housing Problems is a Critical Issue

At the heart of the debate over housing policy for the elderly are questions about what constitutes housing problems, which of these problems should take priority on the public agenda so that some action is taken to address them, and how efficiently in terms of resource utilization different programs are likely to solve the problems. For several decades, public attention focused on poor housing quality stock—for example, on lack of indoor plumbing, hot and cold running water, or complete kitchens—and overcrowding. More recently, the definition of housing quality has expanded to include how well certain parts of the home function, for example the reliability of the heating and plumbing.

Housing Quality Has Been Improving But Problems Remain

The importance of the early attention to improving housing quality has been confirmed by the dramatic impact that has been demonstrated in the lives of older persons who have moved from older housing in the private housing stock to new units, most frequently public or Section 202 housing. However, by the mid-1970s housing quality problems were being viewed as residual, affecting certain pockets of the population, such as those persons living in rural areas and inner-city slums. The gradual improvement in the quality of most of the stock also lessened the strength of the argument that new construction was necessary to improve mental and physical health (Fig. 2.1).

During this period, policy analysts began to expand the definition of housing problems to emphasize not only dwelling quality but also affordability (how much of a person's income was spent on housing), suitability (how well the housing and its neighborhood met physical and service needs), and availability (whether enough units were available that were affordable and fit the needs of potential occupants) (Pynoos, Schafer, and Hartman, 1980). They also began to examine other programs, such as housing allowances and shared housing, that might solve housing problems at less expense than the construction of new units.

Affordability and Suitability Problems Should Receive Increased Attention

In this context, in the early 1980s research began to stress the affordability problem. The number of older persons who were judged to pay excessive amounts of income for housing (over 35 percent of annual income) approached 2.3 million, far exceeding the 1 million who were considered to be living in deficient dwelling units. Unfortunately, analysis of other dimensions of housing was and continues to be hindered by the limited amount of information collected. For example, even though suitability in terms of neighborhood and housing fit are vitally important to older persons, and several articles in this book address such issues, adequate measures have not yet been developed. Consequently, housing goals based only on excessive housing expenditures and condition underestimate the extent of housing problems, especially for the old-old.

FIGURE 2.1 While housing conditions have generally improved, problems remain as indicated by this picture of an older person living in a single room occupancy hotel. *Source:* Ira Nowinski.

The objectives discussed below, many of which are derived from the research presented in this volume, present a context within which to begin to judge our overall housing effort for the elderly.

Policy Objectives

This chapter and those that follow take the overall perspective that housing policy for the elderly is a purposive course of action intended to promote better housing and to deal with general housing problems. In this context, policy is dealt with at both the macro and the micro levels. "Macro-policy" refers to broad objectives where overall public interest is involved, such as promoting housing choice. Macro-policy analysis raises questions such as: What housing problems are we trying to solve? Who is the population to be served? What alternative ways have been proposed to solve the problems? What are the costs and benefits of different approaches? And where does support lie for programs?

Although micro-policy includes some of the same questions, it is more focused at the project level involving the interaction between older persons and the environment. Micro-level issues include management policies, which often set the overall parameter for project operations—such as how much resident control there is in decision making—as well as the kinds of services that are available on-site. Both macro- and micro-policy issues are discussed below.

Although actual measures of program effectiveness include objectives such as cost per occupied dwelling, preservation of stock, and administrative simplicity, which should be included in any evaluation (Struyk and Soldo, 1980), this chapter focuses on objectives considered to be particularly relevant to an elderly population. These include:

- Promoting housing choice
- Providing an appropriate neighborhood and service supports
- Maximizing independence
- Ensuring housing fit
- Providing adaptable or accommodating housing
- Enhancing residential satisfaction and control

Table 2.1 presents a matrix that identifies which authors address these major policy objectives.

Promoting Housing Choice

Older persons vary enormously in their preferences for different housing settings and in their competencies for coping with different living environments. However, for almost 20 years federal policy has concentrated primarily on building new units—for the well, active, older person—under such programs as public housing and Section 202, which now house over 700,000 elderly. Although there were initial concerns that such settings might result in older persons becoming physically and socially isolated from the rest of society, research findings have pointed to positive effects, such as improved morale and life satisfaction, greater activity, increased social interaction, better perceptions of health status, and even increased longevity (Fig. 2.2).

Only a Small Number of Older People Have Benefited from Housing Assistance Programs: Although new housing appears to be generally beneficial, researchers have begun to raise questions about the exclusive focus on such developments and have begun pro-

TABLE 2.1. Policy Objectives Strongly Addressed or Recognized by Authors

Authors	Promoting Housing Choice	Providing an Appropriate Neighborhood and Service Supports	Maximizing Independence	Ensuring Housing Fit	Providing Adaptable or Accommodating Housing	Enhancing Residential Satisfaction and Control
Carp	+	0	0	+	+	+
Cranz		0		+		+
Christensen		0		0		+
Butterfield				+		+
Hartman		+	0	+		+
Moos			+	+	+	+
Regnier	0	+		+		0
Heumann	+	+	+	0	0	
Struyk	+	0	+		+	
Pynoos	0	0	+	+	+	
Steinfeld			+	+	+	
Hiatt				+	+	0
Koncelik			+	+	0	+
Osterberg			+	+		0
Hunt			+	+		+
Weisman			+	+		+

Key + = *objective strongly addressed*
      0 = *objective recognized but not strongly addressed*

FIGURE 2.2 A typical public housing project built in Illinois in the 1970s.

moting policies that provide a greater diversity of residential settings to accommodate what has been acknowledged as a heterogeneous group of older persons. Such a shift in thinking recognizes that while new projects often have had large waiting lists, due to their high costs and the limited federal resource made available to housing assistance programs, only a relatively small percentage of the elderly (3 percent) have benefited from them.

In addition, it has been acknowledged that older persons live in a variety of community settings, such as single-family homes, apartments, cooperatives, mobile homes, and retirement communities. The major program for the elderly up until recently—public housing—required that an older person move to a project in order to take advantage of the public subsidy that the government offered to those in need. However, there were many elderly with similar housing needs who instead preferred to stay in their own familiar homes and neighborhoods. Consequently, researchers have begun to examine alternative living arrangements that include programs that support older persons in their own homes; an important consideration in that approximately 70 percent of the elderly are homeowners.

Providing an Appropriate Neighborhood and Service Supports

When people consume housing, they purchase or rent more than the dwelling unit and its characteristics. They are also concerned with such diverse factors as health, security, privacy, neighborhood and social relations, community facilities, service, and transportation. Being ill-housed can mean deprivation along any or all of these dimensions and can lead to discontent.

For many older persons, research suggests that neighborhood-related problems such as safety seem to be of much higher concern than problems within the house per se. Neighborhood-related problems such as lack of services or transportation become especially salient when older persons become more frail and their home range diminishes. Unfortunately, although many of our housing practices have stressed the importance of site location, few policies have gone beyond shelter to include neighborhood services such as transportation, convenience stores, and emergency medical care.

Maximizing Independence

Public policy in the United States has supported living arrangements primarily at two ends of the spectrum: middle- to large-sized housing projects for the well, active elderly; and nursing homes for those who need medical attention and personal care services.

The emphasis on housing projects for the well, active elderly was fostered in part by the concern of many researchers that overly protective, service-rich environments might encourage passivity and lead to health declines and that more traditional housing aimed at these elderly should be associated with challenge and continued independent behavior.

An Increase in the Over-75 Segment of the Elderly Population Demands a New Look at Supportive Housing Arrangements: As the number of older persons over age 75, with serious physical limitations, continues to expand, increasing emphasis is being placed on housing with supportive services that enhance residents' feelings of security and enable them to function at their optimal level. The need for more supportive environments is demonstrated by recent findings which suggest that old-old persons often desire secure residential environments with on-site medical and personal care services (Fig. 2.3).

In order to avoid "overly supportive" settings, researchers are suggesting that services be custom-fitted to individual needs. For example, in England this concept of supplemental care has been designed to allow older persons to live as independently as their functional abilities allow with support provided only at their margin of need.

FIGURE 2.3   This health care facility located adjacent to an elderly housing project is an example of a housing plan that integrates supportive services.

Ensuring Housing Fit

Multi-family housing designers are somewhat notorious for working without a great deal of client contact. Instead they rely on meetings with the prime sponsor and the analysis of other similar facilities for direction. Such approaches are understandable given that the actual residents of a facility are generally not known beforehand and that the building, financing, and zoning requirements often leave little room for discretion.

Nevertheless, in order to ensure that housing better fits the needs of its residents, attention has been turned toward ways in which potential users can be involved on a more interactive and on-going basis as design and program decisions are actually made. Similarly, researchers have begun to extend the design process beyond the actual physical construction of the building to include post-occupancy evaluations from actual residents so that more can be learned about how the facility meets residents' needs, where it might have missed the mark, what can be done to correct problems, and lessons that can be applied to future projects. Both participatory user/needs surveys and post-occupancy evaluations require the allocation of special funds and the creation of new methodologies to communicate visual and program concepts to older persons.

Providing Adaptable or Accommodating Housing

Because the physical environment has generally been viewed as having a permanent quality and physical changes are often expensive, public policy has tended to provide incentives for older persons to move out of their residences to more supportive environments when they become frail. However, serious problems have often been associated with relocation, and it has been found that most older persons prefer to stay in their own homes for as long as possible.

The increasing magnitude of this concern is emphasized by two recent studies of Section 202 housing, which found that the average age of residents is rising dramatically and is accompanied by a corresponding rise in need for services that are available in such settings only in a patchwork fashion (U.S. Senate, 1984; Lawton, Moss, and Grimes, 1985). Similarly, housing and neighborhoods where older people live were originally designed for younger and healthier persons and do not necessarily easily accommodate the needs of an older, impaired population. As a result, research has begun to focus on housing and neighborhood prototypes that adapt to people's needs as they become more frail as well as on ways in which programs can be devised to assist frail persons in modifying their homes to meet changing needs.

Enhancing Residential Satisfaction and Control

Due to the newness of the concept, early research on planned housing for the elderly tended to concentrate on the impact of moving to such novel physical settings and the types of social interaction that occurred. However, it is now clear that other factors such as management policies affect the success of any housing project by encouraging or discouraging activities and the use of space. For example, management policies affecting resident control and involvement are related to resident satisfaction and level of activity. In fact, it appears that variations in management programming may have an even greater effect on resident satisfaction than variations in physical design, although clearly the two are related (Fig. 2.4).

For example, research suggests that restrictive management policies contribute to depression, a sense of helplessness, and accelerated physical decline. On the other hand, participation in setting rules and personalizing the environment seems to encourage a sense of ownership among older tenants. There are areas, however, such as selection of staff, where administrators may need to make decisions in order to avoid potential conflicts among resi-

FIGURE 2.4 Involving elderly residents in the design and management of housing can help ensure that the development meets their needs and results in high tenant satisfaction.

dents. Consequently, research suggests the need to create a balance between individual freedom and institutional order. Yet, managers have been primarily trained to handle the technical aspects of the job such as maintenance of the premises and rent collection. Rarely are they trained in the equally important areas of stimulating group activities, building a supportive community, counseling residents, or encouraging the use of existing spaces for programs.

New Directions

There is clearly a move away from federal government financing of new construction for low-income persons. Although it is as yet unclear what role the government will play, several major strategies have emerged during the 1980s:

- Making better use of the existing housing stocks
- Increasingly relying on the housing resources of the elderly
- Using housing allowances
- Integrating housing with long-term care services

Making Better Use of the Existing Stock

Housing solutions for the elderly have begun to focus on making better use of the existing stock. A number of neighborhood-oriented housing improvement strategies have begun to emerge, such as Neighborhood Housing Services (NAS) and home repair and energy assistance programs that are administered locally and are often used to upgrade existing housing. Given the preference of most older persons to stay in their own homes, these programs have been viewed positively among older people because they contribute to the emerging philosophy of allowing older residents to "age in place." Since the emphasis on such programs is relatively recent, what needs to be determined are the incentives required to encourage older persons to modify their environments and their behavior, the types of educational programs that will be effective in alerting older persons about problems, and the changes that will reduce accidents, improve the housing stock, and minimize housing expenditures.

More Reliance on Housing Resources of the Elderly to Create Alternative Housing Options

Recent fiscal austerity measures have led to major cutbacks and, in some cases, the elimination of many federal housing programs. For example, President Reagan's Commission on Housing suggested that many housing shortage problems could be resolved not by building new units but rather by encouraging older people who were living alone in "underutilized" (more than three rooms per person) dwelling units to share housing with others (President's Commission on Housing, 1982). Consequently, as the government has reduced its overall outlays for housing assistance programs, there has been an increased emphasis on programs—such as house sharing, accessory apartments, and home equity conversions—in which the elderly rely on their own housing resources to improve their income and housing situation. Such approaches received the strong endorsement of the President's Commission on Housing, a conservative group of advisers appointed by President Reagan in 1981 to chart the future of housing policy.

Using data from the annual housing survey, the Commission pointed out that in 1979 there were 12.2 million one- or two-person households headed by homeowners 55 or older which contained five or more rooms. This is far above the standard of one person per room and, therefore, was viewed as offering the potential for homesharing in which two or more unrelated individuals share a dwelling unit. Other evidence suggests, however, that the housing stock occupied by older persons is not as underutilized as once considered and that only marginal gains result when it turns over to new residents (Lane and Feins, 1985). And although shared housing potentially offers older persons reduced housing expenditures, assistance with tasks, and companionship, issues remain of how to match compatible persons, what type of spaces and tasks persons are willing to share, how long matches are likely to last, and what level of resources agencies need to carry out adequate screening and follow-up (Fig. 2.5).

FIGURE 2.5 Large homes occupied by single older persons such as this one offer the potential for house sharing, a program intended to make better use of existing housing resources.

The Commission also pointed to the $30–40 billion potential market for home equity conversion or reverse annuity mortgages and assumed that such programs like shared housing would require little federal intervention or expenditures (President's Commission on Housing, 1982). It has yet to be determined, however, for whom such housing options are appropriate, how many older persons will try to take advantage of them, and to what extent they will be effective. Will reverse annuity mortgages work for persons whose homes are worth a moderate amount as well as those who have relatively expensive homes? How will they be received by older persons whose home is their major asset? Can adequate safeguards be built in so that the older person's rights to stay and continue to receive benefits from government programs such as SSI, Medicare, and Medicaid are protected?

It has also yet to be determined what types of incentives or financing mechanisms will make such options as echo housing and accessory apartments available to lower-income older persons. These approaches often require zoning amendments. Although a number of communities have made provisions for them, concern has been expressed about the secondary effects of echo housing and accessory apartments on neighborhood services, parking, and aesthetics. There is also the possibility that a potential backlash might occur if echo housing and accessory apartments become so widespread that other residents perceive that the character of their community is drastically changing.

Better Integration of Housing and Long-Term Care

For over 10 years, professionals have advocated better housing and service-program integration to foster the independence of older persons and allow them to live in the least restrictive setting. The problems of an increasingly older population with accompanying health and functional impairments present a serious challenge to find ways in which housing can be adapted and long-term care services provided to meet the needs of the frail. Thus far three service models have evolved: continuum of care retirement communities, congregate housing, and home modification programs and in-home services.

Continuum of Care Retirement Communities (*CCRCs*): There are approximately 400–600 CCRCs in the United States, which house over 100,000 older persons. These communities have a relatively full continuum of care that includes independent housing, housing with services (for example, home health, personal care units), and nursing home facilities. Because of their relatively high entrance fees (averaging $38,000) and monthly costs (averaging $600), CCRCs cater primarily to middle- to upper-income elders (Pynoos, 1985; Pynoos, Regnier, and O'Brien, 1983). These communities clearly aim at keeping older persons in the least restrictive envi-

FIGURE 2.6 Continuum of care retirement communities typically include independent housing (pictured above), housing with services, and a nursing home and community facilities aimed at an old-old population interested in and able to afford its relatively high costs, which include medical and long-term care services.

ronment. They also provide easy opportunities for visiting by residents should an older person need to move to the personal care or nursing home component of the facility (Fig. 2.6).

Nevertheless, a number of important issues still remain to be addressed. For example, are CCRCs able to provide cost savings through their ability to act as gatekeepers and providers of long-term care? Do residents live longer than their counterparts in the community or is apparent increased longevity due to preselection along income and health lines? Are there ways to provide the benefits of CCRCs to less affluent segments of the population?

Congregate Housing: A second model for providing health services to frail residents, this does not generally have nursing facilities on the premises. However, compared to typical planned housing, congregate housing is service-rich, including meals and nonmedical services for residents who need them. Congregate housing ranges from projects that house 30–40 residents to small group homes with 4–8 residents. A variation of this approach is found in the British sheltered housing program, in which 20–40 residents living in small facilities are assisted by neighborhood lay wardens who visit, help organize activities, and coordinate services.

The stumbling block for congregate housing in the United States continues to be the issue of who will pay for it. Previous efforts have been thwarted by the "39-year gap"—Department of Housing and Urban Development (HUD) loan programs such as Section 202 have supported 40-year mortgages while the Department of Health and Human Services has generally only been able to fund services on a year to year basis—as well as HUD's reluctance to go beyond shelter into services. In addition, both Congress and the federal administration have been hesitant to launch an expanded congregate program without evidence that this housing type is cost-effective in preventing or delaying institutionalization. Issues that need further investigation include what proportion of the elderly population will need congregate housing, what types of services should be included, and what mixture of staff and residents is appropriate.

Home Modification and In-Home Supports: This is a third model for housing frail older persons, given the expense of building new units and the desire among many older persons to stay in their own homes as long as possible. Home modification and in-home supports rely on bringing services to people rather than moving people to new settings (Pynoos and Salend, 1982). Such approaches may require modifications in homes to make them more supportive as well as the provision of services such as homemaking, home health aide, and meals on wheels. Budgetary problems similar to those experienced by congregate housing have hindered the creation of a home-care system (Fig. 2.7).

FIGURE 2.7 Home modification programs that stress safety and independent living can help prevent accidents through adaptions such as this Port Orford Cedar bench installed in a shower.

There is concern that if such services were widely available, the costs would be prohibitive, since many older persons who now make it on their own or with the help of friends and relatives would become increasingly reliant on government support. In addition, establishing who needs such assistance has continued to be a methodological and policy concern. It is also unclear to what extent physical modifications in the home can substitute for the provision of services and what the long-range trade-offs of these two approaches would be. Consequently, home care remains fragmented and uncoordinated, with large gaps existing in the continuum of care.

Housing Allowances

In line with concern over excessive housing expenditures and an increased reliance on the existing housing stock, the federal government has been moving toward a direct cash assistance program intended to reduce the amount of income that lower-income persons pay for housing to approximately 30 percent. Such a program has the advantage of allowing such persons greater freedom of choice, especially to stay in their own residence, and could be applied to homeowners as well as to renters. Because this program requires a participant to live in a unit that meets certain housing standards, those persons living in lower quality units may not qualify unless they move or upgrade their unit.

This program approach may work poorly for elderly who move less often than the rest of the population and who may have difficulties either contracting for repairs or, in the case of renters, inducing their landlords to make improvements. As a result, important questions remain about elderly participation in a housing allowance program, the degree to which housing allowances will encourage housing rehabilitation in those units occupied by older persons, and the types of assistance older persons will need to succeed in the program.

An Unfinished Agenda

It is clear that the elderly have been a prime beneficiary of federally subsidized housing programs. According to a recent analysis of housing and urban development data (Zais et al., 1982), roughly 1.2 million households headed by the elderly were assisted in 1980 through HUD's housing programs (for example, public housing, Section 8, Section 202). The elderly constitute about 39 percent of all assisted households, even though they represented a smaller proportion of the eligible population and there is significant variation in how well individual programs serve the elderly. The elderly benefit proportionally more than the nonelderly from programs that created new construction (such as Section 202 and Section 8/new construction) and public housing.

Still, it is important to note that only 3 percent of the elderly have benefited from these programs and that the needs of several million elderly for housing that is affordable, safe, accessible, and suitable in terms of neighborhood amenities and services have gone unaddressed. Housing problems remain especially severe for minorities, renters, and older persons who live in rural areas. In this respect, the federal government's reduction of housing assistance programs bodes poorly for the well-being of older persons. Unless the supply of housing rises overall and adequate levels of assistance are available, there will be continuing pressure on private sector housing. In turn, this demand will result in rent increases and insecurity, especially for low- and moderate-income tenants. Although the private sector is moving with some rapidity in addressing issues of elderly housing, it is unlikely that it will address the problems of poor and inadequately housed older persons.

The extent to which states and localities can pick up the slack through floating their own bonds to finance housing is yet to be determined. Consequently, increased attention is likely to be paid to those programs that entail limited government funding such as shared housing, reverse annuity mortgages, and accessory apartments.

Perhaps the most serious future housing problem revolves around the needs of frail older persons for supportive housing environments. There is a serious lack of congregate housing or home care available for frail persons who need personal and health care services other than the skilled nursing care found in more institutional settings. Addressing such needs will provide a difficult challenge in the coming decade.

PLANNED HOUSING
FOR THE WELL ELDERLY

3

THE IMPACT OF PLANNED HOUSING
A Longitudinal Study

Frances Carp

I n the early 1960s a new term was introduced into the architectural vocabulary: age-segregated high-rise pub- licly subsidized elderly housing. The response to this new architectural form was controversial. Some saw it as the first dan- gerous step, funded at public expense, toward the creation of an age-segregated society. Others argued that the victimization and alienation of older persons in traditional public housing required a safer form of accommodation. A major research question was: How would older people adapt to high-rise contemporary housing? Psychologists and social scientists questioned the adaptability of older persons to such a radical new lifestyle and were split on questions regarding well-being and satisfaction.

Nearly 600,000 older people now live in Housing and Urban Development (HUD)-sponsored housing for the elderly, most of them in high-rise apartment structures. In order to assess these facilities and to enlighten policy and planning with regard to future housing for the elderly, it is imperative to evaluate effects on inmovers.

The study reviewed in this chapter was the first systematic, lon- gitudinal look at the effects of age-segregated high-rise publicly

Various phases of the study were provided by grants from the Hogg Foundation for Mental Health, the University of Texas; an intramural grant from the Aging Program, the National Institute for Child Health and Human Development and research grant R01 HD 03643 from the same Institute; research grant AA-4-70-087 from the Administration on Aging; and research grant R01 MH/AG 32668 from the Center on Aging, the National Institute of Mental Health.

subsidized elderly housing upon its tenants. The impact of moving to this new building was generally favorable on all indices of well-being. These findings serve as a background upon which to view residents' responses to siting considerations and architectural features, which compose the focus of this chapter and provide a record upon which to base directives for improved planning and design.

Related Research

Positive reactions were observed among residents of a low-rent apartment house (Donahue, 1966) and of a relatively affluent retirement community (Hamovitch, 1968). However, the issue of whether residents are better off than they would have been without the move to special housing cannot be resolved without comparing inmovers to people in similar conditions who do not move. Studies where these comparisons were made (Bultena and Wood, 1969; Lipman, 1968; Sherman, 1973) reported associations between better housing and well-being. Still, these comparisons were cross-sectional. Accurate measurement requires observation before rehousing as well as after the new housing has had an opportunity to produce effects. Lawton and Cohen (1974), studying five housing environments with a before-and-after design, demonstrated similar findings. All the studies used data from approximately the first year of tenancy. Critics suggested that the favorable response reflects the rosy bias of a "honeymoon" period.

The Victoria Plaza Study

To avoid the methodological limitations cited above, the Victoria Plaza (VP) study compared inmovers to a similar nonmover control group at three points in time: pre-move, and 1 and 8 years post-move. This "validation across time" suggested that the favorable social and psychological impacts observed at the end of the first year were more than "honeymoon" effects. Victoria Plaza residents continued to lead more active and more sociable lives, to be better satisfied with their use of time and their interpersonal relationships, to have higher morale and life satisfaction, and to have better self-perceived health. Some people might not be impressed with findings on these "soft" measures of well-being. However, they were supported by the fact that the death rate was lower among the residents of VP than among the comparison group.

Before going into detail regarding these effects, it seems appropriate to provide some information about the study. The following section describes the building in terms of siting, general design, and special design features.

The Site, the Building, and Special Design Features

Victoria Plaza is located on a 2.5 acre property, 0.7 of a mile from the center of San Antonio (The Alamo), Texas. When VP was built this area was a slum. By the time of final data collection, it bordered on the Hemisfair, and adjacent areas were drastically altered by urban renewal projects and a freeway system (Fig. 3.1).

FIGURE 3.1   Victoria Plaza is located in a marginal neighborhood south of downtown San Antonio.

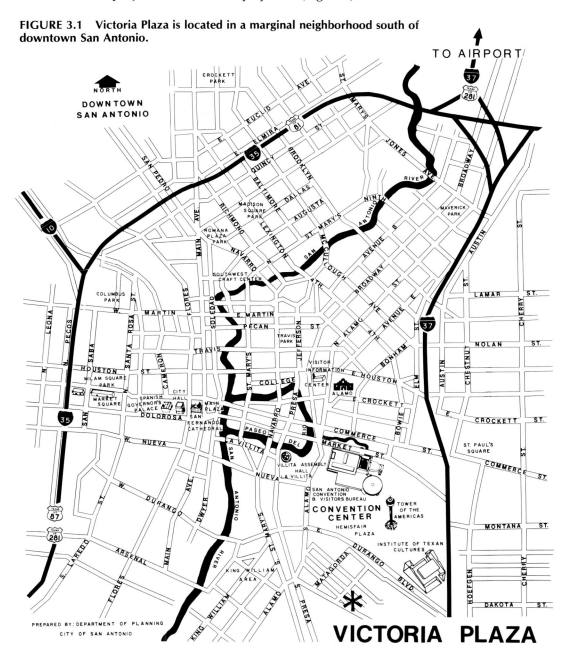

Building Design: The structure was the first high-rise apartment building in the city. Nine stories high and shaped in the form of a modified T, the building has an open balcony, a single-loaded corridor oriented toward the prevailing breeze, which provides excellent cross-ventilation. The building design is bold and the decoration bright and strong. Behind the building are a parking lot and a loading area. A roque court (hard surface croquet) that was originally provided was eliminated after a time, and an area was set aside for small gardens. A shuffleboard court, located on the patio on the side of the building, has also been added. A covered walkway enclosed on both sides leads from the lobby area to this patio, which is surrounded by an 8-foot brick wall to provide protection from the street and neighborhood. The patio has planted areas, benches, and several pieces of modern sculpture. A small medical clinic at one rear corner has a separate entry from the street. A laundry room is located on each floor with washers, dryers, and tubs for hand washing (Fig. 3.2).

FIGURE 3.2 Victoria Plaza ground floor plan: The ground floor plan contains a recreation room (Senior Center), a lobby, and several special purpose rooms (library, arts and crafts).

Diagram of First Floor of Victoria Plaza

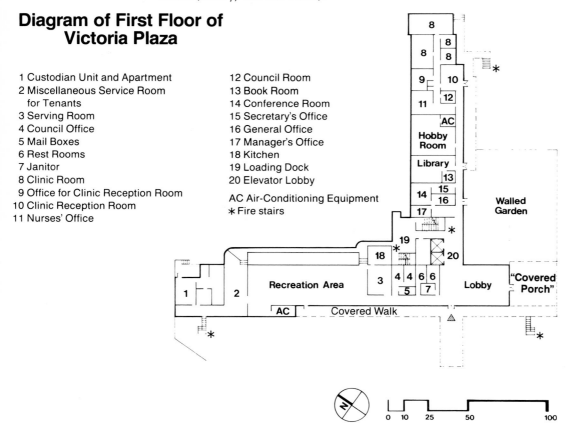

1 Custodian Unit and Apartment
2 Miscellaneous Service Room
  for Tenants
3 Serving Room
4 Council Office
5 Mail Boxes
6 Rest Rooms
7 Janitor
8 Clinic Room
9 Office for Clinic Reception Room
10 Clinic Reception Room
11 Nurses' Office

12 Council Room
13 Book Room
14 Conference Room
15 Secretary's Office
16 General Office
17 Manager's Office
18 Kitchen
19 Loading Dock
20 Elevator Lobby

AC Air-Conditioning Equipment
✳ Fire stairs

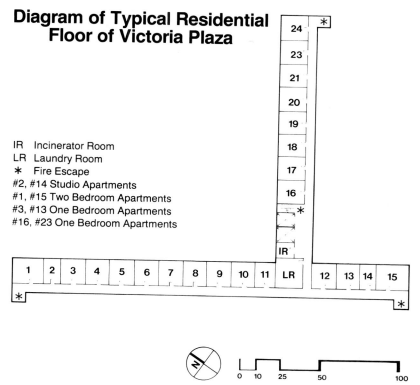

Diagram of Typical Residential Floor of Victoria Plaza

IR Incinerator Room
LR Laundry Room
∗ Fire Escape
#2, #14 Studio Apartments
#1, #15 Two Bedroom Apartments
#3, #13 One Bedroom Apartments
#16, #23 One Bedroom Apartments

0 10 25 50 100

FIGURE 3.3 Victoria Plaza typical residential floor: The upper floors typically contain 2 efficiency units, 2 two-bedroom units, and 19 one-bedroom units. A decentralized laundry is also located on each floor.

Apartment Design: Eight identical residential floors provide a total of 184 units: 16 two-bedroom, 16 efficiency, and 152 one-bedroom apartments. There are electric ranges and central heating. Residents may add air conditioners and telephones. An apartment can be turned into one big room or separated into areas through the use of movable closet units. The kitchen is separated from the living room by a screen covered with light vinyl fabric for easy upkeep. The dining area is near a window that opens onto the exterior balcony corridor. This corridor provides access to other apartments on the same floor and to the two elevators. Standard opaque drapes were provided on apartment windows to ensure a consistent external view of the building (Fig. 3.3).

Special Design Features: The apartments include special features intended to make them safe and convenient for elderly tenants. Shelves and light fixtures are mounted low. Kitchen stoves have controls at the back of the cooking surface. Refrigerators are set on 14-inch platforms to avoid the need to stoop or squat. Doors have lever handles instead of knobs for easier turning and are wide enough for wheelchairs to pass through. Bathrooms have showers rather than tubs, for greater safety. The showers have wood seats to provide security, and tempered doors rather than curtains to provide safety while getting in and out. An emergency button in the bathroom rings a bell mounted in the exterior corridor. Continuous handrails are provided throughout the building and grounds.

The Senior Center: The Senior Center occupies most of the ground floor. Its location within the public-housing facility was both innovative and controversial.

The Senior Center is entered through the main entrance and lobby, where the elevators are located. The lobby area has an open plan with comfortable furniture arranged in conversation groups, a billiard table, and a television set. Piped music has been added. A small residential-scale kitchen for parties or meetings is located next to the lobby. Adjacent to the kitchen is a recreation room, which contains card tables, a piano, an organ, and a public-address system. Living-room type furniture was later replaced by modular seating, which makes it easier to accommodate varied activities such as club meetings, luncheons, and dances.

Beyond the recreation room, a large area was originally reserved for future development. When VP opened, this area was bare except for some donated self-service beauty shop equipment. About half of the area has become the Embassy Room, a small meeting room originally outfitted with black-out curtains and a screen for showing movies and slides. Later this room was used as office space for personnel from various social and health service agencies. Still later, the Embassy Room was used for Housing Authority Training Programs. The remainder of the space is devoted to storage and to vending machines from which employees, residents, and other participants in Center activities can purchase soft drinks, candy, and other snack foods.

Other Services and Features: The ground floor contains offices for Housing Authority and Senior Center staff. Adjoining these offices is a hobby room with equipment for various arts and crafts. The hobby room has been remodeled; an acoustical ceiling, additional lighting, and metal storage cabinets have been installed. Next to it is the library to which a bookmobile comes weekly from the public library.

Methodological and Data Analysis

Initial data were collected from 352 applicants who had been qualified as eligible by the Housing Authority (204 were to be inmovers and 148 were not). Subsequent data were collected from 190 surviving tenants and 105 surviving comparison respondents at the end of the first year of VP's operation, and 127 tenants and 62 comparison respondents at the end of 8 years.

Applicant Profile

The average age of applicants was 72.24; 21 percent were men and 79 percent women. All had low incomes, qualifying them for public housing, yet their median income was similar to that reported by the United States census for older people on Social Security. Their education level was typical for their generation (mostly, eighth grade). Housing Authority standards required the ability to live independently; thus, the seriously ill and handicapped were denied admission.

Housing Quality Differences Between Applicants' Housing and Victoria Plaza Were Great

Generally applicants were living in physically substandard units. The majority resided in housing where wallpaper was peeling, carpets were worn, lighting was inadequate, sanitation was poor, and roaches and rats were prevalent. The typical applicant lived in a converted apartment consisting of a small room partitioned out of a larger one on the upper floor of an old, single-family house. Often antiquated wallpaper hung from two walls while the others were of raw fiberboard. Typically the ad hoc partitions cut out cross-ventilation. Consequently the heat during the long Texas summers was truly dreadful. Most had some form of heating in the winter, although the mechanism was often neither adequate nor safe.

Cooking arrangements were equally substandard. Many had only a hot-plate in one corner of the room, shared refrigerator space in the downstairs kitchen, and garbage cans in the alley. Most had access to a commode inside the building, although it was usually shared with other renters and often was on a different floor. Generally, the bathroom and kitchen fixtures were old and in poor repair. A washing machine was available, although not necessarily convenient, to only one applicant in five.

Social Isolation: It was difficult for applicants to negotiate the dangerous stairways (poorly lit, covered with torn carpet), and they did so only for essential tasks of daily living. It was equally difficult for their friends (usually age peers) to visit. Most applicants were hard-working, middle-class people reduced to poverty by circumstances beyond their control and did not want friends to see them in such circumstances. One woman had spoken to no one, except the boy who delivered her groceries, for the 3 months preceding her first interview. Such isolation was not of her choice. She had broken her hip several years earlier and feared another fall, particularly since her medical insurance was inadequate and she had no family to help her in case of emergency.

General Hypothesis for the Study

Living in the superior environment of VP was expected to have favorable impacts, in general. That is, over time, VP residents would be in better shape than they would have been had they not made the move. This was tested by comparing change over time for movers with change over the same time periods for similar people who did not make the move. Since the average age was over 72 when first interviewed, decrements in health status, activity rate, and other indexes were expected. Therefore the central issue was the differential change between groups. Less loss could index favorable impact.[1]

Findings

Morale and Life Satisfaction

It was predicted that morale or life satisfaction would improve for residents of VP relative to comparison respondents. Several measures were employed to test this hypothesis.[2]

Victoria Plaza Residents Had a Lower Incidence of Major Problems: Among VP tenants, housing had practically disappeared as a "major problem" by the end of the first year, and it did not reappear after eight. However, housing as a major life problem continued to plague a very high and increasing percentage of the comparison group. Aside from housing, at the end of the first year of tenancy, about three-quarters (74 percent) of VP residents but less than a third (29 percent) of the comparison respondents reported no major problems. This difference persisted: at the end of 8 years, over three-quarters (78 percent) of the residents but only a third of the nonresidents reported no major problems other than housing. It would seem that relieving housing problems does not result in greater awareness of other problems. Instead, increased satisfaction with living arrangements was associated with a decrease in the report of other major life problems (Fig. 3.4).

---

[1] *Data Analysis*: When all were applicants, comparison respondents were similar to VP inmovers on demographic descriptions and on variables to be assessed for change over time. To compare change over time among movers with that among comparison respondents in a way that would compensate for any initial difference between groups that might exist, a regression model analysis of covariance (Bottenberg & Ward, 1963) was used with continuous and ordered variables, as was the McNemar Change Test (McNemar, 1962), with dichotomous variables. The 5 percent level of confidence was required as indicative of a statistically significant differential change between groups. All differences reported are significant.

[2] For an indepth analysis of the pre-move to 1 year post-move evaluation, see Carp (1966). The 8-year follow-up study was published as a series of articles that include Carp 1975a, 1975b, 1977; Carp and Carp, 1980.

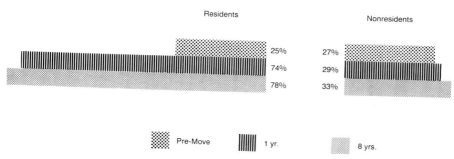

Residents   Nonresidents

25%   27%
74%   29%
78%   33%

Pre-Move   1 yr.   8 yrs.

FIGURE 3.4 Victoria Plaza residents relieved of their housing problem consistently reported fewer major problems than comparison residents.

Fewer Victoria Plaza Residents Considered the Present to Be the Unhappiest Period of Their Lives: A year after the move only 1 percent of VP tenants considered the present to be the unhappiest period of their lives, while 25 percent of the nonresidents did. After 8 years, about the same number of residents considered the present to be the unhappiest period of their lives as they had when the study began, but the proportion of the comparison group who gave that answer had nearly quadrupled, showing a clear trend toward a more negative view of life. Scores on the Happiness Scale of Cavan, Burgess, Havighurst, and Goldhammer (1949) confirmed these results.

Victoria Plaza Residents Were More Confident About the Future: After 1 year, less than half as many residents as nonresidents (7 percent to 15 percent) said they had "no future." Half the residents felt secure about their future, while few (4 percent) were unsure; whereas only 9 percent of the nonresidents felt secure and nearly a quarter were unsure. By the end of 8 years, many members of both groups were "just living from day to day" (46 percent of residents and 58 percent of nonresidents). Still, more residents felt secure about the future (9 percent compared to none of the nonresidents), fewer felt they had no future (4 percent to 12 percent), and more said they did not worry about the future (37 percent to 23 percent).

General Findings: The indicators selected for morale or life satisfaction showed that residence in VP had a positive effect: its tenants tended to show either improvement or less loss than similar persons who remained in living environments like those the VP tenants had left.

Activity, Sociability, and Disengagement

The relationship between activity and well-being remains highly controversial. Some investigators and theorists follow Havighurst's (1963) proposition that activity promotes well-being; some follow the disengagement hypothesis of Cumming and Henry (1961); others stress the importance of individual differences and the "fit" between a person's proclivity for activity and the activity resources in the environment (for example, Brown, 1974; Carp, 1968; Lowenthal and Bolar, 1965; Maddox, 1964).

Most applications for apartments in VP expressed interest in activities they would like to do "if circumstances permitted." The rich supply of neighbors and the Senior Center at VP promised a good fit between desire and opportunity for most residents. Thus, the hypothesis was that movers would become more active, relative to nonmovers, either by increasing involvement or showing less loss over time. This hypothesis was tested for activity rate, sociable behavior, and general disengagement (Carp, 1978; Carp and Carp, 1980).

Activity Rate and Quality

Victoria Plaza Residents Were Involved in a Greater Number of Leisure Pastimes: During each interview, a list of leisure pastimes was presented and the respondent was asked to identify those in which he or she had participated frequently during the past 6 months. This information produced two scores: total number of pastimes and percentage of pastimes that were precoded "active." Across time, the tendency was an increment among tenants and decrement among comparison respondents in both. After 8 years, the average number of leisure pastimes was 15 for the VP group as compared to 8 for nonresidents, and the percentages of active pastimes were 69 percent for residents and 56 percent for nonresidents.

Component items exemplify the differences these scores represent. After 8 years, nearly two-thirds of VP tenants participated in club meetings compared to a quarter of their counterparts. Many more (45 percent to 8 percent) played table games. More read (75 percent to 34 percent), went visiting (72 percent to 62 percent), wrote letters (47 percent to 23 percent), gardened (23 percent to 12 percent), and attended theaters and plays (10 percent to 4 percent). Participation rates among VP tenants in the following pastimes were: community service or charity work, 28 percent; painting, 19 percent; crafts, 14 percent; singing, 11 percent; putting on skits, 10 percent; going to movies, 19 percent; attending football or baseball games, 10 percent; attending discussion groups or lectures, 8 percent; playing musical instruments, 8 percent; doing book reviews, 7 percent; attending concerts, 7 percent; attending school, 6 percent; dancing, 4 percent; modeling clothes, 4 percent; and writing books or articles, 3 percent. None of these pastimes was reported by nontenants.

Passive Use of Time Increased Less for Victoria Plaza Residents: Most members of both groups reported napping and resting as a leisure pastime. The incidence of these activities increased over time for both groups, but less among VP tenants. The most prevalent pastime among nonresidents was "just sitting." At the final data collection less than half of the VP tenants reported "just sitting" as a common pastime, whereas 81 percent of the nontenants did.

At each data collection, respondents recorded 7-day activity diaries that were scored for average time spent per day in 15 categories of time use. After 8 years, VP residents averaged less than 1 hour but comparison respondents nearly 3 hours a day "just sitting" or "doing nothing." Time spent watching television was about two-thirds as much for VP tenants as for comparison respondents.

Fewer Victoria Plaza Residents Decreased Activity Participation: During each interview, people were asked whether their current rate of activity was more, less, or about the same as when they were 55 years old. Less loss over time was noted for VP tenants. At the end of 8 years, over a quarter of VP tenants, compared to only 7 percent of other respondents, said their current rate of participation in activities was "more" than at age 55. Eighteen percent of tenants and a third of nontenants said it was "less" (Fig. 3.5).

Initial Differences in Activity Proved Important: Effects of VP on activity were not expected to be uniform. Those with the greatest proclivity for activity, when they were applicants, were expected to show greatest increases in activity rate following the move, while those with little interest in activity were expected to show little increase. This expectation was borne out. Persons with the most activities and the highest proportion of active pastimes, as applicants, were the residents who made the greatest gains in activity scores after the move. For the minority who originally had high scores on "lost" and passive time use, activity rate remained constant or declined. The activities available in VP were utilized by most inmovers, who had desired activities impossible in their previous situations; however, the same environment accelerated the tendency to sleep and nap, indulge in activities precoded "passive," and to "lose time" among persons who, as applicants, had shown a strong tendency toward passivity.

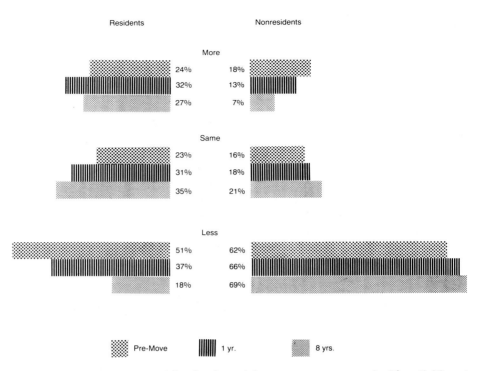

Residents   Nonresidents

More
24%   18%
32%   13%
27%   7%

Same
23%   16%
31%   18%
35%   21%

Less
51%   62%
37%   66%
18%   69%

Pre-Move   1 yr.   8 yrs.

FIGURE 3.5 Participation in activity programs compared with activities at age 55: Victoria Plaza residents consistently reported higher activity program participation rates than nonresidents.

Sociability

Loneliness was a burden to many applicants. The move from an isolated living environment to one rich in social opportunity was expected to increase the rate of social interaction and improve satisfaction with socializing. At the end of the first year, 1 percent of residents and 18 percent of comparison respondents reported companionship as a major problem. After 8 years, no residents reported this, whereas 22 percent of nonresidents did. Another important indicator of sociability was the percentage of pastimes usually carried out in the company of others. At both 1 and 8 years, VP residents reported significantly higher scores. For example, while members of both groups named shopping (including "just looking") as a major leisure pastime in almost identical proportions (84 percent and 85 percent), VP residents were much less likely to go shopping alone (15 percent to 54 percent). The frequency of taking walks was similar between groups, but most comparison respondents walked alone (86 percent) while VP residents usually walked with others (75 percent). Even "watching people" was more companionable for VP tenants; a third of them did their people-watching in the company of others, while 100 percent of the comparison group watched activities of others alone.

Friendships Increased for Victoria Plaza Residents: Residence in VP seemed to increase new friendships while not interfering with old ones. At the end of 8 years, only 3 percent of the comparison group had made new friends in the past year, while 57 percent of VP residents had done so. By the eighth year, tenants had an average of 11.4 "close friends," whereas nonresidents had an average of only 7.5; and no VP resident but 13 percent of nonresidents had "no close friend." The proportion of VP residents who visited friends every day rose from 4 percent when they were applicants to 39 percent at the end of the first year and to 45 percent at the end of year 8. Friendly visiting remained essentially stable for the comparison group (6, 13, and 7 percent). Satisfaction with friends, as measured by the Cavan et al. (1949) scale, clearly improved for VP residents relative to comparison respondents.

Victoria Plaza Residents Spent More Time in Organized Group Activities: With the Senior Center in the building, it was predicted that tenants would participate in more organized activities. According to their 7-day diaries, at the end of 1 year VP residents spent more than twice as much time as comparison respondents at meetings; at the end of 8 years, three times as much. Over time, VP tenants showed an increase in number of memberships in organizations, while comparison respondents showed a loss.

Initial Differences in Sociability Proved Important: Applicants who were the most sociable tended to make the greatest gains in sociable activity and in satisfaction with socialization in VP. However, the minority with a low rate of sociable behavior as applicants experienced a decline over time in sociable participation and in satisfaction. For these introverted people, the resources of the Senior Center and the more than 200 other people under the same roof may have created demands inconsistent with their own natures.

Disengagement

Living in VP slowed or reversed the tendency to disengage for most tenants. However, this effect was not constant across residents. Disengagement was slowed and/or reversed for people who were not very disengaged as applicants. However, the VP environment tended to maintain or increase disengagement in those already disengaged to a considerable extent before the move. Comparison of movers and nonmovers who were at the high end of the disengagement score when they were applicants showed that VP residents became, over time, even more disengaged than comparison respondents with similar initial scores. In an environment where most people re-engaged, a minority disengaged more quickly than they probably would have, had they not moved there.

Self-Perceived Health of Tenants Was Better Than for Community Residents

Attitude toward health as measured by the Cavan et al. (1949) scale showed benefits to VP residents. Two-thirds of comparison respondents but less than half of VP tenants found health was "beginning to be a burden" at the 8-year interval. At the end of the first year, health was reported as a "major" problem by only 4 percent of VP tenants as compared to 18 percent of others; and, at the end of the eighth year, by 11 percent of Plaza residents and 27 percent of comparison respondents (Fig. 3.6).

Health checklist findings demonstrated the same trend. Over time, the number of ailments increased for both groups, but more greatly for comparison respondents. Restrictions on activity due to health showed a greater increase over time for comparison respondents, as did frequency of contact with physicians.

Victoria Plaza Residents Lived Longer

While the findings cited above suggest that residence in VP had a beneficial effect upon health, these self-report data may be subject to bias. Therefore, the groups were compared on a more objective index (Carp, 1977). Comparison was made on the basis of those persons who, on an arbitrarily selected day, had died or were in terminal status in a hospital versus those who were neither. At the end of 8 years, 26 percent of the original inmovers to VP and 37 percent of the comparison respondents were dead or dying. The

FIGURE 3.6 Health was reported as a major problem for a higher percentage of comparison respondents.

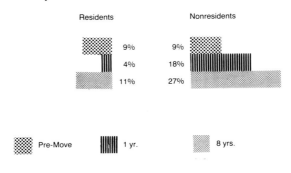

Residents   Nonresidents

9%   9%
4%   18%
11%   27%

Pre-Move   1 yr.   8 yrs.

objective index of officially recorded death plus hospitalization for short-term, terminal care supported the evidence of "softer" indices in indicating that the living environment of VP had a beneficial effect upon health and life expectancy.

Effects Spontaneously Reported by Residents

At the end of the first year of tenancy and again at the 8-year interval, residents were asked an open-ended question about what effect living in VP had upon their lifestyles (Carp, 1975b). Few tenants felt that it had no effect (10 percent at 1 year and 1 percent at 8).

The most frequently reported effect was an increased sense of security (mentioned by 44 percent at both intervals). This security had two components. One was the feeling that they probably could remain in their very nice environment for the remainder of their days. This was a contrast to the insecurity of tenure many had experienced before the move, in old buildings threatened by urban renewal, freeway projects, and rising rental costs. The other component was the sense of physical safety within their apartments and inside VP.

Increased awareness of their age group, its characteristics, and its problems were seldom mentioned the first year (4 percent) but fairly often (21 percent) after 8 years. Apparently there had been some consciousness raising with regard to being elderly as a consequence of living in VP. Anticipation of an extended life-span followed a similar pattern of increase over the years, from 8 percent to 15 percent. These people felt that living in VP would increase their longevity. Increased sense of independence, better opportunity to make friends, and improved feeling of dignity were other perceived effects upon life style.

In General, the Well-Being of Victoria Plaza Residents Was Higher

Comparisons of original VP inmovers with people similar to them but who did not live in that facility support the conclusion that, over the long run as well as the short, the VP environment was generally favorable to many aspects of well-being: morale or life satisfaction, social contact and satisfaction with social relationships, self-perceived health, and death rate. For the majority of people who were selected by staff and who were self-selected to move into VP, the environment was clearly beneficial. Differential rates of improvements and decrements among residents demonstrate the importance of individual differences in people with regard to environmental characteristics. What is a welcome "resource" for one person may be an unwelcome "demand" for the next. The fact that VP was a highly successful living environment for nearly all its original tenants does not justify the conclusion that this type of housing is the best for all elderly persons. However, in view of the overwhelmingly favorable general findings, it is important to know what the respondents thought about this living environment—the siting, architectural design, and special features designed to compensate for age decrements of tenants.

Reactions After the First Tour of the Building

As soon as the building was completed, applicants who had been selected first by the Housing Authority for admission were taken on tours, in groups of eight, for a 2-hour period, to see the common areas of the building and grounds and two apartments.

Positive Reactions Prevailed: The initial reactions to the structure were generally of delight. Regarding choice of apartments, most people were easy to please. When preferences were expressed, they tended to be highly idiosyncratic. Some chose apartments (usually that they had not seen) because it was their "lucky number." Some requested the top floor so they could shake the dust cloth out the window where the wind would be strongest to blow away the dirt, justifying the preference of others to be on the top floor in order to avoid such results of others' house cleaning. While the fourth floor was most often preferred during the visit, the two top floors (the eighth and ninth) were the first to be fully occupied.

Many Applicants Dropped Out After the Tour: Even on the brief visit, reservations were voiced. As the tour ended, potential residents said they would not move. Later, more came to that decision. Over a third (51) of the 148 applicants who did not move into VP were on the first list of people offered apartments. After that, Housing Authority offers and decisions by applicants were so fast and complex that it was impossible to keep an accurate tally. However, it seems clear that a significant proportion of the applicants, once they had seen VP, decided it was not for them.

Why Did Some Qualified Applicants Refuse?

Why did people in clearly deleterious living situations, who had made strenuous and sustained efforts to move to VP, decide—after touring it—that they preferred to remain where they were or to seek other options?

Location of Victoria Plaza Was a Problem: The site may have influenced the choice. Applicants were in search of better housing in a better neighborhood. Victoria Plaza represented a tremendous improvement in housing, but the area surrounding it was an urban slum. While housing ranks second only to spouse in importance for older persons, characteristics of the neighborhood may be even more decisive than those of the living unit in determining "housing satisfaction" (Carp, 1966; Havighurst, 1969; Lawton and Cohen, 1974; Toseland and Rasch, 1978). Because the neighborhood around VP was no better or worse than that in which the applicants resided, the move may have appeared less attractive.

Another influence was the location of VP on the South side, a traditional Mexican-American community. Only 3 percent of the applicants were Mexican-American. For a variety of reasons, the Mexican-American elderly of the city did not hear about or express interest in VP (Carp, 1969, 1970). Therefore, for the vast majority of applicants, VP was outside their "home territory." Moving to VP from the North side, which almost all applicants would have to do, in many ways would be like moving to a foreign country. The separation from family and friends that a move to VP would entail was a problem. The only applicants who lived in the immediate area were residents of a conventional public-housing facility located across the street. Even some of them decided that VP's location across the street would separate them from old friends.

The High-Rise Design Bothered Some: The structure of VP, while delightful to most applicants when they toured it, drew aversive reactions from some. The compact, high-rise construction made some people feel "too hemmed in," with people on all sides and the necessity to go down in an elevator and across a large lobby to gain access to outdoors (Fig. 3.7). Others felt they could never be comfortable in a building in which halls were exterior galleries, or they worried about the safety of the gallery for grandchildren. Some commented about the lack of a ventilating fan in the elevator and the lack of seating, especially when the elevator stalled, as it frequently did during the tours. While some people instantly began mentally arranging their furniture in the new apartment, others realized that their old furniture would not be appropriate in such a fine apartment or would not fit under 8-foot ceilings. The struggle between better housing and keeping old and well-loved personal items was settled sometimes by moving, sometimes by staying.

Certain Design Features Were Criticized: Even on the brief tour, applicants pointed out that some special-design elements, introduced to facilitate daily living for elderly tenants, might instead prove especially difficult in view of their own sensory-motor problems. The back-control stove was one ("I'll have to be awful careful leaning over the hot burner to turn it off"; "I can't hardly see back there where you have to turn things"). The height of the refrigerator seemed inconvenient ("Wouldn't it be better to have the

FIGURE 3.7 Elevation Victoria Plaza: The single-loaded exterior corridor design provided light to both sides of the typical unit.

refrigerator set on the floor?''; ''I'll never be able to use the top shelf''). The lack of bathtubs was noted with regret (''I don't know if I can learn to take a shower''; ''Gee, I really love to sit and soak; I'll miss that''). There were comments that one could not see oneself in the only mirror in the bathroom (''How the hell can I see to shave?''). Some commented that the most important place for a phone jack was the bedroom, not the living-dining area, since they would most likely need to summon help from bed. Many noted the unusually low positioning of the clothes rods in the closets and wondered if their clothes would touch the floor.

People Chose Environments Which Fit Their Needs: The reaction of most of those who decided not to accept the offer of an apartment, after the long months and even years of keeping their applications active, is best summed up by the regretful comment: "It is a *wonderful* place—but not for *me*." While it is clear from findings presented earlier in this chapter that the overall effects of VP were beneficial for the large majority of tenants, there were insignificant and even deleterious results for a small minority, who seemed to have personal characteristics inconsistent with the physical and social milieux. Consciously or unconsciously, people sought settings in which they would best fit. Most qualified applicants who refused apartments, once they toured VP, realized that there was a misfit of their capabilities, needs, and desired lifestyles with the resources, expectations, and demands of the facility. This self-selection may have increased favorable adjustment among residents by eliminating applicants who might not have been happy or well adjusted in VP.

Reaction at the End of One Year of Residency

After a year, the 204 people who had been interviewed while they were applicants and who had moved into VP were interviewed again (Carp, 1966).

Location Continued to Be a Problem: With regard to siting, ambivalence seemed to characterize reactions. The location was considered either good or bad, but rarely neutral or unimportant. Residents enjoyed the fact that VP was less than a mile (within walking distance in good weather) from the major downtown shopping district, and that a bus to that district stopped in front of their door. However, they criticized the immediate neighborhood for its lack of food stores and inexpensive restaurants. They strongly disliked VP's location because the building "looked out of place" in the slums, the streets were not safe, and there were "not the right kind of people" in the area.

Residents Adjusted Well to the Architecture and the Design of the Building: The modern, high-rise design was enthusiastically appreciated by its residents after a year of living there. During planning and building stages there was apprehension that older people might not like the modern high-rise construction, which was so unusual in the city at that time, and that they might not be able to adapt to the single-loaded open galleries that provide the only means of access. However, most tenants (82 percent) found no fault with the building design. A controlled view courtyard provided views from the community spaces and the front entry. Residents used this secure out door space to rest or relax (Fig. 3.8). They especially enjoyed its compactness, which made upkeep of apart-

FIGURE 3.8   A walled exterior courtyard provides views to the lobby and corridor areas.

ments easy and access to other residents convenient. They were aware of the careful planning that utilized ordinary building materials to provide beauty—such as the sunscreens of inexpensive building tile that are not only functional but that also cast interesting, changing patterns of light and shade. They enjoyed the bright, cheerful colors and bold design.

Certain design features—placement of phone, mirror, refrigerator, closet rods, and stove controls, as well as the lack of a bathtub—proved to be real problems. All doors were specified to be wide enough to accommodate wheelchairs. While it was possible to wheel a wheelchair into the bathroom, once there the chair filled the floor space so that the occupant could not transfer from it to any place except the shower.

Elevator Design and Location Were Questioned: The elevators were considered a God-send after years of negotiating unpleasant and unsafe stairways. There were minor complaints (6 percent) about fear of getting stuck in the elevators, which was not wholly unreasonable in view of their performance record. Poor ventilation and lack of seats in the elevators enhanced this fear. Many mentioned the need for a service elevator to transport the sick, dying, and dead rather than taking them through the common area of the lobby and Senior Center.

The Mail Drop Was Another Problem: A mailbox was located some distance from the front door, and residents resented the necessity of walking outdoors to post letters, especially because the mailman came into the building to deliver mail. Ironically, the location of the mail chute resulted from a carefully considered decision on the part of staff to get people out-of-doors. Residents were also required to go across the street to the main Housing Authority office to pay their monthly rent, though the Housing Authority had offices on the ground floor of VP. This arrangement was considered beneficial by the staff but was much resented by residents.

Shared Spaces Posed Some Problems: There were numerous complaints about the difficulty of opening the heavy doors to the outside, and one door was soon replaced by an automatic sliding door. Apprehension was expressed about unlocked outer doors, because of the neighborhood's reputation. A night watchman was posted, and a reception desk at which residents served on a volunteer basis was created to resolve the problem. The open design of apartment porches and the lobby area was criticized by some residents as conducive to nosiness and gossip. However, others approved because the open design provided opportunities to watch what everyone was doing and talk with friends.

Residents thought the location of individual mailboxes in the downstairs lobby was "too public." They did not want everyone in the vicinity (especially those who planned to be there for this purpose) to see what mail they received—particularly when there was none.

Phone contacts were very important to residents. For some it was the only way to keep in touch with friends and family members. Yet often they preferred to forego these calls because of the "public" location of the pay phone. Those who could afford it had phones installed in their apartments.

When asked how future residential facilities for the elderly could be bettered with regard to general design features, tenants suggested a mail drop on each floor, a service elevator with an entry not off the main lobby, and maintenance on washers and dryers in the laundry rooms so that they would not be out of order so often. The largest nomination was for some place in the building in which to buy a meal.

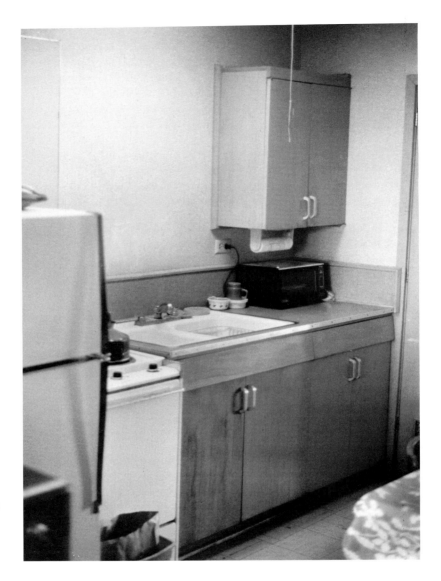

FIGURE 3.9 This compact kitchen area was considered a definite improvement over shared arrangements and substandard conditions Victoria Plaza's residents had experienced in prior housing.

Residents Were Delighted with Most Aspects of the Apartments: The "modern conveniences" were most frequently perceived as being better than expected (65 percent). Though staff were apprehensive about the ability of elderly tenants to cope with up-to-date household equipment, and some prospective tenants voiced the same concern during the orientation tour, there was no problem (Fig. 3.9). Residents were delighted with modern bathrooms and kitchens in their apartments, the laundry rooms conveniently located, and the elevators providing access to all residential floors, the Senior Center, and the world outside. They appreciated the division of space into living, sleeping, kitchen, and bathroom

FIGURE 3.10 Stub walls between apartments defined sitting areas in front of each unit and adjacent to the open single-loaded corridor.

areas, although doors closing off the bedroom area would have been welcome. They enjoyed the fact that activities could be carried on within the privacy of their own apartments and that they did not have to share most facilities. They remarked on the ease of upkeep of the "low" (actually standard) ceilings, the new windows, freshly decorated walls, and unbroken flooring. They appreciated the well-functioning kitchen and bathroom equipment. They were grateful for the trash chute, and delighted by the absence of roaches and rats. One thing that did make housekeeping difficult was the lack of storage space for damp mops and cleaning cloths. Putting them on the porch was unthinkable as well as pro-

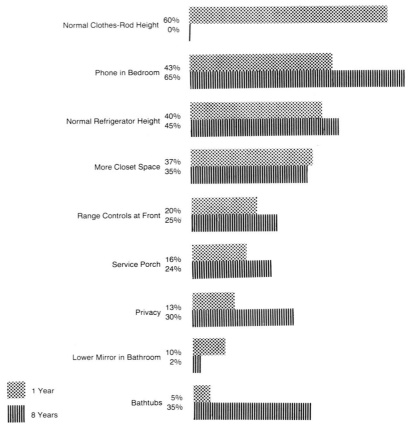

FIGURE 3.11   Spontaneously mentioned improvements to apartments: Awkwardly designed kitchen equipment and a lack of closet space bothered residents.

hibited. It was necessary to keep them in unventilated closets, which created an unpleasant odor.

They enjoyed the view, both the panoramic view of the city on one side and the intimate view of the lives of other residents on the other. They were grateful for the excellent cross-ventilation in summer and the dependable heat in winter. The assiduous care of apartments, and the irate reactions against the few residents who did not take such care, supported the verbal statements of satisfaction, pride, and pleasure in the new home.

Large windows face the open gallery, and it is almost impossible for anyone to walk along the corridor without automatically glancing into each apartment (Fig. 3.10). Tenants had the choice of closing the standard drapes—which cut out light, air, and the view—or of living a fishbowl existence. In the intense heat of the long Texas summer, this was a serious dilemma to many who could not afford air conditioners.

Summary of Improvements for Future Apartments: When tenants were asked an open-ended question about how future buildings could improve upon VP apartments, suggestions included: phone in bedrooms, more closet space, refrigerators at normal height, kitchen ranges with controls anywhere but at the back of the cook-top, a service porch for each apartment to give drying space for mops and cleaning clothes, change the window arrangement for privacy, and lower medicine chests so people could see themselves in the mirrors. Half the male residents of VP spontaneously made the last suggestion regarding future facilities, due to difficulties in shaving (Fig. 3.11). (Subsequently the medicine cupboards in VP were rehung.)

Reactions to the Senior Center

By the end of the first year of residency, 90 percent of VP tenants used the Senior Center. Three-quarters habitually went to the Center for a variety of activities. Over a third participated in some activity every day; and two-thirds, two or three times a week. One-quarter used it "only as a lobby," simply passing through it on their way in and out of the building, and some wished they did not have to do even that. Only 5 percent of the comparison group had been in the Center. This is a typical participation rate for community residents in a senior center (Blenkner, 1961; Rosow, 1967; NCOA, 1975). Clearly, VP residents far outnumbered other respondents in participation in the Center, despite persistent efforts by Center staff to open its activities to all elderly persons. The following reactions about the Center came from VP tenants.

"Lobby Sitters" Were Considered a Problem by Some: These individuals spent most of their time sitting, looking, and discussing the passing scene. Membership in the group was fairly stable, and if one member missed something interesting, another member was glad to fill him or her in. Members passed many enjoyable hours watching and commenting on the behavior of other people. On the other hand, the most heated criticism of the Center was with respect to the openness of this area, which provided a perfect place for "nosey people who have nothing to do but sit and watch and gossip about everyone else's business."

Group Meetings Were Well Attended: Twenty percent of the residents, who either had no television sets or who preferred companionable viewing, went to the Center to watch favorite programs. Nearly two-thirds attended special programs, such as a touring boys' choir or a dance group. Over a third regularly attended a weekly bingo session. About a third went to the weekly movie. Fifteen percent regularly participated in the Sunday evening sing-along, an informal occasion involving singing favorite and familiar songs. Half considered the Center their "place of recreation," much as they would a family room in their own home. They played cards, pool, or dominoes, or started a discussion with someone, depending on their mood and who else was present.

Nearly a third belonged to a Center garden club. The Victoria Plaza grounds had been landscaped and maintenance was provided, but these "green thumbs" cared for plants in the lobby and obtained permission to garden 5-foot plots in an area behind the building where they cultivated vegetables and flowers. Only one in five (mostly women) used the hobby room, but it was kept busy with biweekly visits from a city recreation department instructor.

Noise Was a Problem: The location of various types of activity within one large area caused problems. Television viewers and hi-fi enthusiasts found the pool game, as well as each other, disturbing. Billiard players felt their game was ruined by distracting noises from the television, hi-fi, and card players. Card players couldn't hear each others' bids because of competing activities and noise. Several ladies considered it "disgraceful" to have visitors immediate confront "tobacco-chewing old men in their shirt sleeves" and having to pass through a "pool-hall atmosphere" in order to visit friends.

Book Selections Were a Problem: Only 15 percent used the library, partly because of the unfortunate selection of books provided by the city library. Residents were not interested in how-to books but in reading for entertainment. ("What do I want a cookbook for? My cooking's kept my husband happy for nearly 50 years." "Why can't we have some light fiction?" "How about some who-done-its?" "These books are older than we are.") Resentment was added to disappointment when books donated by family, friends, or tenants themselves did not appear on the shelves after going through the central library for processing. Again, there was a discrepancy between library staff perceptions of what was "suitable for the elderly" and what the tenants wanted.

Medical Services Were a Problem: A similarly small number (15 percent) used the on-site clinic for health-maintenance services (blood pressure or temperature readings). There were many complaints about the clinic. Residents felt that it was primarily a well-baby clinic and offered minimal assistance to old people. If a medical service was to take up space in their building, it should be for them, or at least for adults.

How the Senior Center Could Be Improved: When asked how future buildings could be improved with regard to a senior center, some suggested that a center should not be included or, if it were, there should be access to living quarters without having to pass through it. Others thought it should be restricted to the use of residents and their invited guests. Despite the staff's best efforts, there was resentment of "outsiders." Tenants *knew* that the Center was for all elderly in the county but they *felt* that the area was their own living room.

Overall Impressions of the Building

It is important to put the criticisms in perspective. Residents were overwhelmingly delighted with and grateful for being in the building. Most of the critical points were brought out in discussion of how future facilities could be made even better. With respect to their own circumstances, tenants could express nothing but thanks.

Reactions After Eight Years of Tenancy

The first year may be a "honeymoon" period, after which enthusiasm fades. People growing older might view features of VP differently as those features become barriers or are recognized as facilitators of independent living (Carp, 1975b).

Very Few Left Victoria Plaza Voluntarily: Failing health was almost the only cause for moving out. A low voluntary move-out rate is not firm evidence of satisfaction. By moving to VP, residents foreclosed other options. Cheap apartments were lost, families readjusted their living space, and residents' contingency funds were exhausted. However, evaluations after 8 years were overwhelmingly positive and decisive, which suggests that satisfaction was real and persistent. At the end of the first year, 96 percent of the surviving original tenants decribed VP as a "good" or "very good" place to live; 98 percent did so at the end of 8 years. At the end of the first year, 74 percent gave it the highest rating on a five-point scale; after 8 years, 89 percent did. On the other hand, the proportion who reported that there was "nothing bad" about VP decreased from 47 percent in the first year to 16 percent in the eighth. Still, familiarity did not desensitize residents to good points or to problems.

There was Some Adjustment to an Undesireable Location: At the end of 8 years, a majority of tenants still found the location disadvantageous. Over a third found it convenient, and availability of public transportation was the rationale for convenience in every case. Over a quarter mentioned a second desirable aspect of the location: they could walk to the center of town and the main shopping district. Apparently residents did not adjust to the neighborhood but found ways to avoid it. Disappointments with location centered around fear of being on the street and lack of stores, churches, and eating places. All of these complaints increased from the end of the first year to the end of the eighth.

Design Was the Most Consistently Appreciated Feature of Victoria Plaza: After 8 years of living in the building, 84 percent of the tenants found no fault with the building design. Its "modern conveniences" continued to be by far the major consideration (61 percent). Residents remained aware of and appreciated the physical housing.

Design Problems Remained: Concern over the lack of a service elevator coupled with the location of the elevators in the center of the lobby, and the resulting problem of removing ill, dead, and dying residents through the middle of the lobby and recreation area rose eightfold from the first year to the eighth. Complaints about gossip and lack of privacy were also more pervasive. They rose from 13 percent at the end of 1 year to 30 percent at the end of 8 as the "worst thing" about VP. Design sources of lack of privacy were the window arrangements in apartments, opening onto the galleries; the openness of the downstairs lobby and Senior Center, which nicely accommodated the "lobby sitters"; and the apartment patios opening onto the back of the building, which provided opportunities for a similar group, the "porch watchers." Inconvenience and hazard of the raised refrigerators and back-control stoves increased over time, as did regret at the absence of bathtubs.

The Order of Suggested Improvements for Future Buildings Changed Somewhat: Provision of some place to buy meals was mentioned more often and was the foremost recommended improvement (78 percent). Inclusion of a service elevator (35 percent) and a phone in the bedroom (65 percent) also increased. Provision of bathtubs, even if shared, was mentioned by over a third (35 percent), whereas this improvement was mentioned by only a few at the 1-year interval. Increased closet space, especially for damp cleaning equipment, gained mention (35 percent), as did service porches (24 percent), a mail drop on each floor (20 percent), and different window treatment to provide privacy (17 percent).

These percentages represent tenants who spontaneously mentioned each feature in response to an open-ended question (Fig. 3.12). They must not be mistaken for the proportions of tenants who might agree that the feature would improve future buildings for the elderly. Tenants offered these suggestions not in criticism of VP but in hopes that their experience living there might provide a basis for even better planning and construction of other buildings.

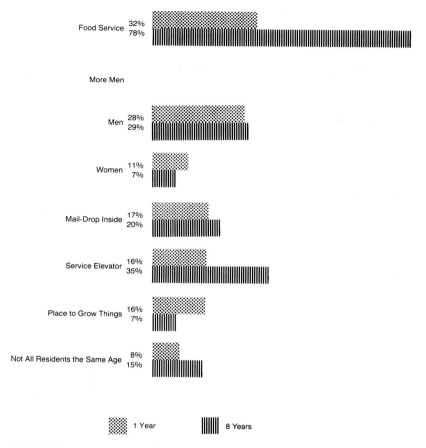

Food Service   32%
           78%

More Men

Men   28%
    29%

Women   11%
     7%

Mail-Drop Inside   17%
        20%

Service Elevator   16%
        35%

Place to Grow Things   16%
         7%

Not All Residents the Same Age   8%
          15%

▒ 1 Year   ‖‖ 8 Years

FIGURE 3.12   Spontaneously mentioned improvements to the building: Lack of food service continued to be a major problem for residents.

Would It Be Better If?

After the open-ended questions, tenants were asked if they would like VP better if it had certain specific characteristics. The responses for both time periods are reported together to highlight changes and constancies across time.

Loss of one's yard was anticipated to be a problem to many, but it was not. At the end of the first year 16 percent said they would like it better if they had a place to grow things; at the end of 8 years, 7 percent said so. This diminution may reflect the provision of garden plots and permission to work on the landscaped areas in the interim.

Men Would Appreciate More Male Peers: A sizeable minority of men (28 percent at 1 year and 29 percent at year 8) and a lesser percentage of women (11 percent and 8 percent) said they would like it better if there were more men. Older men are in scarcer supply than are older women, and the difficulty of attracting them to such facilities has been noted. Apparently a dearth of men decreases their attractiveness for men. One source of satisfaction for male residents was "providing a good place for the wife when I'm gone"; another was the billiard table and its regular clientele (Fig. 3.13).

Victoria Plaza Residents Wanted to Be Nearer Old Friends: This feeling grew over time (12 percent at 1 year to 27 percent at 8 years). It seemed to reflect the increasing difficulty in visiting and being visited by friends outside VP rather than a growing preference for old friends over new. The idea that VP would be a better place if residents were not "all the same age" was a minor issue; however, those expressing it doubled over time (from 8 percent to 15 percent).

Meal Provision Was the Most Consistently Desired Service: Other questions regarding whether VP would be "better if" were asked only at year 8. The most consistent response (83 percent) was in regard to inclusion of some place they could buy meals at reasonable cost. This is consistent with the fact that lack of restaurants in the area was mentioned as a disadvantage of the location of VP and that, when asked how future buildings could be improved, spontaneous mention of inclusion of food service was made by about a third of tenants at the end of the first year and by over three-quarters at the end of 8 years. The opportunity to purchase meals was strongly and pervasively desired. This increased interest in food service may reflect, in part, personal decrements with the passage of years. Residents were also asked whether future facilities should include individual kitchens in each apartment. The large majority (89 percent) favored them but 11 percent (surprisingly, all women) did not.

Medical Services Were Also Desired: Like the interest in meal service, responses regarding medical facilities and services may be due in part to the fact that the survivors tended to be more frail after 8 years. About two-thirds said they would like VP better if it had a full-scale hospital unit; almost as many, if nursing care was available in the clinic on the ground floor, around the clock, and in their apartments when needed; and over half, if there was a full-scale medical clinic. Most other answers were "it would depend," with very few negative reactions.

Most would like the security of knowing they could have hospital care within VP, without the dislocation of being taken to a hospital. The existing nursing services, which had increased over time, served important functions for residents, but did not meet the needs of those who became ill or fell after working hours. A

FIGURE 3.13 The billiard table became a "hang-out" for the minority population of men in Victoria Plaza.

clinic, while desired by the majority, was considered less urgent because residents were able to visit a doctor's office or clinic in the community for routine checkups and medical problems.

The desirability of medical services depended upon their location and degree of intrusion into normal activities. On-site nursing, physician, and hospital care were favored by the large majority. These facilities should be easily accessible to tenants at all hours, and easy for friends to visit, however, not too close to apartments or group activity areas.

The Senior Center Was More Popular But Gossip Was a Greater Problem: After 8 years, nearly two-thirds of the tenants went to the Center for programs or parties, and the same percentage used it for informal socializing much as they would the living room of their home. In fact, many referred to the Center as such. Nearly half the residents habitually went to the game nights. Over a third regularly went to the weekly movie, and nearly as many took part in garden club activities. A quarter habitually watched television in the Center, and the same number regularly used the hobby room. Smaller numbers used the library, attended church meetings, or worked in the patio planting areas.

The greatest source of dissatisfaction was the gossip in the Senior Center. This was mentioned by 13 percent at the end of the first year and by three times as many at the end of 8 years. Among those who mentioned any disliked aspect, gossip and nosiness were named by 38 percent at the end of the first year and by 68 percent at the end of 8 years.

Food Service Was Desired: The most common improvement suggested for the Senior Center was addition of a cafeteria, coffee shop, or cafe. The provision of a place to buy meals was suggested by many more (49 percent) at 8 years than it was previously (12 percent). At both times, addition of a food service was recommended by about 90 percent of those who suggested a change of any kind.

Should a Senior Center Be Housed in a Residential Facility for the Elderly?:   In terms of benefits to tenants, the results suggest that inclusion of a center provides a significant enrichment of opportunities for activity and socializing. By far the majority of participants in center activities were VP residents, and their rate of attendance far exceeds any figures in the literature for community-resident elderly attending a center outside the building in which they live. Few of those who did not move into the Plaza attended events in the center; however, their rate of participation approximates published figures for attendance at senior centers in various cities, suggesting that a senior center incorporated into public housing for the elderly has no more and no less impact upon non-residents than does a free-standing senior center.

Conclusions

Residence in VP was beneficial to the vast majority of its original tenants, over the long as well as the short run. Comparisons with similar nonresidents showed that VP tenants experienced improved morale and life satisfaction, greater activity, more satisfaction with use of time, increased social interaction, improved satisfaction with sociability, less disengagement, better perceptions of health status, and a lower death rate. A small minority showed no change or a reverse tendency.

A Wide Variety of Design Approaches are Preferable

The fit or congruence between individual and environment seems salient to these results. Housing Authority selection procedures ensured that all qualified applicants were competent to live independently. For VP residents, congruence between person and environment was improved by the self-selection of applicants who accepted or refused the offer to move there, following the orientation tour. This finding supports the need for a wide variety of design approaches to housing the elderly and careful attention to matching tenants with facilities. The fact that VP and similar facilities have been successful in improving the lives of most of their tenants does not justify the conclusion that this type of residential setting is the best for every older person.

Planned Housing for the Elderly Is Highly Satisfying to Its Residents

In the long and short run, the original tenants of VP were well satisfied, and the cornerstone of this staunch satisfaction was physical characteristics of the setting. Awareness and delight with the physical environment is perhaps not surprising at the end of the first year, but it is impressive that this sensitivity and appreciation were maintained and even grew to the end of the eighth year. The overall finding was that "good housing" was an immediate joy and a continuing source of gratification.

The Participation of Older Persons in the Design Process May Prevent Some Problems

While well satisfied with their own situation and sharply critical of anyone who had a bad word to say about "their" building, residents saw some faults and were forthcoming with suggestions about how future facilities could be better. Some design features based on staff interpretation of what is good for old people (that is, placement of the mail drop) were not pleasing to tenants. Some special design features based on architects' and planners' views of what would fit the capabilities of elderly people and support them in independent living were not successful. Standard kitchens (refrigerator height and stove type), standard placement of clothes rods, and placement of mirrored medicine chests could have been more satisfactory than the special arrangements that were made. Even on the first brief tour, many applicants noticed these features.

These findings support the growing recognition that designers and architects may not see eye to eye with users and that older people should participate in planning and design of housing for the elderly. Those who are not designers or architects have difficulty in imagining the reality of an environment by reading plans, drawings, and specifications. Simulation techniques may often be feasible and, in the long run, economical. The decision to place refrigerators on 14-inch blocks and to use "safety stoves" designed with children in mind might have been seriously reconsidered if prospective tenants had seen the kitchen plans. The cost of removing the blocks and replacing the stoves was prohibitive, and they remained inconveniences at best, hazards at worst, for VP tenants.

DESIGN DIRECTIVES

DESIGN DIRECTIVE **ONE**	*The provision of meal services in the building or in the surrounding neighborhood should be considered.*

1. After year 1 and year 8, VP residents continued to rate the provision of some place to buy meals as most important.

2. The neighborhood within which VP was situated had few opportunities available for inexpensive meals.

DESIGN DIRECTIVE **TWO**	*Provision of medical services within the building must be considered from the very beginning.*

1. After year 8, nearly two-thirds of the sample suggested that they would like VP better if it had a full-scale hospital unit or 24-hour nursing care available in the clinic on the ground floor.

2. Some residents, who had a strong desire to keep the medical care convenient, also wanted it to be as unobtrusive as possible.

DESIGN DIRECTIVE **THREE**	*A separate service elevator that provides quick access to an exterior loading dock for emergency purposes is highly desirable.*

1. Victoria Plaza residents complained about the central location of the elevator and the fact that dead and dying residents were transported through the senior center on the way to an emergency vehicle.

2. A second elevator with a large platform situated near the edge of the building that allows for emergency services as well as the movement of furniture and other large pieces of equipment should always be considered.

DESIGN DIRECTIVE **FOUR**	*If the senior citizen center is planned as part of a housing development, it should be located near the edge of the site with a separate entrance to encourage community residents.*

1. The central location of the senior center on the first floor of the VP building created problems for both residents and community users. Victoria Plaza tenants consider community residents as invading their "living room." Community residents may have been discouraged by strong feelings of territoriality expressed by VP residents.

2. The undifferentiated open space in the senior center created acoustical and noise interference problems. The provision of privacy in community spaces must be considered equal to the need for providing spaces that allow for new friendship formation and exchange.

If showers are specified as a standard feature, communal bathtubs should be considered as an additional feature.

DESIGN DIRECTIVE
FIVE

1. Showers were specified for safety reasons, although some residents expressed the desire for access to a communal bathtub.

2. Some individuals went as far as to purchase plastic tubs that they placed on the floor of their showers in order to simulate a bathtub experience.

The neighborhood within which a housing project is placed has an extremely important effect on housing satisfaction.

DESIGN DIRECTIVE
SIX

1. Fifty percent of VP residents considered the location to be disadvantageous even after 8 years. The only positive attributes listed about the neighborhood were "convenient bus transportation" and being "within walking distance to downtown." Both of these attributes provide opportunities to leave the local neighborhood.

2. A well-chosen neighborhood surrounded by community services, shopping opportunities, and restaurants may mitigate future service-need problems.

Architectural and design features were the most consistently appreciated qualities of Victoria Plaza.

DESIGN DIRECTIVE
SEVEN

1. Architecture and design features were considered from the first day as one of the most positive attributes of this new living situation. Victoria Plaza represented a great increase in standard of living for most individuals who chose to move.

2. The "worst thing" about VP was gossip and the lack of privacy. Specific sources include apartment windows that open onto the single-loaded exterior gallery corridor, the openness of the downstairs lobby that accommodated "lobby sitters," and patios that were open to the back of the building and accommodated the "porch watchers."

3. Although residents could be candid and critical of some of the building's less successful features, they were fiercely loyal and extremely proud of the Plaza. The building itself became a strong symbolic representation of their own social status.

POLICY CONSIDERATIONS

POLICY CONSIDERATION **ONE**	*Government programs should include planned housing for the elderly.*

Comparisons between community residents and VP residents showed marked increase at the end of year 1 and year 8 with regard to improved morale, life satisfaction, greater activity, more satisfaction of the use of time, increased social interaction, improved satisfaction with sociability, less disengagement, better perceptions of health status, and a lower death rate. We must be careful not to attribute all of these improvements to the housing form alone. Residents of VP may have been able to accrue higher discretionary income that could be used for better health care or higher quality food. Nevertheless, such findings provide strong evidence that planned housing programs for the elderly should be continued.

POLICY CONSIDERATION **TWO**	*Choice and variety should characterize housing policies that lead to the provision, production, and development of alternative housing arrangements for older people.*

Although VP was considered an outstanding environment by its residents, it must be noted that this population may have represented a self-selected group. After a tour of the building, a number of older people who had been offered residency chose to turn down an apartment at VP. Some of these individuals were hesitant to leave familiar neighborhoods and strong social ties, others intuitively seemed to know that this was not right for them. Consequently, the variety of housing types and programs available to older persons should be expanded.

POLICY CONSIDERATION **THREE**	*The interconnection between planned housing for the elderly and its surrounding area needs to be carefully considered.*

The concept of person–environment fit should be considered in the development of new housing policies and housing choices. Care should be taken in the development of community spaces that theoretically will serve the resident population and the community. Feelings of territoriality may create a setting where both tenants and community residents feel ill at ease. The development of a senior center that is located on "neutral territory" adjacent and connected to the building but open to the neighborhood may be a good solution.

The planning and design process for a building such as this should involve older people from the very beginning.

Many of the criticisms voiced at the end of the tour, on the first day that applicants viewed the building, were valid criticisms that haunted the architects and planners for years. If at all possible, the architect and designer should involve the potential user in the design of the housing arrangement. This could take place in a number of ways. For example, older people could be taken on tours of comparable buildings and asked to comment on what they like or dislike about that setting. Also, mock-ups of critical spaces (that is, kitchen and bathroom) could be developed, allowing older people to preview the arrangement and comment.

The staff and management plan for the building should consider the needs, preferences, and desires of the older people as paramount.

The Victoria Plaza staff decided that a mail drop outside of the building would encourage individuals to leave the dwelling every day. The staff considered that the opportunity to pay rent at a housing authority office across the street would allow for another "excuse" to get out of the building. Both of these activities could very easily have taken place in the building and were resented by many older residents.

4

EVALUATING THE PHYSICAL ENVIRONMENT
Conclusions from Eight Housing Projects

Galen Cranz

P ost-occupancy evaluations of housing projects are providing architects with insightful glimpses as to how their buildings are being used, valued adjusted, and modified by tenants and management. The study reported in this chapter first appeared in 1975 as a report (Cranz and Schumacher) that documented the environmental attitudes and preferences of 280 older tenants of eight low- to moderate-income housing projects in New Jersey. Since then, the findings from the study have occasioned interest and discussion, stimulated further study (Christensen and Cranz, 1982), and influenced design (Stephans, 1981). This chapter reports the findings and conclusions that in retrospect have proved to be of greatest interest to researchers and policy makers.

Related Research

Because very little comparable baseline data had been generated regarding the preferences and attitudes of older people about "special built" housing, the researchers chose to develop a broad comprehensive instrument. Since the publication of this study, scores of evaluations have been conducted and published. Some of the more noteworthy contributions have been from Lawton (1975), Zeisel et al. (1977), Green et al. (1978), Howell (1980), and Zeisel et al. (1983). The findings from this study fit well between national surveys and single building evaluations. National survey evaluations, because of the structure of their research design, often deliver recommendations that are broad and general. Single building evaluations, in contrast, concentrate on the special individual chemistry of building form, management policy, and tenant characteristics for a particular structure.

Methodology and Data Analysis

Broadly speaking, the logic of the study was to develop first a social analysis of the elderly tenant in public housing, based on responses to an attitude questionnaire, and then to develop performance criteria for public housing of the elderly from this social analysis. The questionnaire order was conceived as a continuum representing a progression from questions relating to the small scale of the individual apartment unit to questions relating to the larger scale of the entire community in which the building was situated.

Tenant satisfaction follows an uneven path downward from the micro- to the macro-level. Architects have apparently learned more about designing kitchens and bathrooms for elderly individuals than about designing open or communal spaces for elderly groups. Therefore, findings and conclusions from this study will develop with particular emphasis at the site design scale.

General Characteristics of the Eight Projects

Table 4.1 describes some important characteristics of public housing where the 280 respondents lived. The respondents were capable of and their apartments were designed for "independent living." The particular sites were selected for four reasons. First, they were designed, at least in part, for the elderly. Second, they were low- to moderate-income units, the type of housing with which the client, the New Jersey Department of Community Affairs, was most involved. Third, they were independent living situations supported by state and federal programs so that any findings were in principle applicable to this new, relatively unstudied building type. Fourth, the eight projects were located within a highly urbanized New Jersey context but represented a range of alternatives from garden to high-rise, small to large, urban to suburban, with or without private open space, "integrated" with housing for younger people or not, and with or without bathtubs.

Preliminary Observations: Before designing the questionnaire, researchers visited Trent Center, Josephson-Abbott, and French Towers (all in Trenton), New Brunswick Homes in New Brunswick, and Lloyd Terrace in Princeton. This phase was initiated with certain preconceptions concerning the use of public and private space. Some of these, such as the needs for street orientation and public open space in front of the buildings, were confirmed. Oth-

TABLE 4.1   Criteria for Site Selection

Site	Type of Buildings	Number of Units	Context Density	Income Level	Location	Balconies or Patios	Elderly Only or Mixed	Baths or Showers Only
Camiano (Lodi)	Garden complex	40	Medium	Low	North	Yes	Elderly only	Baths
Columbus (Newark)	High-rise complex	1,500	High	Low	North	No	Mixed	Baths
Hanson (Perth Amboy)	Single high-rise	100	Medium	Low	North	No	Elderly only	Showers only
Bethany (Keyport)	Single high-rise	230	Low	Moderate	Central	No	Elderly only	Baths
Oakhurst (Oakhurst)	Garden complex	90	Medium	Moderate	Central	No	Elderly only	Baths
Trent Center (Trenton)	Single high-rise	158	High	Moderate	Central	No	Elderly only	Baths
Josephson (Trenton)	Single high-rise	152	High	Low	Central	Yes	Elderly only	Baths
Tarklin (Vineland)	Garden complex	150	Low	Low	South	Yes	Elderly only	Baths

ers, such as the possible desirability of integrating elderly and younger age groups, were strongly contraindicated.

Age Segregated Projects Seemed to Be More Satisfactory than Age Integrated Ones: At French Towers and Josephson-Abbott, projects that are reasonably insulated from younger persons, difficulties with youths were among the least frequent complaints. At New Brunswick Homes, a project that contains one elderly tower among a series of family buildings, the elderly residents behaved like prisoners, afraid to venture forth into other portions of the site.

Formal Social Organizations Often Overcame Physical Problems of the Site and the Neighborhood: The desire for and dependency of tenants on various forms of social organization were a surprise. In Trent Center, French Towers, and Josephson-Abbott, the maintenance of highly institutionalized social groups and cliques caused some amount of tension between residents. These social structures, however, provided numerous opportunities for social integration on sites and in neighborhoods that did not otherwise lend themselves to social interaction and integration. Did the neighborhood and site conditions foster the coalescing of these social groups? It is hard to determine. A more agreeable neighborhood and a less obtrusive architectural form might have fostered greater social integration with surrounding churches, clubs, and community recreational activities.

FIGURE 4.1 High management visibility such as illustrated in this upper-income hotel example can be a source of security.

The dependency on the site for social exchange also seemed to encourage a close relationship between tenants and management. Architecturally this relationship was aided by the management's literal visibility in the project. For example, in Josephson-Abbott, Trent Center, and French Towers—all large, high-rise projects— management offices were located in central positions and were easily accessible. This observation led to the question of whether personalities or design, or both, had most influence on the development of tenant-management relationships (Fig. 4.1).

The use of "shared spaces" such as lobby, entrance, and circulation was of particular interest. In French Towers, for example, the management maintained a policy that precluded sitting in the lobby. This was based on an aesthetic anxiety, that is, that older people "in bathrobes" sitting around the lobby would make it seem like an old-age home. Therefore, in French Towers, as in other sites, a different configuration of public space might have supported informal gathering and socializing. The degree to which management concerns for cleanliness and ease of maintenance affected such attitudes was questioned, and questionnaire items were devised to test this.

Characteristics of the 280 Respondents

In general, the study dealt with low- and moderate-income persons living under relatively ordinary conditions in apartment complexes. They were "independent"—sufficiently mobile and healthy to require little or no continuous aid by the resident staff. The average resident was 73 years old. There were no significant differences in the age structure of the population among the eight different sites.

As in the nation as a whole, women in this age group dramatically outnumbered the men. The sample had 72 percent women and only 28 percent men. Tarklin Acres, within the sprawling low density metropolitan district of Vineland, had the highest proportion of men (42 percent). The almost exclusively Italian community of Camiano Homes in Lodi had the lowest (17 percent). Not surprisingly, those sites with the more than average numbers of men also had a younger overall age group.

Most of the women were presumed to be widowed based on data from the managers questionnaire. Their estimate of the number of widowed persons on each site averaged around 80 percent.

The sample included a slightly higher than national average of black persons (17 percent). This was to be expected, since publicly assisted housing were used disproportionately by lower income groups. With the exception of one black person reported at Camiano Homes in Lodi, all the blacks were located in three sites: Columbus Homes in Newark, Josephson in Trenton, and Tarklin Acres in Vineland. Whites were virtually the only other racial group in this sample.

Boldly stated, government assisted housing in New Jersey for older persons required meeting the needs of white women in their 70s, although the proportions of blacks and men were significant enough and often concentrated in specific sites to demand the planner's attention.

Expectations from Previous Housing Experience

Some further idea of the population can be derived from an account of its previous housing experience derived from questionnaire responses. Housing specifically designed for the elderly is always occupied by people who have nearly a lifetime's prior housing experience, so their expectations must loom large in design considerations.

The great majority of respondents had lived for more than 2 years in the housing where they were interviewed. Not surprisingly, the most frequently mentioned reason for moving to this housing was economic.

While people lived in these projects because they were inexpensive, it was more significant that they were inexpensive for the value. When asked what they liked best about their apartments, few respondents spontaneously mentioned low rent. They emphasized rather that they liked "everything" about their apartment, especially its convenience for upkeep by one person.

Most Respondents Lived Nearby and Didn't Miss Their Old Neighborhoods: Two-thirds of the sample lived nearby before moving. The people who came from another neighborhood were slightly more likely to miss their old neighborhood. Thus, the practice of drawing people from the surrounding community did seem to lower the chances of people feeling homesick for their old neighborhoods, but not dramatically. Hence, a policy of attracting local residents would seem helpful but not essential. The move launches the resident into a new social world, even if he or she had lived right next door.

Respondents Were Nearly Split Between Preference for a Suburban or Urban Site: Respondents were asked if they would ideally prefer living in an urban, suburban, or rural setting. Only a handful chose a rural setting (8 percent), while suburban and urban choices were nearly equal (45 percent and 47 percent respectively). It could be inferred from these figures that the residents of these projects were not noticeably frustrated or discontented with the high-density settings in which most of them were located.

Slightly over half (56 percent) of the sample had been living in an apartment, rather than a house, before the move. Only two sites, Oakhurst and Tarklin Acres, had less than half (40 percent) who had been living in an apartment prior to their move. Happily, since these were also the garden apartment sites in our sample, those people who had little experience with apartment house living were the ones supplied with low-rise semi-detached units.

Prior to moving, more than half (58 percent) did not have a garden or a yard; hence they were probably not acutely disappointed by the absence of private plots of outdoor space in their new homes.

Findings

Bathtub or Shower: A Major Question

One important question the sponsor of the research wanted to resolve was: Could showers be substituted for bathtub/showers to save money? The argument was that if baths were not being used because people could not get in and out of them readily, then they might as well be abandoned in favor of a well-designed shower, possibly a molded unit with a built-in seat. Another assumption was that older people might not be used to showers, since their widespread use was relatively recent in the United States, but that they could learn to like them once they got used to the idea. Our findings did not support the assumption that baths were not used. People preferred baths to showers nearly two to one.

Half of the Respondents Residing in Units with Only Showers Still Preferred Bathtubs: We purposely selected Hanson Homes in Perth Amboy to see how people felt about baths when they had only showers available. Whether one interpreted this situation as one of limitation, or as an opportunity to learn to prefer showers, the findings were the same: half the people in Hanson Homes still preferred baths. The half that preferred showering seemed to be learning to like what they had been given the opportunity to experience, although the showers, even in this case, were still not overwhelmingly popular.

Sex had some influence; over two-thirds of the women preferred baths over showers. Among the men, the division between those liking baths or showers was more equal. When the residents had only showers, as in Hanson Homes, men adapted to showers more readily than women. Women reported more trouble entering the shower or tub than did men.

Cleaning the tub or shower was a problem for 13 percent of the sample. Further research into the precise nature of the difficulty would be helpful in order to see if it could be solved by a design change without increasing costs.

A Shared Bathtub Is a Sensible Compromise: Thinking that installing only a shower in each unit might save money, and yet aware of the advantages of a bath, an arrangement was conceived that could also have important social and medical benefits. A bathing room with a sauna and a physical therapist (like Japanese, Turkish, Russian, or Roman baths) could become a significant source of preventive medical care.

A major difference between this image and that of conventional American bathing was that it would occur in the presence of others. To emphasize this, but at the same time to emphasize its practical purpose, we formulated a question that explicitly mentioned having an attendant present: Would you be in favor of or against having a place with an attendant to help people into and out of the tub?

Given the extent to which this idea intentionally contradicted the dominant cultural practices, we were surprised to find one-third (34 percent) in favor of the proposal. The older person's attitude toward this idea did not vary by age, sex, or race. Thinking that the semipublic nature of the bathing room might be related to fear of others, we correlated this item with a standard indicator of paranoia: Do you think anyone has taken advantage of you here? The results showed no such correlation.

In brief, baths are overwhelmingly the favorite of older people, especially women. Should a policy maker decide to eliminate them from individual apartments for the sake of economy, showers specified in their place should be be particularly comfortable with built-in seats, and the developer might consider a shared bathing room as a complement.

Outdoor Open Space: Private

Slightly over one-third (36 percent) of the sample units had either a patio or balcony. Of those who did not have them, two-fifths (39 percent) thought that having a balcony would add a lot; one-quarter (25 percent) thought that they would be more trouble than they were worth; and over a third (35 percent) were indifferent about them, saying it did not matter or that they had no opinion.

Almost All Respondents Who Had a Balcony or Patio Valued It: These findings were particularly interesting in contrast with findings concerning those who had balconies or patios. Less than 1 percent did not like these spaces at all, over four-fifths (82 percent) valued them very much, and less than one-fifth (17 percent) were only lukewarm in their attitude toward them (Fig. 4.2).

Previous experience with private open space affected the residents' judgments about how desirable a balcony or patio would be. Those who had a garden before they moved thought that a patio would be desirable. Those who did not had no opinion.

The general conclusion one could draw from this was that once a person had a balcony or some experience with private outdoor space she valued it and probably would not want to give it up. Those without such experience might not be sure just how much they would use one and therefore would not be convinced that one would add a lot to their lives.

Balconies and Patios Were Amenities That Some People Truly Appreciated: This evidence suggests that balconies would not be actively missed by a majority if excluded from a plan. However, this does not justify leaving them out. For some they symbolized the difference between having the bare minimum and having something extra. People did not have high expectations for any part of the environment beyond the walls of their unit. Even though a closely coupled patio space was clearly part of "their" unit, it was still similar enough to public outdoor space to be subject to dis-ownership. Therefore the use of balconies and patios might best be treated as an option for some tenants who, because of previous experience or a strong disposition toward outdoor space, might appreciate and enjoy them.

FIGURE 4.2 Balconies provide a controlled view and are generally highly valued.

Getting the Mail

Half (50 percent) of the respondents actively used the mail room. If we excluded from the sample the garden apartment sites, which had no mail rooms, then the proportion increased to two-thirds (67 percent). Field observations suggested that the mail delivery was an important and exciting part of the day.

The research suggests that the mail area should be prominent and might best be furnished with chairs for informal meetings, lamps for reading mail, and possibly a writing desk for jotting notes. More research examining the role of mail delivery in a tenant's everyday life would be a valuable investigation.

Open Outdoor Space: Public

About half the survey population never walked to a grocery or drug store, a barber shop or beauty parlor, a restaurant, or a place of worship. Although public transportation was used for various purposes, clearly the private automobile played a large role in movement outdoors. A design implication of this phenomenon is that walking needs to be encouraged.

The most basic question about open space was whether or not it was wasted. Four-fifths of the residents (82 percent) said that they sat outside in the summer. This activity was popular regardless of building type or quality of the surrounding neighborhood. On the basis of these data we cannot conclude that low-rise housing is always the best way to facilitate use of the outdoors, since Columbus Homes, the high-rise, showed a similar rate of outdoor space use when compared to the two garden apartments.

Outdoor Areas on the Housing Site Received Consistent and Heavy Use: Nearly half (46 percent) sat outside every day that weather permitted, another quarter (26 percent) sat out almost always, and the remaining quarter (26 percent) used it occasionally. Thus, three-quarters of the population sat outdoors frequently and only 2 percent said they almost never sat outside. At three sites (Hanson, Trent Center, and Josephson) a large number of residents who never used the outdoors was combined with a high number who used the outdoors every day. The most practical kinds of open space were outdoor sitting areas (used by 55 percent), the flower gardens (25 percent), and outdoor recreation areas, such as shuffleboard (22 percent) (Fig. 4.3).

The Most Popular Sitting Areas Were Those That Provided a View of On-Site and Neighborhood Activity: Examining site activity at each individual building provided some insights regarding what elements best set the stage for outdoor sitting. Camiano and Josephson had the highest percentage of site use in front of the building. At Camiano, garden apartment two-story units were entered through porches that were large enough for chairs. The entrances, which faced one another, formed enclosed courtyard-like spaces. A lack of paving at the rear discouraged approaching the apartment from the back. At Josephson a critical mass of activity—including the street, parking lot, bus service, and canopied bus stop—were in the front. The activity associated with the front drew users, despite elaborate design elements intended to facilitate use of the backyard: sliding doors from the kitchen to the outdoors, shuffleboard, benches with backs, a garden, benches in the garden, and a clothes drying area.

Columbus and Oakhurst showed higher rates of site use in the back of the building and elsewhere as compared to other sites. At Columbus the front and back were not clearly distinguished in terms of physical design. At Oakhurst there were no activities to watch and only single family homes on all sides.

Trent Center responses indicated that a place other than the front or back was used often. This actively used place was a row

FIGURE 4.3 Pleasant outdoor seating areas are almost always appreciated by tenants.

of benches and trees that paralleled the street at the front of the lot, which was not directly in front of the building. In Bethany Manor the back was used frequently because of a special aviary and garden and because the front was not situated near the street.

These observations suggested that people wanted to sit where the action was. Usually this was the street, but if the building was not closely situated to the street, if some special facility was provided away from the street, or if one entry was as busy as another or was as close to a busy street as another then residents would sit elsewhere.

Respondents Seemed to Retain a Strong Sense of Front and Back Building to Site Relationships: One tenet of modern architecture suggests that a building should be designed as a free standing object in undifferentiated open space. This notion was tested by examining where residents sat when outside, whether or not they thought the grounds should be larger, and where they would like to see additional open space placed. Over half (55 percent) of the residents claimed that they sat in front facing the street as opposed to the back or elsewhere. This confirmed that despite the theoretical possibility of making all sides equally important, our culture retains a strong sense of front and back. The entry was preferred by most because it faced the street, accommodated a stream of activity, and was a symbolic as well as literal link to the rest of society.

Very few (9 percent) thought the grounds should be larger. From this one could conclude that a little open space would go a long way because the areas that interested people the most—the loci of activity, such as paths and entry ways—did not require much space. The small percentage who wanted to see more space were split between wanting it in the front and back.

Highly Detailed But Passive Small Scale Outdoor Spaces Were Preferred Over Open Green Space: When residents were asked what they would like to see in the grounds, the modal response (31 percent) was a garden. Although we did not know for sure if they meant a flower or vegetable garden, we assume that most meant the former.

Less than a tenth (7 percent) chose grass, the most minimal way to provide "open green space." An expanse of green could be a monotonous sight compared with a garden. Yet even fewer (2 percent) preferred sports, which would have added variety to the grounds through equipment and the motions of the participants themselves. Since they were not selected, one could assume that visual variety was not the sole criterion at work. Older people experienced reduced physical ability and lowered expectations about the ability to do sports. Gardens (31 percent) and trees (26 percent), the two most popular choices, represented visual variety combined with physical passivity. The choice of gardens and trees over open undifferentiated space suggests a preference for a treatment of outdoor space emphasizing color, texture, pattern, and individual plant specimens.

Further evidence of the preference for small-scale landscaping comes from residents' opinions of the views from their apartments. The highest percentage of people who found their views attractive came from Bethany Homes, a high-rise with an aviary and a garden on the grounds, and Tarklin Acres, garden apartments with views across planted courts (83 percent and 80 percent respectively). Columbus, the Newark high-rise, had the lowest (20 percent). The elderly seemed to appreciate small landscaped areas more than vast ground level panoramas.

Residents Preferred Views to Street and Neighborhood Activity: Related to the issue of the differentiation of open space and to the issue of privacy and public safety, one question asked if the tenant would like to see the outside space closed off so that no one could look in, or open so that he or she could see people go by. In keeping with preferences for a strong street relationship was an overwhelming preference to watch people go by. In light of the anxiety about deteriorating surrounding neighborhoods, the importance of the psychological need to watch traffic and people cannot be overstressed (Fig. 4.4).

In order to understand more about preferences for open or closed space, a series of correlations between preference for open or closed space and other variables was conducted. A significant relationship was identified between the quality of the view from one's apartment and preference for open (versus closed) outdoor space. Those who preferred open space felt that their view was attractive, whereas those who wanted enclosed space felt their view was ordinary or ugly. An attractive outdoor area seems to be a universal desire. Further investigation should focus on the types of activity or landscape elements that contribute most to outdoor attractiveness.

Residents Who Feared the Surrounding Neighborhood Wanted Outdoor Space Closed Off: A difference was observed between people who felt that their neighborhood had deteriorated since they moved there and those who felt it had stayed the same. Those who viewed their neighborhood as deteriorating tended to want out-

FIGURE 4.4 A sheltered drop-off area provides residents with a place to wait for rides and a view of the surrounding neighborhood.

FIGURE 4.5 Street views from the lobby can provide a source of constant activity.

door space closed off so that no one could look in. Neighborhood decline was usually interpreted as a racial or economic change. Fear and repulsion were the two major barriers between the predominantly white female tenant and their love of street watching.

In neighborhoods where tenants felt comfortable, failure to provide sitting areas overlooking the street, entry, or other source of constant activity would be simple negligence. In other neighborhoods, spatial and social relationships may be more difficult to resolve.

Design solutions should allow visual contact and surveillance from the lobby to sitting areas outside. The route from outside sitting areas to the safety of the building should be visible from one's seat outdoors. Well-defined but not visually opaque boundaries should separate the site from the street (Fig. 4.5).

Age Segregation/Integration

One of the lingering controversies in the literature on planning for older persons is the degree to which housing for older people should be integrated with young people. Some of the arguments against integration are that children's noise and boisterous play annoy older adults, that older people may be victimized by adolescent boys, and that the contrast with youthfulness might increase feelings of despondency about being old, having physical disabilities, being retired, or approaching death.

Some argue that older people have more in common with people their own age, and furthermore that they should be able to initiate contact with other age groups on their terms and not be dependent on younger people for companionship and service. The arguments in favor of integration are that segregation makes people feel cut off from the rest of society and exacerbates feelings of uselessness, stigmatizes the aged, and hurts the young by cutting them off from the older generation. Housing integration is also thought to be one way to help resist tendencies to withdraw from society.

Most public-assisted housing projects for older persons in New Jersey were exclusively for people over the age of 62. This reflected prevailing beliefs that the disadvantages of integration—family noise, children's boisterous play, invidious comparisons, fear of teenage gangs—overshadowed the advantages. The researchers wanted to check to make sure that this policy was still wise and so included several questions about living near children, teens, and families. One site, Columbus Homes, which accommodated both families and older people, was selected in order to make comparisons of satisfaction.

Age Integration Was Not Preferred: In the seven sites that were exclusively for the elderly, the dominant majority (84 percent) opposed having families living in the development. The few who did want younger people did not come from any particular site. Neither did opinion on this matter change by age. We found no systematic way to differentiate between those who wanted segregated living and those who did not; hence, the decision to design separate buildings for older and younger people seemed sound.

Most residents (69 percent) reported no trouble with children and teenagers living in the area, no doubt because few sites included children. Thus, children's noise was a complaint for only 6 percent. In Columbus Homes, where children and older people lived in the same building, complaints about children's noise jumped to 22 percent. General noise in the apartments was also twice the problem in Columbus Homes than for the other seven sites, another by-product of mixing elderly and young. Children from outside the site annoyed the respondents, who complained that children interfered or were a security problem.

Camiano Homes had especially pronounced problems with teenagers and children as a threat to security (48 percent), while Hanson Homes and Josephson had extra trouble with interference in the yard, 57 percent and 27 percent respectively. Since one-fifth of the sample was concerned with maintaining territorial control, one must conclude that planners have not been highly successful in handling the problems of territoriality and control of access to semiprivate space.

In Columbus Homes, where older people and younger residents lived together, 50 percent of the older people claimed never to socialize with younger people. Only 11 percent said they did often and 40 percent said they did sometimes. Without social programming to provide social structures, through which people could come to interact with and know one another, the advantages of closeness will remain lost to half of this population.

Security

The feeling of safety and security was a recurrent issue in this research. When asked directly if security was a problem in the building, one-quarter (24 percent) replied that it was. By site, most of the problems seemed to be at Columbus Homes and Trent Center, where a murder had occurred the night before the second day of interviewing, no doubt exaggerating this response. Columbus Homes was in such a poor neighborhood and so poorly maintained that security was consistently a problem.

Respondents Felt the Best Strategy for Improving Security Was More Police Protection: When asked what were the best of eight ways to improve security, the top choice was increased police protection (32 percent). This is opposite to what Jane Jacobs and Oscar Newman have suggested. They and other researchers have argued that police protection could never be an adequate substitute for informal, spontaneous, continuous surveillance by people who live in or otherwise use the area. Our translation of this concept, "increase visibility where people walk and sit," was an unpopular choice (6 percent). Skillfully handled, a social worker or resident activist could increase the sense of control and power by devising surveillance or community organizing schemes for a population that sees itself as dependent on outside protection (Fig. 4.6).

FIGURE 4.6 Security equipment can also be used to stimulate interest in planned social activity. In this project decentralized monitors list activities planned for the day.

Residents of two sites did not select increased police protection or having a "safe" neighborhood as the best ways to improve security. At Columbus Homes residents chose better locks, perhaps because the current type was inadequate. More likely, in this age-integrated building older tenants may have tightened their sense of controllable territory to include only the individual unit, so improved locks may have offered the best hope of improving security.

Trent Center showed a high percentage of "other" suggestions (40 percent). A murder had occurred between the 2 days of interviewing there and people were clamoring for hired guards. The manager there insisted that guards would not help as long as the residents themselves continued to let in unidentified people without questioning them. Again, we see the need for better ways to enfranchise older people with power and responsibility for their own welfare.

Medical Care

Since health care becomes more important as a person ages, the researchers examined attitudes toward health services being provided within the building in great detail. Almost two-thirds (64 percent), when asked if they felt the need for better access to a doctor or medical facility, said "no, prefer private doctor." Yet, when asked to rank in order of importance eight ways to improve medical service, methods that brought medical service to the building were ranked higher than methods that took the patient to his private doctor.

Residents wanted, in decreasing order: an infirmary area within the building, better drug delivery to the building, better arrangements for ambulance service, safety and revival equipment within the building, regular visits by a doctor or a nurse, and bus trips or car pools to take people to a clinic or doctor. Their commitment to a private doctor did not keep older people from wanting more convenient sources of health care.

The Need for Social Programming

Almost two-thirds (62 percent) did not know everyone in the complex by sight. The sites varied considerably. The presence or absence of an active social center or tenant association was more important than the presence or absence of a single entry or even the size of the total project population in accounting for recognition. Social structures therefore were much more important than physical structures in facilitating social interaction among older persons in group living situations.

Another way of demonstrating this point comes from looking at the geographic distribution of best friends. After the first two months, about half of the residents found their best friends evenly divided between the building and outside. Tenants never switched entirely to the building as a source of friends, and having lived nearby before the move they could and did keep many past friends.

Creative Social Programming Can Be Used to Develop Stronger Informal Helping Networks: The solution to problems of social isolation is best met through innovations in social programming and not through physical design alone. For instance, one-third of this sample rarely or never exchanged favors with neighbors. This symbolizes a missed opportunity between people that might warrant experimentation with social programs to increase informal day-to-day interaction.

No one complained that the apartment was too private and isolated. On the open-ended questions, a significant number of tenants valued the atmosphere of privacy, quiet, and security, which they felt characterized their building. Yet one-quarter of the sample felt bored occasionally, leading one to speculate that privacy and boredom constitute two different dimensions. We infer that people in this culture must have both individual privacy and opportunities for social interaction in order to feel fulfilled. The sites where boredom was most acute (Camiano, Hanson Homes, Tarklin Acres) were missing both internal activity (social programs) and external street activity. This underscored the importance of treating activity as seriously as personal security. Access to activities without security tended to be anxiety provoking, but security without access to activity would lead to boredom.

Those who did not have company in their apartment tended to be bored more often than those who did. This confirmed the mental health model, which assumes that contact with others is important to a sense of well-being. Generally, this culture is sensitive to the individual's need for privacy but less sensitive to the collective need for interaction with others. Public housing policy makers must self-consciously strive to continue to respect the individual at the same time that they meet needs for social exchange.

The findings confirmed the idea that there were distinct types of adjustment, since there were nearly as many whose activity level had decreased, increased, or stayed the same since moving to the building, and because the majority (91 percent) felt that their current level of activity was good for them.

When a site has only two types of responses—those whose activity had decreased and those whose activity had stayed the same (as in Columbus Homes)—policy makers could conclude that the social programs and activities offered may be inadequate to meet the needs of residents. In sites where all three responses are equally well represented, managers can assume that social programs are working.

Conclusions

This chapter has underscored some of the most important findings from a sample of eight age-segregated housing projects for low- to moderate-income people in New Jersey. Some of the more important and interesting findings relate to the use of open space, concerns with security, unit design features, the benefits/costs of age integration, and the desire for various on-site services. Lost design opportunities and misunderstandings seemed to be more common at the larger scale building and site design scale. With few exceptions, architectural design details in the unit and in common circulation spaces did not pose major problems.

Outdoor space was considered effective when coupled with various activities that animated the space, providing more stimulation. Security was a major concern; residents might benefit from community organizing techniques that, as a by-product, might create informal networks for mutual aid and assistance. Age-homogeneous settings were also found to be associated with a greater perception of security.

Finally, the need for a better understanding of "who" the client group was likely to be would lead to better decisions regarding the popularity of various common activities; the provision of equipment for social, recreational, and educational purposes; and the specification of specific kitchen and bathroom equipment.

DESIGN DIRECTIVES

<table>
<tr>
<td>

DESIGN DIRECTIVE

ONE

</td>
<td>

Kitchens should be designed that fully consider the reach capacity, finger control problems, convenience needs, and limited muscular strength of older residents.

</td>
</tr>
</table>

1. Storage areas that require a reach of over 63 inches should be limited. Visual as well as physical accessibility should be considered. If cupboards are built over the counter, the height of the top shelf should not exceed 4 feet 8 inches above the floor.

2. The refrigerator model should have an easily opened door. Double door models should have handles that cannot cause injury on closing. Refrigerators of 6 cubic foot capacity are regarded as minimum. Ideally, refrigerators should be self-defrosting and equipped with a large frozen-food compartment.

3. Poor vision calls for a higher than normal lighting level, especially over sinks and stoves. Supplementary light sources are therefore recommended. Lights over work spaces help avoid shadows.

4. The size of the kitchen that is generally recommended for the elderly is about 50 square feet. This is the area of a standard minimum usable kitchen and appears to be quite well-suited to the needs of a single older person. Space for eating in the kitchen would require an additional 20–30 square feet. Of the several possible arrangements—that is, pullman kitchen, kitchen alcove, or separate kitchen—the full-scale separate kitchen is preferred. The compactness of the pullman kitchen can cause extremely hazardous working conditions.

5. Pantry cupboards should have bi-fold or swing doors, but not sliding doors. Swing doors should be as narrow as possible to avoid projecting beyond the counter top.

6. Controls should be at the front of the stove, easy to reach, and identifiable by both sight and touch. For reasons of safety, electric stoves are recommended over gas stoves.

<table>
<tr>
<td>

DESIGN DIRECTIVE

TWO

</td>
<td>

Although stall showers were not preferred as much as bathtubs, they may be a safer, cleaner, and more invigorating alternative.

</td>
</tr>
</table>

1. Stall shower advantages generally include that they use less water, have no high sides to climb, present no danger of users' dozing off and drowning, and can be outfitted with a seat so the user can rest if necessary.

2. Stall shower disadvantages include that they cannot be used for soaking—which is pleasurable, is good for circulation, and softens the feet—and that there is sometimes a reluctance to use them because they are new and different.

Outdoor private balconies and patios, although not necessary, can be an important and valued amenity to some individuals.

1. Balconies provide a psychological outlet as well as function for growing flowers, sitting, eating, cleaning rugs, etc. They are essential in many contexts.

2. The design of balconies must create a feeling of security. A sense of security can be achieved by providing semirecessed balconies and a railing at a height of about 3 feet 10 inches to 4 feet 2 inches, which is secure in both function and appearance.

3. Balconies should allow maximum sun penetration as well as providing a view from the sitting position.

4. They should provide privacy from adjacent balconies with a minimum threshold height to allow easy access from the unit.

5. If individual balconies are not provided for each apartment in a multistory building, thought should be given to providing at least one general-use balcony for each floor.

Site development should take advantage of the indigenous activities in the neighborhood and the circulation patterns and interaction spaces on-site.

1. Outdoor areas should consist of several kinds of spaces to provide variety and permit elderly people to watch normal street activities, sit unobserved in a secluded quiet spot, sit in the sun, sit under a roof in the shade, sit in a large group, play outdoor games such as shuffleboard, and see greenery and/or hear water.

2. Benches with backs and arms should be provided and grouped to encourage conversation. Other small furnishings should be movable.

3. Flower beds should be provided, with some raised to a height of 2–3 feet to allow close viewing and gardening without stooping.

4. When easy walking access to the neighborhood is impossible, the grounds should be landscaped in such a way as to invite walking. Possible ways to do this include providing routes through the site with different textures and minor grade changes, seasonally changing bedding plants, vegetables that mature and change over the course of a summer, or tiny "strip gardens" tended by tenants.

5. Movement and activity in landscape design—fountains, brooks, fish, waterfalls, mobiles, bird feeders, etc.—are very desirable.

6. Preferably outdoor space would be open, rather than closed off, so that the elderly are able to watch people go by. Terraces and protected sitting or walking areas that overlook project and street traffic are desirable. A seating area should ideally be located "where the action is," which is usually the street edge of the site.

7. In neighborhoods where residents do not feel secure sitting outside, design solutions should provide a sense of visual surveillance from those in the lobby to those sitting outside. The entire route back into the safety of the building should be visible from one's seat outdoors. Absolute and/or symbolic boundaries, which are visually open, should separate the housing project from the street.

8. Glaring reflections from hard surfaced areas should be avoided by careful selection of materials and surface texture. Walkways at night should be well illuminated to allow safe use.

POLICY CONSIDERATIONS

Age segregated housing is preferable to age integrated housing because security and opportunities for social exchange are increased.

POLICY CONSIDERATION
ONE

When mixing age groups one must realize the elderly are usually less tolerant of noise than younger people. The residence, especially sleeping rooms, should be well insulated from surrounding noise. Older and younger low- to moderate-income people may experience some conflict when sharing the same building. In some instances, however, this problem may be rectified by separating the two parties from one another in different buildings that share a common site. This would enable elderly tenants to be somewhat isolated from their younger counterparts and alleviate unnecessary tension.

Management must take some responsibility for initiating various activity programs as well as encouraging tenants to create strong, sound, and supportive relationships.

POLICY CONSIDE
TWO

Project managers should be responsible for planning social programs, since a majority of the residents put a great deal of trust in building management. Managers are also perceived more as friends than as professionals, which places them in a good position to initiate social programming without making it seem institutional.

In creating the built-environment for "independent" living by the elderly, one might question the necessity of having management, rather than the tenants themselves, plan social programs. In some cases, tenant associations could take on some of the responsibility for social programming, but where there is no such association or where it is not strong, management should take responsibility.

Among the programs and services that management can initiate and administer are the following:

- Access to medical care, including on-site infirmaries, visiting doctors and nurses, ambulance and drug delivery services, transportation to doctors and clinics;
- Car pools or limousine service for groups to community services (grocery stores, drug stores, hairdressers, barber shops, restaurants, etc.), which substitute for the present high reliance on the private automobile and for poor public transportation, which residents may find difficult to use;

- Collective self governance of the main lobby and other public and semipublic spaces (who should use it and for what purpose);
- Psychologically "safe" contact between residents and neighbors in the surrounding community through such devices as exchange programs between elderly and young (for example, multimedia oral histories in exchange for escort service, cleaning, errands, etc.);
- Advising and differentiating prospective and future tenants, especially those coming from larger homes, to ease their process of accommodation and ensure success in their new environment.

EXAMINING PHYSICAL AND MANAGERIAL ASPECTS OF URBAN HOUSING FOR THE ELDERLY

David Christensen and Galen Cranz

V iewed from a historical perspective, publicly assisted housing for the elderly is a relatively new institution in the United States. Originating in the early 1960s, the federal government established and funded a variety of programs designed to meet the housing needs of low-income older people. Among these efforts, public housing constitutes the single most important source of publicly assisted housing with almost a half million elderly-occupied units. Currently, public housing provides a home for one out of every ten renters age 62 and older in the United States (Lawton, 1980; USDHUD, 1979).

Given the large investment required to construct and operate housing projects for older residents, it is not surprising that these facilities have become the focus for a large and growing body of gerontological research. The volume of work in this area is now great enough to support a periodical entirely devoted to the subject (*The Journal of Housing for the Elderly*). Ideally, studies of completed projects can yield information that is useful to housing managers in improving the operation of existing facilities, as well as producing information relevant to the planning and design of future projects. Both levels of information will be addressed in this chapter.

Related Research

Gutman and Westergaard (1974) have described some of the difficulties involved in environmental design evaluation, including the primitive nature of theory building in man-environment relations, uncertainty concerning the proper units to evaluate, the large degree of personal variation found in response to the built environment, and the lesser importance of the physical environment relative to other factors in user satisfaction. Bechtel (1976), Gans (1967), and Marans (1976) have argued that the social environment dominates physical aspects in determining human well-being. In point of fact, research in gerontology clearly demonstrates the salience of the social milieu for elderly residents in terms of the age profile of their neighbors (Rosow, 1967; Gubrium, 1970; Teaff et al., 1978). However, physical aspects of the housing environment also have been identified as important determinants of satisfaction among the elderly (Lawton, 1978, 1980; Christensen, 1984). Based on an 8-year case study of one of the first public housing projects for the elderly, Carp (1976) concluded that, "the good quality of physical housing was originally and continued to be the outstanding best feature in the eyes of its residents." To be most effective, physical and social components of housing projects must be coordinated carefully. Unfortunately, too often federally assisted housing for the elderly has demonstrated something less than optimum orchestration of physical and social aspects of the residential environment (Christensen and Robinson, 1975). This situation is particularly unfortunate given the problematic nature of the lower-income elderly population and their dependence on vital social supports and services (Harel and Harel, 1978).

Methodology and Data Analysis

The focus of primary concern in this research was the performance of the housing environment as experienced by elderly residents. Data for the study consisted of interviews with 190 elderly residents of six age-segregated public housing buildings in San Francisco. The interview protocol was a revised version of the Schumacher and Cranz (1975) instrument, and incorporated an outcome measure of life satisfaction (LSIB; Neugarten et al., 1961). The interview covered a comprehensive range of physical and social issues using three basic types of behavioral indicators: cognitive judgments, reported activities, and expressed preferences (Marans, 1976). The importance of specific judgment and activity measures was gauged by their correlation with general indicators of housing satisfaction and life satisfaction. Items associated with global satisfaction of tenants with their housing or life in general were deemed to be of greater importance than items that were unrelated to these objectives.

Projects Were Selected to Facilitate Comparisons of Site Design, Development Density, and Common Space Location

The San Francisco Housing Authority Departments of Planning and Senior Citizen Social Services selected six sites, chosen to allow analytical comparisons of specific environmental variables (Fig. 5.1). For example, Sites #1 and #4 (Figs. 5.2 and 5.5) were selected because they are fairly small, low-rise buildings that may be compared with larger projects represented by Sites #2 and #3 (Figs. 5.3 and 5.4). The location of shared social spaces and the effect of location on social activity were issues in the selection of Sites #1 and #3, because shared spaces in these buildings, except for the entrance lobby, are located on the second floor. Sites #5 and #6 (Figs. 5.6 and 5.7) are separate buildings that share the same parcel; however, almost all the shared activity spaces are located within the premises of Site #5. Sites #4 and #6 have awkward entrance configurations and lack seating in the front entry areas. In addition to these design features, sites were selected to achieve ethnic and racial balance. For technical information on how the study was conducted, and for a more detailed presentation of the statistical

San Francisco

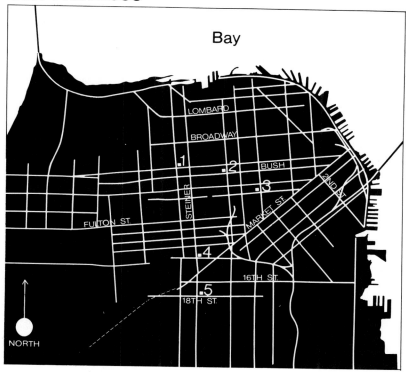

FIGURE 5.1 Location of study sites: Sites were chosen to represent a continuum from high density, downtown commercial areas (Site #3) to medium density, single-family residential neighborhoods (Sites #1, #5, and #6).

FIGURE 5.2   Study Site #1: This low-rise, brown shingle building was judged as attractive by most residents.

FIGURE 5.3   Study Site #2: This mid-rise, concrete block building was considered attractive by most residents.

FIGURE 5.4 Study Site #3: This high-rise concrete building received intermediate ratings for exterior appearance.

FIGURE 5.5 Study Site #4: Most residents felt this low-rise, natural finish redwood structure should be painted.

FIGURE 5.6   Study Site #5: This mid-rise building located most common facilities on the ground floor, except for the laundry room, which was located on the fifth floor.

FIGURE 5.7   Study Site #6: This companion building for Site #5 lacks common facilities.

results, the reader should refer to our final report to the Housing Authority (Cranz et al., 1977).

Findings: Physical Issues

Site Design Should Facilitate Diverse Outdoor Activities

Relatively little research has addressed the effect of landscaping and exterior design features on housing satisfaction for the elderly. While two recent publications have proposed minimum landscaping criteria (Green et al., 1975; Cranz and Schumacher, 1975), earlier works such as that of Musson and Heusinkveld (1963) de-emphasized gardens because "they run down after a while," pointedly noting that "terraces, walks, and paving are cheaper to maintain than grass and flowers."

In the present study, tenants were asked what landscape elements, sports equipment, or seating they would like to see added to the grounds. About half of our respondents evaluated their yard and landscaping as "OK the way it is." Of the 91 respondents who did want a change, over three-fourths specified plant materials over other choices. Flower and vegetable gardens were most frequently mentioned as desired landscape elements.

Another question asked tenants if they would use an outdoor clothesline if one were available. (They did not exist at any of the study sites.) About two-fifths of those responding to the question indicated they would use an outdoor clothesline if it were made available, and this estimate is consistent with the use of such facilities reported by Schumacher and Cranz (1975).

High-Rise and Low-Rise Buildings Have Equal Appeal

The publication of Oscar Newman's (1972) studies of "defensible space" in public housing generated new interest in how the design of buildings affects territorial perceptions and behaviors among residents. While Newman's work has been subjected to criticism on methodological and ideological levels (Adams, 1973; Ellis, 1974; Hillier, 1973; Kaplan, 1973), the issues he raised, and some of the solutions he proposed, remain relevant today.

One of the factors that Newman considered to be critical for the development of mutually protective social relationships among public housing tenants was the height of the building. Other recent research, including work by Newman himself (1976), indicates that elderly residents in age-segregated housing may not perceive building height as a crucial issue (Cranz and Schumacher, 1977). Hartman et al. (1976) reported that their sample of San Francisco elderly was evenly divided over the desirability of high-rise versus low-rise buildings. They concluded that "this is more a matter to be decided on the basis of developer's economic and policy considerations and broader urban design factors." Lawton et al. (1975) found building height contributed only about 1 percent to the variance in housing satisfaction after controlling for tenant characteristics and other factors.

We asked our sample to choose whether "ideally" they would prefer living in a high-rise building or a "two-story walkup." High-rise and two-story buildings were each chosen by about 40 percent of our respondents, while 18 percent expressed no particular preference. When tenant characteristics were correlated with preferences for higher versus lower buildings, only occupational status proved significant. Higher occupational status was associated with high-rise preference.

Our results suggest that building size may be an important factor for some older residents. We found preferences for building type were significantly correlated with housing satisfaction: respondents who preferred high-rise buildings also tended to be more satisfied with their current housing. Since all sites were at least four to five stories in height, many residents may have considered their buildings to be of the high-rise type and were actually expressing their general satisfaction or dissatisfaction with their building.

At present, the weight of available evidence supports Lawton's view that "a satisfying life style is possible in any building type, given the other positive features of housing for the elderly" (Lawton et al., 1975). However, a substantial segment of the elderly population seems to prefer buildings of smaller scale. In this matter, as in others, the ideal arrangement would provide for environmental diversity so that tenants can choose a setting congruent with their personal values and lifestyle.

Exterior Appearance Should "Fit" the Surrounding Environment

Respondents were asked to rate their satisfaction with "the appearance of the building from the outside." Responses to this question were significantly correlated with housing satisfaction and were generally favorable. Almost 90 percent of the total sample expressed some degree of satisfaction, and 44 percent indicated they were "very satisfied" with the appearance of the building. The very satisfied were located disproportionately in two sites: over two-thirds of the respondents at Sites #1 and #2 were very satisfied, whereas only 12 percent at Site #4 gave their building the highest rating. The remaining sites ranged from 26 to 47 percent very satisfied.

The two sites with the highest ratings for appearance are physically quite different. Site #1 is a five-story structure finished in stucco and wood shingles; Site #2 is a seven-story building of concrete block and glass. Both buildings are conventional, conservative, and modern looking. The architectural style of Site #4, a five-story wood frame structure clad in natural redwood plywood, is the most distinctive of the study sites. However, many respondents felt that the natural wood facade was unattractive, unfinished, and in need of paint. This unfavorable evaluation also reflects the jarring contrast between the project building and painted Victorian houses that predominate on the block. Designers should be sensitive to the social stigma that is often attached to subsidized housing, and they should resist the temptation to make an architectural statement at the expense of future residents. Fortunately, paint is a design element that can be changed without incurring major capital costs. In the interval since these data were collected, the façade of this site has been redone to make it more consistent with the prevailing street aesthetic.

Laundry Rooms Should Be Convenient But Unobtrusive

Laundry rooms have received considerable attention in housing guidelines for independent elderly. A review of current standards for laundry locations indicates widespread agreement that convenient access to these facilities is important for older residents. However, there is less consensus in the specific recommendations for locating laundry facilities. Schumacher and Cranz recommend centralized laundry facilities in multistory buildings, and the SFHA Planning and Design Criteria suggest that this laundry be located near the community room or specialized activity room. On the other hand, Green et al. (1975) recommend that laundry facilities be located on each floor of medium- and high-rise buildings to ensure convenient access for all tenants. Lawton (1975) notes that decentralized laundries are sometimes advocated as informal social spaces, but his own research indicates that socializing in decentralized laundries typically does not occur. Finally, Howell (1981) and Zeisel (1982) point out that residents should not be forced to traverse public spaces, like the community room or building lobby, in order to reach the laundry area.

During the interview, we asked how frequently the laundry facilities were used and what locations were preferred. Most residents said they used their laundry and were satisfied with its location. Only 9 percent indicated that they would prefer a laundry on each floor. However, responses concerning usage of laundry facilities varied significantly among sites. The lowest frequencies for both laundry use and preference for current location were found among the residents of Site #6. While this building and Site #5 are officially considered one project, they are separate buildings and front on different streets. The problem is that only one laundry room was provided for the two buildings, and it is located on the top floor of Site #5. The other site with notably low satisfaction with the location of the laundry was Site #4 where over one-third of the respondents expressed a preference for a different location. The laundry facility for this site is located directly opposite the main entrance, a position that many residents considered offensive and inappropriate. Clearly, the placement of laundry facilities must recognize the difference between "front stage" activities, such as greeting guests and socializing in the lobby, versus "back stage" work activities, like doing the washing.

Kitchen Design Should Respect the Anthropometric Abilities of Older Clients

Of all the daily activities older people must perform, none is more important to their health and continued independence than meal preparation. When asked how they handled this activity, a large majority of our sample responded that they usually cook for themselves; 10 percent said they often share the task with others, while 6 percent take meals elsewhere. Women were only slightly more likely to cook for themselves than men.

Tenants reported few difficulties when asked about possible problems with kitchen features and appliances. However, about one-third of our respondents indicated dissatisfaction with the height of kitchen cabinets. Satisfaction with cabinet height did not relate to life satisfaction, but it did correlate significantly with housing satisfaction. Furthermore, those who were dissatisfied with cabinet height were also more likely to express a desire for a larger kitchen. Apparently, the lack of conveniently located storage space was translated into a general perception that space in the kitchen was inadequate.

Differences among sites were striking. At Sites #5 and #6 almost two-thirds of our respondents complained about the cabinet height, while only 11 percent at Site #3 found it a problem. (The lowest shelf was 4 inches from the floor at all sites.) Site #3, which had the fewest complaints about the height of kitchen cabinets, was also the site with the lowest top shelf (4 feet 8 inches). At Sites #5 and #6 the top shelf was 7 feet 4 inches from the floor, much too high for the convenience and safety of elderly tenants. These results confirm those reported by Lawton and Nahemow (1979) and Christensen (1984), and they serve to underscore the special importance of providing adequate facilities for meal preparation when designing living units for older residents.

Bathroom Design Must Emphasize Convenience and Safety

The bathroom is another basic facility for sustaining the independence of older people. Numerous design requirements for bathrooms are contained in the HUD Minimum Property Standards

(USDHUD, 1973) including provisions for grab bars, slip-resistant finishes for bathtubs, and access requirements for wheelchairs. One topic of ongoing controversy involves the relative merits of bathtubs versus showers for elderly tenants. Stall shower units are less expensive and are considered to have safety advantages; but older residents often prefer the comfort of soaking in a tub. In a longitudinal study of housing for the elderly, Carp (1976) found that tenants were initially willing to accept units with shower facilities only. However, after a period of a few years, over one-third expressed a desire for a bathtub. Almost two-thirds of our sample indicated they prefer baths, while the rest chose showers, sponge baths, or some other arrangement. Since safety in the bathroom is a major concern, designers should give special attention to the provision and placement of hand rails, light fixtures, and other safety-related features in this area.

None of the projects in this study had specially designed bathrooms for the disabled. Therefore, it is likely that those in wheelchairs would have difficulty managing these spaces. In fact, one disabled tenant indicated that he had his bathroom door removed so that he could get his wheelchair in and out. In most other respects, tenants appeared to be very satisfied with bathroom features. Less than 10 percent reported difficulty with shower knobs or toilets, and only 2 percent indicated that the bathroom was too small.

Balconies Are Desired and Appreciated by Most Tenants

The use of balconies is another controversial issue in projects for older adults. Researchers have evaluated balconies using criteria such as their use, whether people want them, or whether they are valued when specified. Lawton (1975) questioned their value when he reported that no more than 5 percent of the residents of buildings with private balconies could be found to use them at a given time. Alternatively, Hartman et al. (1976) emphasized desire, reporting that over four-fifths of the residents of a San Francisco project wanted balconies. Schumacher and Cranz also found widespread support for balconies, with 82 percent of their respondents who had balconies reporting that they liked them "very much."

In the present study, residents without balconies were asked if a balcony would "add a lot to their apartment," and one-half of the total sample said that it would. Of those with balconies about three-fourths said that they liked them very much. Furthermore, tenants' satisfaction with their balcony was significantly related to general housing satisfaction. Our findings also corroborate the importance of a balcony for residents in poor health as suggested by Hartman et al. Among those without balconies, respondents whose health prevented them from walking one or two blocks were significantly more likely to express a desire for this amenity.

Findings: Social Issues

Crime Is Perceived to Be a Problem in the Neighborhood and on Site

The Hartman et al. (1976) study reported that the most salient housing need among the elderly was for "personal safety, not so much of the 'grab bar' variety, but of the interpersonal street and public safety variety." Schumacher and Cranz found security was second only to "low rent" as the most frequently selected reason for moving to public housing.

Children and teenagers are often characterized as posing major threats to the safety of older people. Teaff et al. (1978) found elderly residents of "higher density" projects were more satisfied with neighborhoods that had fewer children, but this relationship did not hold for "lower density" projects. When asked about problems with children in the neighborhood, one-fourth of our respondents indicated that children presented problems because of security and noise.

Most tenants felt that crime problems were more severe on streets surrounding the project rather than on-site. Significant differences in the perceived level of crime were found among sites, however. Located in a primarily residential and somewhat more affluent neighborhood, Site #1 had the lowest incidence of perceived crime problems (10 percent). Two-thirds of the tenants reported problems with crime at Sites #2, #3, and #4, which are all located closer to downtown in higher density areas. Perceived crime problems were also relatively high at Site #6 for reasons of site design rather than site location alone.

Access to Community Facilities and Social Services Should Be Included in Criteria for Site Selection

The importance of choosing sites with good access to grocery stores and public transportation is widely recognized. On the other hand, comparatively little attention has been devoted to socially oriented facilities such as restaurants, beauty parlors, parks, libraries, churches, and senior centers. One way to determine the importance of these facilities is to examine how frequently they are used. In this study, we found the three most frequently used socially oriented facilities were restaurants, churches, and beauty/barber shops. These destinations were visited at least monthly by 55 percent, 50 percent, and 47 percent of our sample, respectively. Parks were used on a monthly basis by about 30 percent of our sample, senior centers by 21 percent, and libraries by 18 percent. If we judge salience or importance by frequency of use, churches, restaurants, beauty parlors, and barber shops would be considered the more important social facilities.

Another method of assessing the value of these resources is to correlate facility use with global indicators such as life satisfaction (Christensen and Robinson, 1975; Knapp, 1976). For this sample, church attendance and participation in senior center activities were positively correlated with life satisfaction, while monthly use of parks was significantly correlated with housing satisfaction. These results suggest that frequency of facility use was fairly independent of the importance of facility use as measured by correlations with our global indicators. We conclude that both approaches can be useful in gauging the value of community facilities for the elderly. The low frequency of library use and the lack of significant correlations with housing or life satisfaction suggests that access to these facilities should not be emphasized in selecting sites for elderly housing projects.

Neighborhood Interaction Areas—The Territory in Front of the Building Is an Important Location for Outdoor Seating

The six sites differed considerably in the design treatment of front entrance areas (Figs. 5.8–5.15). This "front porch" space may be significant as a setting for informal social contact among tenants, or between tenants and neighbors. If properly designed, it can also provide residents with a base for informal monitoring of the neighborhood, thereby increasing real and perceived security (Jacobs, 1961; Newman, 1972).

To examine the usage of front entrance areas we asked our respondents if they sat outside regularly in good weather, and if so, where. About one-half of the sample indicated that they did sit outside, with the largest percentage choosing to sit "in front facing the street." About one-fourth of those who sat outside used the back portion of the site, and another 29 percent sat elsewhere. Thus, the territory in front of the building was the single most popular location for outdoor sitting. Our analysis also indicated that those who regularly spent time in this area had significantly higher housing satisfaction scores than those who did not. No significant relationship was found between life satisfaction and sitting outside in general, but small significant correlations were found for those who sat in front, indicating that this activity may be valuable beyond its association with housing satisfaction.

The projects vary considerably in their provisions to accommodate outdoor sitting, and this variation was mirrored in the behavior of our respondents. Twenty-three percent of the entire sample reported they sat in front of their building regularly. At Sites #1 and #2, where benches are provided near the entry, a majority of the residents used this area regularly (Figures 5.8–5.11). Site #3 has a low wall in front of the building, which some residents used

FIGURE 5.8　Front seating area, Site #1: These benches with backs are protected from the sun and rain.

FIGURE 5.9　Exterior
plan, Site #1: The bench
seating area is set back a
few feet from the
sidewalk.

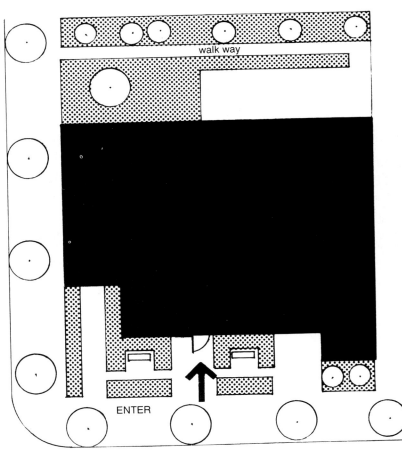

walk way

ENTER

FIGURE 5.10 Front seating area, Site #2: The benches located near the corners provide shelter from cool breezes.

FIGURE 5.11 Exterior plan, Site #2: An extensive front yard area allows residents to choose sun or shade, public or private sitting space.

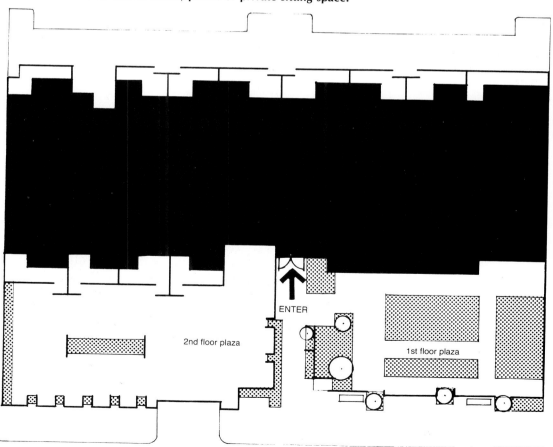

FIGURE 5.12 Front entrance, Site #4: The narrow path to the front entrance is awkward and uninviting.

for sitting, but chairs or benches are not available due to the small size of the lot, combined with problems of crime and loitering in the neighborhood. Sites #4, #5, and #6 had the fewest residents who reported they sat in front of the building. Site #5 has a concrete retaining wall that could be used for sitting, but even such makeshift provisions are absent at Sites #4 and #6 (Figs. 5.12–5.15). These results clearly demonstrate that the design and specification of seating opportunities has a major impact on user behavior (Whyte, 1980). Without an adequate architectural program, even simple activities like this one may get overlooked in the course of the design process.

Informal social activity fostered by sitting spaces near the entry may also act as a deterrent to crime. Residents at Sites #3, #4, and #6 (sites with the lowest rates for front area sitting) were more

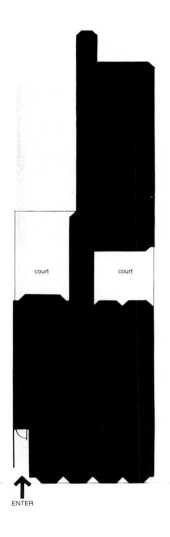

court

court

ENTER

FIGURE 5.13 Exterior plan, Site #4: No front yard space is provided for sitting and socializing at this site.

likely to report security problems. Tenants at Site #6, in particular, complained about the poor visibility of their building entrance, channeled on either side by high walls. In fact, several residents had been victimized while entering or leaving this building.

Tenant Interaction Patterns Are Influenced Both by Social Programming and by Building Design

Social relations in age-concentrated housing for the elderly may be examined from various perspectives. Higher rates of informal social interaction among neighbors typically are found in age-segregated compared to age-integrated housing (Messer, 1967; Gubrium, 1970; Hochschild, 1973; Sherman, 1975). However, formal organized social activities may be just as important as informal

FIGURE 5.14   Front entrance, Site #6: The entrance has poor visibility and lacks outdoor seating.

social exchanges. Several studies have found participation in organized tenant activities is associated with well-being among elderly residents (Carp, 1966; Bley et al., 1972; Christensen and Robinson, 1975). Furthermore, formal activities can be used by housing managers as a vehicle to stimulate informal friendship formation. Therefore, the provision of space for organized tenant activities is required by HUD in all subsidized projects for the elderly. In our study, sites were selected to allow comparisons of larger and smaller projects and different community space configurations. It should be noted, however, that our small sample of projects included a variety of idiosyncratic conditions in addition to the characteristics we were interested in examining. Thus, our findings should be understood as preliminary and tentative until they may be confirmed with a larger sample of sites.

Analysis of the interview data show that projects differed significantly in terms of residents knowing each other by sight, res-

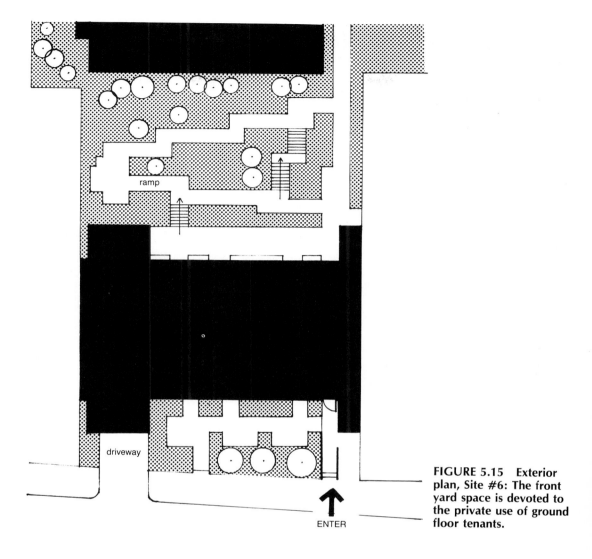

ramp

driveway

ENTER

FIGURE 5.15 Exterior plan, Site #6: The front yard space is devoted to the private use of ground floor tenants.

idents having best friends in the building, and the frequency of informal service exchange among tenants. The two largest projects (Site #2 with 108 units and Site #3 with 100 units) were found to have the lowest proportion of respondents who felt that they knew other tenants by sight. These two sites also had lower than average rates of having best friends in the building. Site #3 had the lowest percentage of residents who said they sometimes exchanged services with other tenants (35 percent). Site #2, on the other hand, had a slightly higher than average proportion of residents who reported this activity (60 percent). One important difference between these sites was the amount of social service staff time provided. Site #2 had a full-time social worker assigned to the building, whereas Site #3 had a professional social worker available only

FIGURE 5.16 Entrance lobby, Site #5: The simple but adequate provision of seating with a view of adjacent street activity is adjacent to the main entry.

one day per week. The more intensive social service program may have been responsible for fostering a higher rate of mutual service exchange among tenants.

Informal social contact among residents was closely linked to the design of the entrance lobby. The three sites with the largest lobbies (Site #1, 480 square feet; Site #2, 300 square feet; and Site #5, 620 square feet) had the highest frequency of reported socializing among residents. Site #6 has no entrance lobby, and responses from this site referred to the entrance lobby in the adjoining Site #5 (Fig. 5.16). Site #4 also has no entrance lobby, although the laundry room was sometimes used for this purpose. Site #3 has a very small lobby (200 square feet) and no seating. Nevertheless, even this minimal space was occasionally used for socializing by determinedly gregarious residents. Most of those respondents who believed that socializing took place in the lobby also felt that it was a desirable kind of activity (82 percent), and this attitude was significantly correlated with general housing satisfaction.

Another issue of interest in this study was whether the location of the community room had any detectable influence on tenants' participation in organized social activities. In her analysis of four Cambridge housing projects, Howell (1981) concluded that the relationship of the community room to major circulation paths was very influential in stimulating activity in these shared social spaces. While the sizes of community rooms in our study did not vary greatly, considerable variation was evident in their placement within the buildings. At Sites #2 and #5 this space is located on the ground floor near the entrance lobby; at Sites #1 and #3 the community room is on the second floor; while at Site #4 the community room is at the rear of the building on the floor below the main entry level. As previously noted, residents of Site #6 used the community room in Site #5. Despite these locational differences, we found no significant variation in the use of community rooms as reported by residents. Apparently, social service programming and the capacity of tenant groups to organize formal activities in the community room were more important than the physical layout in affecting usage of these spaces.

Services That Promote the Independence of Older Tenants Should Be Encouraged

Despite evidence indicating the need for a variety of supportive services in age-segregated projects for the elderly, achieving the delivery of these services has proved to be a difficult task. For example, Lawton (1975) notes that few local housing authorities have adequate funding to support medical programs in their projects for the elderly. This places management in the position of "begging" for services from other community organizations. Robinson makes the same point regarding social services and calls for joint HUD and HHS funding to provide each building with a full-time social worker to act as an intake and referral coordinator, short-term counsellor, and contact person for medical and psychiatric emergencies (Christensen and Robinson, 1975). Others have reported the value of supportive services—such as limited nursing care, housekeeping assistance, and meal services—when needed as preferable alternatives to eviction or institutionalization of marginally competent older residents (Kistin and Morris, 1972; Bell, 1973; Harel and Harel, 1978). Considerable interest in these services has also been expressed by the elderly themselves (Beyer and Woods, 1963; Lawton, 1969).

On-Site Management: This is a housing-related service generally considered important in buildings for the elderly (Lawton, 1975; Green et al., 1975). The SFHA Planning and Design Criteria require that elderly housing projects provide at least one and preferably two offices for management functions and social service delivery. These criteria also require the inclusion of a two-bedroom manager's apartment in each elderly housing project. However, three study sites were still without resident managers when interviewing for this study began. At the three sites with a resident manager, significantly more of our respondents expressed the belief that "management lived up to its end of the bargain." Site #6 had the lowest proportion of residents who felt that management was keeping its end of the bargain, thereby reflecting the lack of both facilities and on-site management. The importance of on-site staff is also indicated by our finding that the "helpfulness" of the manager, as perceived by residents, was significantly correlated with their general level of housing satisfaction.

Tenants Identified Security Services as an Especially Important Issue: The 1974 Community Development Act specifically designated security personnel as an eligible operating cost for public housing, but funding for this purpose remains scarce. When tenants in this study were asked to evaluate alternative approaches to improving security in their projects, the method chosen most frequently was "increased police protection." Alternative strategies for improving security through better locks and improved lighting were selected less frequently. This finding is consistent with those reported by Schumacher and Cranz that increased police protection is likely to be appreciated most by elderly residents, despite Jacobs' (1961) thoughtful admonitions about the limitations of this approach.

A Majority of Respondents Indicated Some Medical Service in the Building Was Needed: The most popular suggestion for the improvement of medical services (27 percent) was for car pools to get people to doctors. However, when all recommendations for increased on-site medical care were compared with all transportation oriented suggestions, an equal interest in these two approaches was revealed. Lawton (1975) observes that one major obstacle to developing on-site health care services is the great variation in the health status and service needs of elderly tenants. A second difficulty lies in providing easy access to medical care for those who require it, while avoiding an institutional atmosphere. As project populations age, and average levels of health and capacity decline, on-site medical services may become more acceptable (Lawton et al., 1980). Our results indicate the value of providing variety in health care services, in both type and degree.

The interview also addressed the issue of possible tenant interest in heat and water therapy such as a health spa or sauna bath. A similar query in the New Jersey study found about one-third of the elderly respondents interested in a supervised shared bathing facility (Schumacher and Cranz, 1975). Results of the present study show about 40 percent of our sample in favor of such a facility, primarily for medical rather than recreational reasons. Interest in this amenity seems widespread enough to warrant further investigation (Cranz and DeVoe, 1977).

The Size of the Apartment May Limit Its Capacity to Support Informal Social Activity

Christensen and Robinson found the apartment to be the primary arena for informal socializing among tenants. In the present study, 80 percent of our respondents indicated they visit with friends in their apartments, 11 percent in the halls and lobby, and 9 percent in community room activities.

Use of the apartment as a setting for social interaction was examined in terms of the frequency of socializing in this area. Of those who responded to the question, 15 percent said they had company every day, 31 percent once a week, 19 percent once a month, and 35 percent hardly ever. Sadly, over half of those interviewed had company once a month or less. A significant relationship was also found between how often tenants had company in their apartment and their evaluation of its spatial adequacy. Those who frequently entertained guests were more likely to perceive the small size of their apartment to be a problem. While correlations cannot prove causation, these findings support the contention that insufficient living space can exert a negative influence on the social activities of older tenants (Christensen and Robinson, 1975).

Conclusions

This study illustrates the kind of information that may be obtained from post-occupancy, user-oriented evaluations. The results support the utility of examining both physical and social issues using multiple indicators of environmental quality (Carp, 1969). Perhaps the most important conclusion to be drawn from our findings is that the built environment does make a measurable difference in the quality of life as perceived by elderly residents. Problems of loneliness, fear of crime, and difficulties with activities of daily living appear to be associated with conditions in the physical environment. For example, the evidence suggests that opportunities for older people to engage in informal social interaction are dependent upon the provision of adequate facilities within tenants' apartments, near the main entrance, and in the immediate neighborhood. Likewise, residents' perceptions of safety from crime seem to be strongly influenced by the density and character of adjacent land use and by provisions for informal monitoring of the street entry area. Also worthy of note are findings that indicate the importance of proper design for basic instrumental activities such as meal preparation, bathing, and laundering. Ideally, each of these issues should be addressed at the beginning of the design process in programmatic performance criteria. If the architectural program is sufficiently clear and comprehensive, it will help the designer keep track of the great diversity of important environmental issues that must be addressed and will facilitate the evaluation of alternative design proposals.

Finally, a word of caution should accompany the discussion of these findings. Our results are most relevant and generalizable to Housing Authorities and other sponsors of subsidized housing. Because only six sites were studied, the generalizability of our findings beyond these sites is uncertain. This would be particularly important where the environmental context is markedly different from that in northern California. With that caveat in mind, we offer the following policy and design guidelines.

ACKNOWLEDGMENTS

The authors wish to thank the many people who participated in this study and assisted in the preparation of the final report. We are especially indebted to Evert Heynneman, Director of Planning of the San Francisco Housing Authority, and Effie Robinson, Director of Senior Citizen Social Services, for their enthusiastic assistance and that of their staffs. The Gerontological Society of America, the Center for Environmental Design Research, and the Department of Architecture at the University of California, Berkeley, provided necessary funding and logistical support. We would also like to thank Sam Dyer, Sharrie Brooks, and other students of Dr. Cranz's graduate seminars who helped collect, analyze, and prepare this material.

DESIGN DIRECTIVES

Site design and building appearance should respect the functional needs and aesthetic values of the resident community.

1. Landscape designs utilizing flowering plants and including space for tenant controlled and maintained gardens provide useful links to previous housing experiences.

2. A clothesline adjacent to the laundry room and screened from public view can provide a less expensive and desired option for drying laundry.

3. Many older residents seem to prefer modern but conventional looking buildings. To avoid problems of stigmatization, subsidized projects should be compatible with the architectural character of the neighborhood.

4. High-rise buildings are acceptable to most elderly, particularly when they fit well with the surrounding development. However, a sizable minority of older adults prefer low-rise buildings, and this submarket should not be neglected.

Design treatment of interior and exterior spaces should provide for the social and territorial needs of elderly residents.

1. Comfortable benches near the main entrance can foster perceptions of safety and sociability while providing residents with interesting views of street activities. Seating areas should offer a choice of sunny and shaded locations.

2. The entrance lobby should be adjacent to the tenants' mail boxes but also partially screened from the main circulation path. Comfortable seating in the lobby should provide a clear view of the passenger loading zone on the street.

3. Every multi-unit building for the elderly should provide a laundry room with an adequate number of washers and dryers. Laundry rooms should have ironing boards, tables for folding clothes, and facilities for doing hand washing. A sitting area near a window with a view should be provided, and coin operated hair dryers might be considered in larger projects. Because of the laundry room's potential as an informal social center, it should be located on a main floor and not tucked away in a basement. However, clothes washing is a "back stage" activity and should not be in view of the main entrance.

Design of the apartment unit should recognize its importance as the primary locus of daily activities and help compensate for the diminished capacities of many older people to perform these activities.

1. Adequate storage space should be provided in the kitchen and elsewhere in the living unit. For the safety and convenience of frail residents, the top shelf in storage areas should not exceed a height of about five feet from the floor.

2. Bathtubs are preferred to stall showers by most elderly residents. Their design should include durable nonslip surfaces, lever-type controls, and grab bars that are logically placed and securely anchored.

3. Apartment design should facilitate informal entertaining and visiting activities. Provide a living room at least adequate to accommodate a full-size sofa, stuffed chair, and a console television. The living room should be separate from the bedroom and screened from view of the kitchen and bathroom. Studio apartments are not recommended, even for those who live alone.

4. Private balconies are valued amenities, and in temperate climates most apartments should provide them. However, north-facing units should not sacrifice daylight exposure in order to provide a balcony.

POLICY CONSIDERATIONS

Evaluation can improve the quality of housing.

User-oriented evaluations can play a key role in improving the environmental quality of existing and future housing projects. Responsible agencies should establish procedures for evaluating their projects and incorporating this information in their planning and managerial activities.

POLICY CONSIDERATION
ONE

Site selection should emphasize safety and accessibility.

Safety and accessibility to important and frequently used facilities should be specified in criteria for site selection. Access to public transportation and grocery stores is primary, but the accessibility of socially oriented facilities such as barber shops, beauty parlors, restaurants, parks, churches, and senior centers also should be considered. A good site will be located within one-quarter mile of each of these facilities. Projects also should be located in neighborhoods having high densities of potential residents in order to minimize the disruption of fragile social networks. Nevertheless, unsafe or declining neighborhoods generally should be avoided, even if the remaining population tends to be elderly.

POLICY CONSIDERATION
TWO

Service facilities should be incorporated into the plan.

Architectural and social components of the program for a new facility should be closely coordinated. Community rooms for organized tenant activities, two-bedroom managers' apartments, and offices for outposting social workers should be included in all new projects. Offices for security guards and/or health services also should be provided, even if staffing is not immediately available, since adding these facilities later will be more difficult.

POLICY CONSIDERATION
THREE

Security is a high priority.

Ongoing efforts are needed to maintain the optimum level of safety, both on site and in the immediate neighborhood. In higher density areas, a security guard service may be necessary. At the same time, management should make tenants aware of the role they must play in informal surveillance and reporting, rather than depending entirely on professional security services.

POLICY CONSIDERATION
FOUR

POLICY CONSIDERATION
FIVE

Health services will be increasingly important as residents age.

On-site medical programs such as blood pressure clinics and visiting nurses play a vital role in preserving the independence of elderly tenants. These programs may require expansion as residents become more frail with age. Management also should consider sponsoring preventive health care programs that help deter physical decline. If public transportation is not fully accessible to frail elderly, special transport service to medical centers should be substituted.

6

HOUSING SATISFACTION OF THE ELDERLY

Dorothy Butterfield and Sue Weidemann

R esearch dealing with resident housing satisfaction supports the importance of management, maintenance, and
aesthetics for housing the elderly (Francescato et al., 1979;
Weidemann and Anderson, 1981; Carp, 1976; Butterfield et al.,
1981). These components of the housing environment are particularly important because they can be manipulated by environmental designers and managers. Furthermore, since management,
maintenance, and aesthetics are each affected by decisions concerning the allocation of resources, an effective strategy to increase
resident satisfaction would concentrate on improvement in these
areas.

Management Contributes Directly and Indirectly to Resident Satisfaction

By establishing rules and policies, management provides a direct
link between residents and owners. The manner in which rules
are established and policies carried out is also important. Not only
must management develop reasonable rules and policies, but they
must be fairly and consistently enforced as well.

Indirectly, management serves as a role model for the type of
behavior expected from residents. It may also serve as an informal
communication system between residents. Supportive, effective

The U.S. Department of Housing and Urban Development (HUD) and the National
Endowment for the Arts (NEA) provided additional financial support for the publication of its results.

management can contribute greatly toward providing a pleasant and satisfying environment. Incompetent, nonsupportive management can accentuate existing problems and lead to resident unrest.

Maintenance Contributes Directly to the Perception Residents Have of the Physical Environment

A well-maintained housing site gives the impression that residents care about their home and is therefore more likely to encourage residents to respect the environment and contribute to the continuation of a high level of maintenance. Conversely, a poorly maintained site, no matter how beautiful the design, will detract from resident satisfaction. A setting of this type will be viewed by residents as an indication that management is lackadaisical. Residents will be less willing to contribute any effort toward keeping the environment attractive and functional. Both residents and outsiders are more likely to vandalize poorly maintained areas because they look as if they are neglected and unappreciated.

Aesthetics Contributes to an Attractive Setting

Although specific design tastes vary, to be aesthetically pleasing an environment must include a concern for high quality materials. Consideration of the context within which it is placed is also important. Amenities, such as trees and sitting spaces, which are visually pleasing and supportive, should be provided. The design of an aesthetically pleasing environment symbolically indicates to the person living in that setting that he is an asset to society. Such an environment may be particularly important to the elderly, many of whom may have suffered a loss in status at retirement. An attractive environment contributes to a "home-like" atmosphere. It also promotes the perception that the environment is a safe place to live (Weidemann et al., 1981).

Although management, maintenance, and aesthetics are each distinct characteristics of housing, to emphasize one component and ignore the others will defeat attempts to provide a supportive, satisfying environment for elderly residents.

Related Research

Resident satisfaction has recently become commonly accepted as a valid measure of assessing housing adequacy. Fried and Gleicher (1961) were among the first to stress its importance. Before that time, evaluation criteria were economic (proportion of rent to income), physical (the presence of plumbing), or social (the degree of crowding). However, after major public housing failures (Pruitt-Igoe in St. Louis and Rosengaard in Malmo, Sweden), more attention has been given to "user satisfaction" as a criterion for success. These projects ironically met most of the traditional economic and physical criteria but failed as communities.

Several recent studies have examined housing adequacy in terms of user needs and their relationship to the physical and social environment (Cooper, 1975; Hempel, 1977; Galster and Heser, 1981; Davis and Fine-Davis, 1981). Research, which relates satisfaction with one's housing to overall quality of life, demonstrates the appropriateness of such a shift in emphasis (Mulvihill, 1977; Campbell et al., 1976). The research on elderly residents, like that of the general population, indicates a strong relationship of housing satisfaction to general well-being or quality of life (Kozmo, 1983; Lawton, 1983; Lawton et al., 1978; Lawton et al., 1974). The relationship of housing satisfaction to the environment is very important because, as Marans and Williams (1979) point out, it is much easier to manipulate design and management variables than other personal aspects that define the quality of life, such as health or economic well-being.

Resident Satisfaction Studies Show That Neighborhood Is Important

Unfortunately, very little research has been conducted on resident satisfaction for the elderly. In a study by Lawton et al. (1974), which was primarily designed to evaluate the well-being of elderly tenants of federally assisted housing, six measures of well-being were examined, which included "housing satisfaction." The results supported the hypothesis that housing satisfaction is strongly related to neighborhood characteristics. This study also determined that satisfaction was greater in "age-segregated sites located in smaller communities with high quality neighborhoods where the risk of crime was considered low."

Jirovec et al. (1985) found the neighborhood to be overwhelmingly the most important predictor of housing satisfaction for urban elderly men. In addition, familiarity, sense of community, and safety "explained a small percentage of the variance accounted for in housing satisfaction." Even though the percentage of explained variance was small (7 percent), the inclusion of these characteristics was considered important "because they represent the aesthetic qualities of a dwelling unit."

Privacy, Security, Friends, and Unit Features Also Affect Housing Satisfaction

Other studies of housing satisfaction for the elderly have shown privacy (Carp, 1966; Hamovitch and Peterson, 1969; Lake, 1962), age-segregated housing (Lawton et al., 1980; Teaff et al., 1978), perceptions of safety and security (Carp, 1975; Clemente and Kleiman,

1976; Sherman, 1972; Toseland and Rosch, 1978), and a network of friends and relations (Lawton, 1978) to be important. Lawton and Nahemow (1979) found that physical features of the housing environment—total kitchen storage, amount of counter space, amount of closet space, and presence of a yard or patio—increased satisfaction.

Devlin (1980) examined differences in satisfaction for residents of low- and high-rise housing. She found that the physical aspects of the environment and proximity to nature were important for the low-rise residents, while the social environment was more important for the high-rise residents. There is also some evidence to suggest that housing satisfaction may also be dependent upon the previous life experiences of the residents. For example, housing satisfaction for residents of Victoria Plaza increased when they acquired such modern conveniences as a toilet, refrigerator, or a stove as a result of their move into the building (Carp, 1976).

This chapter presents two research projects that examine the effects of maintenance, management, aesthetics, and other issues on resident satisfaction. The first study was conducted with a number of housing sites throughout the country and provides general information concerning the relative importance of components of the housing environment that contribute to housing satisfaction. The second study was conducted at one multifamily housing project where 20 percent of the residents were elderly. These data explore site specific issues related to housing satisfaction.

Methodology and Data Analysis

Study 1: A National Sample

The first study in this research program was undertaken during the period from 1972 through 1978 by Francescato, Weidemann, Anderson, and Chenoweth (1979). The research phase included the development of multiple methods of evaluating the residential environment as well as a basic theoretical model.

The study had two major research goals: the development of valid and reliable research measures for assessing residents' satisfaction, and the evaluation of a number of housing sites for the purpose of identifying and measuring aspects of the physical environment, social environment, and management style that influence residents' satisfaction (Francescato et al., 1979).

Thirty-seven Sites in Ten States Were Selected: Sites that displayed as much variety as possible were selected. The dimensions along which the housing developments vary include building type, location, population, design, and age of the occupants. Ten of the developments were public housing while the others had publicly assisted financing but were privately owned. Locations ranged from central cities to rural communities. All except one were designed to house an age-integrated population. The exception was a project specifically designed as housing for elderly persons.

Racial composition of residents ranged from 100 percent white to 100 percent black. Building heights also varied. Twenty-nine sites were low-rise (one to three stories); three sites were mid-rise (three to five stories); and five sites were high-rise apartment buildings (over five stories). The length of time that the buildings were occupied varied from 3 months to 33 years.

The study used a multimethod approach. Methodological tools included questionnaires, interviews, assessments of the physical environment, observations of the residents' behavior, and examinations of the records held by managers, housing authorities, and architectural firms.

Questionnaire Data Were Scrutinized by a Two-Step Process: Questionnaire data were analyzed to determine the aspects of the housing environment most likely to contribute to residents' satisfaction. A two-step process was performed using multivariate statistical techniques. This process first used principal component analysis to group together highly correlated, individual items into sets of related variables called *factors*, in which each represented a single concept. Multiple regression was then used to determine the relative importance of these concepts (and other variables) in predicting residents' satisfaction. The particular housing-related issues that were most important to this sample's satisfaction were determined by these methods.

Twenty Independent Variables Were Examined by Regression Analysis: These 20 variables were examined to determine the degree to which they could predict residents' satisfaction with their housing. Table 6.1 outlines these variables. They consisted of variables measuring physical site characteristics, demographic and housing experience, and evaluations of current housing. The evaluations of current housing consisted of six factors obtained by factor analysis of 16 general evaluative items from the resident questionnaire. The dependent variable used as the criterion of housing success was: How satisfied are you with living here?

Study 2: A Post-Occupancy Evaluation

The second study was undertaken at the request of the Decatur, Illinois, Housing Authority to review modernization efforts and make recommendations for their participation in the Urban Initiatives Anti-Crime Demonstration Program. The study used a research process similar to the first study and offered an opportunity to evaluate previous changes in the environment and to conduct research at a specific site.

TABLE 6.1   Variable Definitions

Independent Variables
1. Number of units in site: number of units
2. Number of units/acre: number of units divided by lot size
3. Age heterogeneity: sum of squared deviations from
                                                 distribution (6 intervals, age range
                                                 from 24 and under to 65 and older)
4. Sex of respondent: female (1) male (2)
5. Number in home: number of people
6. Education: grade school (1) to some beyond
                                                 college (7)
7. Time in town: number of years
8. Time on site: number of months
9. Choice of unit: no choice (1) to many (more than six)
                                                 places (5)
10. Choice of site: no choice (1) to many (more than six)
                                                 places (5)
11. Appearance of last residence: worse (1) to better (3)
12. Last residence better: worse (1) to better (3)
13. Prior housing type: no single family (1), some single
                                                 family (2), all single family (3)
14. Age difference: median age of residents on same site–
                                                 respondents' age
15. Appearance satisfaction (Factor 1):   complete factor score matrix for
                                                 Factor 1
16. Changes allowed satisfaction   complete factor score matrix for
    (Factor 2):   Factor 2
17. Facilities satisfaction (Factor 3):   complete factor score matrix for
                                                 Factor 3
18. Management satisfaction (Factor 4):   complete factor score matrix for
                                                 Factor 4
19. Privacy satisfaction (Factor 5):   complete factor score matrix for
                                                 Factor 5
20. People/community access   complete factor score matrix for
    satisfaction (Factor 6):   Factor 6

Dependent Variable
1. Satisfaction with living here: very dissatisfied (1) to very satisfied (5)

Site Characteristics: Longview Place is a low-income, publicly
subsidized, multifamily housing site in central Illinois. Its residents
are primarily black, single-parent families. There are about 1,100
persons at the site. Ninety percent are black, slightly more than
half are children, and about 20 percent are elderly. Most of the
elderly are single, white females. There are, however, a few couples and a small number of black elderly persons.

The site is composed of 63 two-story rowhouses in a six-block
area of the inner city (Fig. 6.1). There are a total of 418 units each,
including one to four bedrooms each. Older residents are scattered
throughout the site. The size of a unit given to a family is dependent upon the number of family members. Therefore, the larger

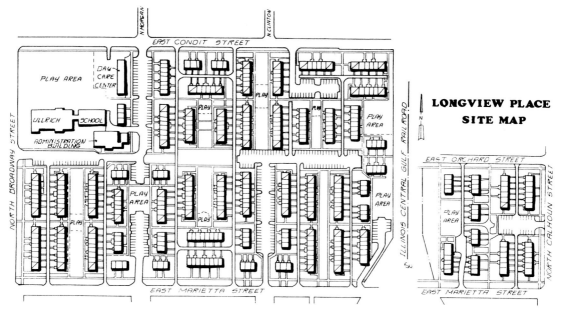

FIGURE 6.1 Longview Place site map.

units tend to have several children, while the one-bedroom units house either single persons or childless couples.

Longview Place is bordered on the north and south by older homes. A major north-south artery is located to the west of the complex. Commercial and residential structures lie to the west and a large industrial land use to the south. The eastern portion of the site contains a one-block area, separated from the rest of the site by an Illinois Central Gulf Railroad right-of-way.

In addition to housing units, the site contains a community building, an administration building, a day care center, and a kindergarten. Other social services include the "Open Door," a rest and relaxation program sponsored by the YWCA, and a social service information center. Recreational facilities, varying in scale and designed for the use of young residents who range in age from preschool to teens, are placed throughout the project. A basketball court is located near the Illinois Central Gulf tracks, and common spaces, located near the center of the project and the parking lots, are also used for active play by the young residents.

After Longview Place was built in 1945, it remained substantially unchanged for 30 years. In 1972, substantial modernization was begun. Over a period of about 5 years, changes were made to both the interior and exterior of the units. In 1976, additional funds were available and used for renovations concentrated in the one-block area that is separated from the main site. The concentration of design modifications in this area provided an opportunity to see what, if any, differences were perceived by the residents.

Data Collection: The information gathering process included meetings with the housing authority, visits to the site, a review of previous documents, and a self-report questionnaire. The questionnaire used to gather information employed the Study 1 instrument, a safety and security instrument developed by HUD (1978), and some additional items related to site specific issues. Data obtained from the survey were analyzed by multivariate techniques (factor analysis and multiple regression) to determine which aspects of the residential environment were most strongly related to residents' perceptions of satisfaction.

Data Analysis: The process for analysis was a two-step method similar to that used in Study 1. First, the multivariate technique of principal component analysis was performed. This technique was used to group the individual questionnaire items into highly correlated factors so that the data were more manageable. The solution generated 23 factors. Multiple regression was then performed to determine which of these 23 factors was the best predictor of resident satisfaction. The criterion variable (dependent variable: *resident satisfaction*) for this study was an index developed from the average score of highly correlated items:

"How long do you want to live in this housing development?"

"If you move again, would you like to live in another place like this?"

"Would you recommend this place to friends if they were looking for a place to live?"

"How satisfied are you with living here?"

The data from elderly persons in the sample were separated and the multiple regression performed, to determine which of the same 23 factors were the best predictors of *residents' satisfaction* for older residents.

Findings From Study 1

Several Factors Were Related to Resident Satisfaction

Eight of the independent variables used in the regression analysis were found to be significant predictors of resident satisfaction. These are represented in Figure 6.2. The arrow width illustrates their relative contribution. The most important of these predictors was privacy. The next predictors were satisfaction with facilities, the interaction between choice of site and privacy, and the inter-

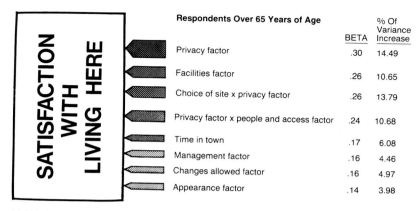

Respondents Over 65 Years of Age	BETA	% Of Variance Increase
Privacy factor	.30	14.49
Facilities factor	.26	10.65
Choice of site x privacy factor	.26	13.79
Privacy factor x people and access factor	.24	10.68
Time in town	.17	6.08
Management factor	.16	4.46
Changes allowed factor	.16	4.97
Appearance factor	.14	3.98

Multiple R = .728   R² = 53%   N = 120

Privacy Factor
Amount of privacy from neighbors
Amount of privacy from family

Facilities Factor
Laundry facilities
Recreation facilities
Parking arrangements
Protection from crime and vandals

People and Access Factor
People outside development
Residents in development
Access to the community

Management Factor
Management rules
Management

Freedom to Make Changes Factor
Freedom to change inside home
Freedom to change outside home

Appearance Factor
Appearance of the development
Appearance of the outside of home
Appearance of the grounds

FIGURE 6.2   Predictors of "satisfaction with living here": Study 1.

action between privacy and people/community access. The final predictors, which were less important but still included, were management, freedom to make changes, and appearance. Several of these variables concern issues of management, maintenance, and aesthetics (Fig. 6.2).

Privacy Was the Most Important Predictor

Results from Study 1 show that the most important predictor of resident satisfaction for elderly residents was satisfaction with privacy, in terms of the amount of privacy from both neighbors and families. Privacy, in conceptual terms, reflects the ability for one to control those factors that directly interfere with its actualization—such as control over visual, aural, or physical intrusions. The extent to which one may maintain privacy depends upon one's ability to control access to both one's home and one's person.

Two items were included in the privacy factor. The first item, "privacy from one's neighbors," implies that one can control those elements that ensure seclusion from other residents—such as a quiet unit free from outside noise and a personally controlled space in front of and behind one's unit. It also applies to the location of one's unit, whether it be near larger family units or other older persons.

The second item is the amount of "privacy from one's family." This issue is important not only for elderly persons who live with other family members but also for those who live alone and have family members who visit. It implies that one has a "personal space." Often this space is a separate bedroom.

Satisfaction with Facilities Was a Moderate Predictor

An issue that turned out to be a moderate predictor of resident satisfaction for elderly persons was satisfaction with the various facilities provided, such as laundry, recreation, and parking. Thus, the relationship of maintenance, management, and aesthetics to these facilities needs to be carefully considered because of their potential to enhance resident satisfaction.

Management, Freedom to Make Changes, and Aesthetics Were Also Important

Management was considered satisfactory by residents if it was accessible to residents for conversations, complaints were followed up quickly, and it was perceived that rules met the residents' needs and, once established, were consistently and fairly enforced.

The factor of freedom to make changes is a concept that is dependent upon management and management policies. Residents were more satisfied with the housing development when they felt free to change their environment.

The appearance factor was also a predictor of resident satisfaction for the elderly. Items in this factor included satisfaction with the appearance of the development and the exterior of the home and the grounds. An attractive, aesthetically pleasing, and well-maintained housing development added to the older person's satisfaction; that is, the more pleasant the residents perceived the housing environment to be, the more pleased they were with where they were living.

Findings From Study 2

Attractiveness, Maintenance, Safety, and Apartment Suitability Rated High

The most important factor predicting resident satisfaction in Study 2 for elderly persons was one that included a variety of items grouped under the label of "attractiveness." Three additional fac-

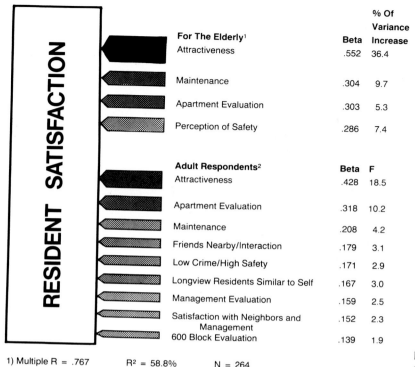

	Beta	% Of Variance Increase
For The Elderly[1]		
Attractiveness	.552	36.4
Maintenance	.304	9.7
Apartment Evaluation	.303	5.3
Perception of Safety	.286	7.4

	Beta	F
Adult Respondents[2]		
Attractiveness	.428	18.5
Apartment Evaluation	.318	10.2
Maintenance	.208	4.2
Friends Nearby/Interaction	.179	3.1
Low Crime/High Safety	.171	2.9
Longview Residents Similar to Self	.167	3.0
Management Evaluation	.159	2.5
Satisfaction with Neighbors and Management	.152	2.3
600 Block Evaluation	.139	1.9

1) Multiple R = .767 R^2 = 58.8%   N = 264
2) Multiple R = .681 R^2 = 46.4%   N = 41

FIGURE 6.3 Factors predicting resident satisfaction: Study 2.

tors were significant predictors of satisfaction: maintenance, apartment evaluation, and perception of safety. These predictors are slightly different from those that are shown in Figure 6.3, which are related to the general adult population.

Items that contributed to satisfaction with attractiveness included a noninstitutional exterior, a home-like appearance, the ability to find one's way around the site easily, special recreation areas for different age groups, provision of a pleasant community building, and suitable interior units.

The attractiveness of the environment was affected by the level of maintenance. A well-kept, neatly maintained housing environment was reported to add to the general pleasantness of an area. For the elderly persons in this study, the appearance of well-maintained parking areas and garbage areas were also important (see Fig. 6.4). High levels of maintenance in each of these areas denoted a tidy, well-cared-for atmosphere.

Additional maintenance concerns were related to both function and aesthetics. Residents desired well-maintained window glass and screens. Broken glass and torn screens were considered symbolic of "nonownership" in a slum area. In addition to the aesthetic

FIGURE 6.4 Garbage area: Screening the refuse/garbage area and locating it near the back door of the unit makes maintenance easier.

blight posed by such conditions, it was also considered dangerous and unsafe for the health and well-being of the residents.

Night Lighting Contributes to the Perceptions of Safety: Since the perception of safety also was important to resident satisfaction, care should be taken to make sure that the environment not only "looks safe" but is safe. Night lighting allows residents to see and be seen in an environment that may be threatening. Vision, in general, declines with age. Therefore, adequate lighting enhances the ability for elderly tenants to recognize, as well as be recognized by, their neighbors. This provides a type of informal surveillance that aids in the perception of safety.

Playgrounds were also among the areas with which residents were most concerned. Some of their concern may have been due to the unpleasant appearance of trash-littered playgrounds. Another reason for concern might have been for the safety of those children playing on the site—especially those younger children for whom broken glass could be extremely harmful when unnoticed.

Most items in the apartment evaluation factor were concerned with physical comfort, such as the ability to control the apartment's temperature; however, one of the items addressed satisfaction with rules about the apartment. Since this issue was addressed earlier, its inclusion in this factor further emphasizes its important contribution to resident satisfaction. Residents were also concerned with the ability to arrange their furniture attractively. This relates to those residents who come from larger homes and have an overabundance of furniture.

Conclusions

Maintenance, management, and aesthetics are important in terms of their contribution to resident satisfaction. Given their strong interrelationships, it is unlikely that high levels of satisfaction can be obtained by just improving satisfaction with one component.

The relative importance of the conceptual issues that account for residents' satisfaction varies among age groups and between sites. Issues most important to housing satisfaction for elderly persons in Study 1 were privacy, facilities provided, people and community access, quality of management and management rules, freedom to make changes, and the appearance of both the site and its grounds.

For Study 2, the sample of elderly persons at Longview Place, the most important factors contributing to satisfaction were attractiveness, maintenance, apartment evaluation, and perception of safety. Along with the above considerations, several major issues deserve special elaboration.

Elderly Persons Generally Prefer a Home-like Setting

When the individual items identified as predictive factors are considered together, they indicate that the elderly in our sample prefer qualities of the housing environment that give it a home-like appearance. The provisions of a home-like environment imply a spatial hierarchy. In a normal residential setting, spaces range from public (such as the street and sidewalk) to private (such as the interior of the home). A definite progression of spaces is evident in noninstitutional settings. Circulation systems are the most public of the spaces and are usually separated from the more private interiors. Yard spaces are usually semipublic in the front of the residence and semiprivate in the rear. A site design that distinctly separates these areas is one in which there is likely to be less ambiguity about who has control over the territory. In typical residential settings the yard areas are distinct.

"Home-like" also implies a sense of ownership, which is very important to residents. Within residential areas, residents "own" their space. Private sector residents are also aware of the collective ownership of one's housing subdivision or apartment complex. In order to provide residents of public housing with this same sense of ownership, the site must reflect the fact that it is a private, self-contained unit. Indiscriminate paths through the site and facilities requiring residents to share parking spaces destroy this sense of privacy and ownership.

Residents need parking spaces that "belong" to them, along with the assurance that they will not be used by nonresidents. Likewise, pedestrian circulation systems, which cut through the housing site that nonresidents use as shortcuts, violate this concern. Public housing circulation systems should be designed to draw off-site nonresident traffic to one end of a site. Otherwise, the site loses its sense of privacy and is no longer "owned" by the residents because they lose control over it.

Personalization and Variety in the Environment Can Help Individualize the Setting

Closely associated with a home-like environment is the notion that the environment stresses personalization and variety. The bits and pieces that make up the design of exterior spaces present an image to the neighborhood of the residents who live there. The image that is presented may or may not be an honest representation of the resident. However, no matter what image is presented it should be one that is chosen by the residents.

Often, this representation is portrayed through the choice of various landscape materials, lawn furniture, and lawn ornaments. The particular appearance presented varies by occupant. The ability to change and define this image is a function of being a home-owner. Control over one's home is a privilege that most home-owners take for granted. It is important to public housing residents for the same reason. Even though they do not "own" their home, they can at least maintain control over their home space. This free-dom allows the residents two options. First, residents can use the

FIGURE 6.5 Personalization: Management rules and policy which allow the residents to personalize their environment contribute to a "home-like" appearance.

space to meet their needs; and second, they can present and individualize a picture of themselves to the other residents and the community. This freedom and responsibility allow the resident an investment in the environment and should be supported through management policy.

In privately funded housing, an environment is normally created that reflects an image which residents wish to portray to the public. Variety, quality of materials, personal embellishment, and concern for the impression imply ownership. Conversely, a lack of variety in materials, sterile rigidity, and a lack of concern for the total design image imply that the environment is an institutional setting. Individuality within a system of vernacular tolerances is important in maintaining an image of home. Materials that are sturdy and well designed also reinforce this image.

The fact that an owner has the opportunity to control his or her environment guarantees that a certain amount of variety will occur—even if the limits of tolerance for difference are small. An example of limited tolerance for difference is a subdivision that has design covenants and restrictions attached to the deed. Even under such restrictions enormous variety flourishes (Fig. 6.5).

In Age-Integrated Settings, Separate Recreational Areas Are Desirable

Special areas for each group could help relieve the pressures of group squabbles for territory. Conflict between groups was noted by some of the elderly residents. There seemed to be a problem with destruction of resident flowerbeds by children. Their intent was not malicious in nature but was caused by the lack of a designated play area, which would normally contain their childlike energies.

Ability to Find One's Way Is An Important Design Element: The ability to easily find one's way around the site is important to residents. Areas of the site can be differentiated so that each maintains its own character. Environmental cues can be used to create distinct areas. Use of various color coding, selection of plant materials, signage, and other special design features can help differentiate areas. For example, a system of planting designs could be developed which would display variation from one site area to the next. In one entry, white pines could be used as the evergreen planting while in another hemlocks could be used. The design is similar but textures differ. Thus, one could specify the hemlock entry as an easy landmark for a visitor trying to find his way. Such a system could be reinforced through the use of signage and placing of names. Designation of areas through the use of distinct names could also reinforce the character of each area. Large, boldly printed graphics would also make it easier to define one's place on the site.

DESIGN DIRECTIVES

The physical environment and its design are extremely important in providing elderly persons with satisfying housing environments. It should be stressed that the overall conclusions about the desirability of privacy, a home-like appearance, and personalization form the backbone for the following recommendations. Since the following suggestions are based on the two studies previously described, care should be taken when applying the design directives and policy recommendations.

DESIGN DIRECTIVE ONE — *Elderly residents should be provided with at least one bedroom which is separated from general living spaces.*

1. Even those elderly residents who lived alone indicated a need to separate various activities of daily life.

2. When an elderly person is part of a larger household, the living spaces should be large enough to allow family members to retreat from each other so as to provide visual and aural privacy.

DESIGN DIRECTIVE TWO — *Adequate insulation should be installed between common walls and along exterior walls.*

1. The creation of such a sound barrier will give residents privacy from persons living next door.

2. Sound barriers also allow privacy from noise outside the units.

DESIGN DIRECTIVE THREE — *Exterior walkways should be placed away from exterior unit walls.*

1. Exterior unit walls that have windows facing the walkways allow those passing by an interior view of the units, thus preventing a sense of privacy.

2. Sound from residents using such walks destroys the aural privacy of residents.

DESIGN DIRECTIVE FOUR — *The most attractive sturdy building materials affordable should be used.*

1. Although what is attractive is a subjective judgment, the use of sturdy, well-designed materials helps to create a home-like atmosphere comparable to well-designed housing for elderly, middle-class residents.

Buildings and units should be easily differentiated from each other.

	DESIGN DIRECTIVE
	FIVE

1. Variety may add to the feeling that a unit is unique. Differentiation emphasizes the individuality of each resident.

2. Variation in the design of units helps both residents and visitors to orient themselves and spares them the embarrassment of attempting to enter the wrong unit.

3. Variety may be accomplished through use of different colors, trim, type of buildings, shape, or placement of units.

Building and landscaping materials should be chosen for their ability to be easily maintained.

	DESIGN DIRECTIVE
	SIX

1. The importance of site appearance is emphasized by being the second most important predictor of satisfaction by elderly residents.

2. An "attractive" site implies that the area is well maintained.

3. If staff is limited, special care should be given to the choice of materials so that they appear well kept without heavy maintenance. For example, natural wood for fencing should be used rather than painted wood, which requires a higher level of maintenance. Plants with high maintenance levels or those that collect trash should be avoided.

Garbage storage areas should be screened from view but made easily accessible to residents.

	DESIGN DIRECTIVE
	SEVEN

1. Trash is more likely to be deposited in the proper location if receptacles are easily available.

2. Several garbage areas lessen the institutional look of a larger housing development.

Vehicular traffic on site should accommodate only residents and their guests. Facilities that are shared by residents and nonresidents should be located at the periphery of a large site. Both strategies reduce the need for nonresidents to traverse through the site.

	DESIGN DIRECTIVE
	EIGHT

1. Nonresidents who linger on site are seen as a threat to elderly residents. The environment should be designed to discourage entry by nonresidents.

2. If facilities on site are shared by nonresidents, the parking facilities should be designed so that nonresidents do not drive through the site to reach the parking area.

| DESIGN DIRECTIVE **NINE** | *Paths from the periphery to site interior should be placed so that they are easily monitored by residents and should not form an easily available short-cut through the site.* |

1. Use of paths by nonresidents can destroy the sense of ownership important to residents.

| DESIGN DIRECTIVE **TEN** | *Recreation facilities should be provided which are separate and designed for specific age groups.* |

1. Gardening space for adults should be placed away from children's play areas and where the plants are under surveillance by adults.

2. Different age groups often have different needs that do not easily coexist spatially and can create conflicts if not kept separate.

| DESIGN DIRECTIVE **ELEVEN** | *Special attention should be paid to adequate night lighting.* |

1. For elderly residents at Longview Place, night lighting contributed to the perception that it was a safe place to live.

2. Many older persons have difficulty with night vision.

POLICY CONSIDERATIONS

Management should be accessible to the residents.

Since management is responsible for so many of the aspects of the housing environment that affect resident satisfaction, they need to be available. Otherwise, residents are without a means of communicating either positive or negative aspects of their housing environment which concern them.

POLICY CONSIDERATION
ONE

Rules should be stated clearly.

Without clearly stated rules, residents may not be fully aware of their rights and responsibilities concerning their ability to control their environment, thus lessening the potential for increased satisfaction.

POLICY CONSIDERATION
TWO

Management should fairly and consistently enforce rules.

Obviously, even clearly stated rules and regulations lose their effectiveness when enforcement is not fair and consistent. Lack of consistency in enforcement undermines the authority of management and leaves the resident confused about what the rules really mean.

POLICY CONSIDERATION
THREE

Residents should be encouraged to participate in the development of rules.

Resident participation in development of rules allows them to feel they have more control over their housing environment, and residents who are involved in the process are more likely to obey the rules.

POLICY CONSIDERATION
FOUR

Residents should be allowed to participate in decisions concerning their environment, such as choosing wall colors for their apartments.

If residents are allowed to choose their wall colors and participate in other environmental decisions, it is more likely they will have an environment that is aesthetically pleasing to them.

POLICY CONSIDERATION
FIVE

POLICY CONSIDERATION	*Management should encourage residents to be responsible for the orga-*
SIX	*nization of on-site recreational activities.*

Adequate recreational activities add to satisfaction with one's housing, provide opportunities for residents to get acquainted, and allow residents to participate in structuring the social environment.

POLICY CONSIDERATION	*Management should give high priority to establishing a high level of on-*
SEVEN	*site maintenance.*

High-quality maintenance contributes much to resident satisfaction and should be given the emphasis it deserves. Without adequate attention to maintenance, the most beautiful design soon looks trashy.

7

INVOLVING OLDER PERSONS IN DESIGNING HOUSING FOR THE ELDERLY

Chester Hartman, Jerry Horovitz,
and Robert Herman

T he design of housing for the elderly is usually based on indirect solicitations of user needs through such methods as mail surveys, meetings with the prime sponsor, and analyses of other similar facilities. These methods have been employed to provide design guidelines in such areas as building style, entryway, location of mailboxes, and lobby space. While useful as general benchmarks, the traditional behavioral design methods may fail to identify needs and preferences of special groups: ethnic minorities, residents of downtown neighborhoods or rural communities, etc. Moreover, these methods are often limited by the difficulty lay people have in grasping design concepts that are expressed in written words or abstract sketches. Of equal concern is the passive nature of these traditional approaches: information is generally sought at one point early in the design process, rather than on a more interactive and ongoing basis as design decisions are actually made. And, unless the process includes a post-occupancy evaluation from the actual users of the facility, little can be learned about how the building met residents' needs, where it missed the mark, and what should be done to correct any problems.

Perhaps nowhere is the identification of user needs and preferences more difficult than in places where urban redevelopment has dispersed lower-income elderly residents long before replacement housing is constructed—itself a major feat in cities that have opted for "higher and better" uses of urban renewal land. San Francisco's South-of-Market area—site of the 87-acre Yerba Buena Center (YBC) convention hall, office building, and hotel complex—is just such an area. There, a nonprofit residents' organization, Tenants and Owners in Opposition to Redevelopment (TOOR), formed a housing development corporation that won the right to design, develop, and manage some 400 units of low-rent housing to be built on four sites. This housing was to be subsidized through a variety of federal, state, and city sources (including an increase in the city's hotel tax enacted to provide this housing aid).

The Site Formerly Housed Many Low-Income Older People

The YBC site, a light industrial and commercial area, also housed the city's low-rent hotel district. Some 4,000 persons—mainly low-income retired white men—lived in four dozen residential hotels. Rents at the time of land-taking (the late 1960s) were $40–60 a month, and housing conditions—at least until the onset of redevelopment plans—were for the most part modest but decent. The elderly residents found the central location convenient and suitable to their needs, as the South-of-Market area is flat in a generally hilly city and sunny in a city with many foggy neighborhoods. Inexpensive restaurants, second-hand stores, and other important community facilities were close by. The hotels themselves served as small, supportive communities—the men sat around the lobbies, chatted, watched TV, played cards, and looked after each other. This mutual support system was particularly important for those with physical disabilities and alcoholism problems—the latter estimated at 15 percent of the population by the Redevelopment Agency. The principal problem the residents faced was that they were occupying land the city wanted to develop as part of an expanding central office area.

When the Redevelopment Agency began acquiring the hotels and evicting residents in 1967 and 1968, the tactics it used and their inadequate relocation offerings led the residents—many former trade union members and organizers—to organize Tenants and Owners in Opposition to Redevelopment (TOOR). Aided by attorneys from the San Francisco Neighborhood Legal Assistance Foundation, the residents brought suit in November 1969, and, the following April, Federal Judge Stanley Weigel took the unprecedented step of enjoining the entire $385 million project until the Redevelopment Agency revised its relocation plan to provide suitable relocation housing for nearly 4,000 people in a city with a virtually zero percent vacancy rate for low-rent units. (For a complete history of the Yerba Buena Center project, see Hartman, 1984.)

Tenants and Owners in Opposition to Redevelopment Forced the City Through Legal Action to Provide Replacement Housing

In November 1970 the Agency signed a consent decree, agreeing to rehabilitate within 3 years 1,500–1,800 low-rent units outside the redevelopment area, in return for which the injunction was lifted. But by mid-1973 the Agency had produced only 11 of these promised units, and TOOR and their lawyers were back before Judge Weigel. This time, in an effort to rid itself of TOOR's legal challenge once and for all, the Agency and the city agreed to provide additional replacement housing within the Yerba Buena project area itself—something TOOR had demanded all along and the Agency had just as adamantly opposed. The resultant agreement was to raise the city's hotel tax from 5.5 to 6 percent and use the new revenue (estimated at $500,000 a year) for 35 years to finance construction of approximately 400 units on four YBC sites, with some of the money used for rent subsidies. Federal Section 8 funds and other subsidies, if available, could be substituted for the local hotel tax funds. The 400 units were to be over and above the 1,500–1,800 units previously promised by the Agency, which was given an extra year to complete this work. TOOR's housing development corporation, the Tenants and Owners Development Corporation (TODCO), would choose its own architect from a panel of five jointly selected by TODCO and the city, have overall responsibility for design and development, and eventually manage the projects. In exchange for these concessions, TOOR would drop its relocation suit "with prejudice"—that is, without possibility of reinstating it unless the city reneged on its commitments.

Because formal city action was required to implement several points of the May 1973 agreement, the first actual development steps did not commence until January 1974. The TODCO-selected architect faced a twofold task: to develop a master plan for the four TODCO sites and to carry out the design work for the first site. The master plan had to take into account the following elements: the relationship of the four TODCO sites to each other and the existence of three nearby new housing developments for the elderly—the 276-unit Clementina Towers public housing project, the 206-unit Catholic Church-sponsored Alexis Apartments, and the 258-unit Salvation Army-sponsored Silvercrest. It also had to consider the relationship of this housing to Yerba Buena Center; and the existence of substantial amounts of low-rent hotel accom-

FIGURE 7.1 Exterior of Woolf House: The 9-story, 182-unit apartment building has bay windows, broken line parapets, a corner turret, balconies, double-hung windows, and stores on the first floor.

modations and family apartments just to the west of the YBC project area. Figure 7.1 shows the exterior of the completed Woolf House project.

A "User Needs Survey" Was to Precede Preliminary Design Drawings

Even though the timing of replacement housing construction was such that TODCO could not ensure that the 400 units would be occupied by YBC displacees, it wanted to do everything possible to make its housing fit the needs of people similarly situated: elderly single people with low incomes who wanted to live in the downtown area. TODCO believed a study of the needs of such people could guide the architects in designing housing on all four sites.

Methodology and Data Analysis

In line with the activist stance of its client, the team of environmental planners and architects hired by TODCO in 1975 developed a highly participatory user needs survey. The method they employed involved direct solicitation of potential user responses to design alternatives shown through the use of a slide show. These slides illustrated specific design solutions to various portions of the building and were shown to small groups of elderly, with concurrent discussion and "voting."

Slides and Small Group Discussions Were Key Attributes

In order to get some general background on the housing needs and preferences of the TODCO client group, several hotel and housing development managers in the downtown area were interviewed, some 30 YBC relocatees scattered around the city were contacted (most in person, some by phone) to get their views, and the more recent and relevant literature about housing design and attitudes of the elderly was reviewed (Gelwicks and Newcomer, 1974; Zeisel, 1975; McGuire, 1972; Michigan State Housing Development Authority, 1974). The primary investigative tool, however, was small group discussions built around a carefully developed slide presentation. The purpose of this technique was to isolate a group of very specific design questions, present alternative solutions in a highly graphic way, and elicit views, comments, and choices from potential users. The work was as much a testing of technique as it was a search for answers.

A series of discussions among the architects and TODCO staff members narrowed the scope of design issues to be investigated. The guidelines used were:

Relevance to the physical, social, and psychological needs of users

Likely ignorance on the part of (nonelderly) architects

Ease of illustration

Possibility of illumination through group discussion

Relative neglect in the architectural literature

Select Design and Planning Issues Were Explored

Keeping in mind the need to limit the presentation/discussion to the attention and interest span of elderly viewers, 17 issues were selected. These were ordered in a scale sequence, from planning for the street area and outside space, to the building's common spaces, and then to individual units. The issues were:

Street development
Old versus new building style
High-rise versus low-rise
Ground floor use
Relation of building entry to street

Lobby
Open Space
Mailbox location
Laundry facilities
Game rooms
Corridors

Balconies
Kitchens
Storage
Apartment furnishings
Apartment size
Apartment shape

To illustrate each issue, a photographer who had worked in the South-of-Market area for several years took 40 photographs illustrating various design questions and options. This collection comprised the visual presentation.

Small Group Sessions Were Organized at Meal Programs

Organizing groups to whom the slide show could be presented was a problem. The original intention was to program 15–18 shows over a 4-week period in the three new South-of-Market developments, in the older YBC-like hotels still standing in the South-of-Market area just west of YBC, and in the Agency-rehabilitated hotels in the North-of-Market area. Arranging such meetings proved time-consuming and frustrating. There was no assurance of an adequate turnout if nothing was done other than posting a notice, and going door-to-door produced suspicion and further difficulties. Consideration was given to asking selected tenants to invite neighbors into their apartments, but this too was unsuccessful: most did not want to have their apartments used in that way or go to the trouble of inviting neighbors in, and arranging to use common space often led to time-consuming bureaucratic delays.

An excellent solution emerged at the suggestion of TODCO's chairman, an activist in the city's senior organizations. Presentations were arranged at various senior luncheon programs in the downtown area (run by a church, a settlement house, the Salvation Army, and one of the new South-of-Market developments) where large numbers of people gather daily, many of whom were willing to remain after lunch for the presentation. A short announcement/invitation was made during lunch, and there was no trouble assembling a small group after the meal. Some meal programs began as early as 10:30, while others served until early afternoon; thus, two slide sessions could be programmed in a single day.

In all, 17 small group sessions were held (including an initial "shakedown" session, following which slight revisions were made in the presentation). Groups ranged from 4 to 10 persons, and in all 123 persons participated. Drawing on the lunch program clientele produced the desired diversity in the sample. Of the 123 participants, 48 percent were male, 52 percent female, 83 percent were white (including several Spanish-speaking persons), 17 percent black or Oriental; geographically, the group represented a good cross-section of downtown residential areas, plus some outlying parts of the city. Virtually everyone was elderly and retired, and, given their residential locations and participation in the senior lunch programs, it is likely that almost all had incomes low enough to make them eligible for TODCO's housing. The method of selecting participants probably resulted in an overrepresentation of more outgoing, sociable, activity-oriented persons (those who participate in the lunch programs and accepted the invitation to join the slide showing), and the "respectable" poor (those without severe social disorders such as alcoholism). But it is likely that any method of selection would lead to moderate overrepresentation in this direction.

Slides and a Script Were Used to Elicit Participant Design Choices

Two persons ran each session; one operated the slide projector, gave the narration, and posed the questions, while the other recorded responses. A form was developed to record the choices of each participant, together with some basic demographic characteristics. The recorder also took down any interesting comments made by the viewers. All three architects in the firm, plus the TODCO staff member, helped run one or more sessions so they would have first-hand experience with the process.

The sessions began with a brief introductory statement as to TODCO's plans, the reasons for soliciting views from the elderly, and the mechanics of the presentation. The slides were shown in blocks of two to five slides each, with a narrative explaining the issue under investigation. Participants were then asked to express preference for one of the alternatives presented and, if they wished, the reasons behind that preference. Following the slide presentation, comments or preferences were solicited on design issues not covered in the illustrations. Sessions lasted 30–40 minutes, which seemed to be just the right length.

Illustrating the procedure are: 1. four slides used to describe the building style and building height; 2. four slides demonstrating alternatives to the location of the building entry. Most of the design questions were presented with two slide alternatives, some with just one to introduce the issue. In only a few cases were there as

A

FIGURE 7.2A–D
Illustrations of
building style and
building height options
are shown as part of
small group sessions.
Photographer:
Ira Nowinski.

B

C

D

many as four or five slides used to illustrate an issue. Using more than this number makes it difficult for the viewer to retain the image of the differences being shown, even if the series is projected more than once. A typical narration accompanying the slides is also offered. No "script" was used—a method that seemed preferable—but the verbal descriptions accompanying the slides were generally very similar from session to session.

1. Building Style and Height: This series followed immediately the first series of two slides, showing options for developing Clementina Street, the narrow one-way route around which the existing and proposed developments are centered (Fig. 7.2).

> Now we're going to show a series of four slides [Fig. 7.2] to get your views on two important questions: Whether you want a tall or short building, and whether you want a building that looks new or one that looks more traditional, because it's possible to build something new that looks as if it's not brand new. Let me run through these pictures to give you an idea of what I mean. First [7.2A] here's a more traditional looking low building, five stories. Next [7.2B] is another traditional looking taller building, ten stories. Third [7.2C], a short low-rise building that is quite modern looking. And finally, [7.2D] a high-rise 12-story building that is modern looking.
>
> Let's first deal with the issue of modern versus traditional architecture. How many of you prefer the older style [reshow 7.2A and B as this is being said], and how many prefer the new style [reshow 7.2C and D as this is being said]? [We asked for a show of hands on each option and then asked whether people wanted to explain their votes; usually two or three people would offer comments.]
>
> Okay, now how about the issue of building height? How many people would prefer a short, low-rise building [reshow 7.2A and C as this is being said] and how many would prefer a taller high-rise structure [reshow 7.2B and D as this is being said]? [Again, a show of hands and comments.]

2. Location of the Building Entry: This series followed immediately a series of two slides showing a building with a corner grocery-liquor store at street level and a row of buildings with no ground floor commercial use, in order to ascertain views about how street level space ought to be used (Fig. 7.3).

> One very important issue in building design is how the entrance to the building relates to the street. We can design the entrance in many ways, as this series of slides will show, and we'd like your views on what kind of building entrance you'd prefer. I'll show you four options [Fig. 7.3] and then go back over them one by one. First [7.3A], you can design the door so it's flush with the sidewalk—the building is entered directly from the sidewalk. Second [7.3B], you can have the entryway a bit recessed, as this slide shows. Third

A

B

C

FIGURE 7.3A–D Illustrations of design
options for building entrance location are
shown as part of small group sessions.
Photographer: Ira Nowinski.

D

[7.3C], we could design an arcade-type entrance. And finally [7.3D], there could be a courtyard—you would enter the building by passing through a small landscaped garden of this type. Let me go through them again and ask which you prefer: the direct sidewalk entrance [reshow 7.3A], the recessed entrance [reshow 7.3B], the arcade [reshow 7.3C], or the courtyard [reshow 7.3D]. Again, the people were asked to indicate by hand vote their preference, with some discussion of reasons. If a person did not vote, we would usually ask her or him specifically to express a preference, although people were not pushed if they either had no clear preference or did not think the issue important.

Findings

The visual slide display technique used in the survey was extremely satisfactory. Participants clearly enjoyed the experience and felt they played a useful role. The problem of assembling groups was finally minimized by taking advantage of existing gatherings (of which lunch programs are only one example). The group size and program length were also satisfactory. The use of slides, accompanied by free discussion, controlled the focus while allowing other issues to be raised. At least 15 such sessions, possibly more, probably are needed to achieve a reliable set of guidelines. Preparation and selection of the illustrations is obviously the central task, and our experience indicates that more preparatory time is needed to avoid the mistakes made in a few areas. The use of sketches rather than photos should be explored further, and several pretesting sessions are advisable.

Photographs That Clearly Illustrated the Choices Worked Best

Illustrations that were as "pure" as possible—that is, they isolated one design variable under investigation and kept all other variables as unobtrusive as possible—worked best. People found it hard to abstract and imagine a project based on verbal instructions, when presented with visual evidence to the contrary. For example, in the slide series on entryways the flush entryway was an older, possibly rundown hotel, whereas the arcade was a modern, prestigious structure. While viewers might be instructed to concentrate only on the spatial relationship of entry to sidewalk and ignore other aspects, their judgment was affected, consciously or subconsciously, by other features. In this instance, they might reject the flush entry because it represents an older, less prestigious building. It is hard to find features that do not contain elements that might bias the respondent.

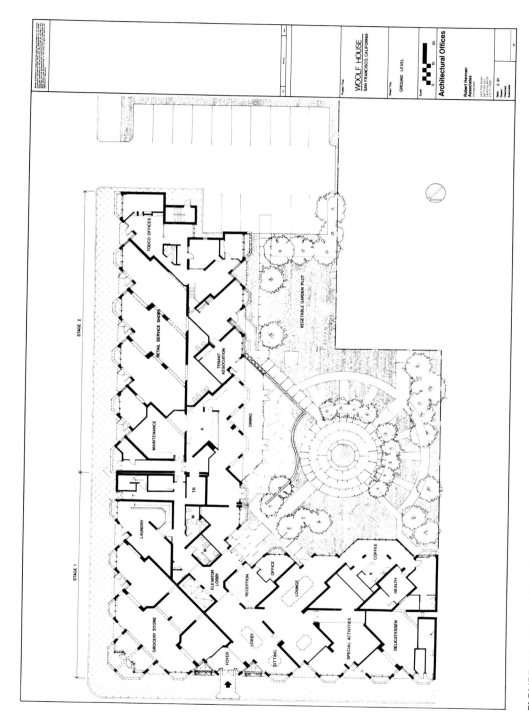

FIGURE 7.4 Ground floorplan of Woolf House: The L-shaped building wraps around a protected courtyard and contains 2,500 square feet of retail space.

165

Innovative Solutions Were Sometimes Difficult to Convey

Similarly, it is difficult to photograph an example of something one would like to present as an option but which may not exist, or may not exist in exactly the form one has in mind. An example from the research project was the discussion of the kitchen. In an attempt to get views about individual versus communal kitchen arrangements, a photo of a standard apartment kitchen from a new development was used, but an illustration of a communal kitchen was hard to produce. A communal kitchen was located in an older hotel near Chinatown; because the men who used it were reluctant to be photographed, the photographer took a shot of the large stove, showing big pots. This illustration not only inadequately communicated the communal aspect of kitchen use, which was described verbally as the slide was being shown, but was also dingy and grubby compared with the kitchen in the new development. The overwhelming preference expressed for individual kitchens probably reflected real choice, but this may have been exaggerated by the nature of the illustrations used.

Consideration was given to creating sketches of things for which adequate photographs were impossible or difficult to obtain, but it seemed that comparing a photograph with a hand-drawn sketch might create even more difficulties.

One important observation is that the weaknesses of specific visual illustrations become immediately apparent through people's reactions and comments, and areas where correction is needed are at once obvious. Probably a more extended time period than was possible in this study—ideally, four of five "shakedown" sessions—would improve the technique considerably.

Conclusions

It is clear that the elderly have important and useful things to say to those involved in producing and designing housing for this group. New techniques must be devised to structure and encourage their participation. The study described here shows that for a relatively minor cost (approximately $4,000), housing design far more sensitive to the needs and desires of future occupants can be obtained.

The process described takes considerable preparation and survey time; nevertheless, the benefits provided by the information collected improve the design and minimize later problems that might otherwise occur concerning the "fit" of the facility to its occupants. Some positive attributes of the participatory survey include:

The survey is a means of collecting current information from local users, which may vary from commonly accepted standards.

The information gathered may uncover unique or subtle design concerns, which cannot be easily dismissed, and can help justify exceptions from local codes and federal standards for the elderly.

The process provides an opportunity to feel the meaning of the information in a way that is far more difficult to achieve with less direct methods, such as mail surveys or literature reviews.

The human contact among designer, client, and (surrogate) user brings the project into realistic human terms at the beginning of the design process, when budgets are being set and before general design solutions are determined.

The client and potential users are an impressive source of ideas, and their participation improves the chances of making solid design/programming advances.

DESIGN DIRECTIVES

Woolf House (honoring the memory of George Woolf, TOOR's first chairman, who died in 1972) opened in June 1979. The nine story, 182-unit apartment building, which was constructed in two phases, resembles a small residential hotel. Woolf House has a modern appearance but is linked to the older streetscape of San Francisco through bay windows, broken line parapets, a corner turret, double-hung windows, simple colors, and a canvas entrance wing. It has a small, intimately scaled foyer, a discreetly defined lobby adjacent to a sitting area and manager's office, wood cabinetry, beveled glass and cove lighting, which one commentator has suggested

> create a genteel ambiance belying the public subsidies that support the housing. Even though the apartments are small, thin bay window configurations and recessed balconies are hardly associated with the term "project" or "replacement" housing ("The New Gray Neighbor," *Progressive Architecture*, August 1981, p. 72).

A major purpose of the participatory design process is to ensure that new developments meet the specific needs of subgroups who are its likely residents. The procedure outlined here was applied to an urban area with a large number of persons who lived in single room occupancy hotels. It is important not to over-generalize the project's findings to all groups of elderly persons because, in some cases, some needs may be different. Nevertheless, several design directives emerged that deserve special highlighting.

The design directives that follow are derived from the participatory user needs survey as well as the post-occupancy evaluation conducted approximately 1 year after residents moved into Woolf House. To assess the impact of the user needs study, one of the two planners involved in the original study visited the project to observe how the space was being used. He spoke with TODCO's Assistant Director of Management, the Assistant Manager of Woolf House, the Site Manager/Social Worker at Woolf House, and the President of Woolf House Residents' Committee. These interviews were supplemented by conversations with residents of the development and detailed notes of a Woolf House tenants meeting which included representatives of TODCO, the California Housing Finance Agency, the management personnel of the building, and the architect.

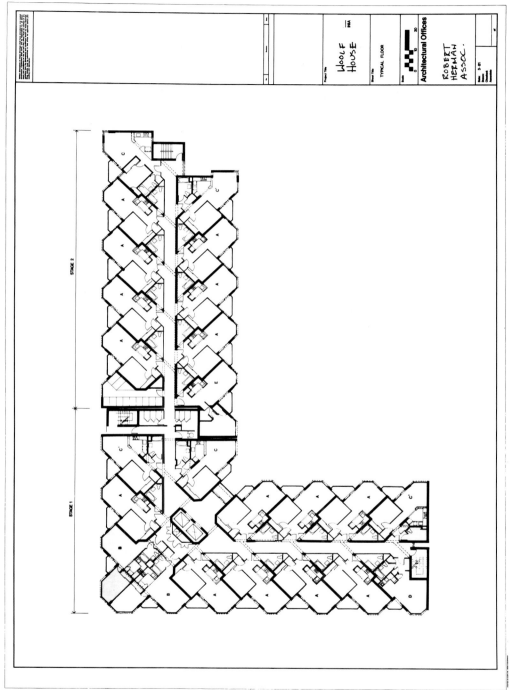

FIGURE 7.5 Typical floorplan of Woolf House. Each floor contains 13 one-bedroom units and 8 studio units rotated at 45° to create balcony niches.

169

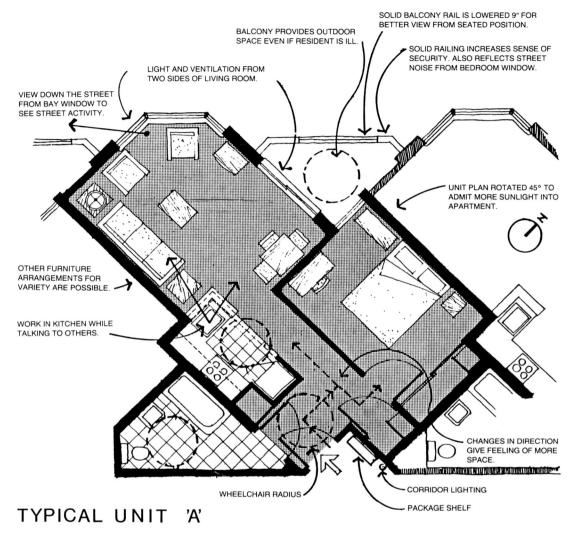

SOLID BALCONY RAIL IS LOWERED 9" FOR BETTER VIEW FROM SEATED POSITION.

BALCONY PROVIDES OUTDOOR SPACE EVEN IF RESIDENT IS ILL.

SOLID RAILING INCREASES SENSE OF SECURITY. ALSO REFLECTS STREET NOISE FROM BEDROOM WINDOW.

LIGHT AND VENTILATION FROM TWO SIDES OF LIVING ROOM.

VIEW DOWN THE STREET FROM BAY WINDOW TO SEE STREET ACTIVITY.

UNIT PLAN ROTATED 45° TO ADMIT MORE SUNLIGHT INTO APARTMENT.

OTHER FURNITURE ARRANGEMENTS FOR VARIETY ARE POSSIBLE.

WORK IN KITCHEN WHILE TALKING TO OTHERS.

CHANGES IN DIRECTION GIVE FEELING OF MORE SPACE.

WHEELCHAIR RADIUS

CORRIDOR LIGHTING

PACKAGE SHELF

TYPICAL UNIT 'A'

FIGURE 7.6 Typical unit layout: The canted exterior wall creates a bay window appearance from the street.

DESIGN DIRECTIVE
ONE

An active street edge can be used to connect the building with its neighborhood.

1. Respondents indicated a strong sentiment in favor of developing the street into an active pedestrian walkway, with some commercial use, as the focus for a mini-neighborhood for the elderly.

DESIGN DIRECTIVE
TWO

Commercial shops should be selected that serve the needs of the residents.

1. A clear majority of respondents desired some commercial use on the ground floor.

2. Participants desired small shops facing the street that provide services, such as a beauty shop, television and appliance repair, and a delicatessen that could both serve the residents and tie the building into the neighborhood.

3. Concern was expressed that shops not cater primarily to outsiders or bring in undesirable and potentially dangerous people (for example, no liquor stores or massage parlors).

4. The idea of a cooperative neighborhood food store, staffed by resident volunteers, of the type existing in many San Francisco neighborhoods, was well received.

5. The post-occupancy evaluations indicated a desire for a nearby ground floor pharmacy, a bank, and a supermarket with ethnic foods to serve residents' needs.

Modern looking structures are looked upon favorably.

DESIGN DIRECTIVE
THREE

1. In spite of the architects' sense that people might want to replicate the apparent comfortableness and homeyness of older hotels and apartments from which they had moved, over four-fifths of the respondents preferred modern looking structures.

2. Both the user needs survey and the post-occupancy evaluation suggested that modern buildings were considered clean, prestigious, and amenity-rich.

Style and detail the building so that it projects a positive, dignified image.

DESIGN DIRECTIVE
FOUR

1. Strong preference was expressed in the user needs survey for features considered to be prestigious, such as wall-to-wall carpeting.

2. Residents acknowledged that subtle colors, such as simple gray carpets in the public areas and light brown elsewhere, as well as the elegant posters and prints, created for them a perception of living in a fine home.

The height of the building should be determined by design and economic considerations.

DESIGN DIRECTIVE
FIVE

1. Opinion was divided equally on whether to have low- or high-rise structures, suggesting that this is more a matter to be decided on the basis of the developer's economic and policy considerations as well as broader design considerations.

Consider designing a separate sitting area off the entryway that also looks out on the street.

DESIGN DIRECTIVE
SIX

1. Three-quarters of the respondents wanted a lobby similar to the kind of "hanging out" space that existed in many of the old hotels.

2. Although most respondents viewed its sociability functions positively, others regarded a lobby sitting area as potentially threatening or discomforting and were afraid that outsiders might use it or that it would be a gathering spot for unruly or inebriated tenants.

3. Many respondents felt that having to walk through a lobby past fellow residents each time one entered or left the building was an invasion of privacy.

DESIGN DIRECTIVE
SEVEN

Balconies should be included as an integral feature.

1. Respondents overwhelmingly expressed a desire that individual balconies, a fairly common feature in new San Francisco apartments, be included for reasons of view, sunlight, an easily accessible place for sitting or growing plants, and a way to get outdoors when one is sick.

2. Private balconies provided for every unit were reported to be heavily used on the sunny sides and, although somewhat less used elsewhere, were nonetheless considered an important element.

3. Even though the communal balconies opposite the elevators at each floor were infrequently used, residents nevertheless liked having them.

DESIGN DIRECTIVE
EIGHT

Safety should be the major consideration in design of the entryway.

1. While considerations of prestige and aesthetics guided many responses, tempting the architect to create a deep, arcaded entry, the dominant concern of respondents was for street safety.

2. Respondents wanted an entrance, clearly visible from the reception desk, which provided quick, secure entry from the street.

3. A landscaped entry courtyard, attractive from an aesthetic standpoint, was widely rejected with comments such as "lovely place for a mugger to hide."

4. Although benches outside were provided for comfort while waiting for rides, the post-occupancy evaluation revealed that residents wanted them removed because they attracted drunks and panhandlers.

DESIGN DIRECTIVE
NINE

Overall safety should be a major design consideration.

1. Even though security considerations such as mailboxes inside the building were incorporated into the original design, the post-occupancy evaluation suggested security remained the major design-related concern.

2. In addition to a safe entryway, designers should incorporate features such as a central intercom or paging system for emergencies; a direct fire alarm hook-up to the fire department; a police call button in the office in case of robbery; control panels in the office for fire alarms and smoke detectors; an emergency phone in the elevator hooked up to the manager's apartment as well as the desk; and television monitors in the office to show locations such as unseen building exits and elevator entrances on upper floors. Several of these features were included in phase two of the project.

Create design features that are easy to maintain and use.

| DESIGN DIRECTIVE |
| **TEN** |

1. Even though slip-proof tile kitchen floors were provided for safety reasons, tenants did not like the dirt that accumulated and discolored the grouting.

2. Bathroom floors were also difficult to maintain; floor drains might have eased the problem.

3. Residents felt that frost-free refrigerators would have greatly eased their home management tasks.

Consider providing some furnished apartments.

| DESIGN DIRECTIVE |
| **ELEVEN** |

1. Respondents were almost evenly split on the furnished versus unfurnished apartment question, with each group feeling strongly about its preference.

2. Those who had furniture previously wanted to retain it when they moved in, for economic savings as well as the emotional meaning of these possessions.

3. Those whose previous lifestyles (long-term residence in furnished hotels and apartments) involved few personal possessions felt equally strong about having furniture supplied, due to the combination of the capital required to furnish an apartment as well as the desire not to have possessions that hinder mobility.

Provide adequate storage space.

| DESIGN DIRECTIVE |
| **TWELVE** |

1. Because the apartment units were relatively small, a number of persons expressed a desire for a storeroom in which to keep extra furniture.

POLICY CONSIDERATIONS

Apart from the specific design issues, some general observations stem from this work with the single elderly urban poor. The first observation is the strong sense of dignity among this group; they are proud, strong-willed, and determined to live complete, active lives to the best of their abilities. Senior citizens are also very conscious of territory; there is an acute sensitivity to individual versus communal spaces and to the designation and use of space for building residents versus outsiders. There is also a need to plan cultural activities, stores, design amenities (for example, signs and ornamentation) that suit the target population of the facility (which, in the case of Woolf House, had a high proportion of Chinese-Americans). But the most salient user need perceived was personal safety, not so much of the "grab bar" but of the interpersonal, street, and public-safety variety. Older people are scared and vulnerable, and big city living gives ample justification for their fears. While "good design" in aesthetic terms is and should be an important criterion, the most important design consideration for elderly residents is to increase their real and perceived security and safety.

POLICY CONSIDERATION **ONE** | *The costs of the participatory design process should be factored into overall project expenditures.*

The participatory design process includes material preparation, pretesting, group meetings, data analysis, and translation of findings into design directives. It can be more time consuming and uncertain than the process normally undertaken by architects, especially when potential clients are dispersed. Nonetheless, its cost is exceedingly modest in terms of total construction expenditures. Ultimate saving should accrue through higher resident satisfaction and spaces designed more appropriate to actual user needs, thereby precluding the need for often prohibitively expensive post-occupancy modifications.

POLICY CONSIDERATION **TWO** | *Some project funds should be reserved or allocated to conduct a post-occupancy evaluation and to correct problems.*

The intense participatory design process that preceded the architectural drawings helped to create a living environment that residents and management judged highly satisfactory. Nevertheless, the post-occupancy evaluation revealed a number of areas in which changes and improvements would add to the overall quality of the facility. Some items were overlooked or underestimated, such as the need for better exterior lighting, increased security, better exhaust fans, lower door peepholes for short persons, a small table next to the bathroom sink, and screens to keep out insects. Other problems arose as the result of changes in the neighborhood. For example, a new office building was constructed across the street, the glass windows of which shone back at the residents' apartments in Woolf House. The see-through drapes, which were intended to allow natural light as well as a view, were insufficient to provide privacy. While one might argue that new buildings should take into account their impact on existing ones, it is also clear that funds should be allocated to address unanticipated problems that arise once a building is occupied.

SUPPORTIVE HOUSING
FOR THE MODERATELY IMPAIRED

PRIORITIES FOR DESIGN AND MANAGEMENT IN RESIDENTIAL SETTINGS FOR THE ELDERLY

Rudolf H. Moos, Sonne Lemke,
and Thomas G. David

D esign decisions are affected by the way designers organize discrete features into an overall conception of the environment, by information about what users desire, and by ideas concerning the impact the setting will have on its residents. In order to obtain better information upon which to base their plans, designers of residential settings have turned to behavioral scientists. What are the most salient aspects of residential settings? What are the underlying patterns of environmental design and programming in existing facilities? What preferences do residents and prospective residents have in regard to such settings? What specific aspects of facilities are most closely related to resident morale and well-being?

We address these issues by providing a framework for approaching design decisions and evaluating designs in terms of their social and behavioral impact. We hope to provide decision makers with models to guide their thinking about environments. In addition, information about preferences and about design-behavior relationships (Holahan, 1982; Moos, 1976; Proshansky, Ittelson,

Preparation of the chapter was supported by NIMH Grants MH16744 and MH28177 and by Veterans Administration Health Systems Research and Development funds.

and Rivlin, 1976) can be used to help inform design choices and guidelines. For example, special priority might be given to facility characteristics that residents prefer and that are positively related to their adaptive functioning.

Our work has highlighted several themes that should be considered in the formation of a design plan for a residential facility for older people. These themes involve the provision of a safe and therapeutic environment, the inclusion of physical design and programming elements to promote resident activity and involvement, and the development of ways to enhance residents' choice and control over their daily lives. Program designers can have an important impact on the quality of life in a residential setting by the design choices they make in these areas.

Our findings have implications for developing broad policies for design decision makers. For example, one overriding concern is the need for diversity in residential settings to accommodate heterogeneous groups of older people (Parsons, 1981). The fact that older people vary greatly in their competence and preferences makes it essential to articulate the trade-offs involved in different design choices. We also highlight the need to consider physical design and programming in conjunction with one another. Furthermore, we believe that information about the probable impact of design elements is as important in formulating design plans as is knowledge about older people's preferences and housing satisfaction. In general, our data suggest that variations in programming have greater effects on residents than variations in physical design. However, this finding may be a function of the somewhat limited range of choices available within current licensing regulations and of professional guidelines about what constitutes good design in residential settings. Moreover, architectural features may become more important as residents' physical and mental abilities decline.

Related Research

Since the construction of better measures of environmental factors is an initial step in formulating design criteria, we first describe the origins of a new procedure for assessing the characteristics of supportive residential settings and then illustrate its use. To structure these efforts, we divide environmental variables into four major domains of resources: physical and architectural, policy and program, suprapersonal, and social-environmental. A growing body of literature indicates that these four domains can be used to characterize social settings and to explore their impacts (Moos, 1976, 1980). We have employed this formulation to develop the Multiphasic Environmental Assessment Procedure (MEAP).

The Multiphasic Environmental Assessment Procedure Assesses Supportive Residential Settings for Older People

The MEAP is a comprehensive, conceptually based procedure for assessing supportive residential settings for older people. Individual MEAP items are grouped into dimensions, which are unified by a common functional implication for residents. The items represent opportunities or environmental "resources" for a given area of functioning. For example, the existence of a lounge by the entry that is furnished for resting and casual conversation offers residents an opportunity to engage in "people watching," to interact with others, and to experience a sense of cohesion, as do other items on the dimension of social-recreational aids. Such a design feature commonly reflects a general philosophy toward the older person that also manifests itself in other ways.

The MEAP was developed on data obtained from a representative sample of 93 residential settings drawn from five counties in California. The procedure was later revised on the basis of data obtained from a national sample of sheltered care settings. Further information on these samples, as well as on the psychometric and normative characteristics of the MEAP dimensions, is provided elsewhere (Moos and Lemke, 1984). The MEAP consists of five instruments that can be used either separately or in conjunction with one another by a facility staff member or outside evaluator. We concentrate here on describing the two parts of the MEAP that assess physical features and program characteristics.[1]

Physical and Architectural Features

A growing body of literature indicates that the physical design of group living facilities can affect the behavior and functioning of older people. Some demonstrations of this linkage deal with the general hypothesis that better physical environments have beneficial impacts on residents, while others test more specific hypotheses about the interrelations of behavior and the physical environment. At the global level, for example, Carp (1976a) has noted that positive physical qualities of the housing environment can influence an elderly person's activity level, social contacts, well-being, and general lifestyle. Moreover, the physical attractiveness of housing has been related to tenant satisfaction (Carp, 1976b),

[1] The MEAP also includes the Resident and Staff Information Form (RESIF), which assesses aspects of the residents and staff in the facility; the Sheltered Care Environment Scale (SCES), which assesses residents' and staff members' perceptions of the facility's social environment; and the Rating Scale (RS), which covers evaluative judgments of the facility by outside observers.

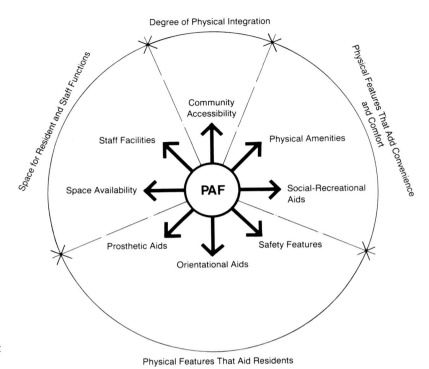

FIGURE 8.1 The Physical and Architectural Features Checklist (PAF) is organized around eight dimensions.

and better physical facilities have been associated with improved resident functioning (Lawton, 1975, 1977; Linn, Gurel, and Linn, 1977).

The first part of the MEAP, the Physical and Architectural Features Checklist (PAF), operationalizes the relevant design factors in terms of more than 175 individual items. The data are obtained through direct observation (Moos and Lemke, 1980). In order to make this information useful to practitioners and researchers, we have organized the items into eight dimensions.[2] The first dimension measures the degree of physical integration between the facility and the surrounding community (community accessibility). The next two dimensions focus on the presence of physical features that add convenience and special comfort and foster social and recreational activities (physical amenities, social-recreational aids). Three dimensions assess physical features that aid residents in activities of daily living and in negotiating the facility environment (prosthetic aids, orientational aids, safety features). The last two dimensions tap the allowance of space for resident and staff functions (space availability and staff facilities) (Fig. 8.1).

[2] The initial version of the PAF was composed of nine dimensions. The dimension of architectural choice was dropped when the PAF was revised. (For details, see Moos and Lemke, 1984.)

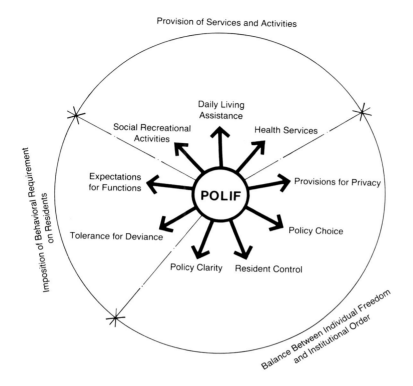

Provision of Services and Activities

Daily Living Assistance

Social Recreational Activities

Health Services

Expectations for Functions

POLIF

Provisions for Privacy

Tolerance for Deviance

Policy Choice

Policy Clarity   Resident Control

Imposition of Behavioral Requirement on Residents

Balance Between Individual Freedom and Institutional Order

FIGURE 8.2   The Policy and Program Information Form (POLIF) is organized around nine dimensions.

Policy and Program Factors

Restrictive policies and an overabundance of services are thought to contribute to the depression, helplessness, and accelerated physical decline observed among some of the elderly in group residential settings. Residents are more alienated in settings that offer less freedom of choice, and there is less life satisfaction and developmental task accomplishment in high constraint settings. Furthermore, Lieberman (1974) found that the outcome of relocation of elderly people was more positive in "facilitative" environments, that is, those that fostered autonomy, placed the locus of control in the hands of residents, and treated residents in an individualized manner.

We operationalized these factors by constructing the Policy and Program Information Form (POLIF), a part of the MEAP that assesses nine dimensions[3] of the policy and programmatic resources of a setting as reported by the administrator or other responsible staff members (Lemke and Moos, 1980). The first two dimensions reflect the degree to which behavioral requirements are imposed

[3] The initial version of the POLIF was composed of ten dimensions. The dimension of selectivity was dropped when the POLIF was revised. (For details, see Moos and Lemke, 1984.)

on residents (expectations for functioning, tolerance for deviance). The second set of dimensions taps the balance that exists between individual freedom and institutional order and continuity (policy choice, resident control, policy clarity, and provisions for privacy), and the third set measures the provision of services and activities in the facility (health services, daily living assistance, and social-recreational activities) (Fig. 8.2).

Describing Supportive Residential Settings

The MEAP Can Be Used to Help Formulate and Modify a Design Plan for a New Facility as Well as to Characterize an Already Existing One: To illustrate the type of summary information that is obtained by these methods, we present the results from an assessment of a congregate apartment facility. The PAF and POLIF scores are expressed as the percentage of the characteristics tapped by a dimension that were actually present in the facility. Thus, for example, just under 90 percent of the social-recreational aids included in our measure were present in Eden Apartments,[4] shown in Figure 8.4. The averages for a normative sample of other apartment facilities are shown by the dotted lines. The PAF and POLIF scores of a facility can also be profiled as standard scores based on a sample of similar types of settings. (For examples, see Lemke and Moos, 1980, and Moos and Lemke, 1980.)

Eden Apartments, currently housing just over 200 residents, was constructed in the mid-1970s under the sponsorship of a local church group. Because it was constructed under Section 231 of the Housing Act, it is less austere than most federally assisted housing projects. However, rents remain moderate for the area, and in addition, over half its residents receive federal rent assistance. Though their income may be somewhat limited, residents are largely middle class in background. Most completed high school and worked in clerical, managerial, or professional occupations. Nearly 90 percent are women, of whom only 6 percent are currently married. In contrast, nearly half the men are currently married. The average age of residents (about 77 years) is similar to the average for our sample as a whole, as is their functional ability.

The PAF results for Eden Apartments reveal a setting rich in social-recreational aids and more spacious and somewhat more secure than the average apartment facility. Eden Apartments' suburban location puts it within easy walking distance of a moderate number of community resources, and the facility includes just an average number of physical features to meet the needs of more impaired residents (average prosthetic aids and orientational aids). The two areas of comparative deficiency at Eden Apartments occur

[4] The name of the facility has been altered to protect its identity.

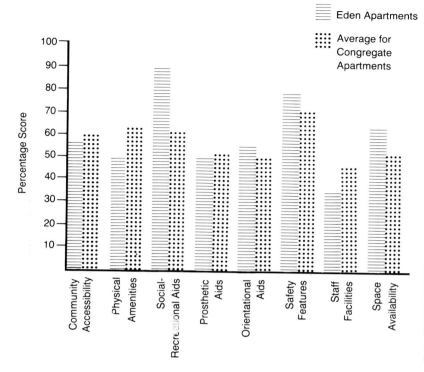

FIGURE 8.3 The physical and architectural resource ratings for the Eden Apartments include a higher than average rating on social-recreational aids and a lower than average rating on physical amenities and staff facilities.

for the provision of physical amenities and staff facilities, both of which are below average for apartments (Fig. 8.3).

The policies in the facility (see Fig. 8.4) reflect an average acceptance of physical disability (expectations for functioning), which is consistent with residents' average functional abilities. However, this attitude of tolerance does not extend to deviant behavior (low tolerance for deviance). The residents are expected to conform to high standards of socially accepted behavior, and these norms are communicated to residents and staff in a clear and systematic manner (high policy clarity). Residents have private apartments and enjoy a fair amount of freedom in the use of their own rooms and in structuring their daily routine (average provision for privacy and policy choice). In addition, there are formal avenues by which residents can influence the operation of the setting (above average resident control). Although the program at Eden Apartments offers no health services, it does provide a reasonably rich array of personal care services and programmed social and recreational activities (high availability of daily living assistance and social-recreational activities).

The MEAP thus permits us to characterize a facility on a number of dimensions and to make systematic comparisons with existing facilities. It can help organize perceptions of a facility into a more differentiated picture. For example, a visit to Eden Apartments

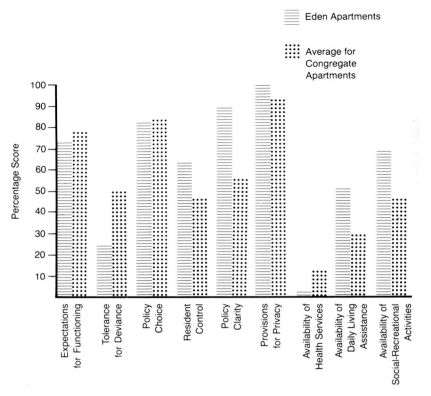

FIGURE 8.4   The policy and program resource ratings for the Eden Apartments show that social conformity is expected (low tolerance for deviance) and that policies are communicated clearly (high policy clarity).

generally results in a global impression of plushness. But the profile reveals that resources are concentrated in the form of social-recreational aids, not as physical amenities or prosthetic aids. In addition, relatively more space at Eden Apartments is devoted to public and private areas for residents and less to staff areas (Fig. 8.5). Standards are demanding in some respects (social conformity) and lenient in others (physical disability). Such information can be used to guide the planning of new facilities or to alter the design of existing ones.

Resident and Staff Design and Program Preferences Can Be Measured

Having developed a way to measure the design and program characteristics of residential settings, we proceeded to construct a parallel method for tapping individual preferences regarding such characteristics. Our goal was to formulate a procedure that could be completed by residents and staff in group living settings, as well as by older people residing in their own homes. We envision several applications for such a procedure. It can be used to compare the preferences of residents of group living settings with those of older people living in their own homes. Person-environment congruence can be measured by contrasting the preferences of current or prospective residents with the actual features of a setting. Finally, individual variations in preferences for different design and program features can be explored. Designers need to consider such variations in planning residential settings that will be populated by heterogeneous groups of older people.

Developing Measures of Preferences

The PAF and POLIF items were reworded to elicit information about individual preferences. Thus, for instance, the PAF item, "Are there handrails in the halls?" (a prosthetic feature), was reworded as, "Should there be handrails in the halls?" We tried to keep the individual items as simple as possible, and, in order to facilitate the administration of the Ideal Form of the PAF and POLIF in either a written questionnaire or an interview format, all items were worded as questions. The majority of the items were answered on a four-point scale varying from "not important" to "desirable," "very important," and "essential." POLIF items that might be viewed as undesirable were answered on a scale ranging from "definitely not" to "preferably not," "preferably yes," and

FIGURE 8.5 This sitting area near a major circulation path is an example of a social-recreational aid.

"definitely yes." After a series of item trials and revisions, we constructed an Ideal Form of the PAF composed of seven of the eight PAF subscales and an Ideal Form of the POLIF composed of all nine of the POLIF subscales.[5]

The Ideal Forms of the PAF and POLIF were administered to several groups of respondents, along with a questionnaire covering sociodemographic and personal characteristics. The four major groups of respondents were older people residing in supportive residential settings, older people living in their own homes and apartments, staff working in residential facilities, and gerontologists active in conducting research and evaluating such facilities. We describe selected portions of the results for the first two groups of respondents here.

The first group is comprised of 371 individuals drawn from eight congregate residential settings (current residents); the second group includes 205 older people living in their own homes or apartments (potential residents). In comparison to current residents, potential residents were more likely to be men and to be currently married. The religious and ethnic backgrounds of the two groups were roughly similar (mostly Protestant or Catholic, white, and U.S.–born), but the potential residents were of somewhat higher socioeconomic status. Overall, the respondents were relatively well educated, with almost two-thirds of both groups having completed at least some post-high school education.

Findings

Residents Considered Safety Features the Most Important Physical Elements

Based on the average rating of items, the seven PAF dimensions can be ranked in order of their relative importance to residents. Safety features received the highest overall rating (Fig. 8.6). Not surprisingly, residents had close to unanimous preferences for such safety features as adequate lighting in outside areas and on steps, nonslip surfaces in appropriate places, strategically located smoke detectors, and call buttons in living areas and bathrooms.

Safety features were followed in importance by prosthetic aids, community accessibility, and orientational aids. Physical amenities, staff facilities, and social-recreational aids received slightly lower overall ratings. This ranking depends in part on the specific items included but nevertheless gives a sense of the relative priority accorded a variety of features thought to be important in facility design. Table 8.1 highlights some of the most preferred items on four of the PAF dimensions.

---

[5] We have not yet been able to develop an item format to tap preferences for space availability.

FIGURE 8.6 Safety features such as good outdoor lighting received close to unanimous approval by residents.

TABLE 8.1 Preference for Selected Physical Features (% Answering "Very Important" or "Essential")

	Current Residents	Potential Residents
Prosthetic Aids		
Front door access for wheelchair	82	86
Handrails in bathrooms	77	81
Handrails in hallways	76	72
Parking reserved for handicapped	70	81
Lift bars next to toilet	58	71
Public phone accessible to wheelchair	56	74
Orientational Aids		
Public bulletin board	77	63
Easy orientation in facility	74	65
Reception area or desk	69	50
Residents' names on doors	67	51
Posted instructions for getting in	61	63
Floors or corridors color coded	54	58
Safety Features		
Steps well lighted	91	93
Main entrance well lighted	86	82
Nonskid surfaces on steps	86	93
Nonslip surfaces in bathrooms	80	88
Apartment or room smoke detectors	72	81
Call button in bathrooms	71	83
Call button in room or apartment	70	72
Bell or call system outside	69	74
Social-Recreational Aids		
Library area	64	53
Visitor parking	64	62
Seating in lobby	61	51
Small tables in lounge	52	53
Comfortable lounge near entrance	51	41

Older People Had Strong Preferences for Prosthetic and Orientational Aids

Residents valued physical features that aid them in activities of daily living and in negotiating the facility environment. Most residents of group living settings preferred such prosthetic aids as parking reserved for handicapped people, handrails in the hallways and bathrooms, lift bars next to the toilet, and wheelchair access. A smaller but still substantial proportion of residents wanted the front door to open and close automatically, to have handrails in apartment areas, and to have such bathroom features as a flexible shower and shower seat. Residents also strongly preferred such orientational aids as a reception desk, posted instructions explaining how to get in if the facility is locked, and a conveniently located bulletin board.

Features That Support Social Interaction and Recreational Activities Were Desired

Although rated somewhat less important, certain social-recreational aids were valued by residents. In fact, more than 50 percent of the respondents in residential settings strongly desired seating in the lobby, a comfortably furnished lounge near the entrance, a patio or open courtyard, small tables around which several people could sit and talk or play games, and a library from which books could be borrowed (Fig. 8.7). Underlining their desire to maintain contacts with the outside community, about two-thirds of the respondents rated adequate parking for visitors very important.

Data such as these concerning preferences can further illuminate the picture of a facility obtained with the MEAP. In this regard, Eden Apartments has most of the physical amenities, social-recreational aids, and safety features desired by its residents (that is, items that were rated "essential" or "very important" by more than 25 percent of the residents). It provides all of the social-recreational aids and most of the safety features listed in Table 8.1. However, some of the bathrooms and living areas do not have call buttons, and there is more than one entrance to the building that is left unlocked. Air conditioning is a desired physical amenity that is not available. Moreover, Eden Apartments lacks prosthetic and orientational aids and staff facilities that residents view as very important. For example, of the preferred prosthetic aids listed in Table 8.1, Eden Apartments does not have reserved parking for the handicapped or a public phone at wheelchair height.

Potential residents generally agreed with current residents in their preferences, although they had even stronger preferences for the prosthetic and safety features. Potential residents would find that Eden Apartments matches their preferences in terms of the availability of social-recreational aids and provisions for safety. As with current residents, they would find that it lacks some desired

FIGURE 8.7 An open patio with tables and chairs where people could sit received a high rating as a social-recreational aid.

prosthetic and orientational aids, staff facilities, and community accessibility. The most striking contrast between the current and potential residents occurs on the physical amenities dimension. Potential residents rate more physical amenities as important, and of these, Eden Apartments has only about half. It lacks such features as air conditioning (rated very important by 67 percent of the potential residents), mirrors in the apartments (60 percent), a public phone (60 percent), seating by the front entrance that is protected from the weather (52 percent), drinking fountains in the hallways, a chapel or meditation room, and window sills wide enough to hold plants (each rated very important by 25–35 percent of the potential residents).

TABLE 8.2 Preferences for Services and Activities (% Answering "Very Important" or "Essential")

	Current Residents	Potential Residents
Health Services		
Doctor on call	49	68
Nurse's hours	47	54
Help with medications	43	52
Doctor's hours	39	49
Physical therapy	33	37
Medical clinic	33	34
Psychotherapy	33	37
Occupational therapy	31	34
Daily Living Assistance		
Dinner each day	59	48
Transportation	56	55
Barber/beauty service	46	28
Lunch each day	34	39
Breakfast each day	30	42
Housekeeping service	29	30
Laundry service	28	26
Assistance with finances	25	26
Assistance with shopping	24	24
Social-Recreational Activities		
Bingo and other games	41	29
Exercise, physical fitness	40	47
Religious services	37	37
Arts and crafts	37	35
Outside entertainment	36	32
Classes	31	32
Social clubs	30	32
Discussion groups	25	28

Residents Value Services and Organized Activities

A critical part of the planning of a supportive residential setting is determining the mix of services and activities that will be offered as part of the facility's program. When current and potential residents were asked to evaluate the importance of these program features, they rated health services as most important overall. Among the health services, residents felt strongest about regularly scheduled doctor's and nurse's hours within the facility, having a doctor on call, and being able to obtain assistance in the use of prescribed medications (see Table 8.2). Although preferences for an on-site medical clinic and for therapeutic services were somewhat less strong, they were still quite substantial.

A majority of residents wanted to have at least one meal served each day, with almost a third of the residents strongly desiring all three meals. A transportation service linking residents to a variety

TABLE 8.3 Preferences for Selected Aspects of Policy Choice and Resident Control (% Answering "Preferably" or "Definitely Yes")

	Current Residents	Potential Residents
Choice in Daily Living		
Choosing time to awaken	90	89
Choosing dinner time	88	92
Choosing seat for dinner	87	92
No curfew	83	71
Choosing bath time	81	93
Unrestricted visiting hours	76	67
Doing laundry in bathroom	64	71
Having wine with meals	53	78
Having liquor in room	49	65
Participation in Facility Operation		
Helping with chores	85	88
Planning orientation	70	84
Planning entertainment	66	76
Planning educational activities	66	79
Planning meal menus	60	75
Participation in Setting Policies		
Resident bulletin board	97	97
House meetings	91	93
Residents' council	88	87
Resident committees	86	88
Resident newsletter	81	86
Dealing with safety hazards	66	72
Deciding on decor in public areas	57	66
Setting meal times	57	71
Handling resident complaints	55	67
Deciding when a resident must leave	39	57
Selecting new residents	28	36

of services in the community was also seen as very important. Other daily living services valued by substantial minorities included a barber or beauty service and assistance with housekeeping and cleaning, laundry, shopping, and financial matters.

A number of social and recreational activities were rated important by residents. The organized activities that were most often preferred included exercise or physical fitness groups, arts and crafts, religious services, organized games such as bingo, and classes and discussion groups.

Most Older People Wanted to Regulate Their Own Daily Activities

In contrast to physical features and program services, facility policies could be rated as either desirable or undesirable. Considerable consensus of opinion emerged as to the importance of policy choice (see Table 8.3). Specifically, over 80 percent of the individuals in each group wanted to be able to choose when to wake up, when to take a bath or shower, where to sit at meals, and when to go to bed. A large proportion also wanted to be allowed to skip breakfast, to sleep late, to have access to alcoholic beverages, to do their laundry in the bathroom, to stay out in the evening as late as they wish, and to have unrestricted visitors' hours. In general, the preferences of individuals in the two groups were relatively similar, except that current residents of group living settings were less likely to feel that residents should have access to alcoholic beverages. This difference may reflect a growing awareness of drinking problems among older residents of congregate settings.

Many Residents Wanted to Participate in Facility Operations and Setting Policies

A large proportion of older individuals stressed the importance of helping with daily chores and of being involved in planning menus, orientation programs, entertainment, and educational activities. The majority of residents wanted to have house meetings and a residents' council that meets regularly. The importance of committees that include residents as members was emphasized, as was a resident newsletter and bulletin board. About half of the current residents wanted to participate in making decisions about meal times, visitors' hours, decor of public areas, safety hazards, and residents' complaints. On the other hand, a majority of respondents felt that residents should not be involved in selecting new residents, deciding whether to move a resident from one room to another or out of the facility, or selecting staff. Both groups of older people showed relatively strong preferences for exerting some influence in planning daily activities and setting facility policies, but current residents wanted to participate somewhat less actively than did potential residents.

As with physical features, we can examine the match between the ideals expressed by current and potential residents and the policies and program offered by a particular facility. For example, the stated preferences of Eden Apartment residents are well matched by the services available to them. There are no health services available at Eden Apartments, but only 10–25 percent of the residents rated these services as very important. Eden Apartments provides transportation, assistance with banking and finances and with shopping, and dinner 5 days a week; these are the personal care services rated most important by the residents. Residents' preferences are also well met by the provisions for privacy at Eden Apartments and by the mechanisms for communicating policies and expectations (policy clarity).

Eden Apartments utilizes the selection criteria preferred by the majority of residents; these criteria are behavioral (residents must be ambulatory) rather than economic or social (no entrance fee or membership requirement). It also offers choice in most of the areas desired by residents. However, they would like more flexibility in the dinner hour and would like to be allowed to choose where to sit at meals. There are greater discrepancies on some of the remaining dimensions. Briefly, Eden Apartment residents would like more control over some areas of life and less over others. For example, a majority would like to see the residents' council meet more often than it does and to have a newsletter written primarily by residents. On the other hand, they generally feel that residents should not be involved in deciding on the decor of public areas, in dealing with residents' complaints, or in selecting new residents. However, these are three areas in which the administration presently seeks to involve them.

Conclusions

Together, these results illustrate several important points. First, older people can respond in a meaningful way to questions about their preferences in design and programming of supportive residential settings. Second, their preferences for some factors are stronger than for others. Thus, for example, safety features and prosthetic and orientational aids are rated very important, as is program flexibility. Design features such as physical amenities and social-recreational aids and program features such as daily living assistance and social-recreational activities are rated as somewhat less important. Third, in some areas of preference a consensus exists among individuals and between various groups of respondents. Features that impact on safety, such as well-lighted steps and a safe neighborhood, or policies that discourage deviant behavior elicit a high level of agreement from respondents. Opinions are more divided concerning the need for accessibility for wheelchairs, policies on alcohol use, whether meals should be served, and what medical services should be offered.

Fourth, preferences can be compared to descriptions of an existing facility to enrich our understanding of its environment. For example, Eden Apartments appears to be well suited to the preferences of its residents and of potential residents. It is not surprising that the residents report Eden Apartments to be a highly cohesive, well organized, and pleasant setting in which residents are encouraged to be independent and to affect policies. Certain contradictions do emerge from the picture. For example, residents would prefer to have features permitting access to wheelchairs and accommodating individuals with other handicaps. However, they feel strongly that residents must be ambulatory to be admitted and that a high level of functioning should be expected of residents remaining at Eden Apartments.

Data About Preferences Must Be Integrated With Information About the Impact of Design and Programming on Resident Behavior: Although information about preferences can be useful in the planning process, it is not sufficient for these purposes. As noted, contradictions exist in people's preferences, and these contradictions must be addressed by the planner. Variations in preferences also pose difficult choices. To supplement information about preferences, it is important to understand the relationships between resident functioning and design and program features. Such data come from two major sources: research examining the interrelationships of environmental factors and studies of the impact of design or program features.

Cohesion is More Likely to Be Present in Residential Setting with Specific Features: We have used the PAF and POLIF to examine the relationship between physical design and program factors and resident morale and behavior. Our results showed that cohesion among residents was more likely to develop in settings with more physical amenities, social-recreational aids, and available personal space. These physical features seem to enhance social interaction among residents and to support social contact by enabling residents to obtain needed privacy. Settings that had these physical features also tended to attract more socially competent and functionally able residents and to develop policies that allowed these residents more flexibility in organizing their daily lives and more opportunity to participate in making decisions about how the setting should be run (Moos, 1980; Moos and Igra, 1980).

Choice and Control are Related to the Quality of Resident Interaction and Adaptation: Another study indicated that the provision of choice and control for residents seemed to help in developing more cohesive, organized, independence-oriented social environments with relatively little conflict. These design and program factors contributed to higher rates of resident participation in facility and community activities, and to lower rates of utilization of health services and daily living assistance, and may have helped to reduce turnover rates by enhancing resident cohesion (David, Moos and Kahn, 1981; Moos, 1981).

Physical Design and Programming Factors Can Have Important Consequences for Health-Related Functioning: In regard to the findings of other studies, the provision of special architectural and physical design features (such as prosthetic and orientational aids and safety features) can have a positive impact on the morale and well-being of older people, especially in conjunction with health and personal care services and easy access to shopping and trans-

FIGURE 8.8 A pleasant dining room space with an emphasis on high quality meal service can improve resident functioning.

portation (Sherwood, Greer, Morris, and Mor, 1981). The provision of attractive dining areas and an emphasis on high-quality meal services that include the availability of snacks (all of which provide an atmosphere for interaction and socialization) can improve resident functioning (Fig. 8.8). Moreover, there is a relationship between enhanced resident autonomy and decreases in morbidity and mortality rates (Rodin, 1980; Schulz and Hanusa, 1979). Group living settings that program challenging activities for residents, that have moderately high expectations of resident behavior, and that treat older people as responsible adults seem to have positive effects (for a review of relevant studies, see Moos and Lemke, 1985).

The most relevant design features appear to be prosthetic, orientational, and safety features, and social-recreational aids. Salient aspects of programming include access to health and personal care services and to recreational activities, as well as the extent to which residents can organize their daily activities and influence facility policies.

DESIGN DIRECTIVES

Although physical design and program choices are intertwined, we discuss them separately for purposes of clarity. These guidelines should be implemented with caution, since trade-offs are likely in all such decisions.

DESIGN DIRECTIVE **ONE**	*Residential environments should include basic safety features.*

1. Older people have strong preferences for features that increase their safety, such as smoke detectors in halls and rooms, call buttons in bathrooms and bedrooms, and nonslip surfaces on steps, ramps, and bathroom floors. Because they have been a major focus of licensing and regulation efforts, nearly all facilities offer most of these basic safety features.

2. One decision facing designers is how far to take the effort to ensure personal safety in light of existing monetary constraints. Features that offer protection from fires, prevent falls, and permit summoning help quickly in case of need are probably cost effective in the long run.

DESIGN DIRECTIVE **TWO**	*In general, surveillance of public areas and provisions against intrusion should be unobtrusive, although the setting should be seen as secure.*

1. A controversial aspect of safety involves surveillance over public areas and provisions against intrusion. The varied opinions of current and potential residents about such features seem to reflect a concern that surveillance may diminish residents' own privacy and imbue the facility with a prison-like atmosphere.

2. Having someone monitoring the entrance, limiting the entrance to a single unlocked door, and having visitors sign in are evaluated as important or essential by a large number of older people though rated not important by a significant minority.

3. The extent of surveillance and protection against intrusion may depend on the neighborhood context, since data indicate a marked variation in preferences for such features from one residential facility to another (Fig. 8.9).

DESIGN DIRECTIVE **THREE**	*A therapeutic environment should be provided that includes the prosthetic and orientational aids and services residents prefer.*

1. Older people, particularly those with some impairment, indicate a strong desire for many prosthetic features, orientational aids, and on-site services.

FIGURE 8.9 This outdoor pavilion near the front door of this elderly housing project provides an opportunity for informal surveillance.

2. The absence of prosthetic features may lead to negative self-labeling. For example, a floor finish that makes walking difficult or seats that make standing up a strain may lead older persons to view themselves as sick or frail.

3. There has been concern that a service-rich environment might maximize satisfaction and comfort among impaired older people but undermine residents' independence. Lawton suggests, for example, that protected, service-rich congregate housing may encourage passive contentment and lead to a decline in health, whereas traditional housing is associated with active strain and continued independent behavior (Lawton, 1976; Lawton and Cohen, 1974). On the other hand, Gutman (1978) found no evidence of differential decline in health status, activity level, or level of interaction with family and friends for older people moving into multilevel facilities as compared to those in housing with fewer services. Sherman (1975a) reached similar conclusions.

4. Although there is a potential for premature dependency, the availability of physical and program supports will enhance residents' feelings of security and enable them to enjoy independence by maintaining themselves at optimal levels.

Prosthetic and orientational aids should be unobtrusive.

DESIGN DIRECTIVE
FOUR

1. Prosthetic features, orientational aids, and on-site services may label older persons as different and less competent.

2. To avoid stigmatizing the elderly, prosthetic and orientational aids should be unobtrusive.

DESIGN DIRECTIVE
FIVE

Environments can be designed to accommodate residents' needs as they age and become more frail.

1. Maintaining a constant environment in which physical features and services do not allow for increasing disabilities can cause considerable disruption of residents' lives when enforced transfers of relatively healthy residents become necessary (Lawton, Greenbaum, and Liebowitz, 1980).

2. Rather than requiring premature institutionalization, administrators often accommodate to the aging of residents by tolerating an extended period of residence despite growing impairments and by relaxing admission requirements.

3. As a result, group living settings often undergo an "aging" process as a function of changes among their residents. The aging of the resident population can eventually reduce the independent character of a congregate housing site and alter the population of new applicants. These changes in the resident population need to be accompanied by adjustments in physical features and services if problems are to be avoided.

DESIGN DIRECTIVE
SIX

Design should search for new ways to allow residents to participate in regulating their own environment.

1. Physical design features can enhance resident choice, which is associated with better health and higher morale and life satisfaction.

2. Individual heating and air conditioning controls, the inclusion of a laundry area and of several communal areas, and the provision of small and large tables in the dining room are examples of design elements that can increase the choices available to residents and provide them with more control over their environment.

DESIGN DIRECTIVE
SEVEN

The environment should be designed to encourage activity and involvement.

1. Continuity in one's pattern of engagement with others and of participation in meaningful activities is an important determinant of satisfaction in old age.

2. The provision of features to support social and recreational activities, the arrangement of private and communal areas, and the availability of formal programs can promote interaction. However, there is some concern that an age homogeneous milieu together with the provision of a rich social program may encourage a limited sphere of social contacts and result in less social involvement with relatives and friends (Sherman, 1974, 1975b).

3. Environments may need to be tailored to residents' activity orientation and functional ability. Individuals accustomed to high engagement and activity generally prefer settings furnished with social-recreational aids and a rich program of organized activities. On the other hand, less socially oriented residents may be uncomfortable in a setting that coerces them into unwanted social contacts and activities. Such residents may show a decline in adaptation and well-being in these settings (Carp and Carp, 1980).

4. To encourage social interaction and use, communal spaces should be located near high traffic or staff work stations or with good views of outside activities. Organized activities in the communal areas also encourage their use.

Facility Policies and Programs Affect Decisions About Physical Design

Decisions in regard to creating a therapeutic environment will depend in part on admission policies and expectations about levels of continued functioning. To what extent will the setting admit and maintain residents of varying levels of functioning? The healthy older people in our study of preferences felt that reductions in functional abilities or in social conformity should not be permitted. Those whose own functioning was lower were somewhat more tolerant of reduced functioning. However, if individuals uniformly prefer to live in settings with others of similar or better functioning and facilities are planned on this basis, then a stratified system of levels of care will inevitably develop. The consequences of such a system for everyone involved, both the residents with high and low functioning and the staff, must be considered.

Resident Choice and Control Should Be Promoted: Residents should be provided with maximum feasible control over their daily activities and over selected facility policies, even though facility management "efficiency" might decrease. Older persons tend to do better in settings programmed to promote choice and control. In fact, the effect of many of the physical design features discussed earlier depends on the degree to which older people control them. Our research indicates that older people want choices concerning mealtimes, seating at meals, and their daily schedule. They also wish to participate in house meetings and resident committees as well as to be involved in planning facility activities.

Policies in Controversial Areas Should Probably Be Set by Administrators: Final decisions about controversial areas that require a set policy and that might create potential management problems should probably rest with program administrators rather than residents. For example, considerable variation exists among older people in their desire to participate in setting policies about the use of alcohol, employment of residents within the facility, selection of staff, decoration of public areas, or handling of safety hazards.

Underlying these divergent opinions may be the fear of some individuals that too much choice and control may lead to disorderly or chaotic living conditions. These elderly may prefer that an administrator make decisions about such areas, thereby avoiding potentially divisive conflicts among residents. In addition, a substantial group of older persons prefers more structured environments in which their activities and behavior are predictable and organized. In dealing with these issues, administrators need to be sensitive to the characteristics of their residents. For example, women may react more positively than men to the provision of choice in daily routines. Similarly, functionally able residents are more likely to desire choice over daily activities than are their frail counterparts (Moos, 1981).

Programming for Activity and Involvement is Valuable: Although physical design features can be helpful, programming and residents' level of disability are likely to be important determinants of how a facility's communal social spaces will be used. A successful program to promote interaction among residents should incorporate resident input in planning, provide flexible rules for participation so as to not place pressure on less socially inclined persons, emphasize community as well as facility activities to counteract insularity, recognize the importance of privacy as an essential element in a design for encouraging meaningful social interaction, and concentrate special attention on physically and mentally impaired residents who need extra encouragement to maintain an active life style.

Some of these issues were considered by Lawton and his colleagues in arranging an environment for mentally impaired older persons. They designed an open central area with bedrooms on the periphery to allow for privacy, to enhance orientation by providing a full view of all important areas, to stimulate social behavior by providing an attractive area with high traffic, and to encourage participation by locating activities in a high density social area. The residents reacted to the changes by spending more time outside their bedrooms and by engaging in more positive, task-oriented behavior and social interaction (Lawton, 1981).

Another example is provided by a nursing home that was involved in an intra-institutional relocation, where we observed resident and staff behavior directly (Moos, David, Lemke, and Postle, 1984). The new building had a more complex floor plan and increased separation between the social areas and the nurses' stations. Neither the communal areas near the main entrance nor the small lounges on individual wards were used very much. Key factors seemed to be the absence of organized activities that would draw residents to these areas, the difficulty of staff monitoring of these areas, and the lack of interesting things to watch. High mental status residents were drawn out of their bedrooms into social spaces, while low mental status residents spent less time in social areas and more in the halls near the nurses' stations, where they could maintain contact with the staff (Lemke and Moos, 1984). Thus, the arrangement and design of communal areas is important. Moreover, designers need to understand that aspects of the program, residents' levels of functioning, and residents' relationship to staff all affect how communal areas will be used.

POLICY CONSIDERATIONS

Our findings underscore the need for designers to take long-term responsibility for evaluating the facilities they create. We see a role for program designers in each of the four major phases in the history of a residential setting: planning, selection, initial post-occupancy evaluation, and long-term post-occupancy evaluation.

The planning process should include behavioral information.

POLICY CONSIDERATION **ONE**

Program factors and expected behavioral implications need to be emphasized during this phase. The input from potential building users should focus on the probable behavioral impacts of design decisions as much as on user preferences. Since the behavior patterns of residents of different ability levels may vary markedly, it is helpful to incorporate information from mentally and physically impaired residents in the planning process.

Selection and orientation of residents is a key factor.

POLICY CONSIDERATION **TWO**

In the identification and recruitment of tenants, designers can use their knowledge about individual preferences and probable design impacts to help select a congruent but also somewhat varied resident group. Participation in the process of orienting prospective residents both before and after they enter a facility will provide designers with useful information about how individuals initially evaluate and adapt to physical design features.

POLICY CONSIDERATION	*An initial post-occupancy evaluation can help overcome unanticipated*
THREE	*problems.*

In the initial or short-term phase, designers can assess changes in preferences and sources of satisfaction over time, as well as problems of adaptation that occur in regard to specific design features. (For an example, see Carp, 1976b.) Possible alterations in programming that may overcome unexpected negative effects of physical features or combine with such features to enhance some aspect of resident or staff behavior can be identified. Detailed behavioral observations and "exit interviews" with individuals who decide to leave the facility can be incorporated in a comprehensive evaluation plan.

POLICY CONSIDERATION	*Long-term post-occupancy evaluations will help develop a knowledge base*
FOUR	*for better designs.*

In regard to the long-term post-occupancy phase, designers should help to plan evaluations of how the characteristics of the facility influence resident and staff morale and adaptation. The history of changes in facility design and programming factors can be recorded, together with the reasons for these changes and their impacts on residents. (For an example, see Sherwood, Greer, Morris, and Mor, 1981.) Longitudinal "case studies" of different types of facilities are essential in the development of a dependable body of knowledge about design-user relationships.

Our assessment procedures may be useful to designers in one or more of the evaluation phases. For instance, the Ideal Forms of the PAF and POLIF can help develop design plans by facilitating the gathering and summarizing of detailed information about the preferences of prospective residents and staff as well as of program managers and designers. The procedures can be used to develop alternative "blueprints" for new settings, to attempt to match resident preferences with facility practices, and to promote the process of orientation and adaptation among new residents. In the post-occupancy phases, the PAF and POLIF can document stability and change in a facility over time, provide ongoing information to program managers about how the setting is functioning, and guide the formulation and evaluation of design modifications that may improve the congruence between participants' preferences and facility practices.

Our recommendations are based on the assumption that a complete design plan necessarily involves an evaluation plan and that the participation of design decision makers in facility evaluations will eventually result in a cumulative body of knowledge about the attitudinal and behavioral effects of architectural and program factors. A national information registry of practices and preferences in different residential settings, their stability and variation over time, and their influence on residents and staff would be valuable in developing the empirical knowledge necessary to formulate data-based design guidelines. Allocating a fraction of 1 percent of building costs to design evaluations is sufficient to implement such a plan. We believe that such a policy innovation would benefit residents and staff of group living settings and promote the future development of the design professions.

ACKNOWLEDGMENTS

We wish to thank Diane Denzler for her assistance in data collection and analysis and Josh Holahan for his helpful comments on an earlier version of the manuscript.

9

PROGRAMMING CONGREGATE HOUSING
The Preferences of Upper Income Elderly

Victor Regnier

O ne of the most critical decisions made in the development of congregate housing is the choice of activities and the types of services and amenities provided as a part of the housing package. The most innovative retirement housing developments have been those that have experimented with various types of supportive services, established strong community ties, and created novel and fulfilling opportunities for social integration.

Methods for Programming Services and Facilities in Congregate Housing

The decision-making process used in the selection of new programs, activities, and amenities for congregate housing has generally been incremental in nature and has avoided radical departures from the status quo.

Method One: Copying a Successful Program: The most common method for selecting service and design features for a proposed housing project has been to copy the services available in existing projects. This method typically involves visiting housing projects and discussing the utility of various design features, amenities, and services with the administrator. Informal observation of successful program features can be helpful. However, one must recognize that the success of various services and features can be accounted for by other influences. For example, management preference for certain programs, features that attract a self-selected resident population, and institutional goals and policies regarding tenant recruitment are but a handful of the influences that can combine to create a unique environment. This environment can mediate the success and acceptance of various design features, amenities, and services.

Another problem with examining existing prototypes is that it requires the examination of past successes to predict future preference. In this case, the lens we utilize to view the future is more like a rear-view mirror. Many researchers believe that upcoming cohorts of older people will have substantially different desires for various amenities and services. Examining past success without examining the changing preferences of future cohorts can lead to the selection of outdated features.

Another problem with copying features and making minor adjustments to account for regional or cultural differences is that features such as the ubiquitous shuffleboard court often become an assumed element of the architectural program. This happens without a great deal of reflection on the relevance, popularity, or appropriateness of this activity for the intended user (Fig. 9.1).

Method Two: Phased Incrementalism: A second equally popular approach to developing an architectural program has been to plan for incremental change in a project as it ages or as resident preferences change. This method works best in making phased additions to facilities. However, it is more effective if the facility has been master planned to respond to various contingencies. Several problems can occur when utilizing this approach. Future contingencies are often impossible to predict at the planning stage. Also, the addition of design features (such as balconies) or of unit adjustments (such as larger kitchens) can be impossible to implement. This method works best when adding spaces or features to the common area. Waiting until "Phase Two" to implement a broad range of amenities may also affect the marketing success of the first phase or can establish unrealistic expectations on the part of current residents. Neither of the two methods described above necessarily involves the formal evaluation of services and features by residents of the facility.

Method Three: Assessing the Community's Preference for Services and Features: The research reviewed in this chapter is based on a third method, which works well when existing models are not available for post-occupancy evaluation or when the preferences of an intended target group have not been clearly established. This method involves assessing the preferences of community residents to a list of features considered as possible amenities and services in planned retirement housing. The format and approach are simple and the results are relatively easy to interpret. Although this

FIGURE 9.1 Shuffle-
board is a recreational
feature that is frequently
assumed to be a popular
amenity. Our research
shows that it is rarely
considered an important/
valuable feature by
middle- to high-income
elderly households.

method seems straightforward, its weakness lies in the link between preference and action. The service or feature an individual
chooses as highly preferable may not always be what he or she
would choose to use.

Keeping this in mind, this research used several procedures
to ensure a clearer, more accurate response from community
residents.

1. During the introductory remarks, respondents were informed about the general type of high-service, supportive
   housing that was under consideration. Specific features,
   such as price range, district location, and general ambience
   were described so that respondents could develop a general
   image of what the housing development might be like.
2. Subjects had higher incomes and could realistically exercise
   choice regarding supportive services and amenities.
3. Subjects were asked to rate each service on a three-point
   scale where extremely positive or negative judgments were
   required with an ambivalent middle choice category.

Related Research

Although the design literature dealing with elderly housing is relatively detailed (Gelwicks and Newcomer, 1974; Green et al., 1975; Howell, 1980; M. P. Lawton, 1975; Urban Land Institute, 1983; Zeisel et al., 1977, 1983), there are few design-oriented publications that address the congregate housing type. The Department of Housing and Urban Development commissioned a comprehensive evaluation of congregate housing in the mid-1970s (Urban Systems Research and Engineering, 1976) to document the "state of the art." However, the design insights from that evaluation were minimal. A new publication by Welch and her colleagues provides useful insights about service and feature preferences of residents of small "congregate house" arrangements. Welch discovered conflicts that result from shared bathrooms and kitchens, which at times caused major problems. (Welch et al., 1984). Work by Hoglund (1986) promises to provide new insights about congregate housing through the examination of European examples.

Lawton (1980) reviewed the work of Carp and others, finding a preference for low-intensity medical services and, to a somewhat lesser degree, a preference for meals services. However, so little work has been published dealing with past and present service preferences that it is difficult to measure the consistency or to identify patterns or changes in residents' expectations for services and features over time. One exception seems to be the issue of security which consistently ranks at the top of most preference surveys (Fig. 9.2).

One source of data on the changing trends in more elaborate life-care communities (Laventhol and Horwath, 1983) reports that the size of units and the percentage of larger two-bedroom units

FIGURE 9.2 Television security monitored from a central location is frequently cited as one of the most important features of purpose-built elderly housing.

has increased dramatically in buildings constructed prior to 1976. This reflects a general increase in housing standards and expectations during the last 15–20 years. Although many experts suspect the preferences of upcoming cohorts of congregate housing residents will be larger and more elaborate units, there is as yet very little empirically based preference data upon which to base programming decisions.

Study One: Methodology and Data Analysis

This research was conducted in 1974, and was based on face-to-face interviews with a representative sample of older, middle- to higher-income elderly households in a large southern city. An income level of $5,000 for one-person households and $7,500 for family households was used as the lowest income eligibility level (1970 income figures). Discounting the income eligibility level to 1969 dollars and comparing this to 1970 census data narrows the sampling range to the highest 19 percent of single-person household incomes and the upper 48 percent of family incomes. The research was structured to investigate the older community resident's preference for services, amenities, and design features that might be considered in a new retirement housing project.

Sample Selection

Selecting the sample for this project involved several steps.

First: Five-hundred fifty-four census blocks with average housing values above $27,000 and/or an average monthly rental of $150.00 were identified (U.S. Department of Commerce, 1970). Although these values seem low by current standards, they were effective in isolating higher-cost housing stock 10 years ago.

Second: A random selection of 90 blocks was made and these blocks were subjected to a complete telephone screening enumeration.

Third: The telephone screening interviews (n = 3,635) identified 584 households that met age and income eligibility requirements.

Fourth: Two hundred twenty-one subjects were randomly selected from the list of qualified households and given face-to-face interviews.

The sample consisted of individuals who were predominately white and living with a spouse or relative in owner-occupied housing. Two-thirds of the respondents were female with reasonably good functional health, retired with an above average income. Table 9.1 outlines basic characteristics of the sample population.

TABLE 9.1 Descriptive Characteristics of Study One Sample[1]

Average Age	70.3 years	Functional Health	
		Does walk 6 blocks easily	66.2%
Race		Does *not* walk 6 blocks easily	33.8%
White	95.9%	Does walk up flight of stairs easily	56.8%
Black	4.1%	Does *not* walk up flight of stairs easily	43.2%
Sex		Income	
Male	31.2%	$5,000–7,500 per year	36.2%
Female	68.8%	$7,500–10,000 per year	23.1%
Living Arrangements		$10,000–15,000 per year	15.4%
Live alone	21.7%	$15,000 +	25.3%
Living with spouse	54.7%		
Living with relative	22.2%	Wording Situation	
Living with friends	1.4%	Working full-time	7.2%
		Working part-time	6.8%
Housing Situation		Retired	52.5%
Own home	77.8%	Housewife	33.5%
Rent home	1.4%		
Rent apartment	10.4%		
Mobile home	3.2%		
Live with children	7.2%		

[1] n = 221

Study One: Findings

The findings from this research have been separated into two categories: total respondents and "potential inmovers." Questions that deal with general philosophies and preferences for retirement housing are addressed by referring to the responses from all subjects.

It was felt that the most meaningful service and feature preference responses would be expressed by individuals interested in moving into a facility such as the one described in the interview. Therefore service and feature preferences have been developed from a sub-sample of the respondents who expressed interest in moving into a congregate housing arrangement.

General Findings Regarding Congregate Housing

All respondents were asked several questions about the concept of retirement housing. One specific question dealt with the degree to which these higher-income individuals embraced the notion of living in an age-segregated retirement setting. Ninety-five percent of the sample thought that a retirement community specifically planned for older people was a good idea.

Another concern was that frail, older people living in the facility might have a negative impact on the acceptance of this housing by younger retirees. The "supra-personal" environment, which

Lawton defines as the characteristics of individuals sharing the same immediate milieu, has been found to create a normative image that, if too debilitating, may discourage younger active retirees from moving into the housing (Lawton, Greenbaum, and Liebowitz, 1980). In response to the question, "Would it bother you if up to 25 percent of the people living there were not as well as you?" 80.1 percent of the total sample reported no, thus providing strong support for the utility of a continuum of care philosophy.

Nearly 91 percent preferred to rent rather than buy their unit. This finding is particularly intriguing considering that 77.4 percent of the sample reported owning their home and that this preference was expressed before recent federal income tax statutes created the opportunity to avoid heavy capital gain taxes at the time of sale. This tax relief option has since made it easier and more desirable for older people to sell owner-occupied property and to rent retirement housing.

Potential Inmover Service Preferences

The most meaningful ranking of preferred services and features, it was felt, would come from respondents who were interested in moving to this type of facility. Therefore, subjects were asked to respond to the following question: "Is it your feeling that you would consider moving into the retirement community?" Nearly one-third (n = 74) responded favorably. The remainder of the findings discussed in this section have been analyzed using this subsample of "interested" potential in-movers. The 74 interested respondents rated 36 different social and health services, recreational activities, site considerations, and architectural features.

To analyze the data, all of the responses that were classified as ambivalent ("not necessary but nice to have") were eliminated. The remainder of the responses, the "must have" and "would not want" choices, were added together to form the denominator for calculations that ascertained the portion of the remaining sample which felt each feature was either very important ("must have") or unnecessary ("would not want"). A differential index was created by subtracting the percentage of "would not want" responses from the percentage of "must have" responses.

For example in the case of security 54 of the 74 responses were "must have" and 4 were "would not want." The remainder (16) were ambivalent ("not necessary but nice to have"). The 16 ambivalent responses were eliminated from the total and the remaining responses summed (58). The portion of the sum devoted to "must have" responses was (54/58) 93.1 percent; the portion of the sum devoted to "would not want" responses was (4/58) 6.9 percent. The index score was developed by subtracting these two

TABLE 9.2   Potential In-Mover Differential Preference Index of Services and Features[1]

Item Rank	Service	Differential Index	Item Rank	Service	Differential Index
1.	Beauty/Barber shop	96.5	19.	Homemaker service	33.2
2.	Infirmary	95.7	20.	Two or more meals	31.5
3.	Pharmacy	92.7	21.	Maid service (optional)	26.8
4.	Small convenience grocery	92.0	22.	Whirlpool/Sauna	16.3
5.	Restaurants	89.7	23.	Meals delivered	0
6.	Security	86.2	24.	Exercise room	−10.0
7.	Public transportation	84.1	25.	Private entertainment room	−10.5
8.	Doctor's office for visit	79.6	26.	Linen (optional)	−18.4
9.	Nurse-on-call	78.1	27.	Greenhouse	−37.0
10.	Physical therapy	72.1	28.	Catering service	−47.8
11.	Gift shop	64.7	29.	Maid service (included)	−54.2
12.	Dry cleaner	60.0	30.	Adult education	−55.9
13.	Nursing home	59.0	31.	Billiard room	−57.0
14.	Private limousine	54.6	32.	Linen (included)	−57.9
15.	Library	51.2	33.	Shuffleboard	−59.0
16.	Card room	46.7	34.	Cocktail lounge	−74.0
17.	Large meeting room	46.1	35.	Swimming pool	−74.5
18.	Craft room	42.0	36.	Tennis court	−100.0

[1] n = 74

figures. In the case of security the score was (93.1−6.9)+ 86.2. The scores displayed in Table 9.2 range from a +96.5 for beauty/barber shop to a −100.0 for tennis court.

Services and Features with Positive Scores Should Be Programmed into the Building: In interpreting Table 9.2, one might consider the 22 services in the positive range to be important or preferable in retirement housing. In this case the number of persons who felt strongly about the need for this service outweigh those who would not want the service. All convenient retail neighborhood facilities, with the exception of the dry cleaner, are located in the upper half of the positively rated services (items 1–11) (Fig. 9.3). Included in this top-11 category is security, public transportation, and several services related to health care.

The lower one-half of the positively rated services and features (items 12–22) include common activity spaces such as the library, card room, a large meeting room, and a crafts room (Fig. 9.4). Also included in this section are the optional support services of homemaker, maid, and meal service. Some amenities that received a surprisingly high relative rating include a nursing home on-site, a whirlpool/sauna, and a private limousine service.

Services with Negative Ratings Include Activities that Require Physical Exertion: Services with slightly negative ratings (items 23–28) include supportive services such as optional linen, delivered meals, and catering service. Also included in this section are unusual common spaces such as a greenhouse, exercise room, and private entertainment room.

FIGURE 9.3 The neighborhood within which the site is selected should provide access to various supportive retail shops and services.

FIGURE 9.4 Spaces that are set aside for social activities should allow residents to participate vicariously in surrounding activity. This two-story atrium space in the Captain Eldridge Congregate House is a very successful example.

The most negatively rated features (items 29–36) include supportive services such as linen and maid services, the price of which was included in the rent, and activities that require heavy physical exertion such as swimming, tennis, and shuffleboard. Also in this category fall features that may project a negative stereotyped image, such as billiards, the cocktail lounge, and shuffleboard.

Study One: Conclusions

The concept of age-segregated retirement housing seems to have strong support from middle- to higher-income community residents in this large southern city. Potential in-movers prefer services and amenities in the general categories of protective, convenience, health, transportation, common spaces, and supportive, in that order. An example of a highly rated protective service is the emergency call button (Fig. 9.5). Services most universally rejected include mandatory support services such as meals, maid, and linen service included in the rent, and recreational amenities that require physical strength and endurance such as tennis, swimming, and shuffleboard.

Study Two: Methodology and Data Collection

The second study was conducted in a very exclusive, high-income Southern California city during 1984. Because of the exclusivity of the community an income screening was not employed. The purpose of the instrument was to establish a priority listing of services for a new congregate housing project planned for the immediate neighborhood.

An expanded four-page mail-out/mail-back instrument containing 77 items was sent to 1,400 community residents over the age of 65. The list included all individuals over the age of 65 who were heads of households and whose names were listed in the telephone directory.

A cover letter on University letterhead and a newsletter explaining the general nature of the project were sent with the questionnaire. Six weeks after the initial mailing, a second wave of letters was sent to residents who had not responded to the initial mailing. Eight weeks after the initial mailing, a final sample of 499 returns was analyzed. This represented a 35.6 percent return rate.

Data Collection and Analysis

The sample of 499 respondents was subjected to several analyses to identify service preference differences between the total sample and various subsamples. Two specific subsamples were identified: respondents over the age of 75 (n = 150), and respondents who recorded that they had difficulty walking five or six blocks easily

FIGURE 9.5 Emergency call buttons are considered by many sponsors as one of the most important features of elderly housing. The specification of an emergency call system should be the first service considered in the development of purpose-built elderly housing.

TABLE 9.3 Descriptive Characteristics of Study Two Sample[1]

Average Age	72.6 years	Function Health	
Sex		Does walk 5–6 blocks easily	85.9
Male	42.0	Does *not* walk 5–6 blocks easily	14.1
Female	58.0	Does walk up flight of stairs easily	80.5
		Does *not* walk up flight of stairs easily	19.5
Living Arrangements			
Live alone	40.0	Working Situation	
Living with spouse	53.5	Working full-time	17.8
Living with relative	5.3	Working part-time	18.2
Living with friend	1.2	Retired	52.7
		Housewife	11.3
Housing Situation			
Own home	27.8		
Rent home	1.9		
Rent apartment	54.0		
Own condominium	13.8		
Children/relative home	2.5		

[1] n = 499

and/or had difficulty walking up a flight of stairs easily (n = 109). These two subsamples provided further elaborations of the preferences of individuals who might be attracted to the supportive services of a congregate housing arrangement. Of primary interest was to identify preferences that were shared by all three subsamples, as well as characteristics unique to and preferred more by individuals over the age of 75 and individuals with mobility and ambulatory limitations.

Service Preferences

The survey outlined 77 services, architectural features, program offerings, spaces, and policies for respondents to rate. Just as in the first study, respondents were asked to select from one of three categories of preference. Was the proposed feature a "must have," "not necessary but nice to have," or "would not want" item? The same procedure outlined in the first study was used to establish a rank ordering of sample preferences. Table 9.3 outlines the basic characteristics of the sample population.

Study Two: Findings
Total Sample Service Preferences

In examining the survey results displayed in Table 9.4, items related to health and physical security seem paramount in the minds of respondents. Within the highly rated top 15 responses were also attributes of the unit, such as kitchenette, kitchen table, and living room large enough to entertain four to six people (Fig. 9.6). Several

TABLE 9.4 Service and Feature Differential Preference Index[1]

Item Rank	Service	Differential Index	Item Rank	Service	Differential Index
1.	Emergency call buttons	98.0	41.	Craft room	15.7
2.	Ergonomically designed kitchen	96.9	42.	Carpenter service	15.1
			43.	Adult education space	14.7
3.	TV security system	95.3	44.	Arrangement with nearby nursing home	10.7
4.	Living room to entertain 4–6	94.5			
5.	24-hour security	93.8	45.	Homemaker service	6.3
6.	Kitchenette	93.3	46.	Private transportation	3.7
7.	Laundry facility	93.1	47.	Private jacuzzi	3.5
8.	Small kitchen table	92.7	48.	Xerox/Typewriter available to residents	0.5
9.	Arrangement with hospital	87.9			
10.	Attendant trained in CPR	87.3	49.	Tours for pleasure	−3.5
11.	Outside landscaped area	83.9	50.	Bathtub instead of shower	−7.3
12.	Public transportation nearby	83.1	51.	Blood pressure equipment	−11.1
13.	Lush landscape	79.5	52.	Room service	−14.9
14.	Staff trained in gerontology	77.5	53.	Weekly visiting nurse	−19.7
15.	Convenience store	73.7	54.	Messy arts and crafts	−25.9
16.	Multipurpose room	70.7	55.	Maid service in rent	−31.9
17.	Post office/mailing center	68.9	56.	Greenhouse	−38.5
18.	Outdoor exercise course	61.9	57.	Pet policy	−41.3
19.	Lounge overlooking activity	61.3	58.	Arrangement with health club	−42.3
20.	Exercise room	59.9			
21.	Beauty/Barber shop	59.2	59.	Workshop	−42.9
22.	Library/Reading room	58.7	60.	Linen not in rent	−43.3
23.	Informal breakfast area	57.0	61.	Room for men only	−50.3
24.	Unit balcony	56.7	62.	Personal counseling	−51.5
25.	Shower instead of bathtub	56.0	63.	Play area for grandchildren	−52.9
26.	Formal parlor	55.5	64.	Gardening space	−57.7
27.	Nurse on call 24 hours	55.1	65.	Putting green	−58.7
28.	Manager trained in gerontology	54.1	66.	Linen included in rent	−65.1
29.	Small pool for exercise	53.7	67.	Shopping assistance	−66.5
30.	Private duty nurse listing	45.7	68.	Shuffleboard court	−66.9
31.	Cafe/Deli	41.1	69.	Billiard room	−73.6
32.	Telephone reassurance	38.5	70.	Catering for parties	−76.7
33.	Home health care services	33.3	71.	Bookkeeping service	−76.9
34.	Office space for resident council	33.3	72.	Horseshoes	−78.7
35.	Dry cleaning pickup	32.5	73.	Small reflecting pool	−83.3
36.	Room for overnight guests	30.3	74.	Aviary	−84.7
37.	Maid services not in rent	30.0	75.	Darkroom	−84.9
38.	Auditorium	29.1	76.	Typing service	−85.7
39.	Physical therapist	25.5	77.	Video game room	−92.1
40.	Doctor's office	21.1			

[1] n = 499

of the highly rated features related to spaces and services—which support everyday activities such as the mailing center (post office), barber/beauty shop, the library/reading room, and the convenience store—all of these were rated above 50 percent.

It is interesting to note that several features relating to exercise—including the exercise room, the outdoor exercise course, and the small lap pool for exercise—were highly rated. The interest in this activity illustrates a most dramatic difference from Study One. The difference could be accounted for by regional preference or by a

FIGURE 9.6 Unit features, such as a full kitchen, are generally considered to be a necessity in middle- to higher-income congregate housing.

FIGURE 9.7 A swimming pool for exercise is gaining popularity in many facilities. This pool arrangement oriented toward units on three sides may not be as good as a smaller lap pool protected from the weather and located adjacent to an exercise room. The swimming pool is generally considered to be more of a therapeutic than a recreational amenity.

change in the image of a swimming pool from a recreational to a therapeutic amenity (Fig. 9.7). Safety features such as the stall shower instead of a bathtub were rated much higher than a bathtub instead of a shower.

Items that were rejected by a majority of the respondents include the outdoor site features of horseshoes, the putting green, and the shuffleboard court. Some of the more unconventional ideas such as a typing service and a pinball-video game room were also soundly rejected. The choice of having maid and linen services offered on an à-la-carte basis and not included in the rent was consistently rated higher than the cost of those services being included in one monthly rental rate.

Services and Features Preferred More by Subsamples

Two analyses were conducted to identify items where the differential service index of subsample respondents was substantially different from the total sample.

The items listed in Table 9.5 represent services where the preferences of the more dependent subsamples (over 75 years, mobility impaired) are stronger than the total sample. Items were listed if their differential index score varied by more than 15 percent from

TABLE 9.5 Services and Features More Highly Preferred by Subsamples 1 and 2

Subsample One:* Respondents Over Age 75 (n = 150)
 **(22.6) Listing of private duty nurse
  (18.0) Room for men to socialize
 **(16.8) Room for physical therapist
 **(16.0) Nurse on call 24 hours
  (15.4) Putting green

Subsample Two:* Respondents With Mobility Impairments (n = 109)
  (46.4) Room service
  (43.2) Home health care services
 **(35.8) Room for physical therapist
  (32.0) Drycleaning and laundry pick-up
  (29.6) Private transportation/limousine
  (29.2) Manager trained in gerontology
  (28.5) Beauty/Barber shop
  (23.0) Assistance in shopping
 **(19.6) Listing of private duty nurses
  (18.6) Adult education space
  (18.0) Cafe/Deli
  (17.7) Homemaker service
 **(16.8) Nurse on call 24 hours

 * The amount in parentheses represents the difference between the total sample and the two listed subsamples. Example: Private duty nurse 68.3 (Subsample 1) − 45.7 (Total Sample) = +22.6.
 ** Services common to Subsample one and two

the rate established for each item based on total sample preferences.

Subsample Two (individuals with ambulatory difficulties) had 13 items that were more strongly preferred than the total sample. They included health services and supportive services, such as nurse on call, physical therapist, home health service, and private transportation. Subsample One, which included those individuals over the age of 75, also strongly preferred the supportive service of a nurse on call, private duty nurse, and physical therapist, as well as a room for men to socialize and a putting green.

Clearly, health services and supportive services are among the items thought to be more important by the older, more impaired segment of the sample.

Services and Features Not as Highly Preferred by Subsamples

Table 9.6 lists the services that were less popular with the subsamples than with the total sample. Subsample Two had 11 items that were less highly preferred than the total sample. These items included activity spaces such as the exercise room, the crafts room, outdoor gardening, outdoor exercise, and the greenhouse. The four items that were less popular with Subsample One include the outdoor exercise course, the library/reading room, the greenhouse, and linen not included in the rent.

TABLE 9.6 Services and Features Less Highly Preferred by Subsamples 1 and 2

Subsample One:* Respondents Over Age 75 (n = 150)
	(−44.2)	Library/Reading room
**	(−25.2)	Linen not included in rent
**	(−21.5)	Greenhouse
**	(−15.8)	Outdoor exercise course

Subsample Two:* Respondents With Mobility Impairments (n = 109)
**	(−33.4)	Linen not included in rent
	(−30.7)	Arrangement with nursing home
**	(−28.6)	Outdoor exercise course
	(−22.6)	Outdoor space for gardening
**	(−22.4)	Greenhouse
	(−22.4)	Lounge/Lobby overlooking activity
	(−22.0)	Space for messy arts and crafts
	(−20.7)	Craft room
	(−20.3)	Maid service included in rent
	(−19.8)	Working arrangement with health club
	(−18.4)	Exercise room

 * The amount in parentheses represents the difference between the total sample and the two listed subsamples. Example: Library 14.5 (Subsample 1) − 58.7 (Total Sample) = −44.2
 ** Services common to Subsample one and two

Most services across all three samples were remarkably similar in ranking and percentage distribution. In fact, the top-rated 12 services in all three categories varied by less than six points. A similar pattern developed with the bottom ten services, which were uniformly rejected by all three samples.

Study Two: Conclusions

Items relating to health and physical security, unit design and configuration, space for traditional activities, equipment and space for exercise, and local neighborhood shops and services were all rated as positive. Outdoor activities, more unconventional activities and spaces, controversial concerns such as a policy to allow pets, and unusual special purpose activities like the darkroom or pinball room were generally rejected.

DESIGN DIRECTIVES

The implications from these research studies are useful to the designer faced with the problem of developing a congregate facility and include recommendations regarding features and services and suggestions for site selection. The following implications are based on a careful review and translation of the research.

Security from personal assault, street robbery, and burglary is a major concern and should be a major consideration in the design of the facility and the selection of a site.

DESIGN DIRECTIVE
ONE

1. Caution should be exercised in design so as not to create the image of a fortress, thus negatively affecting the community's perception of the facility.

Neighborhood service facilities such as a pharmacy and grocery should be conveniently located nearby.

DESIGN DIRECTIVE
TWO

1. Other research conducted primarily with lower-income samples detail critical distances to retail goods and services (Lawton, 1977). The research reviewed in this chapter suggests proximity to various neighborhood resources is also important to higher-income samples.

2. If a site with convenient access to supportive retail goods and services cannot be located, then accessible, frequently scheduled transportation must be made available to these services.

The availability of emergency and outpatient health services is a major consideration to persons considering a move to retirement housing. Access to and procedures for utilizing these services must be dealt with clearly in the program for the facility.

DESIGN DIRECTIVE
THREE

1. Nurse on call, infirmary, and availability of a doctor were rated high by respondents.

2. Access to emergency health (paramedic) services might include working arrangements with local hospitals for physician care.

The institution of mandatory services without choice, included as part of the rent, should be avoided.

DESIGN DIRECTIVE
FOUR

1. If maid, meal, and linen services are to be provided, they would be most acceptable if arranged as an additional expense.

DESIGN DIRECTIVE	*Basic social spaces such as a card room, large meeting room, craft room,*
FIVE	*and library should be considered first before exotic spaces such as a cocktail lounge or billiard room are programmed.*

1. Respondents have reasonably conventional expectations for the types of spaces to be considered within a facility and may be sensitive to activities or features that have negatively stereotyped images.

DESIGN DIRECTIVE	*Services and facilities that require heavy physical exertion, like a tennis*
SIX	*court, are costly to develop and may not be appreciated or used.*

1. Working arrangements with local community centers or country clubs may be preferable to a heavy initial capital outlay for an infrequently-used recreational amenity.

DESIGN DIRECTIVE	*An orientation toward wellness and fitness through the use of exercise*
SEVEN	*features (exercise room, outdoor exercise course, swimming pool) can be attractive.*

1. These services may be more attractive to the younger congregate resident who wishes to maintain optimum health through exercise.

2. An orientation to these services reflects the management's commitment to provide residents the best access possible to services that improve their health and overall physical condition.

POLICY CONSIDERATIONS

This research raises the following housing and neighborhood policy issues.

Neighborhood orientation.

The strong preference voiced for convenient neighborhood services and the concern for security both suggest that locations for elderly housing must be carefully selected. Future neighborhood changes that affect the surrounding public and retail service base are important to anticipate.

POLICY CONSIDERATION
ONE

Marketing implications.

The choices older people make in selecting services and rejecting various service options must be considered in the design of new programs for congregate care. Maximizing choice within the financial feasibility framework established for the project should be of primary consideration.

POLICY CONSIDERATION
TWO

Impacts on the frail.

The problem of growing older and becoming frail in sheltered, retirement housing must be considered from the first day of tenancy. Moving tenants from supportive housing to institutional care or adding services as the competency of the population declines are two strategies that can be developed to better support a population as it ages. A definite management policy should be established to anticipate this problem.

POLICY CONSIDERATION
THREE

Health maintenance continuity.

The strong concern for emergency aid and acute health care suggests that working arrangements with physicians or health maintenance organizations should be developed. The provision of accessible health services should be a basic consideration in the planning of congregate housing.

POLICY CONSIDERATION
FOUR

| POLICY CONSIDERATION | *Accessibility to lower- and middle-income populations.* |
| **FIVE** | The majority of the congregate housing stock in this country is accessible to only higher-income older people. Tax, regulatory, and subsidy incentives should be developed to deal with the inequalities created by the current single tier approach to developing retirement housing with services. |

| POLICY CONSIDERATION | *Training in gerontology and geriatrics.* |
| **SIX** | Older consumers are becoming much more sensitive about the need for personnel who understand more about the unique social and health circumstances which accompany old age. Managers with career training in gerontology and staff with short-term training and sensitivity counseling are rapidly becoming an assumed minimum set of qualifications for personnel. |

10

DEVELOPING SHELTERED HOUSING
Lessons From Britain

Leonard Heumann

S heltered housing is one of several labels attached to long-term assisted independent living for well elderly who lack the physical ability to fully maintain their independence without various supportive social and health services. Grouped housing and congregate housing are synonymous terms within the larger family of sheltered housing programs throughout western society. There are several common attributes between all forms of sheltered housing. First, the housing usually consists of independent apartments or bungalows that resemble conventional units. Each private apartment is "barrier free" to facilitate activities of daily living and to maximize convenience for the functionally impaired. Second, in most sheltered housing, private units are linked to communal spaces that facilitate socializing and aid the provision of domiciliary care as a resident becomes more frail. Third, each unit is connected by intercom or alarm system to a nearby source of help in case of emergency.

Sheltered Housing Prototypes Are Increasing in Popularity

The popularity of this type of housing is on the increase in western industrial countries where birth rates have stabilized, thus increasing the proportion of the elderly population (Katz, 1978; Noam, 1975; Brotman, 1977; Uhlenberg, 1977). In addition, advances in medical treatments that extend and sustain old age, along with changes in the financial and social structure of the family, have increased the number and proportion of frail elderly requiring assistance (Treas, 1977; U.S. Bureau of the Census, 1976; Heumann and Boldy, 1982).

While recognition has been growing that various forms of assistance are needed to maintain frail older people in the community, there is also a fear that too much support and assistance in the form of long-term care can be inappropriate and may lead to premature loss of functional independence (Butler, 1973; Dudley and Hillery, 1977). Past government programs have often failed to recognize that various kinds of support may be needed for individuals of differing competency. As older people age and become more dependent, they also become less able to resist the institutionalizing nature of categorical service programs.

Local attempts at sheltered housing in the United States have tended toward an institutionalized format, either copying large-scale public housing projects or utilizing nursing home designs and management techniques. This research presents the design and management experience of a sample of public and nonprofit managers of sheltered housing in Great Britain and applies their techniques and ideas to our domestic situation.

Sheltered Housing in Britain Is Different for Several Reasons

The British form of sheltered housing was chosen for investigation for several reasons. The British have more elderly residing in sheltered accommodations for a considerably longer period of time than any other western country. This experience has resulted in a larger number and greater variety of schemes accommodating very old populations. The British have 20 years of experience in building sheltered housing and currently house 5 percent of their elderly population in such facilities (DHSS, 1979). In comparison, Sweden and West Germany have sponsored programs for only 10 years that house only 0.8 percent and 0.4 percent of their respective elderly populations (SPRI, 1978; Noam and Donahue, 1976). America doesn't have a formal sheltered program, but the federally assisted congregate housing that exists houses less than 0.2 percent of the elderly population (HUD, 1976).

Related Research

Over the years the British have recognized that variations in sheltered housing are necessary to meet the differing needs and lifestyle characteristics of tenants. There are three variables that account for the variety and differing character of sheltered housing in Britain. These variables are: the size or capacity of the housing scheme, the extent to which a private or communal lifestyle is sought, and the extent to which on-site support services are provided.

Size or Capacity of the Housing Scheme

Variations in size are achieved by varying both the number of units in a building and the cluster of buildings in a given location. Size can affect how well the project is integrated or segregated from the surrounding community. A dispersed allocation of smaller size, 5–35 unit buildings, can allow the elderly to remain in a familiar neighborhood maintaining close family and friendship ties. These family ties can be especially important for elderly with mobility limitations. Small buildings also decrease the complexity associated with tenant organization and shared services. Large schemes, on the other hand (more than 80 units) may be stressful and confusing for residents with failing mobility, eyesight, or hearing. However, among functionally independent elderly there are some who receive a great deal of pleasure from the number and variety of persons and activities available in larger schemes.

Schemes Vary on a Continuum of Privacy to Communality

Sheltered care building designs also vary with regard to the amount of space allocated for private use or communal activity. One extreme might consist of a group of individual bungalows that require the resident to travel outside to reach a communal lounge, dining room, or laundry facility. At the other extreme private bedrooms could be situated in a building where toilet, bathing, eating, and recreation activities are shared. For elderly who find extensive communal intimacy bothersome, a move to such a scheme could produce depression, confusion, or anxiety. For others, a communal setting could produce feelings of belonging, self-worth, security, and novelty.

Provision of On-Site Support Services Can Also Vary

Support services can be provided by on-site staff and can be required for all tenants, or they can be provided when needed by a peripatetic staff. For some, the presence of an on-site staff person is the key to a secure and satisfying arrangement. These residents may have frequent, multiple needs that are best served by a convenient on-site aide. Some may view an on-call staff person as a convenience that allows the resident more time for challenging and rewarding activities. For others the presence of on-site staff can actually result in the resident's premature surrender of independent functions.

A Range of Housing Provides Choice and Facilities Adaptation

National policy and local management in Britain strive to provide multiple sheltered housing arrangements because the British have learned that providing choice is critical to a successful move to assisted independent living. American and other European programs have not developed far enough yet to implement a similar policy effectively. For example, housing with services is characterized in most American communities by one scheme: high-rise apartment buildings usually with more than 100 units, utilizing private apartments with community space and a rich array of on-site services.

Providing only one sheltered living alternative can cause adaptation problems, can result in inappropriate dependencies on support services, may cause some to postpone a move until it is too late to make the transition to assisted independent living, and can result in a homogeneous, frail, service-dependent population. These factors make it difficult to maintain a balance between active and less active tenants, which is considered crucial to the British concept of assisted independent living. In sheltered housing the elderly residents are in control of the social aspects of the housing. A minimum number of active and engaged residents are necessary in order to maintain this type of control. The number can vary depending on the pool of tenant personalities, leadership skills, and support resources. Once tenant control is lost, however, the social life of the housing becomes a staff responsibility and an institutional environment quickly evolves. When this process occurs it is difficult to reverse because active people on the waiting list no longer desire to move into such a setting.

The British Sheltered Housing Prototype Differs from Other Western Countries

Compared to other western countries the British sheltered housing program is unique for several reasons. First, they use small building clusters. Second, they have developed a variety of sheltered housing choices. Third, support services are custom fitted to individual needs. This has resulted in a concept of supplemental care that allows individuals to live as independently as their functional abilities allow, with support provided to persons only at their own margin of need.

The British recognition for the need of choice and variety in sheltered housing arrangements can be traced to their earlier development of "residential homes" in place of "nursing" homes. The residential home differs from sheltered housing in that it is a dependent care environment targeted to a functionally dependent but well population; no nursing staff is present and long-term medical care is not provided. Elderly with chronic illnesses who require long-term medical/nursing care are typically accommodated in geriatric wards of hospitals. Even though the residential homes provided services and a supportive living environment, they maintained a "residential" identity, rejecting the "health provider" image.

The social service agencies that manage British residential homes also provide visiting domiciliary and social services to elderly living in the community. The provision of peripatetic community services helped them to recognize the numerous levels of support available from totally independent to totally dependent living. While management of sheltered housing today is more likely to be the responsibility of public housing authorities or nonprofit associations, social service agencies were the first to visualize the need for assisted independent living and developed peripatetic services that led to some of the current concepts of sheltered housing.

Sheltered Housing Provides More Individual Attention

Residential homes are not classified as nursing care settings and therefore have less rigorous health, fire, and safety standards as well as lower staff requirements. These relaxed standards allow for the economic development of small 20- to 40-unit facilities. As the sheltered housing concept evolved, the British kept this small size and worked hard to integrate each scheme into the surrounding residential neighborhood. Residents benefited because they could stay near lifelong friends and minimize adaptation problems, and the institutional appearance and segregating effect of large-scale, high-density schemes was avoided.

Finally, because residential homes were able to provide extensive personal care using a relatively low-skilled support staff, it was felt that sheltered housing could also be successfully managed by a single on-site lay-manager who they call a "warden." The warden functions as a friendly neighbor and family proxy and is typically a young to middle-aged housewife who lives in or adjacent to the sheltered housing facility with her family. Some of her responsibilities include: visiting with tenants, helping organize and manage social activities, calling for emergency medical care and needed support services, and providing periodic domiciliary support to help augment a resident's individual needs. The warden's role has become more professional over the years but the prime responsibility has remained the same—a dedication to maximizing the independence of residents.

Why Analyze This Prototype?

The British sheltered housing model has evolved through a process of incremental adaptation to the elderly's perceived needs. The British have the longest experience with sheltered housing and the most diversified model. Other countries can benefit from close scrutiny and evaluation of these programs. The following examines three characteristics of the prototype: its small size, the variety of sheltered housing choices available, and the effectiveness of the lay-warden in providing primary care. With regard to these three questions the chapter addresses the following questions: Are local managers maintaining small scheme sizes in the face of growing construction, maintenance, and management costs? What benefits are associated with smaller size schemes? Is there really a variety of sheltered housing types provided at the local level? What kinds of choices does this variety provide the elderly? If a choice is present, what prevents management from using this variety in sheltered support in a "conveyor belt" fashion, shuttling residents to a more dependent environment when they become more frail and disabled? Finally, the chapter explores the role of the lay-warden, the principal service provider in sheltered housing, and addresses whether this role works as the primary source of tenant support.

Methodology and Data Analysis

Most of the findings presented are from interviews with managers and wardens of sheltered housing developments managed by the seven largest public housing authorities and nonprofit housing associations in the West Midlands of England. A random sample of sheltered housing schemes managed by these seven agencies was developed. Thirty-four schemes were chosen, which represent 25 percent of the total universe. One thousand thirty-seven housing units were involved (an average of 30.5 units per scheme). The research was conducted in the spring of 1978.

The analysis procedure involved a structured questionnaire, which was administered to each warden. This instrument covered warden characteristics, duties, and personal characteristics of the 1,198 residents. Another structured interview was conducted with representatives of the seven management agencies. This instrument covered management policy, goals, and activities. Finally, informal observations of social activities at each site were conducted. Where necessary, the research was supplemented by other recent work in sheltered housing schemes, involving managers, wardens, and tenants (Boldy et al., 1973; Boldy, 1976; Griffin and Dean, 1975).

Four Categories of Sheltered Housing Were Analyzed

British sheltered housing was formally divided into two categories in 1969 (MHLG, 1969). Category 1 housing is less supportive and is designed for "more active" elderly. Figure 10.1 illustrates a "typical" Category 1 site plan. Figure 10.2 is a Category 1 project in

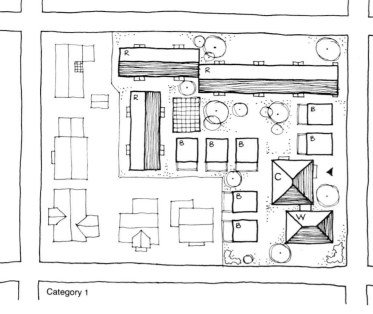

Category 1

FIGURE 10.1 Typical Category 1 Housing: In this sketch the small bungalows (B) and townhouses (R) are separated from the detached common space (C) and warden's dwelling unit (W).

FIGURE 10.2 Typical Category 1 Housing: These are bungalow units in Bucklow Walk, a Category 1 sheltered housing facility located in Birmingham, England.

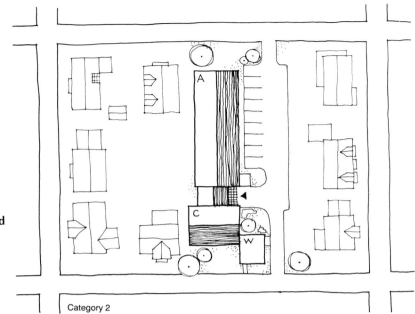

Category 2

FIGURE 10.3 Typical
Category 2 Housing:
Thirty units are arranged
along a double-loaded
corridor (A), with
common rooms (C) and
warden's quarters (W).
The small size fits in
visually with other
housing on the block.

FIGURE 10.4 Typical Category 2 Housing: This scheme in Redditch, England
is managed by the Hanover Housing Association. In this scheme a pedestrain
arcade links the parking area with the main entrance.

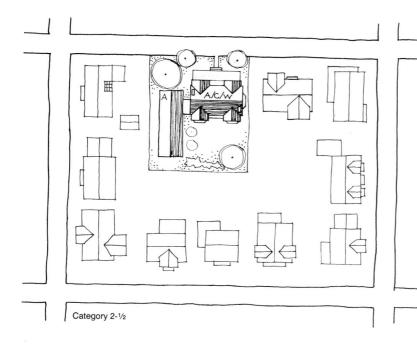

Category 2-½

FIGURE 10.5   Typical
Category 2½ Housing:
This adapts existing
houses to congregate
living for a very small
number of residents
(5–10). In this sketch
a small addition
accommodates eight
private bedrooms (A),
while the existing house
accommodates two more
bedrooms, a common
dining room, and
lounges (C). The resident
warden (W) is called a
housekeeper in this
scheme type.

Birmingham. This category consists of self-contained apartments, bungalows, or row housing with or without adjoining communal spaces.

Category 2 housing consists of a self-contained building of small one-bedroom private apartments or efficiencies linked by interior corridors to communal lounges, a modest kitchen, and a laundry room. Figure 10.3 illustrates a "typical" Category 2 site plan. Figure 10.4 is a Category 2 sheltered housing development in Tamworth near Birmingham. Category 2 is purportedly designed for "less active" elderly. Two additional categories have not been given a formal definition by the national government but are widely recognized by local sponsors.

Category 2½ has full communal dining and normally consists of small efficiency apartments, sometimes with no private kitchen or bathroom facilities. These facilities are often converted existing houses. Figure 10.5 illustrates an existing house with an addition converted to Category 2½. Category 2½ scheme sizes range from 5 to 20 units.

"Linked schemes" represent the final category type, and consist of either Category 2 or 2½ units combined on the same site with a residential home or nursing care facility. Figure 10.6 illustrates a "typical" linked scheme in a residential neighborhood. This creates a smaller version of what is known in the United States as a "continuum of care" facility. Residents of the independent units in linked schemes have access to on-site housekeeping and nursing

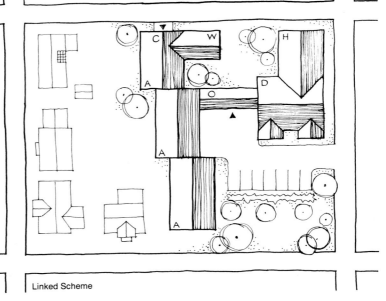

FIGURE 10.6 Typical Linked Scheme: Linked schemes are larger facilities that combine sheltered housing and an old-age home. Many successful schemes are designed at a scale so as to fit into a residential neighborhood. In this sketch 26 single and 4 two-bedroom Category 2 apartments (A), common rooms (C), and warden apartment (W) are linked to offices (O), a 20-bed old-age home (H), and a common dining hall (D).

Linked Scheme

FIGURE 10.7 The entry to the Jack Ball linked scheme in Conventry, England. Design requirements for the old-age home component of this linked scheme are more stringent than requirements for sheltered housing. Sheltered housing residents find elements such as the ambulance access unpleasant and offensive.

services on an episodic basis. Unit clusters normally house 20–40 residents. All four types use a resident warden as a central live-in support person. Figure 10.7 is the Jack Ball House, a linked scheme near Coventry.

The Use of Small Scheme Size

The small number of units allocated to each sheltered housing scheme is due to a British goal that calls for the integration of elderly into the surrounding community and the minimization of on-site social and logistical supports. The British prototype size of 30 units compares to other European and American prototypes of 100 units and more (United Nations, 1967 and 1968; Beyer and Nierstransz, 1967; Noam and Donahue, 1976). National standards define 30 units as the optimum size (MHLG, 1969). This size had been principally determined by the warden's work capacity. Low-key background monitoring is believed to be essential in maintaining an appropriate residential "image."

When interviewed, local managers in this study concurred with this national policy. When asked why larger unit arrangements should not be constructed wardens provided the following rationale.

1. Residents in large schemes tend to be segregated from social ties in the surrounding neighborhood.
   a. Large schemes draw tenants from a larger, more heterogeneous catchment area.
   b. Large building complexes "stick out" because their size and vertical design make them more apparent. This appearance exacerbates institutional and organizational isolation.
2. Social organization, group activities, group identity, and group support in large schemes are more difficult for residents to organize and sustain.
   a. A scheme of greater than 40 units erodes a "sense" of community identity and more often requires support staff to "step in " and manage activities.
   b. Group living in large schemes may appear more confusing for persons with declining functional and mental abilities.

Recent Trends Are Toward Larger Scheme Sizes: Despite the strong philosophical support for small scheme sizes, for economic reasons managers in the West Midlands have been developing larger schemes in recent years. One housing authority has converted an 80-unit high-rise apartment building to sheltered housing and another authority is in the process of converting two 80-unit tower blocks. A third authority was developing a 40-unit scheme with 15 additional self-contained dwellings for independent elderly, all under the supervision of a single warden. The economic

FIGURE 10.8   This patio, off a common room, is shared by dependent residents of the old-age wing (to the left) and independent residents of the sheltered housing wing (to the right) of a linked scheme. This is Gillespie House, located in Rugby near Coventry, England.

rationale for these larger sizes included rising land and construction costs along with staffing economies-of-scale. Some managers were influenced by the results of a study sponsored by the National Department of the Environment (Griffin and Dean, 1975), which concluded that "larger schemes are often justified because they produced more staffing efficiency and flexibility, and because overall tenant satisfaction measures did not vary appreciably among schemes of different size."

These findings are in part suspect because of the way in which the study was conducted. Tenant interviews from only 12 schemes were used. Four of the schemes had over 100 units, four had 50–99 units, and four had 25–49 units. The following four problems may account for some of the differences in tenant satisfaction between large and small schemes:

1. The buildings selected for evaluation were not "pure" examples. Many of the large schemes comprised smaller buildings, each with their own communal spaces and a separate warden. These buildings therefore functioned for all intents and purposes as smaller schemes.

2. Age and physical health were not accounted for in the analysis. Larger schemes typically housed younger, more mobile elderly who are able to overcome some of the problems of larger sized schemes.
3. Interviews were conducted with residents who had chosen these schemes, rather than the total "pool" of applicants, some who had refused to move.
4. Elderly express generally high satisfaction with their living environments irrespective of physical arrangement (Fig. 10.8).

Large-Scale Schemes Have Problems Beyond Tenant Satisfaction:
The study by Griffin and Dean (1975) uncovered some noteworthy problems with larger schemes using measures other than tenant satisfaction.

> Larger schemes tended to have more troublesome access to neighborhood stores and services than smaller schemes.
>
> Considerably less personalized care was provided to tenants in the largest schemes.
>
> Despite an increase in staff efficiency, larger schemes did not provide more services than smaller schemes.
>
> More residents of larger schemes stated they "had no friends."
>
> Common rooms and shared community spaces were used less in larger schemes.

While more definitive evaluations are needed, existing empirical evidence suggests smaller schemes of less than 30 units are more supportive. This is particularly critical for elderly experiencing functional and cognitive decline.

The Variety of Housing Types

Three major research questions were developed to test the importance of different sheltered housing arrangements.

1. Does the provision of a variety of sheltered housing arrangements provide the elderly with choices?
2. Does an initial entry point become the resident's housing for the remainder of his/her life? Or, conversely, does the presence of different sheltered housing types result in a continuum of staging points along which people can move as they become more dependent?
3. Do various types of sheltered housing provide the same level of maximum support and a similar mix of resident characteristics?

For the vast majority of functionally impaired, low-income elderly in America, assisted independent living in a sheltered environment does not exist. There is absolutely no choice other than remaining in conventional housing or moving to an institutional setting. In Great Britain, 5 percent of the elderly are housed in government subsidized sheltered environments, and assisted independent living is an option open to most older people. Nevertheless, even in Great Britain sheltered housing waiting lists average 3 years (Bythway and James, 1978). While sheltered housing has the potential to provide a comfortable, independent life to all other people, the move can be traumatic. This is particularly true if it involves limited choices, necessitates moving out of a familiar neighborhood, or requires a dramatic lifestyle adaptation.

How Much Choice Do the Elderly Have in Selecting Various Categories of Sheltered Housing? Theoretically, the four categories of sheltered housing described earlier provide adequate choice. However, the supply of housing by category limits choice. Table 10.1 demonstrates that, in the West Midlands, Category 2 housing is the predominant type available. Furthermore, three of the four largest nonprofit housing associations interviewed supplied only one type of sheltered housing. Only one sponsor in the sample provided a full range of housing type and location choices within a reasonably short waiting time (6–18 months, depending on whether just type or location or both type and location are requested). However, this one authority was housing over 16 percent of the elderly population in sheltered accommodations. That ratio is more than three times the national average and almost five times more than any other West Midlands sponsor.

The provision of choice among sheltered housing types is even less likely in rural areas because in these sparsely populated areas typically only one housing authority provides sheltered accommodations (Boldy, 1977). Because of the combination of long waiting time for a vacancy caused by an inadequate supply of sheltered

TABLE 10.1 The Character of Sheltered Housing and Sheltered Housing Residents in the West Midlands[1]

		Category 1	Category 2	Category 2½	Linked Schemes	Total
Total units	No.	266	544	91	40	941[2]
	%	28.3	57.8	9.7	4.3	100.0
Average units per scheme		33.3	34.0	15.2	20.3[3]	30.5
Average tenant age		73.0	74.6	79.2	80.3	74.6
% living alone		59.1	77.1	81.7	81.8	71.0
% unable to do heavy housekeeping		17.8	34.1	51.9	97.1	34.7

[1] Based on a 1978 25% random sample of seven public and nonprofit sponsors.
[2] There were actually 1,037 units in the sample. An additional 96 units in schemes that had a mix of Category 1 and 2 units were omitted from this table.
[3] Includes only the sheltered housing portion of the linked scheme.

housing and the inadequate range of choices, it is estimated that almost half of the residents entering British sheltered housing today have no choice. Almost half of the allocations of sheltered housing vacancies nationwide are filled by persons "in emergency situations" who have an immediate need for sheltered support if they are to remain semi-independent in the community (Bythway and James, 1978). People with such immediate need are frequently assigned the first vacancy that becomes available in any of the four category types. Approximately 50 percent of the remaining entering residents are able to shop around, compare several alternatives, and make a choice about housing type, location, and timing of their entry. The accommodation of emergency cases has a profound effect on the character of sheltered housing arrangements.

Even Great Britain, which has a sizeable stock and selection of sheltered housing, needs to expand the supply and variety to meet the growing demand. Persons over the age of 65 currently account for 15 percent of the British population and are predicted to account for 23 percent by 1994 (DHSS, 1979). Currently around 11 percent of the population is over the age of 65 in the United States, and predictions suggest the population will reach 14 percent around the year 2000, peaking at 20 percent by the year 2030 (Katz, 1978).

The Growing 75+ Population Is the Group Most Likely to Require Assisted Independent Living: In the United States, the group of elderly over the age of 75 is estimated to be increasing three times faster than the 65–75 aged population (Brotman, 1977), and it is this group that is most likely to develop emergency needs for sheltered housing. While the proportion of elderly in Great Britain is about 20–30 years ahead of the United States, the need for sheltered housing in the United States is increasing rapidly. To present American elderly with any choice in sheltered housing alternatives, development and construction should start now (Fig. 10.9).

Housing Types: A Permanent Choice or Stages in the Aging Process?

When the national circular (MHLG, 1969) defined Category 1 for "active" elderly and Category 2 for "inactive" elderly, there was some concern among gerontologists that local managers would segregate elderly by functional ability and move them from scheme to scheme as their abilities changed. This has been prevented in part by the high demand and low supply of sheltered housing and the uneven provision of a continuum of sheltered housing types. Vacancies in sheltered housing are too rare to accomplish regular transfers, and very few authorities have a full continuum of sheltered housing types between which they could transfer residents.

Managers were asked how or if they distinguish between category types; whether or not they make checks on tenant functional

FIGURE 10.9 Trinity Close is a Category 2 sheltered housing facility in Birmingham, England. The projected windows are very popular with residents, providing a place to sit and view the street.

ability; and, if needed, do they transfer residents to a more supportive form of sheltered housing? The findings suggest that category types are not segregated models of supportive housing. Public housing authorities who manage more than one housing type make no attempt to transfer less active residents. They often see little or no difference in the level of support provided by different housing types. Once a person is satisfactorily settled in a unit, management normally tries to meet resident needs in that place rather than through a transfer. Nonprofit associations that offer only one housing type, on the other hand, often define their housing by activity level, develop a procedure for checking functional ability, and attempt to transfer tenants when they have difficulty maintaining independence.

Many Wardens View Categories 1 and 2 as Comparable: The most common warden response was also that moves between category types were rare because low vacancy rates made regular, predictable moves impossible. However, many viewed Categories 1 and 2 as equally able to provide similar levels of support at comparable cost. While they recognized that Category 2½ and linked schemes provided better access to on-site staff, in most cases the psychological and social disruptions of moving residents to a more supportive environment when they were experiencing decline were considered too great.

Looking at actual moves from sheltered housing confirms that transfers are rare. Death accounts for the majority (60.4 percent) of all moves from sheltered housing. Transfer to a dependent care facility accounts for 22.3 percent of the moves, 6.9 percent are moves to another sheltered housing arrangement (typically a change in location not category type), 5.3 percent are moves to relatives, and 5.1 percent are moves back to independent/conventional housing. Projects over 10 years old had more moves triggered by death than schemes that were less than 3 years old. Newer schemes have the most mobile residents with an average of 6.4 moves per scheme per year back to conventional housing, compared to only 2.2 such moves per year from schemes that are over 10 years old. The fact that resident mobility declines as a scheme matures and residents age suggests that a phasing of more supportive services should be developed as the competency levels of residents decline.

Resident Characteristics by Category Type: Table 10.1 shows a steady increase in average age, percent living alone, and percent unable to do heavy housekeeping, when comparing Category 1 to Category 2, Category 2½ and linked schemes. The major factor that contributes to this pattern is self-selection. Different categories of sheltered housing appeal to older people with differing dependency needs and lifestyle tastes. Each resident makes the move to sheltered housing at a unique time in their adult development, under different social circumstances, and with different support needs. Reasonably active persons are more likely to choose a Category 1 bungalow, while more frail and inactive persons are more likely to choose the communal setting of Category 2½ or the security of a linked scheme (Fig. 10.10).

FIGURE 10.10   The single-loaded corridor of Queen Mothers Court, a Category 2 facility in Birmingham, England, provides a pleasant view of the surrounding area.

The Critical Role of the Lay-Warden

The British sheltered housing program relies on the resident warden to monitor day-to-day activities. The warden monitors activity and may summon various support services when needed. She is often a service provider, family counselor, and social organizer. So long as the amount and extent of resident support are relatively minor, housewives serving as wardens with no special skills or training are an excellent way of providing patient, loving, and adequate support while minimizing an institutional atmosphere. However, when resident support needs increase beyond a point that the warden can handle, the health, happiness, and safety of residents can be placed in jeopardy. The two major questions that arise in response to the role of the warden are:

1. How frequently and under what conditions are housing arrangements likely to evolve to a point where the lay-warden cannot handle the situation without supplemental professional help?
2. Is the concept of the lay-warden as a proxy to the residents' family modified if the warden is professionally trained and/or has additional support from on-site staff assistants?

The Warden's Role Is Well-Defined: The existing literature and interviews with managers verified the well-defined nature of the warden's role (Boldy, 1976; Chippindale, 1978; Heumann, 1980; Willcocks, 1972). Warden candidates are normally screened for the right personality type. Wardens tend to be warm, gregarious persons dedicated to the functional independence of their tenants. Ninety-four percent of the wardens in the sample had or were in the process of raising families, and 41 percent had children living at home. The average age of the wardens was 52, 23 years younger than the average tenant. Wardens typically receive very low pay. Benefits normally include a rent-free apartment in the scheme and a small stipend. The spouses of married wardens usually hold blue collar or clerical positions. In many schemes the warden comes from the same neighborhood and the same working- to middle-class background as tenants. The warden can often empathize through the proxy role with the resident's own daughter. When asked, most wardens describe their role as being between a friendly neighbor and a close relative.

Spatial proximity facilitates the sharing of experiences and the development of social ties. This communication can provide advanced warning with regard to any episodic illness or crippling disability the resident might develop. Wardens and residents may shop, launder clothing, or converse together over tea. When the resident becomes more dependent, this social relationship with the warden helps to allay fear. As one author has put it, being a warden is not a job, "it's a way of life" (Chippindale, 1978).

Most Wardens Are Able to Balance Their Duties Effectively:
Housing managers in the study were asked to evaluate the 136
wardens they oversee. The seven managers classified 92 percent
as "model" wardens. These wardens are able to judge how much
support was required to meet the problem at hand without creating
unneeded dependencies. Most wardens are skillful in using activity programs to maintain the social awareness and engagement of
residents. The 8 percent classified as "ineffective" tended to either
under-care or over-care. Many didn't like their job and were lax
with their responsibilities. Two types of ineffective wardens over-
cared for their tenants. One type, the elderly dominated warden,
lacked confidence and assertiveness and could not turn down tenant demands. This type of warden found herself overworked but
could not understand why. The other type is the warden who over-
cares by choice. This warden undermines the concept of independent living by controlling the environment. She is overworked and
loves it. Unfortunately, she provides too much for the tenants,
rarely relying on peripatetic help. She often loses her objectivity
regarding what is best for the tenant and may inadvertently create
an institutional environment (Heumann, 1980).

The Diverse and Increasing Workload of the Warden: It is clear
that wardens provide a valuable service. However, many become
increasingly overworked as tenants require more aid and assistance. Interviews with wardens indicate the most common service
they provide is friendly neighboring. This involves paying daily
calls on tenants, contacting relatives and doctors, and arranging
for emergency help when needed. No single event consumes more
of the warden's job each day than making rounds to check on
residents' health. As a resident ages, he/she is often subject to
increasing episodic illness and worsening chronic disabilities.
When this occurs the warden must make more than one check
each day. The more sheltered types of accommodation have residents who require extra visits and attention. In Category 1, 42.1
percent of the residents required at least daily visits from the warden; in Category 2, 54.7 percent; in Category 2½, 63.1 percent;
and in linked schemes, 77.3 percent. In cases where frail residents
have no family or friends, or where support services are slow or
nonexistent (such as evenings and weekends), wardens sometimes
must abandon administrative chores, social support to other residents, and their own families to provide personal or nursing care.

Evolution of the Warden's Role: Twenty-nine potential duties that
a warden might assume were created from existing literature
(Boldy, 1976; Ministry of Housing and Local Government, 1962;
Willcocks, 1972). Wardens were asked if they assumed these duties
and if these duties were voluntarily completed or considered as
part of their job description. Services ranged from neighboring to

caretaker services, from social organizing and counseling to nursing care. In addition, the number of hours devoted to these duties each week was recorded along with the number of residents for which each warden has responsibility.

Results show similarity in the type of duties wardens shouldered in Categories 1 and 2 housing but less similarity in workload. Although Category 1 schemes house on the average the greatest number of tenants, wardens have the shortest workweek—25 hours for both required and voluntary duties. The relatively good health and independence of Category 1 tenants also provide for fewer disruptions during off-duty hours. Category 2 wardens provide on the average 10 more hours of service per week than Category 1 wardens. Most of this extra time is allocated to additional personal visits, home help (shopping, cleaning, etc.), and organizing and directing social activities.

Wardens in Category 2½ and Linked Schemes Work Much Longer Hours: The time allocations of wardens in Category 2½ and linked schemes are quite different from Categories 1 and 2. Category 2½ wardens spend more time shopping for food and planning/cooking meals. Even though the average Category 2½ scheme has only half the tenants of a Category 1 or 2 scheme, the warden works an average of 57 hours per week.

The linked scheme warden, a central support figure and live-in staff member, must oversee a permanent day staff. She works an average of 69 hours per week and her job is more like a full-time nursing home administrator.

Wardens of Categories 1 and 2 housing require similar skills, although the Category 2 job is more demanding. Category 2½ housing requires a warden with additional homemaker skills; in linked schemes a warden requires more nursing administrative skills. Since the average age of all schemes was 8 years old, and the average age of all residents was 75 years old, wardens may face an increasing need for additional skills and may have greater demands on their time in the future (Fig. 10.11).

Warden Workloads Increase as a Scheme Matures: The study design was cross-sectional in nature and thus relied on the impressions of wardens regarding how their jobs had changed over time. Various anecdotal examples of increasing demand for time and work overloads were assembled. Some of these examples range from episodic flu epidemics to a growing need to organize social activities when active tenants were no longer available to provide leadership. Examples also existed of wardens who had to curtail off-site activities, such as shopping for tenant prescriptions or providing social outings for more active tenants, because they were unable to leave the scheme because of frail and housebound elderly tenants.

FIGURE 10.11 The interior court of this Category 2 sheltered housing scheme in Birmingham, England, gives the elderly residents a secure outdoor area where they can interact with other residents.

Boldy (Heumann and Boldy, 1982) found similar trends in a sample of wardens from Devon, England, who were studied over the 4-year period 1973–1977. He found a 50 percent increase in the average workweek of the warden over these 4 years. Particularly time consuming was the increase in "emergency" services. He found reduction in average time spent on housekeeping and administrative duties was necessary to compensate for the increased time spent providing care and support. Boldy's most startling finding was the increased workload outside normal work hours (that is, before breakfast, after evening meals, Saturday and Sunday). The time spent in this period doubled, increasing to one-third of the total workweek.

There is a Growing Need for Professional Training: The increasing warden workload found by Boldy is due in part to an aging and less active elderly population residing in sheltered housing. However, a dramatic increase in such a short time period is likely not to be solely based on tenant aging. A large portion of the increasing workload may be due in part to the poor training a warden receives.

Some wardens may actually create a demand for support rather than respond to tenant needs. Placing an unskilled lay-warden at the nexus of such a potentially complex supportive environment may be a big mistake. A skilled and experienced person may be needed to distinguish between "real" support needs and "false" dependency. The untrained warden without this help and advice may be contributing to her own work overload.

Unskilled wardens also lack the ability to reverse group dynamics toward less dependency when aging and frail elderly live together. Furthermore, lay-wardens increasingly find themselves providing counseling and nursing services in off hours when peripatetic or auxiliary help is not available for residents. In most cases they have not been trained to provide such services but are forced to because other appropriate professionals are unavailable to augment service demand. There are also indicators that lay-wardens may jeopardize their own family's needs when they spend as much as one-third of their free time providing services to residents. Wardens are understandably less happy with heavy workloads and added responsibilities. The Boldy study (Heumann and Boldy, 1982) shows a growing turnover rate among wardens as job responsibilities increase.

Many Recently Hired Wardens Have Nursing Training: Sheltered housing managers screen warden candidates primarily on the basis of personality characteristics, which they believe contribute to the warden's performance as a dedicated family proxy. However, growing recognition exists that other skills and training are helpful, if not necessary. One manager, in conjunction with a local community college, has developed a special training course to provide skills ranging from first-aid to group dynamics. An additional indicator of the trend toward an increased level of professional skill is the fact that 50 percent of the wardens hired between 1977 and 1978 in the West Midlands sample had some nursing training. This compares with only 5 percent of the wardens hired prior to 1977. Boldy (Heumann and Boldy, 1982) discovered a similar trend in his rural sample. This hiring trend recognizes the need for wardens with nursing and social counseling skills.

So far, managers have been able to find women who possess a strong desire to develop close "family" ties with residents, in addition to being well trained in other areas. One might argue (Heumann, 1980) that skilled wardens might become frustrated by day-to-day duties that did not allow them to use their professional skills. As a result a warden with nursing skills might create tenant dependencies that would justify the use of those skills. However, Boldy's research and my recent observations suggest that untrained wardens are the ones more apt to create inappropriate resident dependencies.

In summary, the majority of lay-wardens seem capable of handling expanding job demands, particularly if they receive additional on-the-job training as resident dependencies increase.

Applying the Warden Concept in America

Although purpose-built sheltered housing in the United States, for reasons of financial feasibility, has involved large groups of units in low- or high-rise blocks, the concept of providing support at the margin of individual need coordinated by an on-site warden is a useful design and management option. British high-rise sheltered housing successfully employs the warden concept by breaking the building into small blocks of units and assigning a warden to each block. These blocks are semi-autonomous, with a separate set of communal spaces that contributes to their identification as a small family group. Savings accrue from staffing flexibility especially relief wardens and maintenance staff.

Decentralized Neighborhood-Based Supportive Housing in the Community: There are other ways to adapt the idea of sheltered housing to the United States. One alternative involves the adaptation of a neighborhood or community warden to service elderly residents in decentralized and private single-family housing.

Owner occupied housing currently accommodates over 70 percent of the elderly in America. Many of the elderly live in older single-family neighborhoods located between the edge of central cities and newer suburban areas. Housing and community services in these neighborhoods are largely in good condition. However, the children have all grown, school enrollment is down, and the social infrastructure is dwindling because of the growing number of "empty nests" occupied by single elderly. There are estimates that as many as a million and a half of the homes in areas such as this have already been converted (some illegally, due to zoning difficulties) to create "accessory apartments" (Hare, 1981a).

Accessory apartments are created when elderly owner occupants convert the empty space in their single-family homes into two or more units. When totally separate units are created with private entries, bathrooms, and kitchens, conversion costs are normally in the range of about $10,000 per unit (Hare, 1981b). However, when an elderly owner occupant takes in one or more elderly tenants and they share the house, there are often no conversion costs. This conversion process can provide income to the elderly homeowner, as well as provide new rental housing opportunities for elderly renters (Hare, 1981b). A discussion of the costs associated with this trend is beyond this paper. However, this movement toward shared housing may become an American counterpart to small-scale British sheltered housing.

Share-a-Home is a Successful Shared Housing Prototype: Shared living projects for elderly persons exist in areas where there is both a predominance of elderly homeowners and elderly renters. "Share-A-Home" in the central Florida area is one such program. This program allows older people to stay in their own home with companionship, security, and some additional income. Elderly renters receive companionship and security, and often pay less rent for a more pleasant surrounding than they might otherwise be able to afford. A recent evaluation of 243 Share-A-Home participants revealed that over two-thirds express overall satisfaction with the arrangement (Streib, 1980). Respondents perceived companionship and assistance with household tasks as the major advantages, while loss of privacy and problems with interpersonal relationships are considered the major disadvantages (Streib, 1980). Most of the participants in the program are widows in their early 70's. Program sponsors serve primarily as brokers who match owners and renters. Participants must often learn a new style of shared living that may require counseling and help from a neutral third party. Housemates, initially matched because their needs and resources were complementary, may change to where they exacerbate each others' disabilities. Personality and role relations can change as health declines and dependencies develop. It would seem that such situations could benefit from a "neighborhood warden" concept. A neighborhood warden could visit; monitor daily living; provide shopping, transportation, and domiciliary support; call in support from family, neighbors, or professionals; and serve as a third-party consultant. With the advent of new electronic intercom devices, a neighborhood warden can monitor as many as 50 or more shared homes or conventional elderly households within several city blocks.

Neighborhood Wardens Often Have Problems Providing Adequate Security to the Elderly They Serve: In Great Britain, where they have had both resident and neighborhood wardens, the support provided by neighborhood wardens has been less effective than that provided by resident wardens because they had difficulty providing security to residents located on different residential blocks. Neighborhood wardens easily lost contact with residents whenever they were outside their homes visiting or running errands for their own family or other elderly. They also found it difficult to escape calls at times when they were off duty and wished to be alone with their families. The recent development of portable and stand-in electronic signaling devices provides the neighborhood warden a more efficient, secure, and humane way to coordinate and provide visiting services (Davis, 1979). With these devices, the homes of the elderly being served by neighborhood wardens can be wired by intercom to the warden's home. When on-duty and at home, the warden can speak directly to residents through an intercom. When she is on-duty and away from home visiting residents or running errands, calls can be forwarded by a portable battery-operated shortwave radio system. When she is off duty or when she knows she will be outside the range of her radio signal, the warden can simply switch the intercom call system through her telephone to a nearby warden or a central switchboard shared by a large number of neighborhood wardens.

With a call forwarding service, residents need not dial several numbers to talk to someone who can advise, reassure, or help them. In cases where the elderly have a severe episodic illness or chronic condition that makes it impossible to manipulate the intercom, an electronic companion service can be used that triggers an alarm to signal the warden whenever an individual's normal movement patterns are interrupted for an abnormal length of time. The cost savings combined with personal care of a warden using these time-saving devices make this a very attractive scenario for the future of all peripatetic services to elderly living in the community.

Neighborhood Wardens Could Also Organize Better Informal Care Provision Networks: The use of a neighborhood lay-warden as the primary service coordinator and family proxy to elderly recipients is promising. The warden can provide real economic savings for visiting services by leveraging the support of a network of elderly neighbors under her charge and by calling for expert visiting services only when it is absolutely necessary. Because one person understands the individual's support needs, providers can be informed and coordinated with greater ease. This prevents costly duplication of services and the provision of too much or too many services. By preventing unnecessary dependencies the warden can produce both short- and long-range savings. She also provides the older person with the dedication of a friend and neighbor for daily support and an advocate to prescribe and call in special peripatetic services. The chances of older persons forming the same bond with each visiting home helper, social worker, or public nurse assigned to them are less likely.

Conclusions

The British sheltered housing program consists of several alternative choices in communal living, small scheme sizes, locations in residential neighborhoods, and reliance on a single live-in or nearby staff person (the resident or neighborhood warden) to coordinate support and social activity at the margin of individual need. It is a humane, efficient, and successful model for long-term assisted independent living. The question is, what can prevent adaption of this program in the United States?

The Combination of a Small Scheme Size and the Work Pressures on an On-Site Professional Resident Warden May Be Cost Prohibitive

Whenever wardens or extra on-site assistance is required, scheme size is frequently increased to above 30 units. Development costs in the United States have made it uneconomical to build less than 80–100 units of assisted elderly housing under publicly financed arrangements. Given the substantial demand for public housing units and the great number of older, frail people who should be given priority for new housing, the development of sheltered housing in the United States may require, from the outset, professionally trained personnel and other services.

Such personnel in the United States are likely to be far more costly than their counterparts in Great Britain. The British pay professionally trained wardens a low salary. An average warden, for example, in the West Midlands in 1978 received approximately $35 per week. British wardens, however, receive in-kind benefits such as rent free accommodations and are given free medical care and other social subsidies that supplement their income. Furthermore, the warden's role is a highly respected one, and thus many British women sacrifice financial renumeration for personal gratification. The warden's job in American society is not likely to command the same respect, and a highly skilled warden candidate in America is likely to ask for and get a far higher salary.

Extensive Reliance on Peripatetic Support Services May Be Difficult to Provide

The British resident warden's job is assisted by a well-developed visiting (peripatetic) social and health services system coordinated with the housing system. This type of coordination and cooperation exists in some American cities, but it is not as consistent as that found in Great Britain. Well-established visiting services in the United States often perpetuate individualism and isolation of the elderly instead of encouraging the development of communal networks. Social and health supports in the United States are separate and categorical, and thus they rarely view elderly support needs in a comprehensive manner. For example, a program may be designed to provide demand-responsive vehicles to individuals, but not to organize and pool transportation mobility resources for older community residents.

The warden's role is one of facilitator and organizer. The warden's job involves leveraging assistance within the elderly community. As such they act as case coordinators might in the United States. As mentioned above, "neighborhood wardens" have been developed by British communities to visit and check on the elderly within a residential neighborhood. Their job is to make sure they are receiving emergency aid when needed, to be aware of support services, and to help community members form their own support and social networks within the local neighborhood. Many support services built on existing resources in the community are available in Great Britain. These services are invaluable in supporting frail elderly in or outside of sheltered housing schemes. While the British have had trouble maintaining their support service networks recently due to economic recession and shifting priorities, their networks are typically more comprehensive than community care support networks found throughout American society.

A Lack of Homogeneity Characterizes America's Elderly

Lower-income commonwealth immigrants to Great Britain seldom seek sheltered housing upon reaching old age. As a result, British sheltered housing is overwhelmingly dominated by moderate- to middle-income white protestant natives of the British Isles. When housing in the United States attracts a homogeneous elderly population, such as in a small town or through a religious sponsor, a "family-like" support atmosphere similar to British sheltered housing is easier to develop. However, publicly sponsored congregate housing in the United States draws from a much more heterogeneous pool of residents. This results in a far more difficult task of integrating residents and a far less reliable support network within the housing community. This heterogeneity may require a larger support staff to compensate for the lack of peer support. On the other hand, larger schemes may increase the opportunity for tenants to find a support network of peers with similar cultural tastes and interests.

Viable Neighborhood Support Systems Are Lacking

By using small schemes in residential neighborhoods, the British have been able to maintain socially integrated residents. Small-scale facilities promote interaction with storekeepers and neighbors. Where residents can be retained in decent neighborhoods they have known all their lives, even the most functionally disabled can venture out into the community with confidence and safety. In America, neighborhoods that are safe, densely populated, and offer mixed land uses with convenient stores and services may only exist at the seam between central city and suburban areas. Functionally disabled elderly trapped in older inner-city areas are both isolated and handicapped by the inadequacy of shopping, transportation, and other services; increasing crime rates; and environmental (air and noise) pollution. Newer low-density suburbs are also a problem. These areas are dependent on the automobile and have segregated land-use patterns. Areas characterized by inner-city problems and suburban enclaves with an absence of supportive neighborhood elements will require that sheltered housing have adequate support staff.

In conclusion, the British sheltered prototype provides many important and useful ideas that can assist our attempt at providing independent living for the functionally disabled elderly. By employing the many new advances in electronic and electromechanical technologies, we may be able to duplicate the many humane concepts the British have pioneered in long-term assisted independent living, using more cost efficient means. We must be vigilant, however, and constantly monitor the use of technological devices to be sure they are used to increase service productivity and do not become a substitute for human caring and human interaction. The goal should be to provide older people with more control so that they can maintain active and stimulating lives.

DESIGN DIRECTIVES

This chapter has focused more on housing management and program elements than physical design elements. By focusing on program elements of British sheltered housing, it has been possible to illustrate the varied and dynamic resident needs that must be applied to the design of elderly housing. If there is one overriding directive to give the designer, it must be that elderly housing cannot be limited to one categorical model—it must provide alternative entry point choices to assisted independent living and be flexible in the designed use of spaces without sacrificing feelings of stability, permanence, and security.

Varying the physical configuration, amount of communal space, and on-site support between a range of housing types like the British categories 1, 2, 2½, and linked schemes effectively provides applicants with important choices.

DESIGN DIRECTIVE
ONE

1. Those who would enjoy the benefit of a closer social network can self-select a housing type that accommodates this need; those who prefer more individuality and privacy can select a housing type to accommodate that need.

2. This choice provides for a better matching of individual and environment—which should theoretically lead to higher levels of satisfaction.

Purpose-built housing for the elderly should attempt to "fit" within the neighborhood.

DESIGN DIRECTIVE
TWO

1. Small size schemes that utilize similar architectural scale and material treatment are usually more unobtrusive.

2. Remodeling existing structures to accommodate sheltered housing can help achieve "fit" while taking advantage of existing underutilized buildings.

3. Integration of housing into the social fabric of the neighborhood (that is, churches, fraternal organizations, parks, and retail stores) is as important as physical/stylistic integration.

Common rooms in purpose-built housing must be designed for maximum flexibility.

DESIGN DIRECTIVE
THREE

1. The vast majority of elderly with functional disabilities are able to live out their lives in a barrier-free environment with just a minimum of peripatetic support. However, individual scheme populations can age and require varying degrees of on-site support on an episodic or even permanent basis. Flexibility and sensitivity in the design of common space are therefore critical.

2. Predetermined and highly specialized common rooms are not popular and are inflexible to changing tastes and needs. Flexibility in room size and use is preferred. Changes from a public or semi-private lounge, to a nurses station, to guest living quarters, or to a craft room should be possible to reflect different support needs and/or social interests of the resident population.

3. Some specialty rooms are necessary but they must be adaptable to multiple uses. Laundry rooms, for example, are places where residents often meet while their laundry is washing/drying despite the typical spartan/utility appearance, poor seating, and acoustics.

DESIGN DIRECTIVE
FOUR

Housing choices that accommodate a small number of individuals who share communal responsibilities should be encouraged.

1. The process utilized by the United States Department of Housing and Urban Development to construct purpose-built housing often predetermines the size, scale, and building type used. These factors often result in an elderly housing prototype: a high-rise of 80–100 units in an urban neighborhood.

2. Program requirements for housing with food services narrow the prototype further. The amortization of fixed costs for kitchen equipment and operating costs for meal preparation require, in the view of some planners, a minimum building size of 100 units.

3. Residential-type kitchens that can accommodate the meal preparation requirements of a small number of individuals should be explored. Economies of scale may exist at several different levels depending on the capacity and sophistication of the kitchen equipment specified, the amount of on-site versus off-site food preparation required, and the number of on-site elderly taking meals.

DESIGN DIRECTIVE
FIVE

The use of advanced communication technology to link older people with various emergency peripatetic services should be explored when developing a new building.

1. Intercom systems provide more accurate and personal response to resident needs than alarm systems.

2. New portable communication devices may make it easier to provide emergency support in less time to a larger number of people.

3. An individual caseworker approach, like the British warden, may be the "filter" which is needed to screen and coordinate support services and emergency requests.

| DESIGN DIRECTIVE |
| **SIX** |

1. Shared housing such as this, which is efficient and income producing, can help to improve neighborhoods by reducing the probability that housing stock will be poorly maintained.

2. Older people living together who support each other can experience greater community engagement while lowering the burden of responsibility on the "neighbor warden," family, and visiting services.

POLICY CONSIDERATIONS

POLICY CONSIDERATION
ONE

Consider creating a balanced population for sheltered housing.

A balance should be sought between younger and older, more frail residents in all sheltered housing types. A balance of tenants by functional ability level prevents using the housing types as staging points along which the elderly are moved as their functional limitations increase. All types share a similar goal of assisted independent living and a similar range of support. Only the way the support is provided and style of living vary.

A balance of residents by age, sex, and functional ability enhances the social chemistry of communal space and lessens the wardens' load by reducing the number who need extensive attention. The mixture of ages and activity levels enhances social opportunities by providing a critical mass of active, engaged residents. These individuals are often the catalyst needed to involve less active residents.

POLICY CONSIDERATION
TWO

The warden model has applicability.

The lay warden is a family proxy, neighbor, friend, and helper. She has been a very effective and humane source of assistance when used as an on-site manager or in a neighborhood/community setting. In America, health care systems are beginning to utilize case-coordinators to link the older person with the care delivery system. The lay-warden serves as an important refinement of this model providing individual aid, attention, and friendship.

POLICY CONSIDERATION
THREE

Services must be provided at the margin of need.

Shared or communal housing arrangements providing services at the margin of individual need should be available in the United States. This highly successful European prototype is almost nonexistent in the United States. The examples that exist are sporadic and highly individualistic. Few are integrated with community services, and those that do exist often find it difficult to provide predictable peripatetic assistance.

HOUSING ADAPTATIONS
Needs and Practices

Raymond J. Struyk

I n recent years policy analysts, professionals, politicians, and older retired persons in our society have been justifiably concerned with the system of long-term care for our elderly population. Premature and unnecessary institutionalization of the elderly is costly, and, more importantly, it may have severe negative impacts on persons committed to nursing homes and other facilities. There is a growing recognition that the most humane and cost-effective policies toward the elderly are those that assist as many older people as possible to remain in their communities, rather than be institutionalized. Consequently, considerable attention has been focused on alternatives to institutionalization, such as adult day health center, in-home services, respite care, and congregate living.

One element in this broad strategy is the physical modification of dwelling units to make such units more livable for the elderly who have health problems or mobility limitations and perhaps to relieve pressures toward institutionalization. A crucial factor in considering alternative approaches to assisting the elderly in this important aspect of their lives is knowledge of the extent of the need for such modifications.

The support of the Florence V. Burden Foundation is gratefully acknowledged. A grant from the Aetna Life and Casualty Foundation allowed the basic work to be recast for inclusion in this volume.

Related Research

Factors Leading to the Need for Specially Adapted Living Units Are Poorly Understood

A poorly understood relationship is that between physical impairments, health problems, and limitations in the performance of activities of daily living by the elderly and their need for specially adapted living accommodations. This ambiguity in turn has led to very rough and large estimates of the share of the elderly who "need" a more accessible residential environment. Thus Steinfeld et al. (1979), in reviewing counts of the total (elderly and nonelderly) target population for barrier-free design, conclude:

> . . . a conservative estimate of the principal beneficiaries for elimination of barriers given available data, is from 1.7 to 2.2 percent of the entire population. A moderate estimate is 5.3 percent of the entire population. These estimates exclude many people who might benefit, even though their limitations are less severe, and those in institutions who might be able to pursue more independent lives; but they also may include people who cannot benefit because of the severity of their disability.
>
> A liberal view of the beneficiary population would include not only those who would achieve increased independence in personal care and mobility, but also those who would gain a fuller degree of independence and mobility and more convenience in everyday activities. An estimate of this beneficiary population is the 22.8 million people, or 11.6 percent of the U.S. population, reported by NHIS (1969) to have some limitation in everyday activities, but not necessarily in a major activity.[1]

Applying the same logic to the elderly population yields a "liberal view" that the lives of 46 percent of the elderly would be enhanced through living in specially adapted dwellings. If these estimates are even remotely correct, they could well lead one to conclude that major assistance to the elderly to achieve this objective is required.

Existing Estimates of the Need for Specially Adapted Units Are Probably Too High

There are real questions, however, about such estimates. They largely ignore the possibility that an activity limitation would not affect the suitability of their dwelling. Second, they ignore the substitution of personal assistance for dwelling modifications; for example, spouses helping each other out of the tub instead of installing grab bars. Finally, specialization of tasks in a multiperson

---

[1] Estimates of this type confront numerous and serious definitional problems. See, for example, Haber (1967) or The Urban Institute, Chapter II (1975).

household may mean that no reprogramming is required; the impaired member never performed the task in question. These observations are consistent findings in the relationship between dependency and disability in general. Nagi (1975), for example, found dependency in living conditions to be related to physical disability when combined with specific socioeconomic characteristics.

The purpose of this chapter is to provide basic information on the extent of dwelling adaptations by households headed by a person over the age of 65 living in the community and to make initial estimates for the nation as a whole of the demand for specific dwelling modifications.[2,3] The data used are from the 1978 National Annual Housing Survey—a unique data source for this analysis that includes a special set of questions on health status, activity limitations, and dwelling modifications, in addition to the standard questions on the dwelling and its occupants.[4]

As far as we know, this is the first attempt to estimate the demand, as opposed to the need, for such dwelling modifications. Therefore, there is little highly germane previous work. This allows us fairly free range in discussing the implications of the estimates for design and public policy.

Methodology and Findings

Basic Information from the Annual Housing Survey[5]

The information developed here comes from analysis of the 1978 Annual Housing Survey (AHS), an annual survey of about 70,000 dwelling units and their inhabitants conducted by the Bureau of the Census. Unlike the census at the beginning of each decade, this survey includes a vast amount of information on dwelling unit characteristics and conditions of the neighborhood. In 1978 the respondents were also asked about the health status and activity limitations of each household member and about dwelling modifications that were already in place to assist individuals within the household.

The data presented constitute a representative sample of households, so the results can be said to apply to the nation as a whole. Most of the analysis involves households headed by a person age 65 or older, who reported that at least one person had health

---

[2] "In the community" means not living in an institution or in a public housing project.

[3] This paper does not consider the question of the cost-effectiveness of such modifications, which perhaps should be analyzed first. Since many of these modifications are quite inexpensive, their installation, if reasonably targeted on households in need, seems likely.

[4] For a general description of the survey, see Goering (1980).

[5] The material in this and the next section is reported much more extensively in R. Struyk (1982).

TABLE 11.1 Elderly-Headed Households with at Least One Member with a Health Problem or Mobility Limitation

Health Problems	Number of Households (in thousands)	Percent of Households
Arthritis or rheumatism (or chronic stiffness, limb or back deformity, or paralysis)	5,229	60.8
Heart attack or heart problem	2,425	28.2
Asthma, emphysema, or chronic bronchitis (or tuberculosis or other lung problems)	1,677	19.5
Deafness (or serious hearing problem)	1,419	16.5
Blindness (or serious seeing problem)	937	10.9
Stroke (or cerebral palsy)	585	6.8
Missing arms, hands or fingers	86	1.0
Missing legs or feet	60	0.7
Other	215	2.5
Mobility Limitations		
Going up and down stairs	1,419	16.5
Going in and out of home	963	11.2
Getting around in the dwelling	662	7.7
Using bathroom, kitchen equipment	473	5.5
Completely bedridden	112	1.3
Total number of households (in thousands)	8,600[a]	

Source: Annual Housing Survey, 1978.

[a] Figures do not add to total because respondents could list more than one health problem or mobility limitation.

problems or activity limitations. Using the sample estimates to apply to the 15 million elderly-headed households in the United States, we can say that about 8.6 million households fall into this category.

The types of health problems and activity limitations in such households are displayed in Table 11.1. It is important to note that these percentages involve the assessments of the respondents to the survey and are not the diagnoses of medical experts. Furthermore, the form of the questions asked on the survey suggests that the answers are best interpreted as capturing current health and activity status; there was no probing in the survey for the duration of the condition or for whether or not the condition has been episodic in nature. Neither does the survey probe for the severity of any single health or activity problem.

Arthritis is the Major Reported Health Problem

Despite these limitations, the data in Table 11.1 are especially useful because they include all elderly-headed households with at least one member having one or more of the problems indicated. In the upper half of the table, health problems are listed. As the figures indicate, the most frequent problems are arthritis or rheumatism and related problems of stiffness or paralysis, affecting about 5.25 million households or 60.8 percent of all elderly households that report at least one problem or limitation. The second most cited problem relates to heart conditions, including heart attacks (28.2 percent), followed by asthma and lung-related diseases (19.5 percent). Deafness and hearing limitations (16.5 percent) and blindness or seeing limitations (10.9 percent) also constitute sizable portions of the sample. Overall, these relative frequencies of health problems in elderly-headed households are consistent with the results of other studies (for example, National Center for Health Statistics, 1971).

Going Up and Down Stairs Is the Most Frequently Cited Mobility Limitation

The figures on mobility limitations in the lower half of Table 11.1, however, may strike some readers as small. Very few—less than 2 percent—report that a household member is completely bedridden. That translates into about 112,000 households headed by the elderly, or less than 1 percent of all elderly-headed households. The most frequent mobility limitations are going up and down stairs (16.5 percent) and going in and out of the home (11.2 percent). Only 5.5 percent of our sample of households report having difficulty using kitchen or bathroom facilities—representing about 473,000 households in the total population (Fig. 11.1).

FIGURE 11.1 Going up and down stairs is the most frequently cited mobility limitation: Nearly 1½ million elderly-headed households report this problem.

Taken Together Couples Experienced Fewer Mobility Limitations

These data are particularly useful because they also permit analysis of whether or not more than one member of the household is experiencing health problems or activity limitations. In particular, elderly husband-and-wife households are of special interest because of their potential for helping each other if one spouse is capable. The patterns do demonstrate substantial incidences of joint frequencies for health problems but not for mobility limitations. For example, 55 percent of wives of men with arthritis and related problems also have such problems. Yet in only about 5 percent of the cases respondents report that both husband and wife experience mobility limitations of any kind.

Very Few Older People Employ Adaptive Devices in Their Dwelling Unit

These facts substantially increase our understanding of the elderly who live in their own homes rather than in institutions. They provide us with a more detailed picture than before of the patterns of health and mobility within elderly-headed households. But the newest data to come out of this survey are those pertaining to special features of the dwelling units occupied. It is here that we observe very low percentages of the elderly in units with special adaptations, as shown in Table 11.2.

It is important to note that the percentages in this table apply again to units occupied by elderly-headed households with at least one member with a health or mobility problem—a total of 8.6 million households. Thus, for example, 6.6 percent of such dwellings (or about 568,000 households) have extra handrails or grab bars (Fig. 11.2). Only three other features—sink, faucet, and cabinet modifications (1.2 percent), wall socket light switch adaptations (1.2 percent), and a catch-all "other" category (1.9 percent)—appear in more than 1 percent of the units. In all, about 10.3 percent (or about 886,000 units) have at least one such modification. It is also of some interest that in most cases (about 80 percent) households reported their units having only one such special feature. And despite the fact that one might expect urban areas to have more features due to a wider choice in the rental market and more contractors available to install such modifications, the differences between urban and rural units varied widely according to the type of feature involved, and often made no difference at all.

TABLE 11.2 Dwellings Occupied by Elderly-Headed Households with at Least One Member with Health or Mobility Problems

Modification	Number of Dwellings (in thousands)	Percent of Dwellings
Extra handrails or grab bars	568	6.6
Sink, faucet, cabinet adjustments	103	1.2
Wall socket or light switch adaptions	103	1.2
Elevators or lift chairs	69	0.8
Specially equipped telephone	69	0.8
Ramps	60	0.7
Extra wide doors or hallways	60	0.7
Door handles instead of knobs	26	0.3
Bathroom designed for wheelchair use	26	0.3
Flashing lights	26	0.3
Raised lettering or braille	9	0.1
Push bars on doors	9	0.1
Other features	163	1.9
Total number of dwellings with at least one modification	886	10.3
Total number of dwellings (in thousands)	8,600[a]	

Source: Annual Housing Survey, 1978.

[a] Figures do not add to total since not all dwellings have modifications and some report more than one modification.

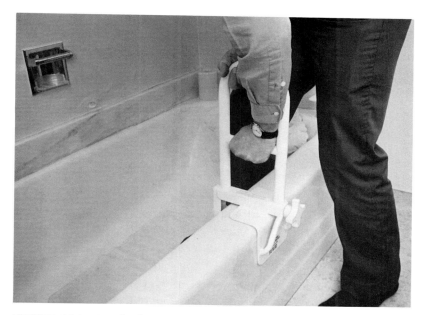

FIGURE 11.2 Handrail and grab bar adaptations are the most commonly cited modification: Nevertheless, only 6.6% of elderly-headed households with at least one member with health or mobility problems have them.

Why Do Some Older People Choose to Adapt and Modify Their Unit?

Although the estimates of mobility limitations in elderly-headed households are lower than might have been expected, the percentage living in units with dwelling modifications is even lower, raising a host of questions about the possible impediments to meeting the demand for such features. The most suitable way to address this question is to examine the factors that cause some elderly households to live in dwellings with special features and impede other households from doing so.

A systematic way of doing this is to construct a theory about which households will have a special feature, and with what probability. The theory employed here is based on economic notions of the demand for such features: in particular, the dependent variables in the analysis are the probabilities that a household of a specified tenure (owner or renter) will live in a unit with a particular special feature—for example, a bathroom equipped for wheelchair use. Based on a series of hypotheses, the likelihood is a function of the household's economic position, the health status and activity limitations of specific members, the potential amount of assistance in the household, the position in the family of the person(s) with the health problem or activity limitations, and the price of special dwelling features.

The model just described was estimated for six separate dwelling modifications, which were chosen in part because they have a relatively high frequency of occurrence and vary in the difficulty and expense necessary to include them in an existing housing unit.

- Extra handrails or grab bars
- Sink, faucet, or cabinet adjustment
- Wall socket or light switch adaptations
- Bathroom designed for wheelchair use
- Specially equipped telephone
- All other features (the final category in Table 11.2)

Those with Health Problems or Activity Limitations Were Examined Separately

A subfile of the full sample described earlier—households headed by a person 65 years of age or older and with at least one member reported to have a health problem or activity limitation—was used for the analysis. The selection was necessitated by the limited coverage of the series used to approximate the price of modifications; in fact, these data were available for only 57 of the 125 metropolitan areas identified on the AHS. (Areas outside of metropolitan areas are identified on the AHS only at the Census region level.) These 57 areas accounted for about 18 percent of the observations on the full sample. After screening on the completeness of the data, a sample of 1,175 observations representing about 2 million households remained: 775 owner-occupants and 400 renters.[6]

Multivariate Techniques Employed Were to Identify the Factors That Influence Changes

The standard statistical technique employed when one has a model with a dichotomous dependent variable is probit or logit analysis. Logit analysis has been used for this estimation. However, all of the multivariate techniques are limited when the absolute number of observations on the event of interest are few. Several of the special features are in only one to four of the units occupied by the sample of households used for estimation. With so few observations—constituting 1 percent or less of all observations—one must judge the statistical results with considerable caution, as the presence of the special feature is almost unique. This circumstance

---

[6] A comparison of the household type and income distributions of households in this sample and the full study population in urban areas revealed no significant differences.

causes the results of the multivariate estimates to be quite sensitive to the exact specification of the model and the statistical technique used in estimations. Consequently, we have complemented the logit analysis by testing for significant differences in the mean values of the independent variables between two subpopulations for each special feature: those households living in a unit with a particular special feature and those who do not. This provides additional information on how to interpret the logit estimates. The observations presented below are based on a combination of the logit model results and the tests of differences in the mean values of the independent variables.

Conclusions

Factors Influencing Dwelling Modifications

The major findings about what factors determine which units are modified are as follows.

Owners Were More Likely to Have Made Modifications than Renters: One expects sharp differences between homeowners and renters. Owners have the legal right to modify their own homes, but renters must generally convince landlords to install special features, or search for a unit that has them. The results do indicate that the specific factors associated with living in a modified unit differ for renters and owners. Still, just knowing information on tenure does not lead to straightforward conclusions about the probability of living in an adapted dwelling.

Income Did Not Determine the Likelihood That a Household Would Have a Unit with Special Features: Surprisingly, household income was generally found not to be a significant determinant of a household having a special feature in its unit. In only one case—bathroom modifications for homeowners—was income significant in explaining its presence. Overall, the results do not suggest that income is a persistent constraint to living in a unit with special features, although the analysis lacked full information on a household's asset position, which may affect whose units are modified.

Severity of Health and Mobility Problems Were Major Determinants of Having a Unit with Special Features: Several dimensions of severity were tested, including the share of family members with such problems and the occurrence of more than one problem per family member. Activity limitations, more than health problems, were especially strong determinants of the likelihood of the presence of modifications. The presence of someone who needs a special appliance and/or personal assistance to get around was also highly predictive. Contrary to expectations, however, difficulty in using the sink, faucets, or cabinets was not related to the presence of special features for handling this problem. Overall, the general picture is one of a strong relationship between severity of need and the presence of special features.

Special Features Are More Likely to Be Present if the Head of the Household Needs Assistance: Surprising results were observed here. Whether or not the impaired person lives alone or is a member of a multiperson household is not especially important in affecting the probability of living in a modified unit. There was, however, evidence that position in the household for those not living alone does matter: special features are more likely to be present if the head needs mechanical assistance or both mechanical and personal assistance than if another member does. Unfortunately, the data do not permit more detailed testing as to why this should be the case.

Households Are Generally Less Likely to Live in Specially Equipped Units if Expensive Modifications Are Needed: More information on the price of features is provided below. In this part of the analysis wage rates were used to estimate the area variation in the price of modifying a unit, because it was assumed that materials costs are generally comparable across geographical areas. The importance of price measured in this way varied, proving significant in some cases and insignificant in others. Generally, however, the higher the "price," the less likely households were to live in specially equipped dwellings.

Eliminating Cost as a Factor, the "Need" for Special Features is Higher

The results just reviewed provide a real test of some of the basic notions about what drives the physical modification of units occupied by the elderly. They can also be used with some strong assumptions to estimate the extent of the "need" for dwelling modifications. The question of need is always a difficult one to address. Some households, for example, might be quite content in providing personal assistance to an impaired member even though a physical modification would substitute for such assistance. Other households with low income may be spending money for modifications that they could otherwise use on other necessities. The question posed here is to what extent "eliminating" income and price constraints, or assuming that personal assistance is no longer available, will change the demand for special features (Fig. 11.3).

Making estimates based on these assumptions results in some interesting findings. We have already noted the low level of current

FIGURE 11.3 Some inexpensive modifications can make daily routines much easier to manage.

features among elderly-headed households. In neither of the estimates just described—eliminating income and price constraints or assuming an end to personal assistance—is the new level of need dramatically greater. On the other hand, the overall level of need found by eliminating income and price constraints alone is on the order of twice the level of the current figures, even though one begins with a very small base.

Roughly 865,000 to a Million Urban and Rural Households "Need" a Special Feature but Do Not Have It

If one assumes for the sake of simplicity that no household demands more than one special feature, these figures imply an increase in the demand by homeowners in urban areas for special features from 12.5 percent of households with an impaired member to about 19 percent. For renters, the increase is from 7 to 11 percent, although in neither case were we able to estimate this for all possible features, due to the insignificance of some of the estimated logit models. One way to compute an upper bound, based generally on these findings, is to assume that roughly an additional 10 percent of all elderly households in urban areas with an impaired member "need" a special feature but do not have it. Since there are about 5.4 million elderly-headed households in urban areas, this constitutes a total of about 540,000 urban households. If rural households are added based on estimates derived for their urban counterparts, we arrive at a total of about 865,000 households.

Since such approximations contain considerable room for error, these figures must be considered rough-and-ready approximations. As a check, it seems wise to calculate an upper limit in another way, by assuming that all households with members having limitations most strongly associated with predicting the presence of special features (that is, going up and down stairs, getting in and out of the unit, needing mechanical and/or personal assistance) need modifications. If we subtract these households that actually have special features, our upper limit estimate is 1.3 million households, rather than 865,000. It seems prudent, considering the pros and cons of either estimate, to use a figure of about 1 million additional elderly-headed households "needing" some special feature.

ACKNOWLEDGMENTS

The author is indebted to a number of people for help in the conduct of this work. Katharine Nelson and Paul Burke of the Department of Housing and Urban Development provided the necessary data tape and guidance about the special features of the Annual Housing Survey in 1978. Debbie Greenstein, M. Powell Lawton, James Zais, and Sandra Newman gave very helpful comments on a draft. Echo de Marets oversaw production of the manuscript.

DESIGN DIRECTIVES

| DESIGN DIRECTIVE **ONE** | *Architects will need to pay more attention to dwelling unit modifications as an aspect of design because the number of older persons with health problems or activity limitations who will need such adaptations is increasing.* |

1. Even though elderly persons are able to adjust to impairments without modifying their dwelling units, it is estimated that a million households that need such features do not have them.

2. The number of persons needing dwelling unit modifications will increase not just because of a growing number of elderly, but also because those over age 75 who are likely to have the most serious physical limitations will grow at about twice the rate of the over age 65 population between now and the year 2010.

3. Policy changes such as a movement away from institutionalization of frail elderly and a cut-back in the federally subsidized development of new specially equipped housing for the elderly will serve to increase the number of older persons whose dwelling units will need modifications.

To help prevent accidents and to make modifications easier, designers should consider specifying features that are relatively low cost in conventional elderly and family housing.

1. Grab bars, adaptations to kitchens, and electrical switches make up the overwhelming majority of modifications made to existing units. Even though their general cost is low, specifying them in the construction of new housing will assure their availability and promote their acceptance.

Cost minimizing design solutions need to be developed for a variety of standard cases and promulgated widely to both contractors and the elderly.

1. The cost of adapting a bathroom and a kitchen of an efficiency apartment or a single-family residence for use by the handicapped is high (see Table 11.3) and can involve major changes (see Fig. 11.4). In 1981 prices, for example, modifications designed by experts for a kitchen in a single-family house, cost about $1850.

2. The high cost of installing special equipment and adapting spaces affects the demand for special features and may discourage their use. Hence, more economical methods (for example, prefabricated kitchen counter modules) that are readily available may allow those impaired elderly who need major modifications greater opportunity to have their needs met.

TABLE 11.3 Estimated Cost of Providing Selected Special Features in Existing and New Structures[a]

Unit Type and Feature	Renovation	New Construction (added cost)
Single-Family Home		
Bathroom adapted	$1,346	$ 416
(grab bars only)[b]	(57)	(122)
Kitchen adapted	1,858	254
Multifamily High-Rise (Efficiency)		
Bathroom adapted	$2,643	410
(Grab bars only)	(116)	(142)
Kitchen adapted	995	119

Source: Schroeder and Steinfeld (1979).

[a] Costs as of 1981; updated by author from 1975 figures using the Commerce Department's Composite Construction Price Index.
[b] Includes reinforcement.

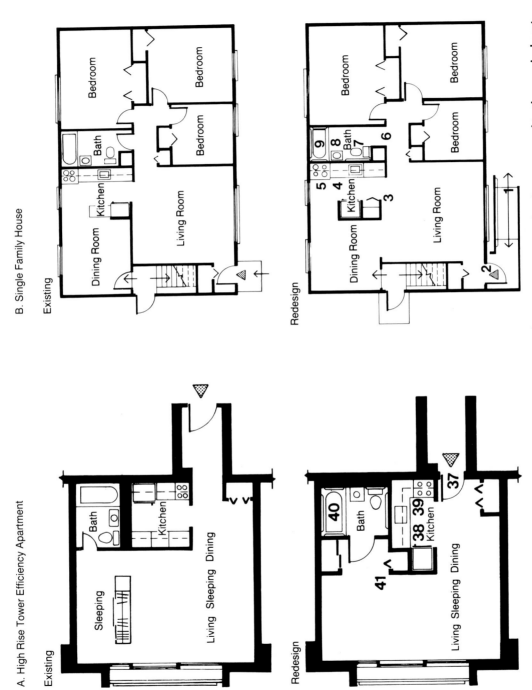

B. Single Family House

Existing

Redesign

A. High Rise Tower Efficiency Apartment

Existing

Redesign

FIGURE 11.4 Dwelling renovation for accessibility: Modifications to existing units are costly when compared to the marginal cost increase of designing adaptable units from the beginning.

Notes to Figure 11.4

Non-Compliance	Compliance Work	High-Rise Efficiency		Single-Family House	
		Work Required	Reference # on Drawing	Work Required	Reference # on Drawing
Entry inaccessible	Provide wider door with adequate clearance at latch side.	X	37	X	
	Construct ramp; install lever-type door hardware; rehang front door.			X	1,2
Kitchen unusable	Adaptable.				
	Provide adjustable mix/sink work areas; provide self-cleaning oven; lower wall cabinets.	X	38,39	X	4,5
	Remove and relocate walls.			X	3
Bathroom unusable	Grab bars at WC and bathtub.	X		X	7
	Install hand-held shower, bathtub seat, single lever faucet in lavatory and drain insulation.	X	40	X	8
	Bifold closet door.	X	41	X	9
	Make entry accessible; relocate sink and medicine cabinet.			X	6
Bedroom unusable	Install wider doors to two rooms; outfit closet in one room.			X	

Source: Schroeder and Steinfeld (1978), pp. 26–27, 62–63.

POLICY CONSIDERATIONS

POLICY CONSIDERATION
ONE

Modification programs should be locally based.

Given the relatively modest number of households nationally that may need help with attaining specially adapted housing, the diversity of their needs, and their geographic dispersion, there is little reason to launch a major federal initiative. Instead, it is more appropriate to create local programs, perhaps supported through broad federal mechanisms such as Community Development Block Grants (CDBG). This does not mean that current federal activity, such as the inclusion of a small number of specially equipped units in any additional subsidized new construction projects, should be discontinued.[7]

The presumption is that local agencies will be better equipped to identify the comparatively small number of households needing help and to provide the appropriate type of assistance.

POLICY CONSIDERATION
TWO

Modification programs should be targeted to those older persons who have activity limitations (for example, those who need personal assistance to get about) and/or who live alone.

Identifying those likely to be in greatest need can be very expensive; however, simply serving those who ask for help can mean overlooking those most in need. Those households with members who need mechanical or personal assistance to get around are much more likely to demand special features than others who are more mobile. The former clearly need to be served first. Other measures of activity limitations generally identified those demanding special features better than health questions. Moreover, there is an interaction between living alone and activity limitations. Hence, in screening applicants or potential applicants, a few questions on activity limitations and their severity may be especially effective.

---

[7] The seeming unimportance of income as a condition for living in a unit with a badly needed special feature may well be the result of the presence of such units and of the repair/improvement programs supported by CDBG funds and Title III (Older Americans Act) and Title XX (Social Security) funds. For a description of the use of these funds for housing, see Struyk-Soldo, chapter 8. There is, however, no comprehensive accounting of the number of units assisted with this type of dwelling modification with these funds.

The fact that the income level of the household was not found to be very important suggests that, in many instances, facilitating services is more important than simple cash in getting modifications made. In the case of renters dealing with a landlord to have minor changes made to a unit (for example, a couple of grab bars in the bathroom) may be effective. In some instances, the best course may simply be for an agency to make the changes itself. For larger features—such as bathrooms large enough for wheelchair use—help with finding a unit is needed. After the agency has given some concrete suggestions, it is important for children and other relatives to help in this process.

For homeowners, the provision of in-kind services may well make sense for the installation of small features, since it may cost little more than providing help in locating a handyperson to do the work. For larger modifications, help in defining what exactly needs to be done and finding a contractor may be as important as cash. As a general concern, economic determinants are too commonly assumed to impede housing adjustments: if the family has adjusted to an activity limitation without installing special features, it should not be pressed to accept them; where they are wanted and needed, the appropriate level of help in securing them—geared to the real impediment—should be provided.

HOME MODIFICATIONS
Improvements That Extend Independence

*Jon Pynoos, Evelyn Cohen, Linda Davis,
and Sharmalee Bernhardt*

T here has been relatively little research on the importance of the designed environment in maintaining the elderly's independent functioning in existing housing, where over 90 percent of this population lives (Faletti, 1983). Instead, most research has been focused on purposefully built housing and institutional settings for seniors which house approximately only 8–9 percent of the elderly population (Lawton, 1979; Howell, 1980; Koncelik, 1976).

Studies have shown clearly that the older population prefers and attempts to live independently in housing of their own choice as long as possible (Struyk and Soldo, 1980; Lawton, 1980). The chronic illness and functional impairment that often accompany advanced age make that goal difficult for many older persons to realize. According to one study (Brotman, 1981), such problems limit the daily activities of about 50 percent of all people 65 and over. Furthermore, with the growth of the population age 75 and over, it is estimated that the size of the chronically impaired population will increase significantly (Brotman, 1981; Harris, 1978). While governmental policies are increasingly directed toward maintaining the older person within the community, professionals have only recently begun to view the existing housing environment as an important part of the support system necessary to achieve these goals.

Given the emphasis on new construction, it is not surprising that little attention has been paid to how modification of the existing environment and the introduction of simple technology or home management skills might enhance the level of the older person's functioning (Faletti, 1981). Similarly, information has not been systematically collected on ways in which activities or the environment can be adapted in order to minimize disabilities, promote safety, or support activities of daily living. Traditionally, it is not until a person is severely disabled or handicapped that an occupational therapist or home health care professional is called in to adapt the home and tasks to meet the specific needs of the patient. Most older people are not specifically disabled and do not view themselves as functionally impaired, yet many may experience problems with activities of daily living; it is believed that they would benefit from a program geared to their specific needs in their existing environment (Lawton, 1980; Hiatt, 1983).

Related Research

Environment and Functional Behavior

Lawton and Nahemow (1973) point to the negative effects that result from an imbalance between the demands of the environment and the functioning level of the individual. Most housing in which older persons live was designed and planned for younger, healthier people and does not facilitate independence among the elderly. The importance of an appropriate "fit" between a person and his surroundings may be a key factor in preventing withdrawal from activities, premature institutionalization, accidents, and even death (Lawton, 1980). Lipman (1968) suggests that independence for the elderly and their ability to maintain an autonomous status will require a reduction of environmental demands and raising of otherwise deficient resources (for example, health, income, and education).

Accidents and Accident Prevention

Research indicates that the elderly not only incur a high rate of accidents but suffer more than twice the amount of resulting deaths compared to other age groups (the Buffalo Organization for Social and Technological Innovation, Inc. [BOSTI], 1982). Most accidents among the elderly occur in the home; home accidents are the fifth leading cause of death for persons 65 and over (National Safety Council, 1980). Falls comprise two-thirds of the over 10,000 fatalities that occur each year among the elderly. Far more suffer from disabling injuries as a result of falls. The U.S. Public Health Service (1980) has estimated that two-thirds of deaths due to falls which have an environmental component are potentially preventable.

Falls Are a Major Source of Accidents Among Older People: Fall-related research (Sheldon, 1960; Clark, 1968; Gray, 1966; Rubenstein, 1983) suggests that, by identifying and eliminating environmental risks in the home, one-quarter to one-half of fall-related accidents could be prevented. A few of the major design factors associated with falls in the home include unsecured area rugs, lack of railings on stairs, lack of grab bars for bathtubs and showers, poor lighting, low beds and toilets, and uneven floor surfaces and stairs (Fig. 12.1). For example, in an analysis of the natural history of falls in 500 aged persons, Sheldon (1960) found that many falls occur on staircases due to missing the last step or group of steps, prematurely thinking that the bottom has been reached. Poorly designed or inadequate handrails, poor lighting (particularly on landings), and the steepness of stairs were found to be major contributing factors in many fall-related accidents. Sheldon also pinpoints other environmental hazards in the home, such as the increasing tendency to accumulate household items with age, which often results in overly cluttered rooms.

In research done by Archea, Collins, and Stahl (1979) for the National Bureau of Standards on causes of residential stair accidents, findings indicate that accidents occurred more frequently on stairs where the first few treads were different from the remainder of the flight and when the design of the stairs was visually distracting or deceptive. While the presence of handrails was not a direct factor in reducing accidents, their importance was emphasized in compensating for the older person's increased diffi-

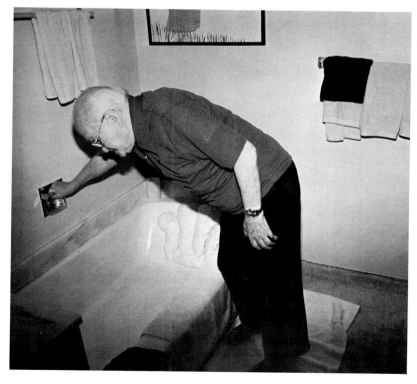

FIGURE 12.1 Getting in and out of the tub is dangerous without adequate supports.

culty and reluctance in maneuvering stairs and was instrumental in reducing the severity of accidents.

Because of changes in visual acuity, the older person has increased vulnerability in maneuvering stairs safely. A major impediment is in perceiving each tread edge. Three dimensional textures or bold, geometric patterns on floor coverings of stairs were found to cause visual confusion and distraction, both of which are major factors in fall-related accidents among elderly. Further, the older person experiences much greater light scatter within the eye as well as a decreased ability to adapt to rapid lighting changes (Weale, 1963). When changes in illumination between the stairs and their immediate surroundings are not gradual, the person may have difficulty in adapting to the general lighting conditions before negotiating stairs, thereby increasing the risk of a fall.

While elderly have fewer stair accidents per capita than people in other age groups, due mainly to their avoidance of steps when possible, they suffer a higher incidence of serious injuries. Over 85 percent of all deaths attributed to stair accidents occur in this age population. Archea et al. (1979) contend that when the figures are adjusted to reflect the less frequent use of stairs by older individuals, findings reveal that they have far more accidents per use than any other age group. The most serious accidents were found to occur in descent.

Lucht (1971) found that the majority of elderly individuals injure themselves in living rooms, with the next most frequent areas being stairs, halls, bedrooms, kitchens, and bathrooms, respectively. Research indicates that elderly, frail women with limited mobility are most at risk from falls (Overstall, 1978). Lucht (1971) found the incidence of falls highest among widows, widowers, and divorcees.

Burns Are the Second Most Common Injury Among the Elderly: The risk of burn injury and mortality increases markedly after age 70, with 93 percent of these accidents occurring in the home (National Burn Information Exchange [NBIE], 1983). Cooking, smoking, the use of matches, and bathing provide the greatest risks. One out of every ten elderly burn victims are burned as a result of bathing in water that is too hot. Providing clearly marked and visible faucet regulators and turning down hot water heaters to 120 degrees are two simple interventions that could prevent a fatal injury from occurring. NBIE estimates that one-half of the burns that occur each year could be prevented through education and design intervention.

Hazardous Environments/Products for the Elderly

In research conducted for the Administration on Aging on accidents and aging, the Buffalo Organization for Social and Technological Innovation, Inc., (1982) identified 49 products and en-

FIGURE 12.2 Bending down to open an oven or broiler is frequently a problem reported by older persons.

vironmental categories that were the most hazardous and costly for elderly people. These products were selected from over 1,000 listed in the National Electronic Injury Surveillance System (NEISS), which contains computerized data on over 14,000 cases recording the number and severity of injuries among persons 55 and older. In-depth investigations, or IDIs, which are narrative detailed descriptions of accidents with selected consumer products and environments, were read and analyzed to select the 49 categories used in the study.

Floors/flooring materials and stairs/steps constituted the two most hazardous product categories and accounted for 41 percent of all injuries. It is not clear what comprises the floors and flooring materials category, as "rugs and carpets" fall into another product category. In developing a hazard scenario, the study cites a change in flooring surface, where a victim might slip or stick while moving from one surface to another, as an example of a type of accident that would involve "floor or flooring materials." While rankings varied with age, when ranked by accident cost these same two items ranked first and second. As one got older, the average severity of the accident increased. The study also focused on the changes and reduced capabilities among the elderly, which may cause accident-producing misfits between the person and his or her environment and products. Sixty-four percent of the accidents occurred in the home. The BOSTI (1982) study estimated that the total number of injuries associated with products in the home was 2.63 times the number of other injuries treated in emergency rooms. Those products associated with the most serious injuries were fire related, such as cigarettes, matches, and stoves (Fig. 12.2).

Elderly Women, Because of Their Involvement in Household Duties, Are More Likely to Suffer Accidents at Home: Droller (1955) found that elderly women were at a substantially higher risk from accidents in the home than men, due mainly to greater activity in household occupations, which can lead to falls. This was substantiated in the BOSTI (1982) study where injuries were associated with traditional gender-related activities and products. For example, while both men and women have an equal incidence of accidents with bathtubs and showers, women suffer five times as many accidents with stepstools. They have a much greater likelihood of accidents with chairs, rugs, carpets, floors, stairs, and steps. As would be expected, men suffer five times as many accidents with lawn mowers and tools such as ladders, nails, and chain saws.

As two important countermeasures in preventing accidents, Haddon (1980) and Baker (1975) point to the requirements of changing the environment and making tasks less demanding. Hogue (1981) indicates that the source in all injuries is energy exchange and that the process of dealing with this in the environment depends on two factors: the performance level of the person and the task demands involved in using the energy. When energy dissipation exceeds human thresholds, an injury is likely to occur.

What these studies indicate is the need to not only evaluate the home for safety but also to develop ways in which we can intervene to make daily tasks easier for the older, frailer person to perform.

Introducing Technology into the Home to Promote Functioning

Faletti (1981, 1984) has carried out considerable research on the design needs of the normal elderly in the home. He differentiates between the interventions utilized by the occupational therapist in both accommodating the person with a specific disability and the necessary adaptations to functional impairment in activities of daily living normally associated with advancing age. The impairments that normally occur in old age are often gradual, multiple reductions in the ability to carry out activities safely. These impairments may be combined with several disabilities or none at all. Techniques aimed at compensatory abilities, as is the case with specific handicaps at all ages, may not be appropriate for the older person. More importantly, older adults experiencing problems with daily living may not view themselves as specifically handicapped or disabled and may be less likely to accept the need for obvious adaptive or therapeutic technologies (Faletti, 1984). While morale may be positively influenced by an environment that facilitates independent functioning, older adults who do not identify with their infirmities may deny their own limitations, thereby increasing the risk of an accident (Lucht, 1971).

Faletti (1981) suggests that technology should not be equated with complexity. The development of a clear understanding of what is needed to support and interface the older person with his or her existing environment will depend upon realistic cost factors and practical technology that is appropriate and acceptable in other age markets.

Safety Education Programs for the Elderly

Gyrfe, Amies, and Ashley (1977), Backett (1965), and Hiatt (1983) suggest that one of the remedial measures to reduce accidents in the home may be through educational programs identifying hazard areas. Hiatt (1983) recommends the development of self-help groups to pinpoint ways in which the environment can be better organized and used to the advantage of the older person. While an educational program might be expected for a younger person who is impaired, objectives for older people stress general social needs and are less directed toward education or change. Faletti (1984) suggests that emphasis should not focus on the impairments as characteristics of the person but, rather, as characteristics of the environment.

Governmental policies are directed toward maintaining the older person within the community. However, emphasis has been on providing a person to carry out daily tasks for the resident rather than on exploring education, the introduction of technology, or other design modifications, which may enable the resident to function independently.

Most educational programs directed toward the elderly have consisted of safety checklists that the older person self-administers at his or her option (for example, the Easter Seal Foundation Checklist). Some checklists also include tips on safe behavior (for example, 58 Do's and Don'ts on Safety). Specialized booklets with tips for easer living or ways in which people with specific disabilities (arthritis, poor vision) can function more effectively in the home are also available to the general public (for example, through the Arthritis Foundation or the American Foundation for the Blind). However, there are no studies that indicate the effectiveness of this informal educational approach or to what extent people make changes in their behavior or homes based on this information.

In-Home Assessment Instruments

The most common in-home assessment instruments are those utilized by home care professionals, such as home economists or occupational therapists. These are related to improving the person's ability to carry out basic activities of daily living, often based on a specific disability. There is limited consistency among these in-

FIGURE 12.3 Loose wires are often cited by professionals as a potential danger.

struments and no systematic approach. Each agency develops its own model of evaluation and none has been validated for either its reliability or validity.

Large surveys, like the National Health Interview Survey, have been conducted to determine the characteristics of the physical environments in which the elderly live and to determine the characteristic functional abilities of the elderly. These are often long and require a subjective judgment on the adequacy of the environment and one's physical ability that may be inconsistent with more objective assessments. Home repair agencies are not consistent in utilizing home assessment instruments prior to providing repair services. The use of a checklist or evaluation form is determined by the particular agency involved.

Further, there is no systematic program to educate professionals assessing the needs of the elderly or handymen in reference to changing physical needs of the older residents in the home. While some written educational material may be provided in flyers, education is not the primary function of such agencies. Repairs or modifications are often based on the older individual's self-assessment of his or her home and are influenced by what the service agency provides. Unsafe areas may be overlooked (for example, an unsecured rug or loose wires—see Figure 12.3) as the focus is not on the overall safety and functioning of the older person but rather on providing products or services—such as installing locks, railings, and grab bars—to qualified residents. In addition, follow-up to determine effectiveness is not consistent among agencies.

Home Repair Programs

Struyk (see Chapter 11 in this volume) found fewer modifications exist in elderly housing than would be expected. Out of 8.5 million elderly households that reported at least one member as having a health impairment or mobility limitation, only 10 percent had modified their home; the majority of the changes were of the grab bar and railing variety. The main motivation in putting in a modification was not based on economics or whether one lived in a home or apartment, but rather on whether or not the head of the household was disabled and the severity of the physical limitation. Struyk and Zais (1982) found that those with activity limitations were more likely to make modifications than those with health problems.

Mayer and Lee (1980) and Curtin, Newman, and Chen (1981) found that those elderly living alone, particularly elderly women, were in greatest need of repairs or modifications. Even though couples or one member of a couple might also have experienced problems in the home, their homes were negatively associated with repairs as the assistance of another person seems to have compensated for deficits.

Identifying Repair Requirements Is a Critical Concern: Research indicates that the need for technical assistance and resources in identifying actual repair and improvement requirements are the most important aspects of a successful home repair program (for example, dealing with landlords to get changes made or locating a handyman). This seems particularly true for elderly, female-headed households who suffer more than half of elderly housing inadequacies (Mayer and Lee, 1980).

Most studies of home repair programs have concentrated on how efficiently services were delivered and the impact of the programs in maintaining and upgrading the housing stock. Questions left unanswered regard how best to provide information and resources, encourage participation, and combat resistance to seeking government aid. Overcoming suspicion in a direct door-to-door approach is a particular problem for many elderly residents, and especially so for women living alone (Mayer and Lee, 1980).

Most research has been mainly aimed at identifying traditional barrier-free modifications within the home (see Steinfield, Chapter 13 in this volume). There has been little information collected on how people may be informally modifying their homes, tasks, or behavior to compensate for reduced strength or physical/cognitive impairments. There is a need to identify the less traditional and more informal changes that older people make, both positive and negative, in order to more effectively develop safety and functioning programs that will be integrated successfully in the community. For example, research on the effectiveness of home repair programs has specifically focused on formal repairs and modifications (such as fixing stairs and installing grab bars) and has not examined the informal modifications (such as rearranging the household for easier access) or the behavioral changes (such as taking a sponge bath rather than using a bathtub) that people may be employing to compensate for activity limitations.

Pilot Programs: Safety and Intervention in the Home

The most recent and inclusive pilot program directed toward providing older people with safety information on hazards in the home as well as the resources to make some modifications and repairs was conducted by the U.S. Product Safety Commission (1984) through funding from the National Council of Older Americans. In this study, trained older citizens were used as safety specialists to deliver the information directly to older persons in their homes while a comparative group received safety checklists by mail and self-administered them. Over 1,000 homes were involved in both Greenbay, Wisconsin, and Philadelphia, Pennsylvania. In Philadelphia, particularly significant problems were directed to public agencies to provide modifications and repairs.

While the program contributed knowledge about safety as well as safety-related changes (one-third of the people modified their environment afterwards), the evaluation raised several issues:

1. Participation in the program was not as wide as expected, and reluctance to become involved with governmental programs that reflected on one's sense of independence was an issue for a segment of the population.
2. The program experienced some difficulties in identifying and reaching the elderly population most in need of this service.
3. While the mail assessment that was self-administered was as effective as the in-home assessment done by the safety specialist, an outreach component that could be a part of the in-home assessment was needed.
4. Safety information needs to be coupled with concrete resources or services, many of which are available in local stores, in catalogs, or in the community. These need to be identified for this population.
5. The design of the checklist was a problem, and a variety of alterations were made to simplify the assessment procedure. The use of other educational tools in developing safety programs for the elderly is called for, including visual aids and the use of sites that are deemed safe and comfortable.

In addition to these issues, it is important to note the specific parameters of the project, which focused on environmental safety rather than on a more broad-based functional approach.

Summary

There is ample evidence that the elderly prefer to live independently for as long as possible. However, chronic illnesses and associated disabilities often make this difficult. In addition, there are older individuals who may not have a specific disability or do not view themselves as having any type of functional impairment but the environmental demands of their homes are such that some assistance becomes necessary in order to maintain an independent lifestyle or to avoid accidents from environmental risks. Several approaches have been tried in order to identify environmental problems, such as checklists and other assessment instruments, but they are not consistently used. Similarly, home repair agencies provide some modifications upon request, but the older person must generally be aware of the need to have a specific change made. Educational programs seem to be an essential ingredient in conveying this information, and researchers have addressed this issue. However, an area of major interest that has received minimal attention concerns the types of informal modifications older persons make on their own and what types of alterations are likely to be effective.

Methodology and Data Analysis

Building upon the perspective discussed above, a pilot project was carried out at the Andrus Gerontology Center in which focus groups from three service programs were convened to discuss the following issues:

1. What are the most common problems you see in the homes of elderly clients?
2. What types of modifications do clients make on their own initiative?
3. What, if any, modifications do you suggest to elderly clients?
4. Do older clients accept modifications in their homes?
5. Are there modifications that you would like to make as an assessor but are unable to?
6. How effective are the modifications that are made?
7. What is involved in a successful home assessment?

In addition, assessment instruments were obtained from over two dozen agencies and organizations. These were reviewed to determine the items covered in each instrument and the approach used to gather information. Further, several groups of older persons met with the researchers to discuss the problems they encounter and the modifications they make in their own homes.

The focus groups consisted of representatives from a visiting nurses' association, a state-wide case management program, and an outpatient program for a hospital. All focus-group participants worked with the frail elderly, with an emphasis on rehabilitation through various types of therapy. Nurses, social workers, physical therapists, and occupational therapists were among the disciplines included in each focus group.

Three members of the research team attended these sessions. Two facilitated the group discussion with probes, and the third recorded the answers from participants on a wall-mounted matrix. Participants were encouraged to contribute in a brain-storming manner. This approach was used to gather a large amount of information quickly and to provide an opportunity for the participants to comment on the problems and solutions mentioned by others. This method also served to remind participants of a problem or solution they may have seen but which did not immediately come to mind until someone else mentioned a related item.

Using a wall-mounted matrix enabled participants to remember what others said and also allowed them to spontaneously respond without being concerned about changing the subject. The information was later transferred from the matrix to concise lists of problems and solutions found in clients' homes. Of the seven questions, 4–7 did not result in information that could be posted on a matrix. The issues were discussed and the session was tape recorded so that a list could be formulated later. An example of

TABLE 12.1 What Are the Most Common Problems You See in the Homes of Elderly Clients?

	Bathing	Food Preparation	Dressing	Grooming	Toileting	Other
Kitchen		No counter space Cabinets too high to reach Possibility of fires/burns from stove burners Hinges on wrong side of oven door, refrigerator Controls on stove are at the back so person has to reach over burners Bending down and opening oven/broiler				
Bathroom	Thresholds or any change in surface Getting on and off toilet Getting in/out of tub Wheelchair can't get in bathroom Slippery rugs Clutter Too many medicines Tub/sink not oriented for stroke patients					
Living Room						Soft chairs Broken chair Clutter Too many wires Not enough outlets Too much furniture
Bedroom			Closets Arrangement of clothing and space is poor Bed height is too low, too soft Can't open closets			Too cold Too dark Bed too high or low
Other						Electric cords Torn carpets Locks don't work Stuck windows Poor lighting No elevator

the common problems identified by one group of service providers is indicated in Table 12.1, which attempted to categorize problems in terms of activities of daily living and the rooms in which such activities usually took place. This proved to have some limitations since some problems were found throughout the home and/or they were not related to any of the specified activities of daily living. For example, a common problem was poor lighting but reading, which requires good light, was not listed as an activity. Typical responses to questions 2 and 3 are illustrated on Tables 12.2 and 12.3. These matrices present various types of modifications that older persons were reported to make on their own and modifications professionals often recommend.

Typology of Home Modifications

Modifications were classified into five categories intended to cover the variety of ways in which older persons might either adapt to their environment or change the environment itself to meet their needs. These categories were: structural changes, special equipment, assistive devices, material adjustments, and behavioral changes. Structural modifications are changes made to the original structure of the house itself or its component parts, such as lowering cabinets or widening door frames. Special equipment, on the other hand, generally included items that are attached to the existing structure, such as grab bars or new handrails. Assistive devices, which include walkers and reachers, refer to items that are generally mobile in nature in that the person manipulates them in order to better carry out activities. Material adjustments refer to alterations in the location of home furnishings, such as moving furniture or throw rugs. And finally, behavior modifications connote changes made in either the location or the way in which older persons might carry out activities, such as taking a sponge bath near the sink rather than soaking in a tub.

Findings

The Most Common Problems

The three focus groups consistently mentioned clutter, scatter rugs, electric cords, phone cords, and lighting as problems throughout the house and particularly in the living room. Access to shelves in the kitchen was a concern, and narrow hallways and entrances made mobility with a wheelchair or walker difficult. Low ovens and broilers presented problems for those elderly who had difficulty bending. The bathroom was cited as the room with the most problems, especially in regard to bathing. Clients had difficulty getting in and out of the tub and were afraid of falling or being burned by scalding water. Finally, the bedroom was usually free of problems except for the height and firmness of the bed.

TABLE 12.2 What Types of Modifications Do People Make on Their Own Initiative?

	Structural Changes	Special Equipment	Assistive Devices	Material Adjustments	Behavioral Changes	Other
Kitchen (Cooking)		Electric can openers Few microwaves purchased (if any)	Hot plates/ toaster ovens	Equipment easily accessible Not using shelves or cabinets Horizontal storage of food	Don't use oven Simplify cooking and food preparation Use T.V. dinners, can goods without heating Eat in another room	
Bathroom (Toileting, Grooming)		Grab bar—rare Bath bench—rare Hand-held shower	Urinal, potty, bedpan	Soap holders, Organizers Plastic container to rinse hair after shampoo	Sponge bath No bath Move medications to kitchen Bathe in kitchen because counter is higher	
Living Room (Visiting, Leisure)	Locks Weatherizing changes	Remote control for TV 45% of clients have a TV, 50% B/W Adjustable sound of telephone 1 Button calls phone # 1 cordless phone Stairlift to 2nd flr.	Purchase small bed for living room Magnifying glass Large numbers on phone Push button phones	Bed is moved from bedroom to living or dining room Dining room table becomes horizontal storage, so does coffee table	Sleep in couch Live in this room only Medication moved here	
Bedroom (Sleeping, Dressing)		Hospital bed Special light to increase light	Use shoe horn Use flashlight	Bed moved to make room for commode Move furniture to accommodate wheelchair Pathways between junk or furniture (fire hazard) Live out of suitcase Lower or raise beds	Sleep in L.R. intermittently or permanently Don't change clothes as frequently Don't dress in street clothes	
Other						

TABLE 12.3 What Types of Modifications Do You Suggest to Elderly Clients?

	Structural Changes	Special Equipment	Assistive Devices	Material Adjustments	Behavioral Changes	Other
Kitchen (Cooking)		Smoke alarms Blender for soft diet foods Toaster oven Small refrigerator on counter or table	Jar opener/reacher special spoons/eating devices Carts to transport food in preparation process Reachers	Move dining room chairs with arms to kitchen for more support	Use an aide to help in meal preparation Hire an aide Education about food poisoning Diet supplement	
Bathroom (Toileting, Grooming)	Take door off frame Widen doorway	Safety rails Toilet seat Use transfer bench Shower head with flexible hose	Walker in bathroom to help wheelchair bound client reach the toilet Put a chair in the bathroom	Remove bath mats	Assistance in bathroom for shower or bath	
Living Room (Visiting, Leisure)		Life line-emergency response unit Install a phone	Remote control for T.V.	Get rid of throw rugs	Put some items away (clutter is #1 problem) Throw away junk (have to be careful, sensitive emotional area) Encourage use of walkers Hire aide to clean	
Bedroom (Sleeping, Dressing)		Hospital beds Fans Portable heaters Trapeze device Side rails on bed	Overbed table for bedridden clients Install a phone	Bedside commode Special pillows Incontinent supplies Window repair Move bed to accommodate commode Lower or raise bed Put clothes in accessible location	Encourage client to change clothes Sleep in living room Make more central space and access to get out in case of fire	
Other	Ramps Outdoor stair railings	Security devices outside				

Modifications Clients Made on Their Own Initiative

A statement made at one focus group session provides a synopsis of our findings: "A high concentration of people change their behavior to adapt to the environment, rather than adapting the environment to meet the changes that come with aging. They don't realize they can change the environment so they automatically compensate." Some examples of compensating include taking sponge baths instead of using the tub and wearing loose-fitting clothing that is easily put on and taken off. Many clients were reported to have created a control center in their living room composed of an easy chair, television, telephone, and a small table so as to have everything in easy reach. This control center often became a place where clients also slept or napped. Another common behavioral change was to stop cooking or to fix meals that were easier to prepare. Frozen foods were common, and many clients used a toaster oven.

Some material adjustments were also made. Clients sometimes added cushions to raise the height of chairs or pieces of wood to

FIGURE 12.4   One simple but effective cabinet adjustment is to place a shelf between the counter top and the bottom edge of upper cabinet. Note also the toaster oven used by many elderly because of its convenience and low energy use.

raise the bed or make it more firm. In the kitchen and bathroom, clients often reorganized items, putting the most frequently used items on counter tops or low shelves within easy reach (Fig. 12.4). Special equipment such as grab bars was rarely found unless the client had received prior assistance from other agencies. However, assistive devices—such as bath benches, remote control for the television, and toaster ovens—were often found in people's homes.

Modifications Professionals Suggested

The predominant modifications professionals suggested were either material adjustments or behavioral in nature, such as removing throw rugs and planning activities to conserve energy. They also recommended that older persons remove the clutter, make a pathway for ambulation, and reorganize possessions so as to be able to reach what was needed frequently and to store items less often in use. Special equipment such as grab bars, transfer benches, and toilet-seat risers were also frequently recommended. Suggested assistive devices included a cart that could be used as a mobility aid when transporting items and a help in meal preparation.

Acceptance of Modifications by Older Persons

A central hypothesis supported by the focus group participants was the underlying theme that the client's perceptions and desires must be considered for modifications to be successful. If elderly persons did not recognize the need for a piece of equipment, and did not have an active role in choosing solutions to the problems that an assessment revealed, clients were less likely to use the modifications. Related issues included the other person's view of their physical disabilities and the sentimental value they attached to various items.

Focus group members reported that it was difficult to convince some older persons that they needed to make a change; rather, they had to realize it themselves. Some older persons would not give up their independence or their lifestyle, including clutter and throw rugs, until they accepted the fact that something had to change or they would have to leave their home. Safety was not reported to be a motivator in such situations, although several service providers were able to prove the value of some modifications by insisting on their installation and then enabling the client to experience greater mobility because of the special equipment or assistive device.

Once the client was willing to have a modification made, another issue arose. Older individuals often reported to have decided on their own what specific type of modification was best, sometimes based on a neighbor's experience. In such situations clients sometimes became quite determined and resistant to the use of any other type of modification, again raising the issue of client choice and control. Specific changes that were often met with resistance included the installation of grab bars, the removal of throw rugs, and the cleaning up or rearranging of clutter. Service providers reported that they first worked to determine the client's preferences and priorities and then to find a plausible solution.

Modifications Assessors Would Like to Make and Constraints

The discussion centered on the constraints faced by service providers. A lack of funding was found to be a primary reason for not suggesting some modifications. Other reasons included the client's perception of certain modifications, the family's view, and the availability of someone to do the actual work. Another constraint was reluctance to spend money on someone else's apartment building. In many situations service providers preferred to provide a removable item that clients could take with them if they moved.

The specific items mentioned as most difficult to provide were mainly structural. There was a desire to widen doorways, provide an open area under the kitchen sink, lower kitchen counters and cabinets, install railings, and change flooring from thick carpeting to something equally aesthetic but more functional.

Effectiveness of Modifications

The most effective modifications from the standpoint of being used and reducing injury or the incidence of problems were reported to be bath benches, transfer benches, hand-held showers, grab bars, toilet-seat risers, railings, doorless entranceways, a cart for the kitchen, and remote control for the television. However, little was known regarding the use of many modifications. For example, some clients were reported not to use items such as grab bars after they had been installed. Other clients may have put throw rugs back on the floor or put a walker in the closet after the therapist or service provider left. If recommended items were used as requested by the service provider, most modifications appeared to be effective.

Components of a Successful Home Assessment

There was tremendous variability in the assessment methodology used by focus group participants, even within the same agency. Recommendations included gaining general information first, involving the client and family, and observing the client or contacting family members to verify responses given about functional abilities.

Some service providers focused on specific rooms that are known to be dangerous, while others tried to determine the concerns of the client first and then assess only those areas in which a problem seemed to exist.

The use of checklists seems to be a common form of assessment. However, several providers recommended letting the client talk about general concerns rather than following a precise question-answer format. One focus group member advocated asking clients what they would like to be doing but are unable to do currently, and whether the inability is because of a physical limitation, the environment, or a combination of both. From this functional base, it might be possible to identify major concerns and the framework for possible solutions.

Conclusions

The focus group discussions were very informative, and this methodology seemed to be well-suited for gathering the information desired. There were some difficulties in that participants were not always clear as to which category was best for specified modifications, and the matrices used did not include some areas of the home that proved worthy of consideration—namely hallways, entrances, and stairwells. The focus group participants also raised some issues that should be addressed in designing future studies. These include the difficulties and unique problems faced by chronic versus acute-care clients, high- versus low-crime area residents, the type of dwelling (for example, one-room apartments, mobile homes, or privately owned homes in wealthy areas), the socio-economic status of clients, depression and affect as it relates to motivation and the acceptance of modifications, cultural impacts on individual preferences, and how clutter may relate to the desire for a locus of control.

In spite of the apparent limitations of a small study done on a particular population of the more frail elderly, several conclusions emerge:

1. The fit of the home environment to the functional capacity of older persons can be extremely important in the lives of the elderly; yet this area has generally been overlooked.
2. Older persons do make some adaptations on their own. Although such modifications tend to focus on the behavioral end of the spectrum in terms of limiting activities and creating control centers, older persons also have made other changes such as using remote control television and toaster ovens.
3. There is a clear need to take a closer look at how the nonfrail elderly modify their own houses.

4. Simple, user-friendly technology, incorporated unobtrusively into the living environment, has the potential to provide support for the functioning of older, more frail elderly.
5. Barriers to modifications come from lack of knowledge of what changes to make, the reluctance of older persons to alter their environment, and the lack of resources for making major modifications.

In general, clients tended to make behavioral changes more often than any other alteration, likely due to the assumption that the physical environment is unalterable. Material adjustments and the use of assistive devices or special equipment were often adopted through the encouragement of a service provider. Structural modifications were rare, and the family seemed to be a major factor in determining whether or not such expensive and extensive alterations are pursued.

DESIGN DIRECTIVES

The following design directives and suggested activities are drawn from the related research and from our study. Care must be taken in interpreting these directives because of the great variations in the capacities, lifestyles, and homes of older persons.

When adapting existing housing to the needs of the resident, consider the introduction of simple modifications and technology as well as more expensive retrofits.

DESIGN DIRECTIVE
ONE

1. If altering cabinet heights is not a practical solution, consider the conversion of a closet into a pantry, the introduction of permanent or portable lazy susan shelves, open shelving under cabinets, pegboards with unslanted pegs, and sliding shelves in bottom cabinets that can be bought in a store.

2. Stoves that are difficult to operate can be replaced with a counter-top broiler oven. It should have an on-off switch, a large door handle with a firmly hinged door, and easy-to-read numbers.

3. If an individual is having difficulty operating sliding glass doors into a bathtub or shower area, removal of the doors and the substitution of a shower curtain is a practical, low-cost solution.

4. Difficulty in turning faucet knobs can be overcome without replacing the unit through the introduction of aides such as tap turners.

5. The use of pantrys and open shelving in conjunction with traditional or adjustable height wall cabinets will facilitate storage accessibility for the older individual.

6. Bottom cabinets with slide out shelves will eliminate the need for bending and make access to items easier.

7. Adequate counter space and/or open shelving in the bathroom is important to store frequently used items such as medications.

8. The use of extra pullout breadboards located at major work centers in the kitchen can provide extra counter space as well as a place for the resident to sit and prepare food.

In adapting housing it is important that the individual physical characteristics of the resident be considered.

DESIGN DIRECTIVE
TWO

1. The placement of grab bars and railings can vary depending upon the height and reaching capabilities of the user, and should be determined with the individual being present to demonstrate his or her abilities and preferences.

2. If furniture is to be selected, careful attention should be paid to purchasing chairs and couches that properly support the person over long periods of time, given that some users actually nap or sleep in them. Seats that are fairly flat and firm yet with some resilience are necessary. The height and seat depth should adequately support the individual and allow for feet to lay flat on the floor. Arm rests that protrude past the edge of the seat will assist the older person in getting in and out without exerting unnecessary energy.

DESIGN DIRECTIVE

THREE

It is important to respect the older person's lifestyle and personal preferences in making recommendations or changes in the home.

1. Many people are reluctant to change the status quo and resist making alterations even though areas are unsafe. Therefore, rather than removing scatter rugs that may have sentimental value, the introduction of two-way tape or nonskid pads allow them to remain without being a hazard.

2. Furniture that may be difficult to get in and out of can be modified through the introduction of adaptive cushions or lifting seats that assist in providing the necessary push.

3. The reorganization of space may be required to eliminate clutter that comes from a psychological need or a lack of storage space. Closet retrofits that include a variety of shelving combinations can be extremely valuable in providing a better utilization of space.

4. Because of vision changes, many elderly can benefit from a rearrangement of clothing by color. This is particularly helpful for those who cannot distinguish colors in the blue-green range. Labeling of drawers can also be advantageous for some people with memory problems.

5. Beds that are too low can be modified through the use of wooden blocks to raise the bed to the desired level. The blocks must be thick and heavy and the legs of the bed securely fitted into the blocks.

6. Ease in bathing can be supported through the introduction of grab bars, hand-held showers, bath benches, and nonskid surfaces on the bathtub or shower floor.

DESIGN DIRECTIVE

FOUR

A design that conserves energy and provides protection will increase the ability of the older individual to retain his or her independence.

1. Self-cleaning ovens, self-defrosting refrigerators, and dishwashers should be provided whenever possible.

2. Wall mounted ovens with interior lights are preferred to free-standing ovens. Ovens and stove tops should always have counter space on either side for ease in transfer of food.

3. A shelf mounted at the outside of an entry will allow a person to put packages down while opening the door.

Safety features and aides should be readily available but unobtrusive and nontherapeutic looking. Older people do not wish to be identified as impaired and will be resistant to design that is institutional in appearance.

DESIGN DIRECTIVE
FIVE

1. Many noninstitutional appearing grab bars of different configurations, materials, and colors are available. These are more likely to be acceptable to a wide range of elderly individuals than the typical therapeutic models.

2. Hand railings made of wood or colored materials should be considered over the metal variety, which is colder and institutional.

3. The use of faucets with contrasting colors to indicate hot and cold (red and blue) can be a nonobtrusive aid for both visually and nonvisually impaired older people in selecting the desired water temperature.

4. Lever type handles are easier for the arthritic user to manipulate than the knob type and should be used whenever possible.

5. Edges on all counter tops, particularly in the bathroom area, should be rounded to protect the older person from accidental injury.

6. Select appliances that have large, easy-to-read numbers and controls located at the front, rather than the rear, of the appliance.

7. Illuminated light switches should be used so that locating the switch is easier when entering a dark room.

8. Provide self-mixing valves on bathtub/shower controls that regulate the water temperature and protect the older person from accidental burns and scalds.

9. Provide an outlet in the hallway in order to create a lighted path from bedroom to bathroom at night.

10. Safety and security for the older person should be considered throughout the home and can be enhanced through the installation of a number of passive systems: smoke detectors, security alarm systems, intercom systems, door peepholes, outdoor lights, locking devices on windows, and metal doors and frames.

Safety in the home should be stressed in a home assessment along with information about resources.

DESIGN DIRECTIVE
SIX

1. A home assessment instrument should include both an emphasis on safety hazards in the home (for example, trailing cords;

poor lighting; loose rugs) as well as activity promotion based on the needs of the residents and what they wish to do (such as extending capabilities in cooking or cleaning).

2. Concrete resources either in the form of facilitating services (dealing with a landlord to get changes made), providing information (handyman service, available aides), or defining what is needed and providing service are essential to success in a safety and assessment program.

DESIGN DIRECTIVE	*Because of their potential contribution in causing accidents, special atten-*
SEVEN	*tion should be paid to stair design. Focus on eliminating ambiguity and providing adequate support for the person to maneuver the stairs safely.*

1. Light switches should be provided at both the top and bottom of stairwells to allow the user to control lighting as needed.

2. Increased lighting should be provided throughout the stairwell with a minimum of 10 foot candles, and illumination should be consistent so that shadows are not created on the stairs or landing. Increase the lighting intensity on the stairwell while decreasing the lighting intensity slightly in surrounding areas.

3. Windows in the stairwell or on a landing should be protected by window coverings that eliminate glare.

4. Polished treads should be designed to minimize any glare that can be disturbing to the older user.

5. In descending, surface and edge cues on each stair must provide a figure-ground relationship in which each tread edge appears as a figure with the tread below appearing as the background. In ascending, each edge should be clearly distinguished from the abutting tread and riser.

6. The bottom and top steps in a stairwell should be in a contrasting color to the other steps to define them clearly. The first and last steps are the most likely to be misjudged when descending stairs and can result in a severe fall.

7. All steps should be of uniform height and depth.

8. Avoid bold patterns on stairs as they may be confusing. When possible, use carpet to absorb noise and reduce the severity of falls.

9. Handrails should be provided on both sides of the stairwell and protrude from 6 to 12 inches beyond the last step for needed support when the last step has been reached. They should be in a color contrasting with the adjacent wall.

10. Combination of low headroom and orientation edges that permit a full view of a room while descending should be avoided, as these are often distracting and are a factor in fall-related accidents on stairs.

Materials that are selected for the home should promote safe mobility for the older person.

1. The pile of carpeting should be limited to low level loop or dense cut pile. This provides the least resistance to walking, wheelchairs, and other mobility aids and provides the greatest traffic-bearing surface.

2. Carpeting not only absorbs sound and noise but also reduces the seriousness of accidental falls. Therefore, it should be used on stair steps and corridors as well as bathroom floors.

3. Lighter, low-intensity colors in flooring material reflect light and aid the person in seeing. Bold patterns can be confusing and may lead to misjudgment of distances.

4. Matte finishes or even a semigloss (such as wood and resilient vinyl floors coated with a nonslip, nonwaxed finish) are preferable to shiny surfaces as they reduce glare that can be uncomfortable or disturbing to the older eye.

Whenever possible, design choices should be based on knowledge of the physical and sensory changes that occur in the normal process of aging and should be supportive of those changes.

1. Thresholds should be flush or with a rise of no more than ½ inch and, if necessary, cued with a color contrast.

2. Vision changes that occur in the older eye suggest that when using color to identify an area it should be of a high contrast in both brightness and value to the surrounding area. A figure-ground contrast can make identification of objects easier for a visually impaired individual (for example, outlining the door frame in a contrasting color to the adjoining wall).

3. Glare from exposed windows can be remedied through either the use of an exterior overhang or through a variety of window treatments (such as light-filtering sheers under draperies, louver type shades).

4. Alarm systems should be both visual and audible. The sound should have intensity and frequency that will attract the attention of persons with partial hearing loss.

5. Light switches that are pressure or rocker type are easier to use than toggle switches for persons with limited hand dexterity or strength.

POLICY CONSIDERATIONS

<table>
<tr><td>POLICY CONSIDERATION
ONE</td><td>*Better assessment and increased coordination among agencies concerning the home environment is desirable.*</td></tr>
</table>

Case managers, visiting nurses, homemakers, and other staff members from a variety of agencies come into contact with frail older persons in their existing homes. Very few of these staff include the home environment as part of their assessment, nor do they systematically evaluate environmental problems or solutions individually or as a group. As a result, problems related to the home environment often fall through the cracks. Whatever attention is paid to the home environment is spotty at best, focusing on simple interventions such as grab bars and ignoring other areas such as behavioral changes or material adjustments that may be just as important.

<table>
<tr><td>POLICY CONSIDERATION
TWO</td><td>*Home repair programs should be expanded to cover home modifications related to safety and independent functioning.*</td></tr>
</table>

With the expected increase in the numbers of older persons who are likely to be frail, the modification of the home environments to support them becomes more important. Such adaptations could be incorporated into the activities of home repair programs that have thus far concentrated on home security (such as locks and window bars) and grab bars. However, such as expansion would require more comprehensive assessments, increased knowledge concerning how to make modifications, a better understanding of what modifications are effective, and the creation of an environmental assessment team possibly including occupational therapists or specially trained interior designers who would work with home repair programs and other agencies.

<table>
<tr><td>POLICY CONSIDERATION
THREE</td><td>*A variety of assessment, education, and remedial models should be created for both the elderly and providers to increase safety and functional abilities.*</td></tr>
</table>

Because the elderly population is highly differentiated, a variety of approaches are needed to increase awareness of the potential of home modifications to increase safety, reduce accidents, and provide comfort and support. Such approaches could range from mass educational programs—such as the one designed by the U.S. Product Safety Commission, which relies on self or volunteer checklist assessments—to a peer approach, in which groups of older persons are trained together on how to assess their own homes and then share successful solutions they have used or observed. In either case, the availability of trained staff to follow up on difficult problems and the identification of resources for physical modifications are likely to be important program components.

Major focus of assessment and education should be on existing housing.

The majority of elderly individuals reside in their own homes and are unlikely to move unless a change in their health and/or functional abilities necessitates a more supportive environment. In addition to the desire of older people to remain at home, there is now an increased emphasis among service providers and advocates of government programs to keep them in their own homes because it is potentially less expensive to do so and relocation problems can thus be avoided. Home assessments and educational programs can serve to alert elderly residents to the problems in their homes (older houses are more likely to have several items in need of repair or modification) and provide information and resources to enable them to make changes. New housing can be designed to overcome future potential problems, but the focus of assessment and education must be targeted at existing housing as that is where most of the frail elderly live and where the problems are most frequently found.

IV

HOUSING ENVIRONMENTS
FOR FRAIL OLDER PERSONS

13

ADAPTING HOUSING FOR OLDER DISABLED PEOPLE

Edward Steinfeld

P urpose-built housing for older people normally includes some design features that improve access and enhance the usability of buildings by people with disabilities. All public or common spaces in housing for the elderly are normally designed to be free from barriers. In addition, apartments often have some features that make them easier for people with impairments to use, such as grab bars at toilets. A few dwelling units within the housing project are usually set aside and designed to be accessible and usable by severely disabled people—in particular, people who are confined to wheelchairs.

The conventional policy toward the provision of accessible housing has been to allocate a certain percentage of units within a building to the handicapped, usually 5–10 percent. The standards employed by the U.S. Department of Housing and Urban Development (HUD) and those of other government agencies require that these units have additional space and design features: large bathrooms, larger kitchens, wider doorways, and appropriately located grab bars.

These units are intended for severely disabled people and purposely held off the market until qualified tenants appear. Although this ensures that they will be rented to disabled tenants, there have been reports, particularly in market-rate housing, that units often remain vacant for a substantial time period. This results in reduced profit to developers or financial liabilities for nonprofit sponsors and adds to the resistance toward broader policies regarding accessible housing.

If accessible dwelling units are not reserved, they will often be rented to able-bodied people. This leads to no increase in the availability of accessible housing, a poor use of resources, and a false perception of low demand for such units. Many disabled people do not know that this housing exists, and thus, without outreach, latent demand does not become effective demand.

Designing Housing for Both Nonambulant and Ambulant Users Requires Flexibility

Two other problems with the conventional policy of providing accessible housing are that not all people who live in one dwelling may be disabled, and not all disabled people have the same needs. Meeting the design needs of both nonambulant and ambulant users requires flexibility. Design requirements often vary among people with the same disability because the degree of impairment differs. The cost of designing for the most severely impaired can be very high. Developers question the installation of features that may not be used, and the institutional appearance that can result may reduce the unit's marketability.

In housing for the elderly, research has demonstrated that the incidence of disability is very high—often higher than the usual percentage of "handicapped" units. With advancing age, older people in such housing are likely to become more disabled. However, the lack of design flexibility in a conventional unit and the unavailability of a handicap unit when needed may require the tenant to relocate, be institutionalized, or become dependent on home-delivered services.

Although it is often overlooked, there is a close relationship between housing policy and the building standards or codes used as a basis for implementing policy. If standards for barrier-free design result in significant increases in construction cost, the scope of application will be limited. Moreover, if those standards, applied universally, result in an environment that is inconvenient for able-bodied residents, implementation of the standard may be viewed as counterproductive. Before 1980, most standards for accessible housing did, in fact, result in significant increases in the cost of a dwelling unit and, if applied universally, would have resulted in inconvenience for people who were not confined to wheelchairs. Moreover, questions were raised regarding the appropriateness of some of the standard requirements, even for the severely disabled.

The ANSI A117.1 and MPS Are the Most Influential Barrier-Free Standards

The two standards that have the most impact on barrier-free design in housing for the elderly are American National Standards Institute (ANSI) A117.1, *Specifications for Making Buildings and Facilities*

Accessible to and Usable by Physically Handicapped People[1] and *the Minimum Property Standards for Multi-Family Housing* (MPS), issued by HUD. Although each state and often each municipality has its own standards, most are based on these two model standards. The MPS differs from ANSI in that the latter is solely concerned with barrier-free design, while the former includes requirements for all aspects of construction, including fire safety, space planning, and material specifications.

The MPS references the ANSI standard for barrier-free concerns other than dwelling-unit design, namely public and common spaces. Until 1980, the ANSI standard had no requirements for the design of dwelling units. The MPS standards for dwelling units have a number of items that resulted in increased cost and/or considerable inconvenience for able-bodied people. These include:

1. a required 5'-0" turning diameter for wheelchairs within a shower (later revised to 4'-0" × 4'-0");
2. kitchen counters at 34" high rather than the standard 36";
3. space under sinks and kitchen work counters and 48" maximum height of top shelf; and
4. a required 5'-0" turning diameter for wheelchairs within a kitchen.

Generally, larger apartments are required to accommodate the MPS standards. On the other hand, significant limitations of the MPS included:

1. excluding the use of bathtubs;
2. lack of detailed concern with appliance design; and
3. lack of minimum circulation clearances for wheelchairs in front of doors and in passageways.

During the 1970s, the interest in improving opportunities for non-institutional living arrangements for disabled people resulted in pressure on the Department of Housing and Urban Development (HUD) to broaden the application of accessibility criteria to include more than a minimum number of dwelling units. However, HUD was reluctant to act because the MPS criteria clearly resulted in higher costs, and many criteria were considered to be of questionable utility in providing barrier-free environments to a great number of people.

Pressure mounted to improve the ANSI A117.1. This standard had been used as the basis for accessibility codes in all 50 states and many federal agencies. However, as its application increased many inadequacies and inconsistencies were identified. When the standard was developed in 1961, public sentiment for barrier-free design and the demographic characteristics of the disabled pop-

---

[1] Until 1980, the title was *Specifications for Making Buildings and Facilities Accessible to and Usable by the Physically Handicapped*.

ulation were very different. As time progressed, the original standard was considered by many agencies as a first step. In the mid-1970s, many states developed their own codes, which caused problems because some items in the codes were of questionable validity.

The Office of Policy Development and Research at HUD, starting in 1974, sponsored research that would lead to an improved data base for barrier-free design recommendations and for revising the ANSI standard to include criteria for dwelling unit design. Part of this research included human-factors studies designed to gather empirical data on the specific problems of physically disabled people. This chapter describe the human-factors research and the recommendations that resulted for housing design. Many of the recommendations were subsequently included in revisions to the ANSI A117.1 standard. A major result of this work was the development of a new philosophical approach to the provision of accessibility—the concept of "adaptable housing." This new concept has implications for the nature of housing design for the elderly. It augments the policy of creating only a few accessible units for severely handicapped people by requiring housing to be "adaptable" for those who suffer from less severe handicaps. The results answer many common design questions that surface during the design process, such as "Should showers be provided instead of bathtubs?" and "What maximum distance should be specified between parking spaces and building entries?"

Related Research

A major goal of the project to revise the ANSI A117.1 standard was to use criteria generated from reliable, empirical research. A review of the existing human factors research on accessibility identified many serious deficiencies in the quality of the underlying research used to develop standards (Steinfeld, 1972a).

The major findings of the literature review addressed accessibility concerns such as movement disabilities, limitations of stamina, and difficulties maintaining balance. Specific findings include the following:

1. Limited empirical data were available about the use of kitchens.
2. Limited empirical data were found regarding the use of doorways.
3. No empirical data on strength and stamina limitations were identified.
4. Conflicting data emerged on the use of ramps.
5. No empirical data were found about the use of bathrooms.
6. Limited empirical data were available regarding navigation in small spaces such as elevators and bathrooms.

7. Limited empirical data dealing with reaching and grasping objects were available. Only anthropometric data were commonly identified.

Although many accessible design standards existed, few were based on reliable empirical data. Most had either an anecdotal source or relied on limited and ambiguous information.

Research Objectives and Questions

It was determined that a series of empirical research studies was necessary to provide a more reliable and valid data base for generating technical criteria that would lead to better standards. The objectives of the research were:

1. to clarify conflicting findings in existing information,
2. to fill gaps where little research was available, and
3. to determine optimal environmental conditions for people with different disabilities, differing degrees of disability, and no disability.

The "optimal conditions" objective was a complicated issue to study. Since voluntary standards such as those of the ANSI must be accepted in a consensus process, the "optimal accessibility" may be defined differently because of varying political, economic, or technological factors. Thus, data was collected and analyzed in such a way as to clarify who would be included, excluded, or limited from using the buildings if design criteria were set at various threshold levels. This approach allowed a more flexible definition of "optimal environment."

In addition to human factors data, consumer acceptance data in the form of an interview survey were collected. The survey sought to answer the following two questions:

1. Do people with disabilities view some, any, or all devices/ design features as stigmatizing?
2. Are any devices or aides viewed more positively than others?

It was also considered important to investigate the kinds of adaptations people made to their own dwelling unit. This identified the type of adaptations consumers considered acceptable, manageable, and necessary. Even though circumstances may force people to use items that they patently dislike, consumers nonetheless were able to rate the devices and equipment they considered useful and appropriate.

In the laboratory, research subjects were interviewed to determine their opinions regarding adaptive devices, equipment, and interior design features. Home visits were also conducted, which provided an opportunity to observe actual adaptations people had made themselves.

Methodology and Data Analysis

Human Factors Study—General Procedures

Disabled and able-bodied people performed simulated tasks of daily living within full-scale mock-ups of public and residential environments. This *in situ* research examined the behavior of older handicapped people in various settings. The following measurements were gathered:

1. Anthropometric tolerances
2. Speed and distance ratings
3. Wheelchair maneuvering clearances (K-turn, U-turns around walls, L-turns from corridors to passageways)
4. Manual strength requirements for push and pull tasks

The following environmental spaces, features, and conditions were considered to be of initial interest:

1. Kitchen work centers—oven, sink, range, refrigerator, mix center, and kitchen layout (the bathroom lavatory was also included in this group due to its similarity with kitchen work centers)
2. Bathroom design—including bathtub, toilet, shower, and bathroom layout
3. Ramp slope and length
4. Doorways
5. Elevator
6. Toilet stall design (Fig. 13.1)
7. Public telephone height
8. Public mailbox use

Simulated everyday tasks were developed in order to test the performance of a variety of different arrangements and configurations. It was also important to involve as many different types of handicapped subjects as possible. Flexible mock-ups were used because field conditions would have limited the study to characteristics of existing settings and would not have provided a sufficient range of observations. Mock-ups were also helpful in identifying optimal conditions and the full range of accessibility problems. Additionally, the cost of building real environments for each of the testing stations and the time required to have each subject use them was prohibitive. The simulation method allowed the research to be realistic within budgetary constraints.

Testing stations were located in a vacant factory building, which served as a laboratory for the project. The testing stations were

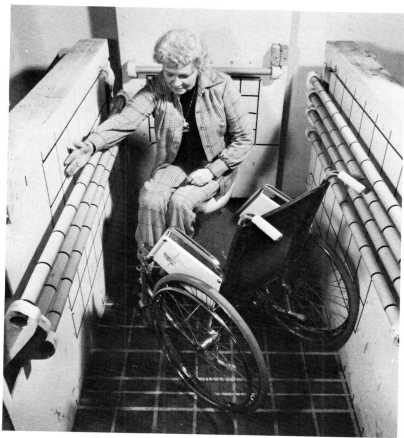

FIGURE 13.1 A wheelchair user is shown after transferring to the toilet apparatus. Findings indicated that a 48″ wide stall width will accommodate most people.

designed to generate the specific data necessary for meeting pre-established information needs and objectives.

Testing procedures were standardized by writing explicit instructions for each testing station. All staff members were trained, and team leaders, who were professional staff, supervised all laboratory work. Subjects were encouraged to experiment creatively with alternative methods of using testing stations when it was apparent that the method they used to accomplish a task was ineffectual. All testing was completed in casual clothing with wheelchair users equipped with their own wheelchairs.

A two-stage approach was used in the research. During the first stage, general performance data for each testing station were obtained. A second stage of testing involved a smaller group of subjects, who represented the lower extreme of the range of abilities for a particular task. The second stage of testing determined the limits of performance for the entire sample by focusing on the abilities of the extreme group. Methods were employed to reduce the effect of training and fatigue on performance. For some stations, two trials defined the parameters of performance. For example, shelves were both lowered and raised until they could not be reached.

Graphic Overlays Were Used to Analyze Data

All testing stations were designed, as much as possible, to allow automatic measurement. For example, ruled measurement grids were applied to equipment so that observers would not need to measure every dimension. This reduced measurement error as well as the time required to take measurements. Methods of analysis and presentation of results were based upon the need to develop standards. Most data were analyzed using frequency distributions. Data analysis for some testing stations involved the use of graphic representations to identify patterns. Figure 13.2 demonstrates the use of this technique for data regarding turning a wheelchair within a small space.

Further statistical analyses were not performed for several reasons. First, there was no way to establish how representative the sample was with respect to functional abilities in the overall disabled population. Data on detailed functional abilities for tasks of daily living had not been gathered for a representative group of the disabled population as a whole. Second, even if such data were available, the major purpose of the research was to develop design criteria that accommodated the range of abilities. The computation of means and standard deviations did not provide any added significant information. In fact, such "average" statistics can disguise major variations. Design criteria based on mean values may poorly accommodate the needs of those on either side of the mean. In some cases, the average may not accommodate anyone. Third, the data was used to develop design criteria, the cost implications of which required compromises to be made. Knowing that in some cases designers would want to exceed minimal criteria, frequency distributions enabled the identification of those people who would not be well served by minimal design criteria. The research provided the designer an idea of how many and who might be accommodated by exceeding minimal criteria.

Three Guidelines Were Used to Judge the Standard

Recommendations were developed by considering and judging the standard's relationship to three general guidelines. First, when no appreciable cost impact resulted, criteria were based on meeting the entire range of abilities. Second, if a cost impact resulted, criteria were set in such a way as to maximize the number who could be accommodated. It was felt that in many cases an individual's disorder was so unique as to defy the development of a successful design feature. Third, criteria were examined to see if their implementation would increase the difficulty of using a building for another segment of the population.

BASIC U-TURN

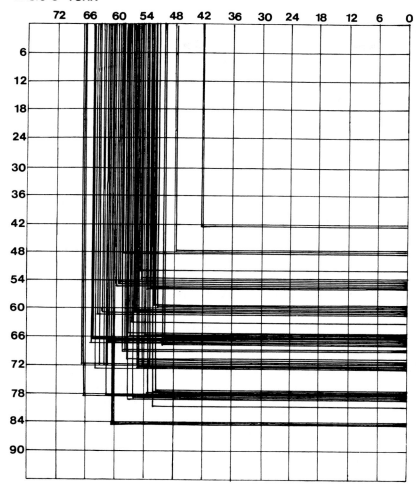

FIGURE 13.2 The minimum space required by each wheelchair user to make a 180° turn was graphically overlayed on a grid. This data demonstrated the need for a rectangular or oval-shaped turning area rather than a circular or square-shaped area.

General principles of human factors design were applied in developing criteria. Tremendous variations in human performance ability require the provision of adjustable environments. For example, the use of adjustable automobile seats rather than a fixed seat set at mid-range accommodates the great variation in the height of drivers. In the review of existing human factors research, principles useful in developing barrier-free design criteria were identified (see Steinfeld, 1979A).

Subject Selection Methods and Recruitment

The research included subjects with problems such as movement disabilities, limitations of stamina/balance, and ambulant, semiambulant, and nonambulant status. Able-bodied subjects also participated in the research. Some of the major disabilities included:

1. Difficulty in coordination and manipulation,
2. Difficulty lifting and reaching,
3. Inability to use lower extremities (wheelchair users),
4. Reliance on walking aids,
5. Difficulty bending and kneeling,
6. Difficulty sitting down or getting out of a chair,
7. Difficulty using stairs, inclines, and walking long distances,
8. Difficulty walking on rough surfaces,
9. Difficulty lifting and reaching combined with difficulty in manipulating fingers,
10. Difficulty lifting and reaching combined with inability to use lower extremities, and
11. Reliance on walking aids combined with difficulty sitting down or getting up.

Disability categories do not, in themselves, establish a description of an individual's potential for independent action. For example, an individual who cannot use his legs may be young, with strong upper arms and good stamina. Another individual who cannot use his legs may be old and frail, obese, and limited in stamina. Differences in impairment and individual/personal characteristics can result in different levels of functional ability, different even though both may suffer from the same impairment (Fig. 13.3).

FIGURE 13.3 Subjects were asked to do a variety of reaching tasks. Many had multiple disabilities.

Functional Ability in Each Disability Group was Examined: To ensure that the selection of subjects reflected differences in functional ability, each disability category was further divided into several functional levels. Functional ability ranged from the most independent level of ability for each disability category to the lowest level of ability that would allow independence in daily activities. A diagnostic interview was developed, utilizing a self-report method that documented performance of tasks of daily living. This was used to identify persons' disabilities and also to specify their functional ability level within each disability category. This screening interview was done by telephone and by nonprofessionals. The lack of a clinical assessment or functional evaluation required the use of a pretest as well as a validation procedure in the laboratory.

Three versions of the diagnostic interview were administered by telephone to a total of 20 people. The accuracy of this interview instrument was checked by home visits from a physical therapist. Most items proved to be valid indications of functional ability, but some corrections and improvements were made following the home visits.

The overall goal of the research was to establish requirements for accessibility and manipulation of the environment for people who were competent enough to live independently. We wanted the sample to be representative of a range of disabilities including some marginally independent people. With such a sample, we could be ensured the results of the laboratory research would apply to the broadest possible population. Our objectives in selecting subjects were:

1. To find people who represented all the disabilities on our list,
2. To find people within each disability category that represented a range of functional abilities,
3. To minimize bias in sample selection, which might result from an individual's dependency on institutional services,
4. To obtain a large enough sample in each ability level and each disability category to make generalizable conclusions, and
5. To minimize bias in sample selection that might result if a high proportion of the sample had received advanced rehabilitation training that would normally not be available to most disabled people.

A Quota Sample of Subjects Was Employed: Demographic data on all these disability categories were not available. Thus, there were no clearly defined subgroup statistics from which we could draw a proportionate sample. Furthermore, because the proportion of people in the general population with these disabilities is well below 20 percent, a random sampling method would have resulted in a major screening effort to identify eligibles. The diagnostic interview, combined with a validation procedure in the laboratory, provided a convenient and accurate method to identify and verify disability and functional level. An arbitrary target, however, was set for the number of subjects in each group. Because the performance of wheelchair users was critical, we over-sampled this group.

A local senior citizen's advocacy organization, the Action Coalition to Create Opportunities for Retirement with Dignity (ACCORD), recruited subjects by telephone. Quality control included reinterviewing a small, random sample of people interviewed by ACCORD workers and checking all interview forms for completion and consistency.

Recruitment was not limited to older people, and a concerted effort was made to recruit subjects of all ages. Recruitment, however, was limited to noninstitutionalized people. A few exceptions to this rule were made, but such individuals were tested in a limited number of stations. Subjects were only tested at stations where their performance was affected by their disability. For example, subjects who had difficulty in manipulating objects were tested for finger dexterity. People who used walking aids or wheelchairs were tested at all testing stations. The total number of subjects was 201.

Testing Took Place in Two Phases

The first phase established a range of performance for each testing station. These data were used to generate proposed standards. The second phase tested the generalizability and validity of the proposed standards, researched some areas in more detail, and tested combinations of design elements such as bathroom and kitchen layouts. Second phase subjects were selected to be representative of various ability levels. Thus, even though small samples were used, the criteria derived from the second phase were expected to satisfy the need to represent the disabled population in general (to the extent that our basic sample reflected the range of functional abilities in the population).

When subjects arrived at the laboratory testing site their actual performance in various tasks was compared with their self-report on the diagnostic interview. This not only validated the diagnostic interview but checked on the current physical status of individuals. There was a change in functional ability for approximately 25 percent of the subjects. The major changes were in the categories of "difficulty lifting and reaching" and "limitations of stamina." Subjects seemed to have some difficulty in judging how high they could reach or how far they could walk without fatigue. A lesser proportion of subjects perceived themselves as more disabled than they actually were.

Initially, we had hoped to recruit a minimum of ten people in

TABLE 13.1 Subjects for First Phase Testing

Disability Categories

Test Stations	Incoordination, Difficulty Manipulating Fingers	Difficulty Lifting and Reaching	Wheelchair Users	Reliance on Walking Aids	Difficulty Bending and Kneeling and Difficulty Sitting Down or Getting Up from a Chair	Difficulty Walking Long Distances	Difficulty Walking on Rough Surfaces	Hook Prosthesis Users	Reliance on Walking Aids and Difficulty Walking Long Distances	Walking Aid Users with Exceptionally Good Abilities	Wheelchair Users with Exceptionally Good Abilities	Total Disabled	Able-Bodied	Total
Kitchen sink		14	57	11	19		23	4	4	6	4	142	11	153
Oven		13	54	11	20		22	4	4	5	4	137	11	149
Cooktop		14	54	11	19		21	4	4	6	4	137	11	148
Mix center		14	58	11	20		22	4	4	6	4	143	11	154
Turning radius			55								4	59		59
Doorways			54	9					4	5	4	78	10	89
Elevators			51	10		4			4	4	4	77	9	86
Bathtub/shower	14	15	53	9	20	29	23	4	4	6	4	181	11	192
Toilet	13	15	54	11	19	28	21	4	4	6	4	179	11	190
Anthropometrics	14	15	55	11	19	29	23	4	4	6	4	184	11	195
Push-pull forces	14	15	53	11		28	22	4	4	6	4	161	11	172
Ramp			53	11		27	19		4	6	4	124	9	133
Telephone												107	11	118
Mailbox	9	15	56	8				3	3	6	4	104	11	115
Bathroom lavatory		13	54	11	17		19	3	4	6	4	131	11	142

each functional ability level in each disability category, except for the category "inability to use lower extremities." In that category, the desire for finer distinctions in ability levels resulted in a quota of five people in each level. In categories where only a few individuals at certain levels were identified, those levels were combined for analysis purposes. Table 13.1 displays the total sample broken down by disability category. Subjects found not to be disabled during the validation procedure were grouped in the able-bodied category.

Description of Subjects

A second interview was administered to all subjects during their first visit to the laboratory. This solicited background information about present living arrangements, use of technical aids, and opinions regarding design features for increasing usability of dwelling units. Tables 13.2, 13.3, and 13.4 describe the sample in terms of age, sex, and living arrangements.

The tables show the sample to have over twice as many women than men, to consist almost entirely of people who live independently, and to be an adult group. Compared to the adult population in general, this sample had a greater proportion of late, middle-aged, and elderly people (over 55 years old). The over-sampling

TABLE 13.2 Age Range of Subjects Compared to US Population (1979 Census)

Age	Distribution Range of Subjects	Age Distribution of Subjects by Percentage		Age Distribution of US Population by Percentage
Under 20	2	1.0		37.9
20–29	16	8.2		14.5
30–39	26	13.3		11.1
40–49	32	16.4		11.8
50–59	46	23.6	61% of total sample	10.4
60–69	40	20.5		7.7
70–79	27	13.8		4.6
80 and above	6	3.1		1.9
Total	195[a]	100.0		99.9

[a] There were six diagnostic interviews with incomplete data on age.

of women is an artifact of the mature nature of the sample. Women outlive men and therefore form a larger proportion of the population in late adulthood.

The sample characteristics suggest this group of people were likely to exhibit generally lower strength and stamina, reduced agility, smaller stature, and greater familiarity with kitchen work than a sample that is younger or more equal in distribution of men and women. Moreover, these people were far less likely, as a group, to have advanced rehabilitation training. This is not necessarily a detriment to the generalizability of the research, since the lower limits of performance are more likely to be represented by our sample. If a less competent sample can be satisfied by design recommendations based on this research, people with better abilities should have fewer difficulties.

Specific findings related to housing for the elderly follow. Readers are referred to the original research report for information regarding detailed findings (Steinfeld et al., 1979b).

TABLE 13.3 Sex of Subjects

	Number	Percent
Male	61	30.3
Female	140	69.9
Total	201	99.9

TABLE 13.4 Residence of Subjects

Type	Number	Percent
Publicly subsidized housing[a]	37	18.3
Private	161	80.1
Home for the aged	1	0.5
Nursing home	1	0.5
Missing data	1	0.5
Total	201	99.9

[a] People in this category lived in housing that was either federally subsidized or public housing.

Findings

Anthropometric Measurements Must Involve Goal Orientation

Subjects were measured as they extended their arms, reaching in several different positions. General data on standing and sitting height, eye height, and wheelchair sizes were obtained. Great variability in reaching abilities existed among the subjects. Moreover, when comparing this data to findings from the other testing stations, we found that actual task performance, which is goal oriented, often exceeded the reaching limits obtained through conventional static anthropometric measurements. This implied that general anthropometric data should not be used as a basis for design decisions when specific task data are available.

Circulation in Tight Spaces Can Be Accommodated in a Variety of Ways

Wheelchair users performed a variety of maneuvers in an effort to navigate within minimum size spaces for various activities. All areas were bounded by portable walls that resisted movement during the course of testing. The findings demonstrated the 60″ diameter turning area used in many standards as a minimum space for making a 180° turn in a wheelchair was inadequate for almost half of the wheelchair users. They need a space that was at least 60″ wide by 78″ deep. It was also demonstrated that those who have difficulty making a 180° U-turn can turn more efficiently using a K-turn. Furthermore, they could complete an L-turn with only 36″ clearance on each leg. These data imply that circulation requirements should not be based upon "turning diameters." For U-turns, an oval space is needed. Spaces that allow other types of maneuvers can be satisfactory and more compact.

Rate and Distance of Travel Are Limited

Subjects were asked to walk or wheel in a straight line at a normal pace. The distance they could travel without stopping and their rate of travel were recorded. The results indicated that disabled people often travel very slowly. One foot per second is not unusual for severely disabled people. One-third of those tested moved at this rate or slower. People with low stamina are the slowest. Only 2 out of 34 (26 wheelchair users) people could not manage a 100-foot distance. Based on this data, 100 feet was recommended as a maximum distance between resting points. Distances between points of origin and destination—for example, parking lot and building entry—can be based upon rate of travel. Assuming a reasonable trip length of 2 minutes between parking space and entry, a distance of 120 feet would be satisfactory. For a trip from apartment to lobby in a one-story building, a distance of 300 feet would be maximum, assuming no rests. Considering a 2-minute test period[2], a distance of 180 feet would be maximum.

Pull/Push Forces Varied Greatly by Subject and Task

An apparatus that simulated motions used to open doors and windows allowed the maximum push or pull force for five different positions to be measured. Great variation existed in the maximum force that could be exerted. Less than half the subjects could exert a force greater than 8 lbf in all positions. People with disabilities that result in difficulty lifting or reaching; difficulty lifting, reaching, and manipulating fingers; poor stamina; and difficulty bending and kneeling are marginal performers in tasks requiring more than 8 lbf. About 10 percent of the sample could exert no more than 5 lbf. The implication of this research is that doors and windows should be easy to manipulate in housing for disabled people.

The data on reaching abilities indicate that controls on the back wall of a tub were not reachable from outside by people who use wheelchairs. Moreover, few people could reach controls when seated in the tub or shower if the controls were at the opposite end.

Ramp Slope and Length Are Interrelated

A 40-foot long ramp that could be adjusted in slope was used to test the ability of subjects to manage ramps of various slopes and lengths. Less than half of the wheelchair users could manage the full length of the ramp with a slope of 1:12, the widely used recommendation for maximum ramp slope. There was a relationship between slope and length. That is, people could negotiate shallow slopes for greater distances than steep slopes. Railings were used frequently by ambulant and semiambulant subjects. A slope of 1:20 was necessary before all people could manage the full length of the ramp.

Toilet Stall Width of 48 Inches Was Sufficient for Most Subjects

In an adjustable toilet stall, fitting trials were used to establish optimal conditions. In the second phase of research, a proposed minimum stall width was tested. The results indicated that many severely disabled people need assistance in using toilets. There are a variety of methods used for toilet transfers from wheelchairs, and

---

[2] At least two minutes are needed for one's pulse rate to return to normal after being elevated.

different arrangements favor different techniques. However, in general a minimum stall width of 48″ will accommodate most people. It was found that wheelchair users do not always use grab bars for transferring, but they are useful for maintaining balance. Optimal grab bar height varied within a very narrow range of 33″–36″. There was also a range of preferred toilet seat height. Generally, wheelchair users preferred a lower height than semiambulant users. A range of 17″–19″ from the floor to the top of the seat satisfied most subjects. The depth of a usable toilet stall is related to its width. We tested different stall sizes with a large adult male using a wheelchair and found that, depending on width, a stall depth of from 56″ to 66″ is necessary. These findings differed significantly from most existing code requirements. We also tested the use of grab bars integral with the seat and swing-away bars. Both were found to be of limited value to all people but valuable to some.

Curbs in Stall Showers Were Obstacles for All Subjects

In studying the use of bathtubs, shower stalls, and bathroom layouts, we used adjustable equipment. Bathtubs and showers were equipped with several sets of bars on all sides of the fixture. Each bar could be moved out of the way so as not to obstruct the use of the fixture during testing. Grids marked on the wall were used to test reaching abilities. The findings indicate that bathtubs are not usable by all disabled people. However, our opinion survey found that half of the sample preferred taking baths. Curbs in shower stalls were definite obstacles for all the subjects tested. Both tubs and shower stalls must have sufficient clearance in front of them for wheelchair users to approach and transfer. It was possible for the wheelchair users to use conventional bathroom layouts of relatively minimum sizes, as long as the fixtures and doors were located in the right places. In particular, with a 5′–0″ by 7′–6″ bathroom, the door must be on the long side and it must open out. Grab bars are very useful for many people at tubs and showers. However, there is great variability in how they are used. It was possible to isolate a limited area on the walls of tub and shower enclosures where grab bars would be generally useful.

Preferred Kitchen Counter Heights Varied by Task and by Person

Several similar pieces of apparatus were constructed that allowed fixtures and countertops, as well as shelves below and above counters, to be adjusted in height. Each apparatus could be tested with both open and closed-in areas underneath. In addition, a

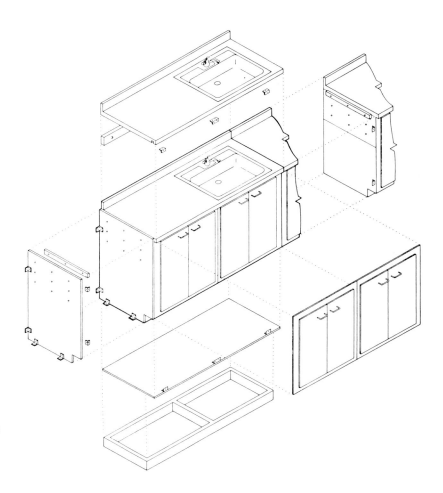

FIGURE 13.4 An adaptable kitchen counter area can be designed by using standard cabinet parts that are affixed to adjoining walls and other cabinets.

complete mock-up of a kitchen was built with modular components so that a variety of different configurations or layouts could be simulated. All subjects performed standardized tasks simulating the use of kitchens and lavatories. Through these fitting trials, preferred design features were identified (Fig. 13.4).

Preferred counter top heights ranged from 26"–36". No compromise height existed that could satisfy all subjects. The pattern of counter height preferences varied for different tasks. For example, higher countertops were preferred for work in the sink. Lower countertops were preferred at mix centers where more force must be exerted for tasks that require upper body strength, such as rolling dough. Each subject was tested for a comfortable range of heights for each task. The "open front" condition dramatically improved the ability to reach to upper shelves; however, many wheelchair users had difficulty reaching shelves mounted higher than 47". All subjects could reach the front of undercounter shelves if the shelf was no lower than 9" above the floor. Reaching to the rear of the shelf, however, was more difficult. Shelves mounted 18″ from the floor were fully accessible to the rear of the shelf by all subjects. A lavatory height of 32″ was preferred by a large majority of subjects as a compromise height, even though it is harder to get a wheelchair under a 32″-high lavatory than the typical 34″ height required by most accessibility codes. Oven heights were also tested in various positions. The major problem with ovens was cleaning. For cooking, the conventional floor model was satisfactory as long as cookware and utensils were lightweight. For heavy objects a counter-height oven tested more satisfactorily. The easiest oven to clean had a side-hinged door and was at counter height. The bottom-hinged door created an obstacle complicating efforts to clean the oven. A counter area with an open space underneath located adjacent to the oven made it easier to use the oven, particularly the counter-level oven.

The results of kitchen layout studies showed a preference for counters mounted at one height, even though studies of individual work centers indicated that preferred heights should vary for different tasks. Minimum Property Standards minimum clearances between opposing counters/cabinets were found to be usable, but good practice would dictate an increase in the width to reduce the number of times wheelchair users bump into cabinets. Minimum sized U-shaped and L-shaped kitchens resulted in fewer bumps and accidents, probably because the clearances were greater than in corridor or galley-type layouts.

Doorways With Clear Width Dimensions of 32 Inches Are Preferred

Doorways with 30″ and 32″ clear widths were constructed. By positioning movable partitions in front of the doors, minimum clearances were identified for different door and corridor configurations. Subjects were tested in three different approaches to the door from the "pull" side. The results indicated that 30″ clear door widths were adequate for those who can negotiate doorways by themselves (very few subjects could not). Thirty-two inch doorways, however, are more convenient and will reduce maintenance problems caused by wheelchairs scraping the door frame and stop. When approaching doors directly from the front, a clear space of 24″ was needed adjacent to the latch side of the door. When approaching from the latch side of the door, a corridor clearance of at least 42″ was needed and, when approaching from the hinge side of the door, a corridor clearance of 54″ and a latch clearance of 36″ was needed. However, a large group of subjects (as much as one-third) could not manage within the minimal corridor clearances. Increasing corridor widths to 48″ on the latch side approach and 60″ on the hinge side approach accommodated almost all of the subjects. Subjects with disabilities common to older people had

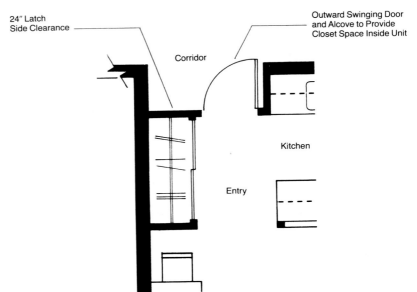

FIGURE 13.5 One of the most difficult design problems in barrier-free housing is providing adequate clearances at doors without increasing the floor area of dwelling units. The research identified the need for a 24″ latch-side door clearance for out-swinging doors where a forward approach must be used.

Figure labels: 24″ Latch Side Clearance; Corridor; Outward Swinging Door and Alcove to Provide Closet Space Inside Unit; Kitchen; Entry

considerably greater difficulties managing doors when clearances were tight. Figure 13.5 illustrates the door swing tolerances for a typical unit.

Standard Elevator Size Was Deemed Adequate

An elevator mock-up allowed us to adjust cab size, measure the time subjects needed to respond to the elevator arrival light, and test acceptable locations for elevator controls. The time needed to respond to the arrival light was consistent with the results of speed/distance data for the 100-foot course. Thus, the shorter distance made no difference in overall speed of the slowest people. The minimum standard elevator size of 2,000-pound capacity was deemed adequate. Most subjects could reach 54″ controls mounted no higher than at either front or side panel locations; only a very small number could not reach a point 48″ high. The front location was slightly easier for subjects to reach.

Telephone and Mailbox Reach Heights Were Tested

A public telephone, a telephone booth, and a U.S. Postal Service free-standing mailbox were used in testing. Fitting trials were used to establish the maximum height for reaching a telephone. The mailbox was tested for mailing letters and small packages. Only one subject could not reach the coin slot on a telephone at 54″ high using either a side or diagonal reach. The only difficulty with the mailbox was holding the door while simultaneously inserting a letter.

Consumer Acceptance Study Findings

Accuracy and usability of the consumer acceptance interview were assured by pretests in home visits with 20 subjects. Photographs of adaptive devices, equipment, and architectural design features were presented along with items that queried the subjects' experiences with various items.

Lower Height Tables Were Often Adapted for Food Preparation: In kitchens, the standard height of countertops (36") was always considered too high for wheelchair users. To compensate for this, TV trays and the kitchen table were often used for meal preparation. Some people employed a typing table with lockable casters for mixing and meal preparation. When unlocked, the table could be used to transport food or dishes. Similarly, utility carts of the two and three shelf variety were used for meal preparation and for transporting items. Sometimes, tables and carts were used for dining in place of a table. Some people used a high kitchen stool to facilitate work at higher counter levels. One individual, who had use of only one arm, propped the refrigerator door open with a TV tray while removing or storing food.

Often additional cabinet tops and even the tops of washing machines or dryers were used to compensate for the lack of counter space at an appropriate height. Because stoves and ovens are difficult for wheelchair users to manipulate, some people preferred portable microwave ovens and electric fry pans, which could be located more conveniently. Peg board clips were used to mount pots, pans, and cooking utensils at more reasonable heights for storage. In one instance, an individual had the upper cabinets in her apartment removed and placed the cabinets directly on the counter to facilitate access.

The bathroom was also creatively adapted. Shower stalls and bathtubs were often used for drying clothes and sometimes for washing large items. Showers were occasionally used as storage areas since many occupants could not transfer into the shower. In place of manufactured shower seats or bathtub seats, some individuals used folding chairs and lawn chairs in the bathtub. Evidence indicated that showers should not be provided exclusive of bathtubs, even though many people cannot use the latter.

Some Adaptive Features Were Considered Unsightly and Undesirable: Summarizing the results of the home visits and opinion survey, the following broad conclusions can be made.

1. There is definitely a dislike for some adaptive devices and architectural features.
2. The architectural features received the best are those that are built into kitchen cabinetry, which are invisible when not in use.

3. Some well-designed and attractive adaptive equipment items are popular, even to those for whom they are not specifically intended.
4. People readily develop adaptations on their own, usually by building or modifying conventional equipment or using something in a different way than was originally intended.

The findings suggest consumers will more readily accept accessible kitchens and bathrooms when they are designed to be convenient but appear to be no different than conventional kitchens and bathrooms. Some important considerations include:

1. Avoid open cabinets and glass cabinet doors in kitchens.
2. Provide the potential to create an unencumbered open space under kitchen sinks.
3. Mount grab bars in bathrooms when and where they are needed for the individual.
4. Avoid the use of bed pans and commode chairs by designing accessible fixtures.

A major finding is that adaptive design features (for example, open or glass cabinets, open space under sinks) or innovative equipment items (for example, lap boards, built-up handles, commode chairs) may be considered unacceptable or undesirable from the consumer point of view. This suggests that an approach to accessibility that focuses solely on design of "special equipment" may be shortsighted. Adaptive items, which are invisible and adaptively designed, such as familiar kitchen equipment, are viewed positively. This suggests that adaptations should strive to be unobtrusive, generally useful to all people, disassociated with specific disabilities, and familiar in appearance.

Conclusions

Many of the findings of this study are comparable with the findings of other human factors research focusing on accessibility and usability of the environment by people with disabilities. In general, the research findings on kitchen counters and shelves are similar to the findings of McCullough and Farnham (1960, 1961) who used a smaller sample drawn mostly from a university community. The results of the testing with telephones confirm the findings of an earlier study completed by AT&T (1975). The ramp and some of the wheelchair maneuver results are also consistent with the findings of Walter (1971) in England, even though his sample was more limited. Another ramp study by Elmer (1957) had results that were radically different; however, these differences can be attributed to his sample selection. Our findings on door clearances differ considerably from previous research. However, most of the differences can be explained by differences in methods and sample selection. This study used a larger and more representative sample compared to previous research studies.

The Adaptable Housing Model

Generally, the findings indicate considerable differences in need between conventional housing provisions and the requirements of disabled people. Conventional dwelling unit plans usually would not provide enough clearance in front of doors to accommodate many of the people in the sample. Most doors used in housing do not have a clear width of 32", particularly those in bathrooms. Bathrooms of minimum size usually do not have their doors on the longest wall. Often toilets are located between tub and lavatory, which precludes the use of wall-mounted grab bars. Kitchen counters are usually 36" high, and the lowest kitchen cabinet shelves are 54" high. Toilet stalls are usually 30"–31" wide by 56" deep, which does not provide enough space for use by people with severe disabilities. Most bathrooms do not have any grab bars or are not equipped with stud blocking for future installation of bars. Elevators often have controls mounted higher than 54". Moreover, the time between the arrival signal and door closing requires much faster movement than most people in this sample could manage. These differences suggest different standards for housing design for disabled people than for able-bodied people. Indeed, there already are such standards. However, comparing the results of this research to existing standards for barrier-free housing identified many areas where existing design criteria for barrier-free housing are too restrictive. These criteria result in increased cost and lack of design flexibility (Fig. 13.6). For example:

1. Larger bathrooms and kitchens are generally not necessary to provide accessibility if clearance is provided at appropriate places underneath the fixtures and cabinets.
2. The sink area should not be the only work center in the kitchen with knee space underneath.
3. Countertops set at 34" are not effective in accommodating a large proportion of people.
4. Most barrier-free design codes do not give enough attention to the oven.
5. Clearances presently required for maneuvering around doors are inadequate.
6. It is impossible to specify one location for a grab bar at showers and tubs that will accommodate everyone.
7. The typical minimum ramp slope of 1:12 is often too steep for wheelchair users.

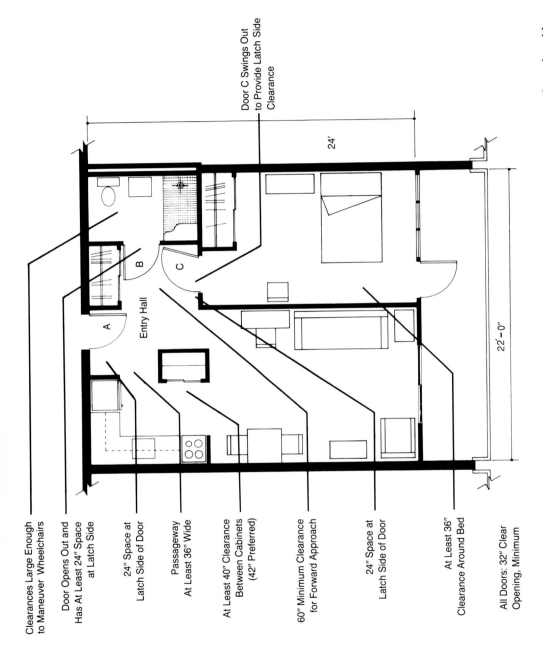

Clearances Large Enough
to Maneuver Wheelchairs

Door Opens Out and
Has At Least 24" Space
at Latch Side

24" Space at
Latch Side of Door

Passageway
At Least 36" Wide

At Least 40" Clearance
Between Cabinets
(42" Preferred)

60" Minimum Clearance
for Forward Approach

24" Space at
Latch Side of Door

At Least 36"
Clearance Around Bed

All Doors: 32" Clear
Opening, Minimum

Door C Swings Out
to Provide Latch Side
Clearance

Entry Hall

A   B   C

24'

22'-0"

FIGURE 13.6 This illustration shows a one-bedroom apartment of 528 square feet. It demonstrates that adaptable housing can be designed that does not exceed the size of typical dwelling units in housing for the elderly.

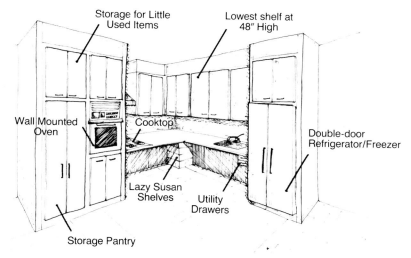

Storage for Little Used Items

Lowest shelf at 48″ High

Wall Mounted Oven

Cooktop

Double-door Refrigerator/Freezer

Lazy Susan Shelves

Utility Drawers

Storage Pantry

FIGURE 13.7 This example illustrates a basic planning approach to kitchen layout—locating full height cabinets/appliances at either end of an open counter unit.

The findings of the consumer acceptance survey, considered along with the results from the human factors study, suggest new approaches in the provision of accessible housing. In particular, the bathroom and kitchen results suggest that, as with many other consumer products, a degree of adjustability should be provided to accommodate the wide range of needs among the disabled (Fig. 13.7).

Older People Are More Likely to Be Marginal Performers

Throughout the research, some people were classified in a "marginal performance" category. These individuals were wheelchair users with severe limitations of arm movement, hemiplegia, or poor stamina. Older people make up a disproportionate share of subjects who, for various testing stations, were categorized as marginal. Moreover, they also are more likely to be at the lower extremes of performance, even if not classified as marginal. Older disabled people often cannot benefit as much from rehabilitation therapy. In fact, many do not receive any therapy or even basic instruction in how to use a wheelchair. They are also much more likely to have multiple disabilities. Thus, in housing for the elderly, minimum guidelines for accessibility should be adjusted to accommodate the frail and weaker older disabled population.

About 46 percent of people over 64 years of age in the United States have a limitation of activity (NHIS, 1969). Residents of housing designed specifically for older people probably have an even higher incidence of limitations and disabilities than the older population at large. Moreover, they constitute a population at risk whose members are likely to become more disabled as they age. This evidence suggests that adaptability and adjustability of critical features in housing for older people should be a basic philosophy in designing the dwelling unit.

DESIGN DIRECTIVES

ONE

Careful attention should be paid to the details of site design features.

1. Signs reserving assigned spaces should be provided.

2. Curb ramps should connect the parking lot with the sidewalk level.

3. Parking spaces should be located relatively close to units.

4. Construction materials that create an irregular walking surface should be avoided.

5. Where site features, such as a recreation trail, cannot be made totally accessible, perhaps a segment can be adapted for handicapped access.

DESIGN DIRECTIVE
TWO

Ramps should be designed no steeper than 1:16 and preferably 1:20.

1. Limit ramps with greater slopes to very short lengths, if they are used at all.

2. The lower slope (1:20) will make it easier for the more physically disabled older frail resident to self-ambulate.

DESIGN DIRECTIVE
THREE

An accessible dwelling unit must have at least one path of travel without stairs from the main entry of the unit to at least the following rooms or spaces: kitchen, dining, bedroom, full bathroom, living room, and storage.

1. Although some codes require 48"-wide hallways, a 36"-wide corridor is sufficient if all doorway clearances are adequate (that is, 32" clear width).

DESIGN DIRECTIVE
FOUR

Kitchen counter heights should be adjustable so as to accommodate the capability level of the individual and the limitations of the wheelchair.

1. When standing, people need a counter height of 35"–36".

2. When sitting in a wheelchair, the best height of the counter will vary depending on whether or not the wheelchair has detachable arms and personal preference. A 1½"-thick counter positioned at about 28" clear dimension is the maximum amount the counter can be lowered and still allow enough room for the knees of a tall person to fit underneath. A 32" clear height will accommodate the arms of a wheelchair.

3. There are several methods of providing adjustable support for the countertop, including metal L-shaped brackets bolted to the back wall with ledger strips at each side of the adjoining cabinet. Adjustable heights can be provided using standard kitchen cabinet parts, with the exception that the countertop itself may need to be structurally reinforced if it spans 60".

4. In adaptable dwellings it is preferable to provide a closet or other storage area conveniently located near the kitchen to make up for the cabinet space lost when base cabinets are removed.

Changes in floor surface height should be limited to no more than ½" and the edge should be beveled.

| DESIGN DIRECTIVE |
| **FIVE** |

1. Thresholds should be eliminated wherever possible.

2. Most wheelchair users can negotiate an abrupt change in height of ½". However, floor surface changes often occur at doorways, where this abrupt change is complicated by the need to simultaneously manipulate a door.

3. Where there are thresholds in doorways, the height of the threshold should be no more than ½", and its edges should be beveled.

Doorways must have a clear opening of 32" and adequate maneuvering clearance on both sides.

| DESIGN DIRECTIVE |
| **SIX** |

1. Maneuvering room is also necessary in front of doors if wheelchair users are to be able to reach door openers and pass through easily. Entry doors to apartments set back in alcoves can be extremely difficult for wheelchair users to open unless there is a clearance at the latch side of the door within the alcove.

2. Bathroom doors should always open out so that if someone falls behind the door, one can still open the door. A side benefit of the out-swinging bathroom door is that space within the bathroom can be kept to a minimum, because less space is needed on the push side of the door than the pull side, and the door swing will not interfere with bathroom fixtures.

Adequate accessible storage space is important to provide in kitchens.

| DESIGN DIRECTIVE |
| **SEVEN** |

1. The inside of the cabinet doors can be outfitted with storage racks so that when a door is opened, equipment and supplies are easily accessible without reaching into the cabinet. Lazy susan shelves, sliding shelves in base cabinets, and the addition of extra drawers are also useful.

2. In adaptable dwelling units, wall cabinets can be used; however, the bottom shelf of such cabinets should not be any higher than 48″ from the floor. In dwelling units where it is known that disabled people will live from the very start, wall cabinets can be omitted in favor of a single 12″ shelf within 48″ of the floor, running above the counter area. Again, the space lost from wall cabinets can be made up by the addition of full height storage units.

3. Conventional ovens and ranges are very difficult for disabled people to clean. Thus, in adaptable dwelling units, the ovens should be self-cleaning or a separate cook-top and wall-hung oven should be provided. Self-cleaning ovens are initially more expensive than others, but energy savings through the increased insulation provided result in a long-term saving on operation costs.

DESIGN DIRECTIVE

EIGHT

The conventional minimum clearance of 42″ between base cabinets is sufficient to provide wheelchair maneuverability only when base cabinet fronts are removed.

1. A 60″ turning radius in L-shaped kitchens is not necessary for basic access because the space under the counters can be used for maneuvering.

2. In a U-shaped kitchen with base cabinets, a 60″ clearance between base cabinets is needed to provide enough space for access to the mix center, sink, and refrigerator. U-shaped and L-shaped kitchens are preferable to galley arrangements.

DESIGN DIRECTIVE

NINE

The most important consideration in space planning of a minimal size accessible bathroom is that the water closet be located parallel and adjacent to an uninterrupted wall so that a grab bar of adequate length can be installed on it.

1. Accessible bathrooms can be provided within the constraints of a conventional 5′ by 7′6″ bathroom, but only if the fixtures and doorway are located so that adequate clearances and maneuvering room for wheelchairs are available (Fig. 13.8).

2. Since the tub or shower must be located on the opposite wall, the door to such bathrooms must be on the long side.

3. Some accessibility codes require a 5′ turning radius in the bathroom. Given adequate clearances, there is no need for a wheelchair user to make a 180° U-turn.

4. The height of water closets in adaptable dwelling units for the elderly should be 17″ to 19″ high, using a wall-hung fixture.

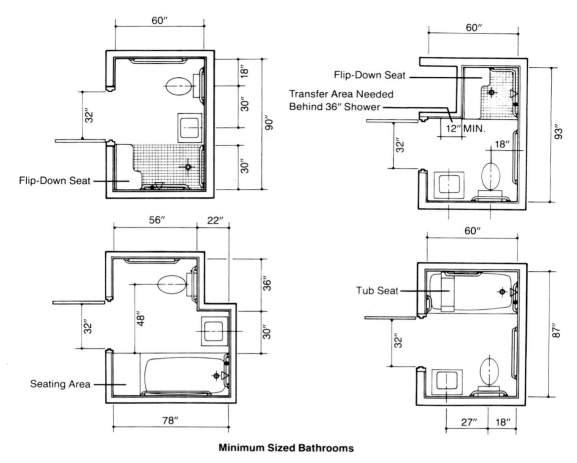

Minimum Sized Bathrooms

Note: Grab Bars and Shower/Tub Seats are Shown in Place but are Not Required in Adaptable Housing.

Symbol Key △ Shower Location
● Bath, Shower Controls
✛ Drain

FIGURE 13.8 These plans illustrate minimum-size bathroom layouts using different types of showers or tubs. The research indicated that each has its own advantages and disadvantages.

Although either tubs or showers can be provided in accessible bathrooms, in service-supported housing for the elderly shower stalls should be provided in all units.

| DESIGN DIRECTIVE |
| **TEN** |

1. Although many disabled people can use bathtubs if they have seats, hand-held shower spray units, and grab bars, there are quite a few who cannot use the tub at all. Since soaking in a bathtub is good therapy, a tub room should be provided somewhere in the building whenever dwelling units do not have bathtubs. If bathtubs are provided, they could have seats; a ledge at the back of the tub can be used as a seat, or portable seats can be used. The seat must be designed and attached so that it will not move as the person transfers into the tub. All bathtubs and shower stalls should be equipped with a hand-held shower spray.

2. There are two types of accessible shower stalls, the small 3' by 3' stall and the 5' long shower stall that takes the same amount of space as a bathtub. The 3'-square stall can be helpful to individuals in maintaining their balance and to catch themselves on the opposite side if they start to fall. The 3' by 5' stall has no advantage over the 3' square stall unless the curb is eliminated. Without a curb, the area within the stall provides additional maneuvering room for people who use wheelchairs and makes a minimum-size bathroom much easier to use. The absence of a curb in a shower stall allows a wheelchair to be pulled into the stall while a person transfers from the wheelchair to a shower seat.

3. Some accessibility codes require a 4' or 5'-square shower stall. These sizes provide no advantage over the stalls described above. Although they may be accessible, they take more room in a bathroom than necessary and may often require custom-made stalls.

4. The 3' shower stall should have a folding seat installed. A seat that is in a fixed open position is not appropriate because a fixed seat that is adequately sized in a stall as small as this would be a barrier to an ambulant resident using the shower. A 5'-long stall has enough space to accommodate a fixed chair or bench (Fig. 13.9).

DESIGN DIRECTIVE

ELEVEN

Walls must be reinforced so as to accommodate the installation of grab bars in flexible locations in or around the shower/tub and the toilet.

1. Residents use grab bars to maintain balance as they transfer into the tub or onto the toilet and for support as they lower themselves down or pull themselves up. The best location for grab bars varies considerably from person to person. Generally, they are needed on each side of tubs or showers and on one side of the toilet. Adaptable dwelling units do not need grab bars initially; they should be installed when needed, according to individual requirements.

2. Side bars near a toilet must project beyond the front of the toilet so that a person can pull him/herself forward. Some people find a bar at the back of the water closet useful.

3. In adapted dwelling units, horizontal grab bars should be installed initially. Vertical bars and diagonal bars do not provide as much safety if a person should start to fall. A single horizontal bar at the toilet is sufficient. At bathtubs, bars should be provided at both ends, and two bars should be provided along the side of the tub. One bar should be about 9" from the top of the tub rim, and another bar should be directly above that one at 33" from the floor

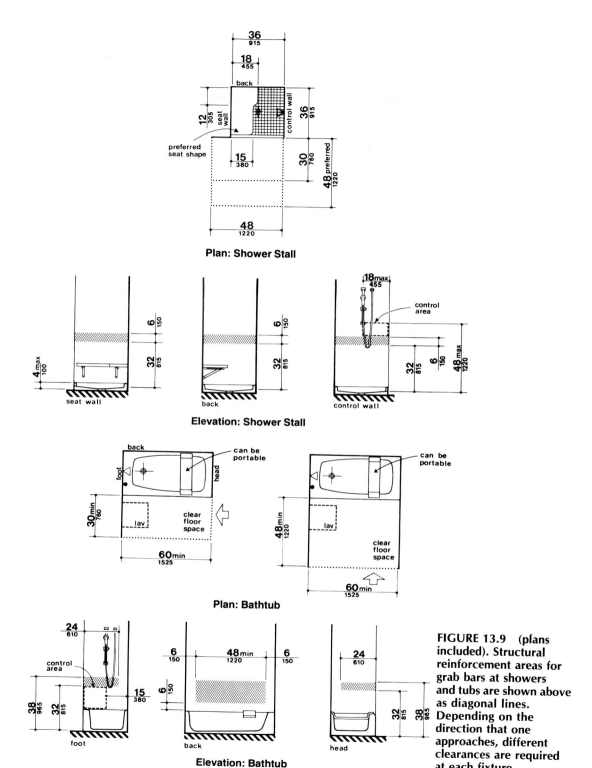

Plan: Shower Stall

Elevation: Shower Stall

Plan: Bathtub

Elevation: Bathtub

FIGURE 13.9 (plans included). Structural reinforcement areas for grab bars at showers and tubs are shown above as diagonal lines. Depending on the direction that one approaches, different clearances are required at each fixture.

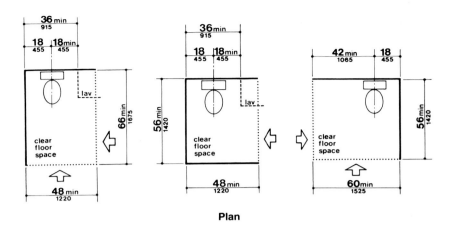

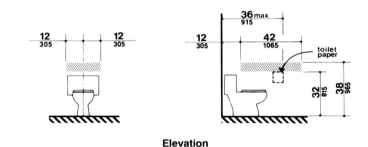

FIGURE 13.10 Structural reinforcement areas for grab bars at toilets are shown above as diagonal lines. Toilet paper holders should be below grab bars so that they do not obstruct the use of the bar.

surface. Both of these bars should be no less than 24″ long, starting at about 12″ from the back wall. At shower stalls, each side of the stall should have a continuous bar mounted at 33″ from the floor. A grab bar is not needed behind the seat of a 36″ shower stall.

DESIGN DIRECTIVE

TWELVE

Adaptable dwelling units should be equipped to allow full access to electrical systems and emergency communications.

1. Equipment is now available that utilizes any convenience outlet as a connection for a flashing unit. A device attached to the emergency controls activates the flashing unit through the building's regular electrical circuits. If such a system is not utilized, the wiring for the emergency visual alarm system must be connected to the emergency power supply. If a deaf person should occupy an adaptable dwelling unit, the emergency light can be connected so that when the fire alarm rings, the light will flash in the individual's apartment. In apartments where it is known that deaf people will live, a visual indicator should also be provided to substitute for doorbells. Vibratory devices can be installed as alternatives to or in addition to visual alarm systems.

2. In adaptable housing, center lines of electrical switches, controls, and thermostats should be located at a height of 48″ and wall outlets no lower than 15″ from the floor.

POLICY CONSIDERATIONS

Adaptable housing should become a key concept in housing the elderly.

Housing planned specifically for the elderly should employ the concept of "adaptable housing" to accommodate the needs of residents as they age and become frail.

The adaptable housing concept ensures the provision of more accessible housing at little additional cost, more choice and flexibility in unit design and adaptation, accessibility to a range of impaired and handicapped residents, and a unit design that does not cater to the most severely disabled at the expense of the less physically disabled. Embracing the adaptable housing concept does not preclude the development of special units that could be adapted to the needs of the severely impaired.

Programs should be designed to make incremental changes to dwelling units as residents need them.

The adaptable housing unit should be coupled with a formal process of evaluating the need to make adaptive changes to the dwelling unit. Theoretically, physical changes in the dwelling unit should coincide with the user's need for a more supportive environment. The environmental flexibility of accommodating change is worthless unless those options are systematically employed when the resident is in need of them.

14

DESIGNING FOR THE VISION AND HEARING IMPAIRMENTS OF THE ELDERLY

Lorraine G. Hiatt

H ave you knowingly visited a building or room that was specially designed to improve the vision and hearing of older people? Few people have. Despite data on vision and hearing changes and available design research, there are few environments that optimize the older person's remaining capabilities or encourage the use of alternative senses (Vision and Aging, 1981; Fozard and Popkin, 1978).

The purposes of this chapter are to present arguments for designing responsive, creative sensory environments; to list typical situations and environmental experiences that are affected by sensory losses; to outline design details for maximizing vision and hearing; and to suggest methods for implementing better design.

The chapter will address older people living in apartments, congregate housing, and nursing homes, as well as the older users of senior centers and rehabilitation facilities. The issues raised may be applicable to those residing in their own homes or in institutions, to workplaces for seniors, to public and commercial buildings, and to landscapes. The emphasis is on individuals whose visual and/or auditory impairments have occurred late in life. References will be made to the gamut from partially to totally impaired individuals. However, due to the sparseness of relevant literature, the needs of profoundly deaf and blind older people will be discussed only incidentally.

Related Research

Reasons for Designing Better Environments for Sensory Impaired Older People

There is good justification in the theoretical and practical literature on aging for designing and renovating environments to meet the needs of sensory impaired older people. The following outlines some of the major issues:

1. The environment is not passive; it both aids and hinders visual and auditory competence (Silver et al., 1978; Snyder et al., 1978; Fozard and Popkin, 1978).

2. Deficiencies in vision and hearing may affect mobility, whether a person walks independently or uses a wheelchair. Mobility and exercise for sensory impaired elderly people need careful consideration so that sensory impairments do not produce undue loss of mobility (Welsh and Blasch, 1980; Hiatt, 1982a, 1981d). Environments may impede or facilitate independent motion, especially for those with diminished senses (Hiatt, 1985).

3. Vision and hearing are often the first changes to be experienced with aging. A person who develops techniques for coping with initial impairments may be more adept at dealing with subsequent changes associated with aging. Many useful coping techniques rely on creative uses of the physical and social environment or technology (Marsh, 1980; Fozard and Popkin, 1978; Fozard, 1981).

4. The environment may serve as an instrument or tool of mental function by maximizing attention or concentration, essential to problem solving (Vygotsky, 1978; Fozard and Popkin, 1978; Fozard, 1981). Sustaining attention can be very demanding when the environment is not well planned or managed (Fig. 14.1).

5. Older people with disabilities may shun assistance (Weissert, 1981; Berkowitz et al., 1979). By expanding the focus from discussion groups and counseling to include practical details of managing one's surroundings, the individual may cope better both practically and emotionally. Environmental design can be an appealing, nonthreatening intervention uniting professionals, families, and older adults in problem solving.

6. The environment is omnipresent. When properly managed, it extends human services and may facilitate independence 24 hours per day (Fozard and Popkin, 1978; Fozard, 1981; Hiatt, 1981a).

7. On any given day, about 4 percent of all elderly are in nursing homes (Kastenbaum and Candy, 1973), yet 25 percent of all seriously visually impaired elderly are in nursing homes (Peterson and Kirchner, 1980). The preponderance

FIGURE 14.1   Corridor glare is often a problem: Any facility looks older and more hazardous with uncontrolled light, reflective surfaces, monochromatic colors, and monolithic textures.

of vision and hearing impaired people in institutions suggests that nursing homes be recipients of design innovation. Improving programs and environments for sensory impaired older persons may help reduce unnecessary or premature institutionalization.

Examining Statistics on Sensory Impairments Can Aid Program Planning and Design

Inferences drawn from statistical and epidemiological profiles of the older sensory impaired person suggest some specific program and design objectives.

Sensory Impairments Characterize the Majority of Elderly People:
Clinical measurements of people age 75–79 indicate that only about

15 percent have 20/20 vision, even with correction, and only 25 percent are free of hearing impairments (Harris, 1978). Most older adults experience moderate changes in vision that affect sensitivity to glare, need for additional light, and difficulties with light-dark adaptation and/or depth perception (Marsh, 1980). Many who are able to pass hearing tests in clinics cannot comprehend speech, especially in noisy places (Fozard, 1981; Elderly Hearing Impaired People, 1981; Vision and Aging, 1981). A facility serving older people should be designed to optimize whatever degree of vision and/or hearing individuals possess. To design for wheelchair access without accommodating sensory needs (as some apartments and public buildings have) is to leave the majority of elders underserved.

Most of This Nation's Sensory Impaired People Are Elderly: Nearly all hearing impaired persons and about half of all visually impaired and blind persons are elderly (Vision and Aging, 1981; Elderly Hearing Impaired People, 1981). However, resources have not been allocated proportionately. Services have focused on children, those in the labor market, and veterans (Hiatt, 1981a). Research, programs, and design specifications appropriate for these groups often do not meet the unique physical, social, and economic needs of older people.

Most "Blind" People Have Some Sight; Most "Deaf" People Have Some Hearing: Terms such as "blind" and "deaf" are construed by the public as total debilitations. (Disability groups achieve fundraising successes and influence enactment of more favorable legislation if the most dramatic needs of the extremes are emphasized.) In reality, rehabilitation services for the blind or deaf typically serve a majority who are partially sighted or hard of hearing. It is this range of impairments, from slight to none, that must be more actively incorporated in policy, program, and design. Older people may avoid information, services, or housing because they perceive themselves as having slight remaining capabilities and hence deign themselves unqualified for useful amenities (Berkowitz et al., 1979). Both 1981 mini–White House Conferences on Vision and Aging and on Hearing and Aging concluded that priorities accorded totally deaf or blind people have resulted in major policy and design omissions for the majority who are partially impaired (Vision and Aging, 1981; Elderly Hearing Impaired People, 1981) (Fig. 14.2).

Generalizations from younger blind or deaf persons may need to be amended before applying them to designs for older persons. Perhaps 3 percent of all Americans 65 and over are totally blind (Kirchner and Lowman, 1978). Rarely do the elders among blind people read braille or have guide dogs (Berkowitz et al., 1979). A slightly larger proportion are totally deaf. Hearing aids do not improve the aural losses of a substantial portion of older people (Elderly Hearing Impaired People, 1981; Sayre, 1980a,b). Design fea-

FIGURE 14.2 Lamp selection can minimize glare: Selecting lamps with globes or shades makes reading more comfortable.

tures have often catered to those in extreme need, much the same as have programs. Design for visually impaired persons has also focused on small scale features. For example, while braille notations in elevators may assist one segment of impaired users, the majority would be better assisted by large, well contrasted, raised print and large, tactile numerals at the opening of the elevator. And why should designers target elevator buttons to the exclusion of many other important building features? The total environment, rather than one notation or communication device, may become increasingly important in supporting the interactive range of impairments affecting older people.

Impairments of the Elderly Typically Occur in Multiples: Most visually deficient older people are impaired in hearing, mobility, or agility (Peterson and Kirchner, 1980). Most policies and programs are targeted toward a single disability (Hiatt, 1981a). This results in fragmentation of resources and information (Berkowitz et al., 1979). Multiply impaired people tend to be older. Advocacy and design for single disability group issues may not fully respond to the experiences of elders. Products and environments have also focused upon singular impairments, failing to consider the interactive effects of several losses (Hiatt, 1981d). Most often this has resulted in overlooking reduced agility, energy, and response time.

Most Sensory Impairments Are Slow to Develop: With some exceptions, the sensory impairments of older people occur gradually, sometimes over periods of forty years (Birren, 1964; Marsh, 1980).

As a result, individuals may not attribute difficulties in daily activities such as attention, mobility, or communication to sensory changes. Older people and professionals alike may inaccurately conclude that changes in behavior signal unremediable mental disorders (Snyder, Pyrek and Smith, 1976; Ohta, Carlin, and Harmon, 1981). Slow onset of impairments also suggests that elderly consumers may not readily identify or vocalize their own needs. Environmental designers must realize that we are designing for a population whose needs are varied and changing.

Two Major Forms of Sensory Impairment

Several excellent reviews of the literature on sensory function in old age have appeared in the past 20 years. These include:

1. Those on vision and hearing (Birren, 1964; Fozard and Popkin, 1978; Marsh, 1980; Koncelik, 1979; Sekular and Blake, 1985);
2. Those on vision, blindness, and visual aspects of sensory impairment (Fozard, Wolf, Bell, McFarland & Podolsky, 1977; Pastalan, 1979; Faye and Hood, 1976; Jolicoeur, 1970); and
3. Those on hearing, deafness, communication, or auditory aspects of sensory impairment (Corso, 1977; Cohen, 1979; Comalli, 1967; Flood, 1979; Galton, 1981).

These references document both the well-known diseases and the lesser-known chronic conditions of impairment. Examples of the diseases and disorders include: cataracts, glaucoma, diabetic retinopathy, presbyopia, presbycusis, and tintinnitus. The second set of factors playing a key role in sensory deterioration are not well recognized by the public, professionals, or designers. They include the changes that affect the lens of the eye (yellowing, thickening, and uneven surface), the muscles around the eye, and changes in hearing organs that influence the perception of speech and of high-pitched sounds.

Evaluations of Sensory Abilities Are Infrequent and Seldom True to Life

Vision and hearing specialists tend to identify impairments that their training has prepared them to treat. This may include diseases or conditions appropriate to refraction, hearing aids, or surgery. Adults are seldom given functional evaluations or techniques and instructions to help them function more efficiently, despite the many other aspects of vision and hearing loss (Figs. 14.3 and 14.4). Light-dark adaptation, night driving capabilities, color perception, and sensitivity to glare or contrasts are seldom measured or discussed (Secular and Blake, 1985; Hiatt, 1985). Hearing measure-

FIGURE 14.3
Decorative lighting can
be a problem: Clear
bulbs that expose the
filament produce hot
spots and problem glare.

FIGURE 14.4 Indirect
lighting is a good solu-
tion to glare: Indirect
fluorescent valance lighting combined with in-
candescent task lighting
provide effective, com-
fortable illumination
(Schnee and Schnee
Designers).

ments are taken in specially soundproof environments and are seldom realistic. Inadequate, superficial measurement of the partial losses of vision and hearing have resulted in fragmented reporting and a tendency to overlook these needs in services and design (Cohen, 1979; Fozard and Popkin, 1978; Sekular and Blake, 1985; Elderly Hearing Impaired People, 1981; Vision and Aging, 1981).

There have been recommendations to improve evaluations by measuring functional performance in realistic circumstances (Willems, 1977). Researchers are perfecting the use of "contrast sensitivity" rather than print legibility as a test of adult vision (Sekular and Blake, 1985) and of evaluating vision in one's own residence (Cullinan, 1980a; Hiatt, 1980c). Hearing assessment techniques are also beginning to rely on tests made in real surroundings rather than clinics and clients are urged to ask their specialists how clinical information will relate to real life circumstances (Sayre, 1980a,b). Ideally, both clinically controlled measures of vision and hearing and those that indicate performance in actual settings are needed. Research comparing the findings between the two would be useful in developing better acoustical and visual settings.

New Services Increasingly Involve Training to Optimize Existing Abilities

Three innovations are emerging in services for older people with sensory limitations: formal training, emphasis on identifying and improving existing skills, and self-help groups.

Services for people who are partially sighted, also called "low vision services," can be an example of all three of these trends. Low vision services involve using a variety of optical aids or special techniques (such as posture, seating, and eye resting) to induce the individual to get the most out of any remaining vision (Faye and Hood, 1976; Rosenbloom, 1981; Genensky, 1980). Similar efforts have been urged by advocacy groups in the field of audition (Cohen, 1979; Sayre, 1980a,b; Elderly Hearing Impaired People, 1981).

While self-help groups are no substitute for rehabilitation services or specialized design, they are increasing the direct participation of older people in self-assessment and are stimulating the assertiveness necessary to cope in challenging social situations. Self-help groups also provide a forum for sharing practical solutions to everyday tasks and environmental problems (Hiatt, Brieff, Horwitz et al., 1982; Elderly Hearing Impaired People, 1981).

Experiences Affected by Sensory Impairments

How do sensory losses affect daily activities? While those who have experienced impairments early in life may have adapted techniques for coping in complex and busy surroundings, the older person

TABLE 14.1   Activities Affected by Vision and Hearing Losses

This table includes some types of activities that can be difficult and need to be accommodated in design.

Difficult for People With Visual Impairments

I. *Close Work*

Reading; financial transactions; telephoning, related searching, and message taking; telling and keeping track of time; locating lost objects; using controls (stove, thermostat, radiator, electronics); sewing; sorting and matching (clothing, decorating); home repairs; handling fire (smoking); preparing and eating meals; table games (cards, bingo); and grooming (shaving, makeup, facial care).

II. *Intermediate Distance Tasks*

Shopping, gardening, pedestrianism, orientation to and location of specific places; recognizing and identifying people; identifying and maintaining order; laundry and housekeeping.

III. *Mobility and Exercise Tasks*

Driving automobiles and bicycles and related safety; depth perception; landmark recognition; avoiding hazards; target sports; transfer of weight and repositioning, as in getting in and out of tubs; entering vehicles and using ramps or escalaters.

Can be Difficult for People With Hearing Impairments

IV. *Communication and Social Situations*

Conversations (with strangers, acquaintances, friends); use of communications technology (telephones, radio, T.V.); functioning in crowds; participation in discussions; correspondence; interactions among people of varying abilities.

May be Difficult for Either or Both

V. *Memory and Learning*

Increased reliance on memory; use of memory cues and props; need for greater time for input and response.

VI. *Security*

Self-protection and sensations of vulnerability; locking and unlocking doors (vision-impaired persons); pedestrian security (both); overhead obstacles (blind persons); changes in ground contour (visually impaired persons).

For reading on techniques taught to mitigate difficulties, see Markle, 1972; Yeadon, 1980; AFB, 1972.

---

may find complex, dense, or highly stimulating environments to be taxing.

Table 14.1 illustrates some of the activities affected by sensory losses. By learning about the adaptation techniques taught by rehabilitation professionals and occupational therapists, designers and decision makers may gain new insights regarding the potential for accommodating these activities.

One particularly difficult task is scanning and the ability to accurately interpret what one initially perceives. Other challenging situations are those that require an immediate response, such as rushing through a revolving door. Both blind and deaf persons can be challenged in unfamiliar places: transportation terminals, medical centers, or public meetings may all be somewhat difficult.

For hearing-impaired persons, groups larger than six to eight may make participatory conversation difficult. Use of amplifiers, visibility of speakers, and conscientious social practices may overcome some of these difficulties for those with partial hearing.

Sounds are information-laden cues. They may signal arrivals, changes, disorders, and even mark passing time. To the city dweller, the din of continual background noise may be familiar and comfortable. For the country dweller, crickets and peepers suggest that all is well. Sound distortions from either physiological or environmental causes may limit the usefulness of life-long cues. Uncontrollable background noises or changes in one's acoustical environment may produce sleep disturbances. The change from intelligible to nonintelligible sounds may be as frustrating as the change from an acoustically rich to a silent world (Zimbardo and Anderson, 1981).

Methodology and Data Analysis

The data for this chapter rely heavily on literature, owing to the lack of facilities developed for sensory impaired older people and the scarce number of post-occupancy studies. Recommendations are derived from:

1. A study of sensory functioning of 200 older persons in a geriatric center (Snyder, Pyrek and Smith, 1978);
2. Abstractions from a mail survey of 1,660 U.S. institutions (apartments to health centers) and site visits to 47 of these (Berkowitz, Hiatt, de Toledo, et al., 1979);
3. Research visitations and consultation to some 300 other institutions over the past 15 years (Snyder and Bowersox, 1976; Snyder, Ostrander and Koncelik, 1973); and
4. Five years with the American Foundation for the Blind working on an evaluation research project on how elders use life-long experiences and arrange the physical environment to compensate for vision, hearing, and memory losses (Hiatt, Brieff, Horwitz and McQueen, 1982).

Findings and Conclusions

The planning and design of environments for sensory impaired adults require knowledge of four fundamental principles: how the user experiences the setting; what activities are affected by sensory impairments; the repertoire of environmental responses available to alleviate difficult situations; and how to implement information.

A Review of Existing Facilities Offers Examples of Fundamental Considerations

Site visits made to nearly 350 U.S. institutions, senior centers, and rehabilitation sites over the past 15 years and consultation to some 80 clients have resulted in these guidelines.

Clarification of Capabilities: Both capabilities and impairments of older sensory-impaired persons need to be clearly understood by service administrators, program planners, and those overseeing design. Users are often more diverse than planners imagine and often have minor multiple impairments rather than serious singular disabilities.

Informal interaction with older people may not reveal the extent of their sensory impairment or the degree of their coping skills. Partial hearing losses, especially with today's subtle hearing aids, and deafness may be undetected. Hearing-impaired people often have few signals to remind those with whom they interact to speak clearly, face them, or speak one at a time (Sayre, 1980a,b; Mc-Cartney and Nadler, 1980) (Fig. 14.5).

Supporting the Services Housed: Generalizations based on stereotypes of leisure time or experience with younger sensory-impaired persons may fail to allow designers to activate the potential of design. Specifics on the activities to be performed need to be incorporated into site selection and landscaping, facility layout, room configuration and size, and material choices. Buildings designed without adequate information on the daily routine may be more costly to manage and may be over-designed for some users and under-designed for others.

FIGURE 14.5   Groups sized for conversation: Small group conversations improve speech intelligibility. Due to physiological changes, hearing problems may likely occur in groups larger than six.

Taking Advantage of Technology: The field of technology and aging is burgeoning with possibilities for overcoming sensory limitations. Professionals may tend to think first of services. They may dismiss products as too costly or unavailable. Some of the most significant environmental improvements for older sensory-impaired people can be made through informed interior design and product selections. Underutilized technologies include lighting, interior surfacing materials, hand-held objects and furniture, and security and communication systems (Hiatt, 1981d).

Reevaluating Design: After a building is occupied, the activities, services, and users' needs are likely to change. Some design adaptations are made every day such as those involving arrangement. However, too often people waste time each day making up for a dysfunctional setting. Changes are deferred on the assumption that older people can work around the poor light or hear announcements through the din. Everyone presumes that older users will adapt. But sometimes their strategy for adapting, particularly in the face of diminished sight and hearing, is to limit participation or to stay away.

The designer can encounter three main barriers to innovation: anxiety regarding precedent setting, time, and cost. Research on vision and hearing needs of older people, for example, are quite recent (Fozard and Popkin, 1978). It takes time for research findings to be translated into structure and products. Decision makers are sometimes reluctant to venture into functional design for sensory-impaired people because they do not know how to meet the needs and cannot identify prototypes. The fear of being first may be revealed by comments such as: "If it were such a good idea, why hasn't it been done before?" There are some good design examples, the locations of which are available through professional societies and literature in gerontology and design. They are still sparse and may require some travel. Addressing barriers to innovation at an early planning session may free up time and energy for creative problem solving.

Time is a concern because it is equated with money. It does take time to plan, but effective planning and orderly decision making can save time.

A sponsor may retain local designers and such firms may or may not have experience in innovative and functional design for sensory-impaired older people—though they may have designed many units of housing or health care facilities for older occupants. Becoming better versed in the options, using the literature, attending conferences, or even retaining consultants early in the thinking process can result in a better initial design concept, one in which board members or owners can have greater confidence, making decisions flow more quickly (Zeisel, 1983).

Finally, designing facilities and selecting products that will maximize the capabilities of older, sensory-impaired persons does not necessarily require greater expense. Often, the choice involves "even money"—making a better selection from equally priced commodities. Many recommendations will yield lower operating and management costs. Better design may require investigating new products (by meeting with sales reps, attending conferences, and touring newer facilities). Many manufacturers recognize that there is a large market in renovation work and have designed products for retrofitting as well as new construction (Philips and Salmen, 1983; McGillivray, 1984).

Planning Techniques

Planning Technique: Clarify the Users: There is a phenomenal gap in most projects between idealized and actual users. Dissatisfactions with new and older buildings often occur for two reasons. Users change, making plans less suitable. They may age, be more diverse than anticipated, or be more impaired as the facility becomes older. Also, planners or designers may have mistaken notions about the users; for example, apprehensions regarding marketability often result in designing for unrealistically independent users. Conferring with too small a constituency may result in designing for the extreme (and articulate) users.

Speak with experienced providers. Visit with managers who have lived through 6 or more years with a population similar to yours and have them speak to the adjustments and changes. Since about 1980, three factors have resulted in more diverse and somewhat more frail housing and health care tenants and more diverse senior center clients: home care and community options have increased so older people stay at home longer; the numbers of apartments for independent older persons—such as housing and continuing care retirement centers—have proliferated, often creaming off the more adept and self-reliant consumers; and more people are living into their 80s and beyond, when sensory impairments are more common. In addition, organizations for professionals such as the National Council on the Aging have developed highly sophisticated educational workshops to train senior citizen center leaders to work with more diverse and impaired populations (Jacobs, 1976).

As consumers become wiser about what can be done to compensate for sensory impairments, facilities that respond appropriately and subtly may have a marketing edge.

Planning Technique: Experience Sensory Impairment on a Personal Level: How does it feel to have less vision or hearing? To understand how patterned, habitual movements are affected involves more than closing one's eyes or cupping the ears. Most planners and designers have not experienced the maturing processes of late adulthood. Even consumer representatives may not have a full understanding of the interactive effects of impairments on the overall experiences of home life or mobility. Empathic techniques engage decision makers in simulating the effects of vision and hearing losses and are especially useful in communicating the effects of glare and background noise (Pastalan, 1980).

Two cautions are urged. Empathic models may exaggerate problems because most older people have had many years to grapple with adaptations; they are not undergoing the sudden changes. As a teaching tool, the empathic model needs to be supplemented by equally dynamic teaching methods that convey individual differences and the potential to offset some of these changes through improved design. Meetings with occupational therapists or designers who have resolved some of the environmental deficiencies can supplement the empathic experience. Empathic techniques combined with audio-visuals may clarify the experiences and stimulate innovation (National Council on Aging, 1985).

Planning Technique: Identify Activities Influenced by Sensory Impairments and Project Their Locations on Plans: Table 14.1 illustrates activities that can be affected by diminished vision and/or hearing. This list may spark planners to identify the specific activities that will be occurring in their own building and help prioritize areas for special design treatment. Architectural details can also minimize the problems associated with glare (Fig. 14.6).

Designers need to gather information from those who will ultimately use a space and expand the traditional architectural program (which details room types and square footage). Consider specially detailing spaces that house close-work, intermediate distance tasks, distant tasks, transactions and communications, and memory dependent tasks; mobility and weight transfer (reaching, getting into a tub); or security. For example, if people are intended to conduct transactions at an office, they should not be required to be in the line of traffic, susceptible to noise or distractions, and in poorly lit surroundings. With specific ideas on how spaces—particularly community rooms, lobbies, and living areas—are to be used, the designer is in a better position to develop specific plans regarding efficient task lighting and to incorporate techniques for minimizing acoustical problems.

Planning Technique: Engage the Intended User in Planning and Evaluating Alternative Decisions: There have been a few examples of planning procedures involving older people, but those who have utilized these "participatory" procedures are generally enthusiastic about the potential benefits (Hartman, Horovitz and Herman, 1976; Howell, 1980). One organization has a self-help kit

FIGURE 14.6
Architectural means of controlling glare: An overhanging roof line and bay windows provide architectural variety and better views while minimizing glare (The Architect's Collaborative).

for use by older people in adapting personal environments to respond to the needs of vision, hearing, and memory (Hiatt, Brieff, Horwitz, and McQueen, 1983).

Environmental inventories that include questions related to sensory functioning have been compiled for use in long-term care facilities (Hiatt, 1981c), senior centers (Jordan, 1978), and households (Remnet, 1976; Sayre, 1981a,b). These can be helpful in raising important discussion issues and in leading the designer to identify important problems.

Planning Technique: Visit Other Facilities and Use Specialists with Knowledge and Experience in Innovative Design: In most cases, becoming aware of models or facilities that have accomplished similar objectives, even if in another state or country, can be very useful (Fig. 14.7). These models may inspire designers, leading to improvements beyond those of the "models." Prototypes may also be useful in convincing boards or review commissions about the value of new design features. Facility engineers and marketers may have some questions, for example, about the public reaction to nonglare surfaces. Putting sponsors in contact with precedents is a method for making "new" ideas more familiar. Journals, conferences, specialists or consultants, and professional organizations may all be sources of information on exemplary design. Though there are few if any "perfect" facilities for older people, there are more and more with elements of good design. Guide touring groups carefully through the model facilities, pointing out highlights. And, plan to deal with questions about shortcomings so that visitors do not become disillusioned with the important features on the basis of unrelated or remediable shortcomings.

FIGURE 14.7 Task lighting in corridors: Indirect, recessed lighting improves the visibility of each resident's door and reduces the light level change between apartment and corridor (Robinson Myrick, Architect).

Design Technique: Consider How New Technology Will Affect Environmental Design: Many new technologies have been introduced to the general market place that fulfill requirements of sensory-impaired users.

In the area of vision, for example, the scope of new products has included laser canes and sonic guides for travel, speech synthesis, and reading techniques, as well as braille translators (Mellor, 1981; Frieberger, 1980). Telephones have been improved for easier dialing and controlled listening. In the home entertainment industry, televisions have been designed that are easier for vision-impaired persons to view. The contrast is crisper and the picture is larger with less distortion. The sound may also be amplified for better listening: individually controlled treble and bass mean that the older person can increase lower tones without raising the volume.

Developments are coming so fast that some national organizations such as the American Foundation for the Blind have allocated a major department to keep track of new products and participate in their development.

Research and technology in lighting seem to have lagged behind other types of products (Rosenbloom, 1982). Touch-on™ lamps, full-spectrum lighting, and multipurpose valance lighting are three improvements that are widely marketed. More research is needed on the impact of halogen lamps on visual performance of older people. Someday, consumers will have simple techniques for judging how effectively different work areas are lit according to their needs.

Products for improving the acoustical environments are not widely advertised. One needs to contact national hearing organizations for information and up-to-date product reviews. One design technique has involved the creation of sophisticated spaces that minimize sound distortion and reduce background noise.

There are stationary amplification devices for assembly halls or meeting places, some of which can be used in conjunction with hearing aids. Some are designed to receive signals transmitted directly from a microphone rather than transmitting sounds through the room itself (which may be noisy, and would amplify distorting background noise, confusing the sensitive listener).

Acoustics have also been improved through portable amplifying systems that do not require modification of the environment. Transmitters are wired into a television or radio, and sound is received by the listener through an earmold or stethoscope-type device. A hearing-impaired person may enjoy television or concerts alongside normally hearing peers. Products have also been adapted that differentially remove problem noise; some of these are like windscreens and facilitate group communication (Alternative Listening Devices, 1981). Some portable devices have short ranges, 300 feet or less, and have been used more in residential-size spaces such as dining or meeting rooms. This field changes so rapidly that contact with national associations such as Self-Help for Hard of Hearing (Bethesda, Maryland) before launching each new project is advised.

The proliferation of graphic computers and telecommunications is suggesting many new ways for sensory-impaired people to share information (Blasch and Hiatt, 1983). Talking signs, clocks, scales, calculators, and key chains are all fairly widely available. Alarm clocks that vibrate and fire signals that have more audible and visual output are also marketed (contact Able Data, Washington, D.C., for current product sources). Communication devices such as Teletypewriters (TTYs) and telecommunications for the deaf (TTDs) permit typed messages to be transmitted through telephones. While such devices are located in some of the larger airports, alternative communications and related security systems have seldom been integrated into the design of senior centers or retirement housing.

Design Technique: Give Sensory Features High Priority: Responsive design starts with consensus on the priority for meeting the needs of sensory-impaired users. Because codes and regulations do not amply incorporate information on sensory function (Blasch and Hiatt, 1983), sponsors and designers must set the priority themselves. Few outside agencies will draw shortcomings to one's attention.

Vision is typically maximized by techniques of glare reduction, increased lighting, and improved contrast between foreground and background. Hearing can be maximized by controlling background noise and substituting lower tones for higher ones in communications or security technologies. Unwanted sounds can also be absorbed by specifying wall finishes that help baffle noise (Fig. 14.8). These approaches are detailed in the Design Directives section.

FIGURE 14.8 Textured wall covering as a backdrop for artwork: This material not only absorbs sound but also offers a backdrop for changing art exhibits.

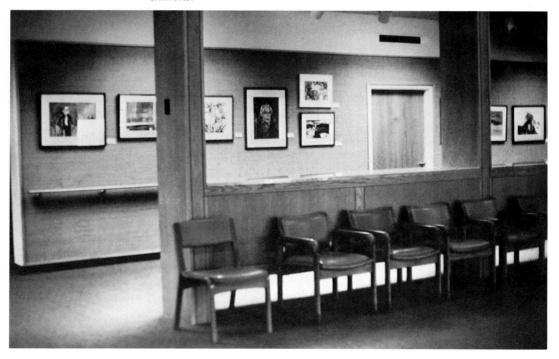

Conclusions

Why Are Sensory Aspects of Environmental Design Being Underutilized or Overlooked?

The gap between knowledge and practice is wide. Some of the reasons for this include:

1. Issues of vision and hearing, ranging from services to facilities, are typically not incorporated into building codes (Blasch and Hiatt, 1983).
2. There is a false assumption that improvements always cost more and that no sources of financing are available to pay for them.
3. Other health issues, particularly acute needs, take precedence over sensory impairments, which typically do not cause pain or visible suffering.
4. Older people and their families do not demand design features that would offset sensory impairments. Sponsors will need to hear the demand or identify clear cut marketing or management advantages before they are convinced that sensory issues are design issues.
5. Administrators, service directors, and designers are unaware of available information sources or design options.
6. Few model programs and environments exist. Therefore, good examples are not readily available and require money and travel. Often the majority of powerful decision makers never visit the prototypes first-hand.
7. Everyone thinks the sensory-impaired person inhabits some other environment, not the one he manages or will build.
8. Few information resources are available to guide remodeling and new facility planning.
9. There is a false assumption that "independent" older people are free of sensory changes.
10. Sponsors mistakenly believe that features that maximize the needs of vision- or hearing-impaired persons will inconvenience users who are younger or less impaired. Features are presumed to be obtrusive and unacceptable by the youth oriented (even if elderly) consumer.

What Can We Expect in the Future?

Unobtrusive Functional Design in Environments and Products:
Recognition of the elderly market of consumers since about 1981 has resulted in the proliferation of subtly designed products and facilities for people with special needs. Function can be beautiful. Designers will become increasingly skilled and competitive about product and facility appearance. As this happens, designs that accommodate and overcome sensory impairments will become more acceptable.

Sensory Efficiency Training: Buildings, spaces, and equipment will motivate the individual to exploit their remaining capabilities. Someday, the blind pedestrian may drive and the deaf musician will hear. Short of that, most elderly people will be instructed in methods for using their residual faculties more effectively in tasks ranging from golf to financial management, from conversing to remembering.

Environments Will Stimulate Fitness: Furniture will be designed and settings arranged to evoke fitness and motivate exercise. These products and settings will be geared toward "gradients of difficulty" with adjustable, self-controlled features. Facilities and products will match our maturing process. We will personally manipulate acoustical and visual environments to accommodate changing needs, and from these changes we will learn more about the limits of our own capabilities. Instead of moving from one level of care to another, environments may well age with us (Lawton, 1981; Hiatt, 1981d).

New Opportunities Will Emerge for Older Workers: As our understanding of functional design increases, so will the application of these findings to places of work. With better lighting, manual laborers may be more efficient and earn the option of working longer. With improved acoustical and visual environments, office workers may continue to perform and intergenerational communication will be improved (Fig. 14.9).

New Methods of Planning Will Emerge: New techniques for collaboration (teleconferencing, use of off-site experts, and more comprehensive facility planning) will emerge. As the result of better communication, better methods for compensating for sensory needs will be developed.

Sensory Transcendent Technology: Technologies will enhance and expand the previous limitations of the senses. Though full organ transplants or mechanical eyes and ears are not yet available, the person who is old will be less reliant upon a 100 percent, perfectly operating body or mind (Hiatt, 1981d).

Developmental Prevention: Throughout life, greater attention will be paid to human performance, activities, and environmental design features that contribute to optimizing health in later life. These include improved early identification of vision and hearing changes, incentives for healthy living, and the adoption of products throughout the life cycle that protect and preserve vision and hearing.

FIGURE 14.9 Controlling noise in public areas: Bookshelves, textured materials, and carpeting help absorb annoying background noise.

Prescriptive Design: Environmental design features will be part of the prescription used to alleviate particular visual and hearing conditions, much the same as pharmaceuticals and exercises are ordered today.

Economic Benefits: Economic benefits will be documented on the costs and savings that result from employing environmental design strategies to help overcome the dependency of older sensory-impaired people. Knowledge of costs will guide developments and help expand the potential of supportive but noninstitutional services. If savings can be documented, institutional facilities for sensory-impaired persons will be improved.

More Information and Less Cost: Professionals and peer groups will emerge to help people deal with the options and resources available. These may include more and better consumer guides on products, self-help groups on how to use environmental design more creatively, clearing houses on housing and health care, and more purchasing clubs that would make such amenities available at a discount.

DESIGN DIRECTIVES

Upgrade lighting levels and direct light as demanded by the task.

1. Lighting levels in households and institutions are typically inadequate for the visual needs of older people (Cullinan, 1980; Hiatt, 1981b; Lefitt, 1980). Task lighting can be increased by better location of the light source in relation to the task (that is, directing light to tables for dining and arts, on a floor near handrails in hallways, up walls for storage and signs). For some tasks, lighting levels will need to be increased (Boyce, 1980; Blackwell and Blackwell, 1971; Fozard et al., 1977; Koncelik, 1979).

2. It has been estimated that older people require about two to three times the light as do younger ones. In the absence of specific empirical research on task lighting, several designers and the State of Virginia have multiplied conventional foot candle requirements and developed the following guidelines:

TABLE 14.2 Lighting Recommendations in Footcandles

Corridor	20
Overall dining	30
At signs	60
Library	150
Bedside	200–300
Average	100

Developed by John Purdy, AIA, Architekton, Inc.; Joan Pease, Partners in Planning, Inc.; and (independently) by the Commonwealth of Virginia.

3. If the building is specifically designed for low vision users or those requiring magnifiers, additional task lighting is needed. Lighting levels should, however, be under individual control as there are occasionally visual conditions in which lower lighting levels are more comfortable.

4. Reduce fatigue by using full spectrum fluorescent lighting sources (Hughes and Neer, 1981). Full spectrum light simulates natural sunlight, giving better color rendition for indoor illumination. It also improves vitamin absorption (Hughes and Neer, 1981). Visual fatigue may be overcome by keeping fluorescent lamps in good working order, that is, by replacing worn out ballasts that tend to cause flickering. Shorter fluorescent tubes are often easier to store, transport, and service than are longer ones.

5. For hallways and paths, the best way to maximize vision, minimize confusion, and reduce risk of falls is to supply evenly spread continuous lighting that is free of shadows or other abrupt changes

(Hughes and Neer, 1981). Incandescent wall sconces and lanterns typically do not adequately or economically meet lighting requirements of older persons.

6. Use accent lighting and color contrasts to alert users to important features of the environment (Hiatt, 1980a; Fozard, 1981; Hughes and Neer, 1981; Sicurella, 1977).

7. All fluorescent and incandescent light should be indirect. This means that bulbs should not be visible to the user. Valances, cove lighting, lamp shades, and diffusers are all methods of concealing the lamp and avoiding visual "hot spots." Can or down lamps should be avoided except when they are directed toward artwork or the wall.

Contrast features or surfaces that need to be differentiated.

DESIGN DIRECTIVE
TWO

1. Use contrast to differentiate edges. Contrast may be achieved through the use of color, texture, materials, size variations, and lighting (Dickman, 1983; Sicurella, 1977; Hiatt, 1980c).

2. To emphasize a focal object, signify a change, or direct attention to important information, increase the contrast between focal object and background. The two surfaces should be two or three values or shades different from each other on a gray scale (Blackwell and Blackwell, 1971; Sicurella, 1977).

3. Minimize contrasts that may inadvertently create optical illusions of objects or surface changes. Even simple stripes or checkered patterns on a floor covering can be perceived as steps or openings (Blackwell and Blackwell, 1971; Sicurella, 1977; Finch, 1981).

Minimize and control glare.

DESIGN DIRECTIVE
THREE

1. Changes in the human eye's lens render the older person more sensitive to glare (Fozard et al., 1977). Glare is produced by the sun or light reflecting off of surfaces or fixtures. It can also be aggravated by fluorescent lights; shiny, lustrous floors; and metal, vinyl, plastic, or veneer furnishings. Use nonreflective surfaces and materials to minimize glare.

2. Architectural features for controlling glare include overhangs, recessed windows, and roof designs that function like an awning. Tinted glass, solar shades, and horizontal window coverings (which can be partly lowered) are interior design methods that help control direct glare from the sun while maximizing natural lighting.

3. Avoid direct glare by minimizing excessively bright or unshielded lighting sources, selecting chandeliers with shades, and using heavily opalescent bulbs rather than crystal ones (Hiatt, 1978; Hughes and Neer, 1981; Welsh and Blasch, 1980).

4. Plan seating arrangements that orient older people away from sunlight or mirrored surfaces. Alter either the location of light, surfaces, or placement of furnishings to avoid exposure glare (Hughes and Neer, 1981; Pastalan, 1979).

5. In existing facilities, glare may be reduced by cleaning dirty lamp lenses or windows and by using nonglare finishes (waxes) on floors.

DESIGN DIRECTIVE	*Avoid confusing vertical surfaces.*
FOUR	

1. Architectural barriers for blind people include overhead branches, protruding fountains or phone booths, and scaffolding or perpendicular signs. Such items may not be detected by the sweep of a cane or the responses of a guide dog. Architectural plans should be detailed to three dimensions, since features on vertical surfaces are often overlooked in two-dimensional floor plans.

2. Uneven ground, changing levels or drop-offs, and curb cuts that flow into traffic without warning create hazards for blind pedestrians (Wardell, 1980). Posture changes with aging and ramps are hazardous for the older pedestrian, particularly when vision is diminished.

3. Avoid surface changes requiring ramps whenever possible. Use firm, sturdy, well-lit handrails and nonslip surfaces if ramps must be used. Ramps without handrails are totally unacceptable. In some instances, one or two steps may be easier to negotiate than a ramp, and dual walkways are advisable.

DESIGN DIRECTIVE	*Use color and texture to create design schemes and set moods.*
FIVE	

1. However, do not rely on color coding alone to identify a room or entry. Color is often so subtle, abstract, or unfamiliar that its value to older people as a distinguishable room identifier is limited. Personally meaningful, identifiable, nameable objects distinguish doorways and may be more easily remembered and used (Hiatt, 1980a).

2. Graphics that contrast to their background surface can be more visible (Blasch and Hiatt, 1982; Dickman, 1983).

3. The eye's lens yellows with normal aging. Colors should be selected with a view to minimizing this discoloration. Blues, greens, and violets placed side by side are often difficult to correctly name. Dark shades, under similar lighting and on the same background, are typically indistinguishable. Pastel tones, under similar conditions, are also hard to differentiate and name. Bold colors blend into one or two values. Walls might best be kept light so that objects are distinguishable. However, to define an edge or end wall, dark or bright tones and all-over textures can be effective. Nearly any color can be rendered more visible by selecting an appropriately light or dark background.

4. Because of the difficulties in perceiving or naming color, texture can be an effective design resource to augment color variation or create an ambiance.

5. Since color perception relies on so many variables, no single set of colors can be guaranteed to elicit a particular response. However, when wall colors dominate a space they may make other details of the environment more difficult to perceive.

Use contrasts such as textures, objects, and size variations to communicate important environmental information.

1. Texture changes are useful cues for both partially sighted and totally blind users. However, repetitious textures can be as monotonous as a singular color scheme.

2. Novelty items, well placed in relation to choices to be made, tend to be most useful for way-finding (see Weisman, chapter 18 in this volume).

3. Contrast also improves print legibility (Ralph, 1982).

4. Size changes such as ceiling heights or landscape changes may also convey importance, especially when these features create a different ambiance in air movement. However, super-graphics or full wall murals may be so large as to be unfamiliar outside the visual field (Hiatt, 1980a).

Use environmental cues to increase awareness of spaces/places that may lead to falls.

1. Three common sites of falls for older people are the bathroom, the area adjacent to the bed, and transitional spaces between rooms and halls or indoors and outside. Design features such as upgraded lighting and matte finishes in transitional areas, sheet rubber rather than reflective tile flooring in bathrooms, and sturdy grasping surfaces at the bedside may all improve stability.

2. With diminished sight, grip becomes more important. Providing stabilizing surfaces or fixtures for holding onto will often help overcome unsteadiness and reduce risks of falls.

3. Nonglare floors and surface treatments may further reduce risks of falls in corridors by making the ground seem more secure and less icy.

DESIGN DIRECTIVE	*Carefully consider the form, size, font style, and location of graphic devices*
EIGHT	*that are intended to clarify orientation and way-finding.*

1. Research on graphic signage has indicated that the simple lines of sans serif (Helvetica style) lettering are more legible for building signs. Letters with serifs (Roman style) are more quickly read in hand-held printed material (Ralph, 1983; Blasch and Hiatt, 1983).

2. Because visually impaired and blind persons may trace door labels manually, recessed letters are preferred. Raised letters may cast shadows and can be misread (for example, a 3 may appear to be an 8). Raised letters of acrylic or plastic are more likely to chip and break.

3. Distance must be considered in selecting lettering size. For door signs meant to be read in close to midrange, lettering should be about 2 inches high on a well-contrasted background and should be at eye level beside the door.

4. Tangible orienting devices may be preferable to abstract symbols and words or letters alone (see Weisman, chapter 18 in this volume).

DESIGN DIRECTIVE	*Control background noise.*
NINE	

Auditory environments, perhaps more than visual ones, are capable of contributing to stress. Excessive stress may have many negative effects upon older people, ranging from increasing paranoia to decreasing attention span and memory. The older person is more sensitive and vulnerable to stress from background noise and unidentifiable sounds than is the younger individual (Marsh, 1980; Fozard, 1981). Noise is also a greater problem when the individual cannot see its source or predict its occurrence (Weiss, 1976).

1. Two types of noise are important to control: background noise and sudden, intense, and uncontrollable noise.

2. Eliminate constant sources of noise to improve speech intelligibility. This includes piped in music that is not the focus of an activity, heating or air conditioning, mechanical systems and dishwashing, and vending or ice machines.

3. One step in the design process should include predicting and analyzing sources of noise from either mechanical systems or social sources in the planning stages.

4. By diagramming sources of noise, alternative locations of mechanical systems or methods of noise separation may be planned. Whatever noise sources cannot be changed can often be isolated behind sound-absorbing walls or baffled through other architectural or landscaping techniques.

5. Ceiling treatments alone have typically been unsatisfactory methods for controlling noise associated with conversation (though ceiling treatments have worked in industrial settings) unless the area is small and ceiling is quite low.

6. Walls may be covered with absorbent materials such as fire-treated carpeting, acoustical panels, dense fabrics, or textured redwood. Such treatments are increasingly common in corridors, dining and activities rooms, and even bedrooms. Most have the advantage of providing a tackable surface for artwork or objects (useful as landmarks) without leaving a mark.

7. Glass absorbs little sound. Large window walls may produce acoustical problems unless heavily draped or covered with acoustical vertical blinds. Lower, more effectively placed windows may actually improve communication and reduce glare.

8. As a last resort, activities may need to be relocated to a more workable location in the building so that conversations can occur more comfortably.

Minimize difficult-to-hear, high pitched sounds.

DESIGN DIRECTIVE
TEN

1. Several hearing disorders commonly associated with old age render the older person less capable of perceiving high pitched tones (Corso, 1977). Ultra-high frequency security systems may interfere with hearing aids.

2. Important sounds like emergency signals or security systems should be of a low frequency with strong reverberations.

3. For the range of the partially to totally deaf older person, sound-emitting signals should be outfitted with a redundant visual warning device, such as a flashing light.

4. Textured signal systems (those emitting heat or vibration) are available for communicating signals to deaf blind persons (contact Able Data, Washington, D.C., an information clearing house, for details).

Seating should be arranged so as to optimize visual and communication abilities.

DESIGN DIRECTIVE
ELEVEN

1. Many totally deaf older people can follow events visually if they are seated so that they can see them clearly. Adjustable rather than fixed seating may allow staggered arrangements that improve visibility.

2. Circular rather than straight-line seating will maximize eye contact and the freedom of movement necessary to orient listeners toward the speaker(s).

3. Individuals should be seated within handshake distance for most effective participatory group discussions. For larger groups, recognize that participation may be diminished and make simple-to-use, flexible amplification systems available.

<table>
<tr><td>DESIGN DIRECTIVE
TWELVE</td><td>*Explore new sound technologies for communal spaces and meeting rooms.*

1. Obtain current information on the latest technologies for sound amplification. Consider the use of technologies for selective amplification.

2. Explore the feasibility of wireless systems that allow users greater choice in seating position and arrangement.</td></tr>
</table>

POLICY CONSIDERATIONS

Explore the implications of comingling partially and severely visually and hearing-impaired people.

The presumption that vision or hearing impairments warrant separate facilities and services is questionable (Wener, 1984). Facilities erected only for the blind or the deaf often result from inadequate community awareness on deafness or blindness and/or admissions requirements to housing or services, which give the impression that such users are less competent than they in fact are.

In fact, the numbers of totally blind and/or deaf persons are typically so small that facilities erected for only these users tend to have marketing difficulties and eventually extend their services to partially impaired users as well. The presumption that special facilities are the only appropriate environment for sensory-impaired persons can be a disservice to many sensory-impaired consumers, depriving them of normalized experiences, role models, informal supports, and conventional stimulation. The population of elderly sensory-impaired persons is not monolithic. By consulting potential users and using research strategies, such as focus groups and ethnographic interviews, planners and policy makers may be better prepared to develop the options most suitable to their constituents.

Better quality data are needed on the full range of functional impairments.

Epidemiological data are needed that quantify the full range of minor to severe impairments and that look at the interactive effects of impairments. Research is also needed on functioning of and design for older deaf or blind persons. With such data, planners would be in a better position to characterize their users. Similarly, longitudinal data on the changes one might anticipate among users of a senior center, retirement housing, or a nursing home would help plan for the full life of a facility.

A clearing house is needed for identifying prototypical products, model facilities, programs, legislation, and funding methods.

With information on examples, widely publicized and frequently updated, planners would be in a better position to advance the state of the art. Dissemination of such information should extend to consumers through home and trade shows, as well as through popular and professional media.

POLICY CONSIDERATION	*Product and technology innovators need information from professionals*
FOUR	*and consumers to develop new products and to disseminate more widely the existing technologies.*

Information is needed on the effectiveness of existing technologies for both consumer and designer purchased products. And, such information needs to be disseminated back into industry. Some companies are still unaware of the need or potential application of their efforts to sensory-impaired clients. Others are unaware of the demand, of available research, or of the concerns of multiply impaired elders. Experienced designers and allied health and human service professionals need to contribute to technological innovations so that they will be more satisfied with the results.

POLICY CONSIDERATION	*Research on lighting levels and acoustical environments is needed and*
FIVE	*should be incorporated into functionally based building standards.*

It is frustrating not to have specific information on how the yellowing of the human eye's lens affects color recognition or differentiation and not to have large scale studies of basic task lighting needs of older people. It is equally exasperating to design without being able to quantify how much background noise renders conversation unintelligible to older listeners. Such data are needed as quickly as possible. With such data, planners and policy makers can begin to incorporate findings into recommendations, standards, and functionally based design guides.

POLICY CONSIDERATION	*Post-occupancy evaluation should be more widely supported, publicly and*
SIX	*privately, as a method of learning from previous building experience.*

Buildings need to be evaluated by teams of professionals. Such reviews should include input from users, would-be users, professionals, and tradespeople. This information could then be incorporated into better design. We need to offset the awards given to unoccupied and new buildings with citations for effective renovations. And we need to develop award programs that are accorded by satisfied users.

POLICY CONSIDERATION	*Information on functional needs of sensory-impaired users needs to be more*
SEVEN	*widely disseminated to interior designers, decorators, and home furnishings trades.*

Many of the recommendations have direct implications for interiors. More conferences, workshops, educational materials, and programs on aging have been offered to architects than to these other important decision makers. To have greater impact on the materials and objects used in environmental design, information on sensory impairments must be directed to the decorating professionals and the home furnishings industry.

Older people must be able to learn more about their vision and hearing and about design as one of the several methods of compensating for disability.	POLICY CONSIDERATION **EIGHT**

Communication among professionals is good. But it is time the message of capability were directed specifically to the older consumer.

15

PRODUCT AND FURNITURE DESIGN FOR THE CHRONICALLY IMPAIRED ELDERLY

Joseph A. Koncelik

T he history of design enterprise is the story of professionals developing buildings and products for people. Ignoring the role of aesthetics, the primary objective has always been meeting human needs. Defining needs and developing an accurate picture of what they might be is the greatest problem that has faced the designer, whether that person is an architect, interior designer/space designer, industrial designer, or graphic designer. For the greater part of the twentieth century, the image of human needs has been a fuzzy or obscure apparition of subjective design. The designer's subjective opinions and judgments have been as important in form giving as the scant information available on human needs. World War II radically changed the situation by making new information about human anthropometrics available. These data were translated into criteria for the creation of environments and products. From the late 1940s through the mid-1960s, the development and use of human performance criteria shaped the way in which the design process was conducted.

Aging as a Component of Human Engineering

However, in spite of the ever-increasing amount of information about human performance and limitations, the image of man has remained abstract. Human performance criteria provided a summarization of man as a young adult, healthful, strong, and capable.

As the wave of young adults peaked in number around the mid-1960s, it became apparent that this image of man was incomplete. Beyond the young market was the unexplored but gradually advancing population of older Americans—increasing in numbers and demanding that their special needs be met. The special characteristics of the aged, viewed as a necessary component of human engineering, has changed the way that designers relate to clients and evaluate the successfulness of the products they create.

Awareness of the aging process has also changed the way we view human factors criteria. The image of man is no longer conceptualized as a steady state. The human being is now viewed as having characteristics that change, and these changes delineate a user group of great diversity, individuality, and capability. The anthropometric limitations for a designed object can be narrowed to fit the average or normal older adult, even though in physiological terms there is no such thing as a "normal" older adult. Anthropometric dimensioning has been used to acquire and classify statistical data on body sizes. Used as a model for defining characteristics of the older adult population, it has given designers a false sense of security. It has created an abstraction of the older adult that may not exist in reality. For example, designers often assume the older population as evenly distributed between the sexes, when in reality past the 80th year the sex ratio of women to men is nearly three to one (Brotman, 1973). A nursing home environment designed for the average older person must reflect this demographic reality.

Design Disciplines Must Coordinate Their Activities

Another critical aspect of designing for the aged ignored by architectural, interior, graphic, and product designers is the interrelationship between the work that results from each discipline. Until now, design specialists have followed a separate and distinct track, ignoring how their work affects other related disciplines. Architects and interior designers largely coordinate the products and visual communication devices designed by industrial and graphic designers. The product designer and graphic designer often develop their work based on an abstract notion of the setting within which their designs will be used. To remedy this dilemma, architects and interior designers must begin to recognize, more than they presently do, the impact of technology and mass production on their work. On the other hand, product and graphic designers must begin to view their work in the context of how a particular environment functions. The intrinsic aesthetic characteristic of the product they design may be less important than the relationship of products and graphics to an overall environmental aesthetic. Products can no longer be regarded as sculpture and graphics as a nonreproducible version of an easel painting.

The Kitchen: Often a Collection of Design Failures

An excellent example of a setting that can profit from a comprehensive understanding of the older user is the kitchen. In this example, all of the elements produced by the collection by previously mentioned design disciplines must combine to support the finite activity of meal preparation. The architectural arrangement of food storage, work space, and appliance location must combine with time keeping devices, telephones, small appliances, and the graphic instructions and information on food products to support meal preparation.

In many kitchen designs, even the most rudimentary architectural and interior considerations for the elderly are ignored. Cooking devices are difficult to operate because controls are hard for the arthritic hand to grasp or difficult for the aging eye to comprehend under glare conditions. Standard ovens are mounted beneath cook-top surfaces and thus require the elderly to bend at the waist or kneel down. Both of these movements can be physiologically difficult and may cause dizziness or loss of strength. Food package graphics will most certainly be printed in typefaces that are impossible to read and on glossy surfaces that produce reflection and glare. The sink will probably have controls that are difficult to grasp and may promote confusion regarding which fixture is hot or cold. Standard cabinetry will require reaches out of range for most elderly women. Finally, almost no sit-to-work opportunities will be designed for the slower pace of meal preparation.

Problems in the kitchen micro-environment are partially caused by lack of available appropriate products. A proper understanding of communications devices, cueing symbols, and readable type faces is not stressed in the training of the graphic designer. As a result, the kitchen not only lacks basic functionality, it could even endanger the older user. It is interesting to note that information exists regarding proper solutions for these design problems. Many solutions are easy to employ but presume that the designer is aware of the problems older people must face. The answers are often not complicated, nor do they require higher technology or sophisticated electronic devices to promulgate change for the better. In fact some major problems could be better resolved with lower levels of technology than consumer products currently utilize. A common belief exists among many designers that sophisticated technology is the only future product design alternative.

Good Design Does Not Necessarily Cost More

Designing for the elderly does not necessarily mean increasing costs of products and buildings. In the area of barrier-free design it has been shown that when the needs of the disabled and non-ambulatory can be accommodated in the planning and design of buildings from the beginning, construction costs will rarely increase beyond 1 percent (National Commission on Architectural Barriers to Rehabilitation of the Handicapped, 1968). If design changes for elderly and handicapped are implemented after construction has begun, the cost can rise to as high as 25 percent. Likewise, changes in products after the basic design decisions have been made will entail increased costs to produce and sell the product. The issue of consumer costs that result from a lack of attention to design is as much of a determinant of success than the technology or form of the product. Designers do not determine the final cost of a product, but their approach to the solution of a problem, whether they employ high or low technology or complexity versus simplification, has a definite effect on the outcome. The sensitivity of product design for older users may increase as the elderly gain in educational status and amass more discretionary income. Future change may occur in two distinct ways.

First, there may be increased militancy among the elderly to demand more satisfactory products and buildings. This change may result in more participation by the elderly in the design process when they serve as consumer panelists or members of architectural review boards. They have time to learn about design concerns and the political savvy to become powerful advocates.

The second method of influencing design may come through legislation. The barrier-free design movement has had an immense influence on the design of buildings and products to accommodate all users. Automotive safety legislation is another example that has greatly affected product design. Unfortunately these examples of design controls have also increased consumer costs. A much more satisfactory response would be voluntary recognition of the importance of design to all users. This might provide a stimulus to greater industrial competition rather than more tedious regulations, which inhibit design creativity.

Related Research

During the last two decades, social scientists have attempted to link concepts such as well being and independence to the environment. In most instances, the environmental linkage has been interpreted as a social environment—the interaction of people with people. However, increasingly there have been attempts, if not successes, to link social and personal outcomes to the physical design of the environment. Robert Sommer's (1970) observations of the behavior of elderly women in a mental institution exemplified some of the initial insights linking furniture placements to behavior:

> The ladies sat side-by-side against the newly painted walls in their chrome chairs and exercised their options of gazing down at the newly-tiled floor or looking up at the new flourescent lights. They

were like strangers in a train station, waiting for a train that never came by. The shoulder-to-shoulder arrangement was unsuitable for sustained conversation even for me. To talk to neighbors, I had to turn my chair and pivot my head 90°. For an older lady, particularly one with difficulties in hearing and comprehension, finding a suitable orientation for conversation was extremely taxing (1970, p. 27).

Much of the information generated about behavior and the physical environment of the elderly came from studies conducted in mental institutions and nursing homes. These settings by their very nature were artificial derivatives of health-care models and did not sufficiently respond to the psychosocial needs of the elderly. Kahana characterized this dilemma best when she remarked:

Even our best institutions for the aged often operate on a pathological model of aging, viewing the individual as a medical-management problem (often) disregarding his (or her) personal identity (1973, pp. 282–283).

Microenvironmental Considerations: The Key to User-Centered Design

Although the problem of how to design institutions for independent or institutionalized living is often touted as the major goal, there is little doubt that the key to designing a good building is in the handling of details in the residents' micro-environment. In an institution the critical interactions between physical environment and the elderly user occur at this personal or micro-environmental level. As Arthur Schwartz has suggested:

Design of micro-environments for the aged must be aimed not only at ameliorating stresses, minimizing the effects of losses, and compensating for deficits, but must do so in ways which enhance the individuals' effectiveness, support their confidence, and thus help them maintain self esteem (1975, p. 289).

Distinctions between the micro-environment and the larger macro-environment are at best vague. Most researchers and designers would agree that the macro-environment is at an architectural scale. It involves space relationships, building form, aesthetic expression, site considerations, and community interactions—the "gestalt" physical environment. Micro-environments are characterized by personal scale—the immediate surroundings of an individual. In essence, the micro-environment is that part of the physical environment that is literally within the reach of the person. The more infirm that person is, the more constrained his or her personal micro-environment becomes. In research conducted at Cornell University (Koncelik, Ostrander, and Snyder, 1972), elderly people interviewed in institutional settings often commented to the question "Where do you live?" by responding "In this chair." For older residents who may be restrained in geriatric chairs for most of the day, the response, although poignant, is unerringly accurate.

Who Specifies the Details of the Micro-Environment?

The design approach followed most consistently in the creation of special environments is a top-down process. Design activity begins with overall planning, often ignoring the personal environment that surrounds each individual. Frequently, the design of the "personal environment" is delegated to an administrator or staff member in the facility who most likely has no design training or experience.

In a recent questionnaire survey of 100 architects within the United States, over 50 percent of those responding stated that they had engaged in the specification of architectural products, while under 20 percent had engaged in the specification of furnishings for facilities for the elderly (Koncelik, 1981). Personal furnishing elements of the micro-environment include: seating, beds, tables, storage units, and appliances. Although social scientists have repeatedly demonstrated the importance of the micro-environment to the well-being of elderly people, this level receives the least amount of formal design attention. The micro-environment is largely a product environment, and spaces that are relevant to critical user activities are often outfitted with an unorganized collection of furnishings, seating, appliances, tables, and lighting. The job of the responsible designer is to coordinate spaces and furnishings so as to create a functional, comfortable, and pleasing environment. Because furnishings and equipment specified for nursing homes come either from hospital designs or commercial vendors, the resulting micro-environment is often less functional.

At present, no systematic approach exists for the design of interrelated products for specific environments. At best, manufacturers provide performance criteria about their products. This information is useful to the degree that it allows matching of one item to another. However, the total effectiveness of the resulting environment is often left up to chance. Matching of components through output performance criteria alone does not provide all of the information necessary for effective design, for other criteria must also be considered. As Lawton (1970) has stated, "Little is known about the factors of design, furnishings, and other features of smaller spaces." This also includes the lack of information about the affective environment or how the micro- or product environment (furnishings, etc.) influences emotional behavior.

Many Design Adaptations Hinge on a Clear Understanding of Sensory Loss

The micro-environment has been described as that part of the physical environment that is within reach. To know that environment is to reach it, touch it, manipulate it, and understand it. One must be able to determine locations of one component relative to another or be able to make adjustments to that environment in order to place it under personal control. In order for these things to be accomplished, information must be processed through sensory channels. Several texts have dealt with how changing physiological and sensory modalities affect one's ability to manipulate the environment (Koncelik, 1976; Pastalan, 1970). These personal changes alter the residents' perception of the environment and thus require the designer to review his perception of the elderly person.

The following four-stage conceptual framework can help the designer understand the environmental needs and priorities of the aging person (Koncelik, 1979). The four relationships the older person more acutely shares with the environment are: warning, interpretation, negotiation, and responsiveness.

Warning: Stimuli are necessary to convey life-threatening situations or harm. For older people these stimuli must be free and clear of confusion from background noise. Signals used to convey harmful or life-threatening situations should be "backed-up" with redundant signals or "cues" that increase the probability that these signals will be received (Fig. 15.1).

Interpretation: This involves the conveyance of information about the environment to the user of that environment, allowing the user

FIGURE 15.1   Warning: Simple and clear signals should be used to convey dangerous situations.

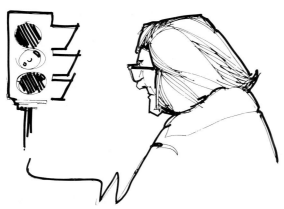

FIGURE 15.2 Interpretation: Information about the environment and its configuration allows the user to understand and comprehend the setting.

to "understand" the place (Fig. 15.2). Without appropriately presented information, the person might be confused about a given place. Correctly interpreting an environment largely depends on two factors: Are there sufficient differences between various parts of a given environment so as to ensure discrimination from place to place? And is there enough information about locations and pathways to ensure the user is aware of his/her position in the environment in relation to other places?

Negotiation: This refers to the aspect of movement—especially continuous and uninterrupted physical movement through an environment. The user of the environment must move from one place to another within an environment without incurring obstacles or becoming confused. There are two major features any environment must have in order to facilitate negotiation. First, all physical barriers must be removed that impede use by the physically handicapped. Second, various design signals and cues should be available to ensure that a person's movement through a space will be guided and will provide the assurance of arrival at an anticipated destination. A simple example of this is the use of a continuous arrow or long band of color to indicate a direction within a corridor (Fig. 15.3).

Responsiveness: Responsiveness is the ability of persons to manipulate their personal environment. The personal environment provides important signals about personal control and self-esteem.

FIGURE 15.3
Negotiation: A successful
environment is one that
is barrier free with
various design cues to
facilitate movement.

Changing the environment to make it one's own can be a significant
aid to health and well-being. For example, in congregate housing
arrangements, the acceptability of residential units without kitchens is being called into question. The primarily female residential
population of these facilities has a strong desire to continue the
role of homemaker. This role is facilitated by food preparation and
storage space in each unit (Fig. 15.4). Evidence from nursing home

FIGURE 15.4
Responsiveness: The
environment should be
manageable and
controllable by the user.

research suggests that the lack of personal control may lead to physical decline (Rodin and Langer, 1977). This conceptual framework provides several important functional themes toward which physical design should be sensitive. Designers using these themes should realize that numerous design recommendations can be made that may adapt a building to populations suffering handicaps or sensory losses. Design-idea testing and implementation are intuitive or common sense processes derived from the recognition of infirmity or sensory loss problems. Good design solutions, not mysterious devices, need to be employed to counteract confusion, disorientation, or impediments to use.

Product Designs for Critical Environments

Research is also being conducted on various portions of the environment and various products that greatly affect the independence of older institutionalized people. The following data are based on research by Koncelik reported in the publication *Designing the Open Nursing Home* (1976). It reports conclusions relating to three environmental settings where proper product design is critical. The functions of these three settings (eating, sleeping, toileting) greatly affect the independence of the institutionalized older person.

The Bedroom and Bed Design: The bed is one of the least scrutinized devices in a nursing home, even though it is occupied for a substantial percentage of time during the day. During the waking hours, napping, resting, reading, snacking, eating, and many other peripheral behaviors also take place in and around the bed. In double occupancy rooms, beds must be considered as places for visitors to sit, for socialization with friends, and even conjugal visitations or lovemaking.

Most nursing homes consider hospital beds as the only viable choice for this piece of furniture. In a hospital, staff must have access to all parts of the bed and all parts of the patient while he is in bed. However, for nursing home application, hospital beds appear to be too high, and they greatly encumber patient freedom by restraint devices that are necessary for only a few patients. Hospital beds also provide articulations that are not necessary for the majority of nursing home residents. Nursing home beds require articulation for only three movements: the head must move up and down, the foot must move up and down, and the entire platform must be able to be raised or lowered.

The bed should lower to normal bed height, which is approximately 20" off the floor. This level allows for dressing without assistance, entrance, and egress. However, the bed should raise for the staff functions of changing, bathing, and assisted feeding. It is often difficult to converse with a resident in a hospital bed because the bed is higher than the normal 20" limit for seating. The

CDA

FIGURE 15.5 The design of this one-bed patient room in a new facility planned for the Motion Picture and Television Fund Country House and Hospital respects the privacy, storage, autonomy, personalization, and display needs of the patient. Unusual features include a large shared balcony and a window seat.

patient bed can be a source of "institutional character" or can be designed, covered, and finished like a piece of residential furniture (Fig. 15.5).

Bed rails mounted to the side and left exposed are also potentially dangerous for the patient and staff. Patients egressing beds with exposed bed rails often tangle their feet and fall. In research conducted at Ohio State University, Koncelik and Bonner (1974) discovered that in one nursing home 60 percent of all injuries due to falls occurred around the bed with patients slipping on wet floors and striking hard metal frames or bed rails. One important aspect of nursing home bed design is that construction cost of a more appropriate nursing home bed could be much less than that of a hospital bed.

Sitting and Dining with Chairs and Tables: Seating devices can be subdivided into lounging and functional seating categories. Re-

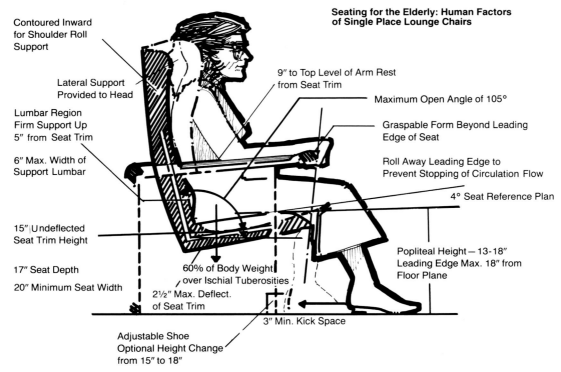

Seating for the Elderly: Human Factors of Single Place Lounge Chairs

Contoured Inward for Shoulder Roll Support

Lateral Support Provided to Head

Lumbar Region Firm Support Up 5" from Seat Trim

6" Max. Width of Support Lumbar

15" Undeflected Seat Trim Height

17" Seat Depth

20" Minimum Seat Width

9" to Top Level of Arm Rest from Seat Trim

Maximum Open Angle of 105°

Graspable Form Beyond Leading Edge of Seat

Roll Away Leading Edge to Prevent Stopping of Circulation Flow

4° Seat Reference Plan

60% of Body Weight over Ischial Tuberosities

2½" Max. Deflect. of Seat Trim

Poplical Height — 13-18" Leading Edge Max. 18" from Floor Plane

3" Min. Kick Space

Adjustable Shoe Optional Height Change from 15" to 18"

NOTE: The Design of Seating for the Institutional Setting Should Place Heavy Reliance on the Anthropometric Characteristics of the Female Population.

FIGURE 15.6   Seat design criteria: Properly designed seating should provide lower back support. The arms should be designed for easy grasp. A higher average seat height will facilitate ease of entry and exit.

search conducted by Koncelik, Ostrander, and Snyder (1972) has shown that the duration of time spent in a seated position ranges from as much as 6 hours for the ambulatory to 12 hours for the restrained nonambulatory nursing home resident. In the majority of institutional environments, seating occupied by nonambulatory residents serves as both lounging and functional seating as well as a major mode of ambulation throughout the facility (Fig. 15.6).

No chair meant for infirm elderly should be without arms. Chair arms should extend forward slightly beyond the leading edge of the chair to facilitate entrance and egress. Seat height from the floor to the leading edge of both categories of chairs should not exceed 17". This is important because older people are somewhat shorter, with the majority of institutionalized women having a standing height of 5'2" or less. Chairs with seat heights above 17" may force the users' feet to dangle, thus cutting off the blood supply to lower limbs and causing weakness or lack of control.

Chairs necessary for dining and other activities can be regarded as functional seating. Back support is an extremely important consideration in functional seating. Younger populations tend to lean forward and away from back supports provided in the chair. However, back support is more important for older people who often suffer loss of strength in the torso, inability to flex the spinal column, greater roll at the shoulders, a tendency to slump forward, and limited side-to-side head movement.

Tables should accommodate the ambulatory and nonambulatory in activity and dining areas by encouraging the greatest possible participation and socialization. Generally a 31"-high table will accommodate both groups of people. This table height might be slightly too high for the smallest person so that a few tables of lower height might be necessary.

The Bathroom's Critical Fixtures Include Showers, Toilets, and Lavatories: The bathroom itself has been the subject of very intensive investigation (Kira, 1975; Steinfeld, 1975). The bulk of this investigation, however, has concentrated on the arrangement of standard hardware and the placement of handrails and supports. Little attention has been given to the design of fixtures and hardware (Fig. 15.7).

The sink, mirror, and storage configuration of the bathroom need to be scrutinized far more than they have been to date. Mirrors should be placed lower to the surface of the sink and canted outward so that wheelchair-bound residents are able to see themselves with little difficulty. The sink should have a shallow draft, and the waste pipe and hot water supply should be shrouded to prevent burns to the legs. Control devices should be graspable and

FIGURE 15.7 The bathroom: Storage and space should be low and manageable, with fixtures that are convenient and easily manipulated. A shroud over waste water pipes will avoid accidental burning, and a canted mirror will allow the wheelchair patient a better view.

easy to actuate for people with very little finger strength and manipulation ability.

Bathtubs have also not been given sufficient design attention. There should be more quasi-seated or semi-supine bathtubs available. With little equipment available except for very inappropriate and old fashioned devices, there is no question about the necessity for innovation in this area. Entrance and egress of both bathtubs and shower stall units are critical movements. Showers are generally considered safer because there is no change of body position from standing to sitting, and no stress is transferred through arms and legs to accommodate awkward positions.

The toilet should vary in height from the floor according to the ambulatory status and arthritic condition of the hips and lower extremities. A major concern is the transfer from the wheelchair or movement to and from the standing position to the surface of the toilet. Grabrails are an essential design feature for the infirm elderly. The closer the proximity of the rail to the surface or edge of the seat, the greater the leverage and amount of force that can be exerted to lift upward or ease downward movement. Grabrails are often placed too far away and too high from the surface of the toilet to be effective assists for moving to and from the surface of the seat.

Methodology and Data Analysis: The Geriatric Personal Furnishings System

The problem of the personal or micro-environment was the subject of an unusual research and product development collaboration. This collaborative effort involved the application of basic and applied research in ergonomics and anthropometrics to the design of a furnishings system for the older nursing home resident. The collaboration was between a designer and manufacturer, and it led to the development of a new line of system furnishings manufactured by the J. G. Furniture Company. The following chronicles this unique design research experience.

The major thrust of the Geriatrics Personal Furnishings (GPF) program was to design a number of interrelated nursing home bedroom products that would form the basis of an environmental system. This system would essentially become the personal space of infirm elderly people who reside in both private residential and institutional settings. The fundamental hypothesis of design was that chronically ill older people are affected both physically and psychologically by their sense of personal control over immediate surroundings. This control is maintained by being able to personalize surroundings, changing the setting to meet personal requirements, and manipulating the amenities available in a space.

The Major Problem Was How to Implement Existing Design Research

Much of the research necessary to carry out design tasks had already been conducted. A major marketing opportunity provided the stimulus for the systems furniture idea. A substantial stock of buildings designed as institutional facilities during the late 1950s and early 1960s were now in need of renovation. While there is and continues to be great pressure to expand the stock of nursing home beds, economic financing and institutional constraints made renovation projects a more viable direction for a product system. Speeding up the renovation process by using a system design and being able to quickly amortize the cost of furniture rather than depreciating the cost of capital expenses were strong incentives in favor of the development of such a system. These incentives were particularly strong for older facilities with multiple bed spaces, which were becoming less competitive.

There were six critical human factors that had to be accommodated in the design of the GPF system. Thirty general performance specifications were developed relating to these areas of human factors (Koncelik, 1980).

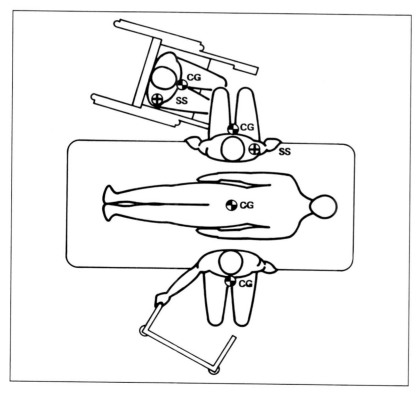

FIGURE 15.8 Ingress and egress from the bed entail a complete set of movements. The strength of the person, rotation around the center of gravity (CG), and the position of the strong side (SS) of the patient next to the bed are necessary for a successful transfer.

Transfer Conditions from the Bed Surface: Transfer conditions from the bed surface must be maintained by providing a bed height at a level equal to that of wheelchairs. Many beds are kept at levels that are too high for elderly people to egress easily from the bed surface without entanglement in bed side rails or other hardware (Fig. 15.8).

Circulation and Clearance Conditions Around the Defined Privacy Area: The most important aspect of circulation is that a distance of 36″ be maintained for passageway to accommodate the necessary swing of a wheelchair inward to the bed for ease of transfer. Clearance from floor level to the surfaces must be maintained at 8″, and no electrical connections should be made at floor level or protrude in such a way as to become an impediment to free movement around the space. All furnishings must provide temporary support for the ambulatory elderly while walking.

Sit-to-Work Conditions: Residency—that sense of living within a space—necessitates personally controlled activities. Hence, sit-to-work situations do occur and must be accommodated in these personal spaces. The critical human factor is that both the ambulatory and nonambulatory person must be provided with the proper dimensional relationships within that situation (Fig. 15.9).

A similar situation exists for the bed itself. Adjustable beds can be used to permit sit-to-work situations. Both independently initiated tasks should be promoted by the products and the staff/resident functions such as therapy sessions, feeding, eating, and other activities (Fig. 15.10).

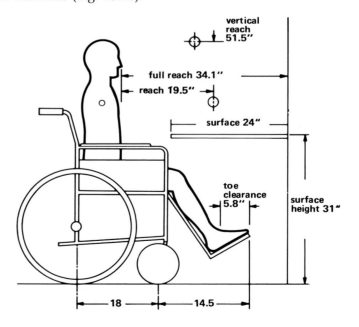

FIGURE 15.9 Effective work conditions require adequate surface and clearance dimensions that accomodate the ambulatory and nonambulatory patient.

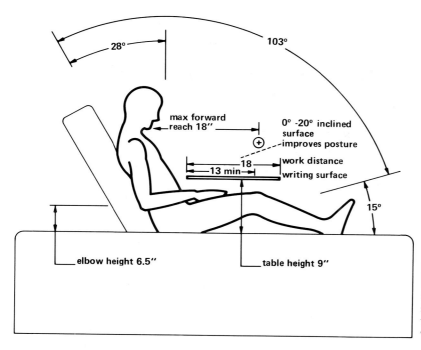

FIGURE 15.10 Over-bed tables required by some states should be sized and positioned to facilitate eating and working.

Manipulative Task Conditions: Manipulative tasks are limited by the presence of arthritis. Grip strength and tip prehension in the fingers are often greatly diminished. Hence, the use of all storage units as well as the actuation of lighting must be carefully considered in terms of the reduced manipulation capacity of the resident.

Criteria for Lighting and Sound Control: Lighting must be designed to accommodate both task and ambient conditions. Task lighting must be designed to assist functional operations in the space. Task lighting should emanate from a source high to the rear or off to the side of the bed. Ambient lighting must be designed to provide general room illumination up to and surpassing code requirements. With both lighting conditions, glare is a serious problem because of the heightened sensitivity of the aging eye. This is due to changes in lens opacity, corneal yellowing, and eye-muscle deterioration. Sound control is an important and often neglected consideration. The baffling of extraneous sounds is essential to privacy.

Findings: The Components of the System Design

The preceding data detailed the anthropometric, ergonomic, and functional requirements that the system needed to meet. The design process led to the creating of three product groupings: the bed, panel and storage, and lighting (Fig. 15.11).

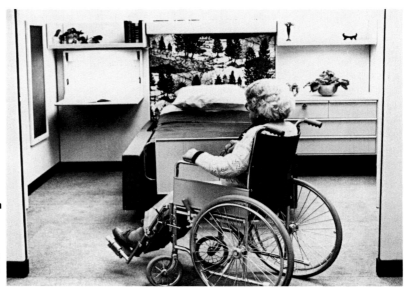

FIGURE 15.11 The Geriatric Personal Furnishings (GPF) system designed for the J. G. Furniture Systems Company represents a systems approach to the provision of institutional furnishings.

Bed Design: The design of the bed utilized a unique "bolster" system that allowed bedside seating, transfers, and protection from bedside hardware. The bed rails were integrated with the bolster and recessed within them for protection of the user. An over-bed table was developed that clamped to the rails and was designed to be stored on the footboard of the bed (Fig. 15.12).

Panels and Storage Units: The second grouping of products are interrelated panels and storage units. A corner storage unit was designed that became a structural element in the design of free-

FIGURE 15.12 The over-bed table is clipped to the footboard of the bed when it is not in use. The soft side bolsters facilitate entrance and egress from the bed.

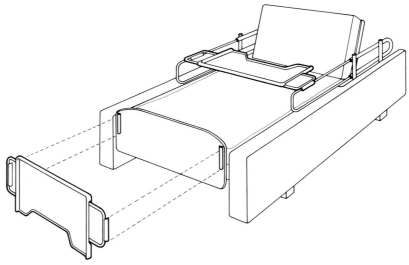

standing panel walls, and a night stand was developed that contained the traditional storage capacity of most other competitive units. The unique fold-down desk also mated with the panels providing for activities such as letter writing, reading, and hobby interests.

Lighting Considerations: The third grouping of products related to lighting. Ambient illumination was provided by recessed fluorescent luminaires inside the panel tops. Task lighting was provided in the fold-down desk, in shelving units, and in an over-bed light.

Conclusions: The Complete System

The system components can be assembled in four consecutive levels of completeness. However, these four levels are only suggested. The major advantage to the panelized system approach is the flexibility of creating numerous design arrangements from the basic components (Fig. 15.13).

Flexibility and Adaptability
Were Key Considerations

The system also needed to accommodate room configurations that were quite dissimilar. A large body of information was available regarding not only dimensional configurations but also room proportion and code requirements. These data were used to derive the number of panels that would work in a variety of room settings. Physiological capabilities of elderly women were used to establish

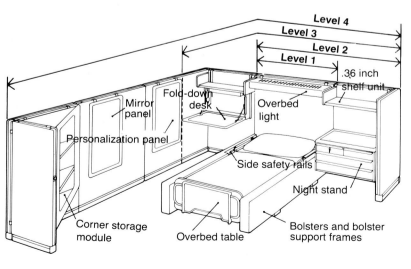

FIGURE 15.13 The GPF system is modular and includes four levels of completeness.

panel heights, locations of suspended components, and reach capacities for storage. In addition, the manufacturer's experience in open office systems was used to create a novel panel arrangement that used stock connector hardware. Using the manufacturer's experience allowed the swift development of the GPF system.

Prototype Testing Consumed 1 Year of the Development Period

The first year of design development included a parallel program that functioned as a cross check on all assumptions regarding the use of the system by elderly people and facility personnel. An occupational therapist with wide experience in assisting infirm and disabled people headed this testing and evaluation process. Each idea regarding transfer, accessibility, operational use of equipment, and system effectiveness was tested, evaluated, and documented. The result of this parallel investigation was a planning manual (Koncelik, 1980). This manual was published by the manufacturer and established the basis for informing potential purchasers about the various options, choices, and levels of application available.

The need to utilize higher levels of technology in production affected many of the design decisions during the second year of operation. During that year, components such as the over-bed light and the fold-down desk were redesigned to utilize injection molding production techniques.

Conclusions

The success of the Geriatric Personal Furnishings System will depend on several important factors. The prolonged credit squeeze of the 1980s has diminished prospects of a new wave of renovation. Large commitments of funding are necessary to initiate a system such as the GPF. Hence, progress in the use and evaluation of the system may be impeded.

Another critical aspect is product acceptance. This system of products was an attempt to match micro-environmental products with human needs. The solution was radically different from products currently available. Will designers, specifiers, or administrators accept this approach, or will it seem too much of a radical departure from currently available products?

The GPF design process is an argument for the participation of older people and allied care-giving professionals in the development of design solutions. The parallel process of design development and research testing is a model that may lead to better solutions rather than the traditional linear process of research translation to design. Task-specific problem solving by an inter-disciplinary group of professionals is a tedious but rewarding process.

Research and design activity in environments for the aging has traditionally developed from a body of knowledge that is based on a functional understanding of resident needs.

The product environment through the arrangement of various furnishing items establishes important functional relationships with the resident client or user. This emergent concept of design holds within it the secret to understanding all human interaction with the environment. Nurtured, developed, and applied carefully in all design activity, this fundamental concept could allow for a significant beneficial change in the process of designing all environments and products for all human beings.

DESIGN DIRECTIVES

DESIGN DIRECTIVE **ONE**	*Ambient background sounds in open reverberating public spaces should be dampened and reduced.*

1. This can be accomplished through the use of baffling materials such as wall hangings of thick woven fabrics or screens, or panels that reduce sound reflection from overhead ceiling surfaces.

DESIGN DIRECTIVE **TWO**	*Seating arrangements in institutions should be no greater than six positions, and preferably four positions, to facilitate conversation and eye contact.*

1. This will help older people concentrate on verbal communication from their neighbors. It will also facilitate the reading of lips and facial expressions.

2. Smaller tables may also facilitate the serving of meals.

DESIGN DIRECTIVE **THREE**	*General background noise in public thoroughfares or corridors can be reduced through the use of carpeting and heavy sound-absorbing textures on ceilings and wall surfaces.*

1. Heavily textured surfaces applied through sprayed techniques can reduce sound reflection, while also providing a surface that allows greater "purchase" for the dry hand of the aging person.

2. Ceilings can be "flocked" with dense sprayed-on materials, which can reduce high frequency background noises.

DESIGN DIRECTIVE **FOUR**	*Elevators can and should be equipped with middle frequency tones which would sound when safe passage is possible to and from the elevator.*

1. This would also serve to warn others in corridors that the elevator has reached that floor and is available, or that it will soon be discharging traffic into the corridor.

2. In settings that have six or fewer floors, tones may ring in accordance with the number of the floor itself—serving as a redundant cue for visual signals that signify the floor for those people who have suffered visual sensory loss.

Canned background music is potentially distressing to the sensory deprived and should be avoided because it makes the environment more uniform rather than maximizing the difference for ease of identification.

1. However, carefully controlled sound sources in specific locations can help to identify the place. Dining rooms have sounds and smells that help to identify them. The locations of these environments can be more easily recognized using carefully chosen background music.

2. Evenness of sound throughout an institutional facility is highly counterproductive, particularly when an attempt is made to encourage self-reliance in the negotiation of the environment.

Visual warning devices such as emergency exits should be backed up with auditory middle frequency sound signals to enhance the identification and location of exit.

1. In the event of fire, many visual signals placed high in the space cannot be seen through accumulated smoke.

The use of color coding to increase recognition of spaces or places can aid way-finding and negotiation.

1. Each floor, for example, can be designed with significant color and decor differences so that a specific color becomes identified with a particular place.

2. Even the partially sighted may be capable of recognizing bold color patterns located in carefully lighted areas.

3. For those people who are suffering hearing losses, there may be an even greater dependency upon visual stimuli for the identification of a specific place.

The "figure-ground" relationships of signage systems should employ a high contrast ratio between the symbol and the background upon which it is situated.

1. It is preferable to use white symbols on dark backgrounds rather than the reverse.

Signs should be located at wheelchair eye heights of approximately 48"–52" because the standing or ambulatory person would still be capable of reading signs at that height.

DESIGN DIRECTIVE **TEN**	*Problems with glare should be mitigated throughout the facility.*

1. Adaptation rates from low light to high light conditions coupled with changes in the aging eye make the elderly extremely susceptible to glare.

2. Carpeting floors and corridors wherever possible and using peripheral indirect lighting to increase the "subjective" total lighting of a space can reduce glare on all surfaces and also provide a better visual sense of the shape of the space.

3. Window walls must be carefully considered. Glazing patterns and units that reduce potential glare should be considered.

4. Entrance and exit areas from public buildings should be designed to accommodate the slower adaptation rate of the older adult eye.

Example: A significant problem of accommodation occurs in highway underpasses that go from a high-lighted to a low-lighted and then back to a high-lighted condition. The elderly eye cannot adapt quickly to these changes, and the consequences can be serious and the situation dangerous.

DESIGN DIRECTIVE **ELEVEN**	*Because older residents have more than one sensory deficit (hearing and sight most frequently affected), there should be markers that identify important places through the use of touch.*

1. The most obvious form of textural communication is braille, which is now found in most public buildings.

2. Other textural markers should be employed such as shape coding of hand rails in nursing homes (in intermediate locations, notches or grooves could be cut in the surfaces of a handrail to identify location) or changes in the texture of wall surfaces.

Warning: Care should be taken to provide sufficient difference in textures so that building users do not become confused.

DESIGN DIRECTIVE **TWELVE**	*A multiplicity of textures and personal artifacts should be available to provide the resident a sense of territoriality and ownership.*

1. Institutional settings in particular are often devoid of richness and variety. For the bedridden, this type of setting can be a desolate place without stimulus.

DESIGN DIRECTIVE **THIRTEEN**	*Architectural hardware used in buildings for the aged should recognize sensory loss and arthritic problems and be easier to manage, change, open-close, and control.*

1. The standard American doorknob encourages ulner deviation, helping to bring about the onset of arthritis (osteoarthritis) through the rotating motion of the bone of the forearm opposite the thumb needed to actuate the device.

2. The inability to manipulate architecture hardware designed for most buildings communicates a loss of capability to the infirm, long before their infirmities reach a point where they do inhibit use.

3. This same principle applies to control devices such as light switches, window latches, sink or lavatory water controls, stoves, ranges, and television sets.

POLICY CONSIDERATIONS

POLICY CONSIDERATION **ONE**	*The design process should employ greater integration of product designer graphic designer and architectural designer.*

The complexities of designing for special user groups requires that architectural designers coordinate their thinking so as to include a clear understanding of how graphic design and product design can be employed. Without this integration, slippage or failure can occur at several different levels, thus accounting for a less successful environmental design setting.

POLICY CONSIDERATION **TWO**	*The testing of product environments should involve both user/resident and employee participation.*

These two distinct perspectives can provide a number of benefits that contribute to the refinement of a particular product design. User feedback will most likely lead to solutions that enhance independence. Employee feedback will lead to solutions that enhance function and manipulability.

POLICY CONSIDERATION **THREE**	*The specification of furnishings should not be left to an untrained novice.*

A brilliant laudable architectural design solution can be irreparably damaged by the specification of inappropriate furnishings.

POLICY CONSIDERATION **FOUR**	*Creative collaborations involving designers and manufacturers may lead to cost effective and practical furnishing solutions in a much shorter time frame.*

Acting as equal partners in a collaboration of this sort, both parties can contribute to an optimization of expertise, practical experience, production efficiency, and cost effectiveness.

16

EVALUATING DESIGN INNOVATIONS IN AN EXTENDED CARE FACILITY

Arvid E. Osterburg

T he problem of designing a stimulating, innovative, and interesting—yet safe, supportive, and satisfying—living arrangement for residents who require continual nursing care is the major challenge facing architects who design long-term care facilities. Because of their physical and sensory limitations, older people in these settings are often extremely dependent on the environment. For this user group a poorly detailed or confusing design solution can have major impacts on independence, self-sufficiency, and satisfaction.

The research presented in this chapter involved the evaluation of a midwestern retirement facility labeled, for purposes of ano-nymity, the "Westside Retirement Home."[1] The evaluation ex-amined important functions that the building was expected to per-form, as well as objectives established by the project's architect.

Research Played an Important Role in the Design of the Building

The Westside Retirement Home was chosen because the architec-ture represented an unusually thoughtful approach toward the cre-ation of a supportive living environment. This approach resulted

[1] This study was supported in part by a grant from the Administration on Aging, Department of Health, Education, and Welfare, and was the basis of a doctoral dissertation at the University of Michigan (see references under Osterberg, 1980).

from a thorough programming and extensive research process undertaken by the home's administration and by the architect for the project.[2]

Several noteworthy attributes characterize the project's design:

1. A residential character was achieved in the design, which is atypical of today's nursing facilities.
2. The setting maximized the independence of residents through the use of environmental cues and color coding.
3. Traditional "images" associated with institutional building types (such as shiny floors and pastel colored walls) were avoided.
4. A surrounding high-crime neighborhood was the catalyst for a design concept that oriented the building toward an interior atrium-court, thus creating a stronger sense of community.

The Facility Was Recycled from Church, Classroom, and Apartment Use

Westside is an adaptive reuse structure. Constructed in 1927, the original building consisted of a church, a classroom wing, and an attached nine-story apartment structure with ground floor shops open to the street. The Westwide Retirement Home started operation in 1963 when three of the apartment floors were converted to nursing floors, with the remaining five designated as apartment floors for the independent elderly.

During the early 1970s the board of trustees of the home considered abandoning the then out-of-date facility and moving to a suburb to construct a more modern building. The neighborhood surrounding the home had changed over the years, and attendance at the church had decreased to only a handful of Sunday worshipers. Additionally, the three nursing floors were considered inadequate and no longer met city and state building code requirements.

When elderly residents of the home learned of the impending move to the suburbs, many became upset and voiced their disapproval. A number of long-time residents claimed that the city was their home and they didn't want to move out of it. They reportedly liked the idea of staying where they had always lived and were willing to tolerate the increased risk of crime. The final decision was to recycle the old church and the three-story educational wing into a modern nursing facility.

When the nursing home remodeling was complete, residents of the three nursing floors in the old wing of the building moved to

---

[2] Nathan Levine, D. Arch, architect for the project, received recognition for the design, which was published in the May 1977 issue of *Architectural Record*. Dr. Leon Pastalan of the University of Michigan was consultant for the project.

rooms in the newly renovated wing of the building. The old nursing floors were recycled into apartments. The capacity of the retirement home at completion in 1978 was 214 residents; the make-up included 94 independent apartment residents, 30 semidependent residents, and 90 skilled care nursing residents.

Related Research

In the past few years, post-occupancy evaluations (POEs) have become an important part of the design process. However, the limited experience with POEs to date has resulted in a sparse and fragmented collection of experiences. As Sommer (1972) points out in *Design Awareness,* the lack of evaluative data has caused bad design features to be repeated through ignorance and good design features to be overlooked. Brill (1974) describes the two basic outcomes of evaluations as information about the usefulness of buildings and information that can improve the design of new buildings. Architects and building designers traditionally receive little feedback about how well their completed buildings have met intended goals. Zeisel and Griffin (1975) concluded from their study that to increase the probability of successful matches between design assumptions and user needs, new methods were needed to feed back evaluation results during early stages in the design process.

Methodology and Data Analysis

A multidimensional research approach was employed to study the response and reactions of residents and staff to the building over a 1-year period. Three basic strategies were used to collect data for the two primary user groups—elderly nursing residents and the staff. The methods employed included: face-to-face interviews, behavioral observation, and record consultation. This multimethod approach offered the primary advantage of providing a broad data base for analysis. Each method provided a data set with overlaps that could be used to validate information obtained from other methods. Resident interviews, nurse and aide interviews, and employee interviews were pretested and revised before data collection began.

Reliance on a formal interview instrument in post-occupancy evaluations can be misleading. Interviews were supplemented by observations and photographs that yielded additional evidence regarding how and when various building features and services were used. One of the less formal data collection procedures involved visiting users over a period of weeks and months. In these social settings, individual users often revealed insights that were not recorded either through previous interviews or observations. This social visiting procedure was particularly beneficial in documenting efforts to adapt to the new building. The architect who designed the renovation of Westside was interviewed at the time of construction. This interview provided a record of intended architectural and programmatic objectives.

Evaluation Took Place During a 1-Year Time Period

A longitudinal research design was chosen to allow the study of user reactions to the building over a 1-year period. Adaptation to the building usually required time; therefore, data gathered at any one point did not necessarily provide an accurate assessment of potential problems. Research conducted in the first month of occupancy is often misleading because users are often preoccupied by or grieving about their former dwelling units. Grieving can sometimes result from the unfamiliarity or novelty of the new setting. Another initial reaction may be a reluctance to recognize or accept environmental changes of any sort, even when these changes are improvements. These effects must also be given time to subside.

Collecting data after a 2-month period offers the advantage of allowing the users to adjust and accept the new environment. Initial negative responses often give way to habituation and acceptance. Habituation, however, can also affect the findings. In some cases, users who have come to know the new setting may prefer it because it is familiar and not necessarily because it is better. Thus, evaluations taken after a year may not result in a clear and accurate listing of all major problems encountered in the move.

Findings

Designing for Visual Legibility Was an Important Goal

The Westside project design employed several innovative design solutions that responded to the problems of age-related sensory losses. The diminution of perception in the areas of sight, hearing, taste, touch, smell, and temperature sensitivity was considered. Vision loss was the sensory loss of paramount concern to the architect of Westside. The design of the nursing floor utilized several principles to increase overall visual legibility.

Visual losses may vary in severity from one individual to another; however, everyone can expect to experience some vision loss after age 70 (Pastalan, Mautz, and Merrill, 1973). Older people are often not aware of these losses because decline in visual ability is gradual. This condition cannot be corrected through eyeglasses; but by using various principles, the environment can be designed to appear more visually responsive, thus offsetting this condition to a certain degree.

Glare Is the Most Common Age-related Vision Loss Problem

A recent study at the University of Michigan by Pastalan, Merrill, Osterberg, and Pomerantz (1975) has shown glare to be the older driver's single largest source of frustration. Varying seasonal and weather conditions create unavoidable glare situations. In an interior environment, however, much can be done to alleviate problems of glare. Solutions range from the specification of appropriate sources of lighting to the use of window screening devices and nonglare surfaces.

In the Westside project, major reductions in glare resulted from the use of carpeting, vinyl wall covering, and balanced lighting. This reduction is apparent when comparing a typical corridor in the old nursing wing to a typical corridor in the new nursing wing (Fig. 16.1). Low reflectivity wall and floor materials around the nurses' station also reduced glare. Figure 16.2 compares the nurses' station in the old building with the new nurses' station.

Improvements in the resident's room such as carpeting and wall covering can reduce reflective glare, but window glare often remains a problem. While it is difficult to eliminate window glare entirely, the use of appropriate shading and diffusion devices can help. Figure 16.3 illustrates a wise choice of furniture, fabric coverings, and wall and floor coverings in a lobby area, which provides a pleasing interior environment without glare problems.

Colors Are Not Perceived as Intensely: In addition to problems with glare, elderly residents with vision impairment do not perceive colors with the same intensity as nonelderly. When asked about their preference for colors on the old nursing floors, several residents of Westside responded: "What colors? There weren't any, were there?" Residents either did not remember or could not discern between the light pastel colors used on the floor.

To compensate for losses in color perception, stronger color stimuli were introduced. Brighter than medium hues were used in carpeting, draperies, and wall coverings. Brightly colored furniture was also specified. Informal visits with residents and staff members verified the favorable response to bright colors inside the building. Resident and staff interviews revealed a higher preference for warm colors and a medium to low preference for colder colors. One color especially disliked was blue.

The Buildings Were Designed to Aid Orientation

The ability to visualize the spatial layout of buildings is extremely important to the elderly who suffer losses of visual and/or mental acuity. Consequently, the design of Westside was studied for its effect on orientation or way-finding.

BEFORE

AFTER

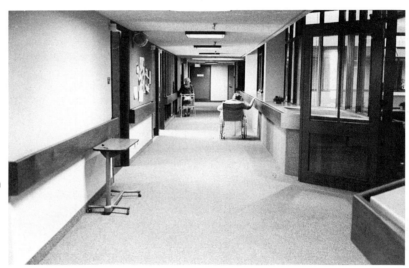

FIGURE 16.1 Comparison of the corridor view in the old and new building: Major reductions in glare were accomplished through the new design.

Orientation can be broadly defined as "the positioning or alignment with respect to a specific direction or reference system and/or the familiarization with or adjustment to a situation" (Morris, 1973). The elderly have increased difficulty in establishing a sense of direction and developing reference points from which to make navigation decisions. To facilitate resident orientation within the environment, the designer must be aware of the consequences of critical design decisions. Certain design strategies can be employed to facilitate orientation.

BEFORE

AFTER

FIGURE 16.2 Comparison of nurse's station in the old and new building: Low reflectivity wall and floor material helped to reduce glare.

The Atrium Provided a Central Point of Orientation: The enclosed and centrally located glass atrium in the Westside building provided an easily identifiable central reference point for all users. The atrium is an element that one can relate to both horizontally and vertically. Building users could maintain a sense of orientation as long as they could place themselves in relation to this central space.

The Loop Hallway Aided Confused and Alert Residents: The "loop hallway" system also helped to achieve a better sense of orientation. As shown in Figure 16.4, the central atrium complements the

FIGURE 16.3   Lobby lounge area overlooking atrium: Attractive furniture, colorful wall coverings, and resilient carpeting create a pleasing environment without glare.

FIGURE 16.4   Typical upper-level plan: The central atrium complements the loop hallway arrangement.

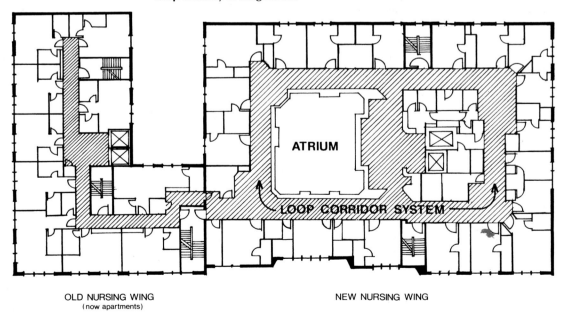

OLD NURSING WING
(now apartments)

NEW NURSING WING

Typical Upper Level

loop hallway arrangement. Together these two elements create a reinforcing image. The loop hallway system offers several advantages. The rectangular shape of the loop facilitates orientation by eliminating building wings with dead-end hallways. Instead, only four right angles exist. If a resident goes for a walk and makes four turns he ends up back where he started. Alert residents benefit from increased confidence because they realize they cannot get lost with this system.

Confused residents using a double-loaded corridor often reach the end and must mentally rotate the plan to maintain their orientation. Rooms that were once on the left are suddenly on the right when one turns around to go in the other direction. In the loop system used at Westside, residents could avoid this problem by moving in one direction. Specific rooms would therefore always remain on the same side.

The Lower Level Was Confusing to Some Residents: While the loop corridor system at Westside facilitated orientation on each of the residential floors, at the lower level a different layout resulted in confusion for some residents (Fig. 16.5). Nursing residents who attended craft workshops and other activities on the lower level often lost their bearings and were temporarily disoriented. Even when assisted by volunteers or staff members, residents became noticeably upset because they were not sure of their location. A contributing factor may have been that the lower level of the building was used less frequently than the upper residential floors.

FIGURE 16.5 Lower-level plan: Residents who attended activities on the lower level (below the atrium) often lost their sense of direction and became temporarily disoriented.

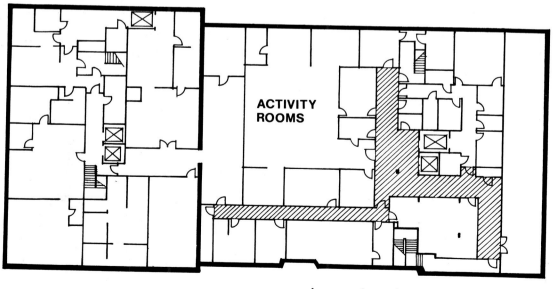

ACTIVITY ROOMS

Lower Level

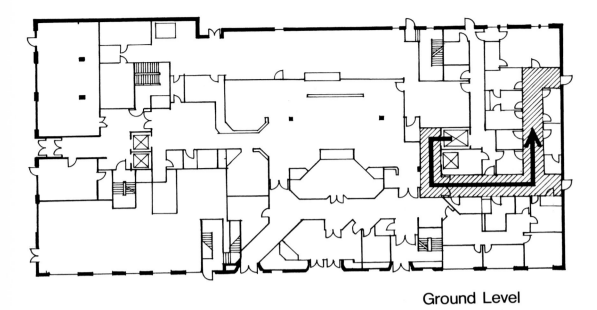

Ground Level

FIGURE 16.6 Ground-level plan: When residents left the elevator to visit the doctor's office in the adjacent space, many were turned around and confused. Arrow indicates path from elevator to medical clinic.

While it would have been impractical for the architect of Westside to repeat the use of the loop corridor and atrium on the lower level of the building, the resident confusion on the lower level underscores the need for considering design alternatives to aid orientation. Behavioral observation on the ground level of the building indicated that when residents left the atrium to visit a doctor in the adjacent medical clinic, many were turned around and confused (Fig. 16.6).

To find the medical clinic a resident was required to make three turns after leaving the elevator. Not only did residents have difficulty finding this area, but they had even more difficulty retracing their steps back to the elevator following the visit. This return trip requires a mirror-image–reversal of the route, substituting left-hand turns for right-hand turns. Because residents infrequently visited the medical clinic, they did not have a chance to learn the route.

Another way a designer can aid users in orientation is to include "nodes," or collecting points, within the building's circulation system. In Westside the four corners of the loop hallway system were treated as nodes. The architect emphasized these nodes by using octagon-shaped recesses in the ceilings and octagonal carpet inlays on the floor (Fig. 16.7).

Color Coding Was Also Used as an Orientation Device: In order for a resident to find his way easily in a building, he must be able to recognize where he is at any point in the building. Because

FIGURE 16.7 Hallway corner: Ceiling and floor treatments at the four corners of the hallway were used to aid orientation.

retirement homes are an assemblage of similar elements, confusion may result from the spatial monotony of the building. At Westside, the layout and design of each of the four nursing floors were the same. The architect was aware of this and color coded the carpet and walls on each of the four floors. The building contains a green, a blue, a yellow, and an orange floor. These colors are used as themes or accent colors rather than dominant colors. The various color themes are expressed by large inlaid areas of carpeting in the dining lounge across from the elevator, inlaid octagonal-shaped carpeting in each of the four corners of the "loop," and colored bulletin boards in the hallways of each floor.

Interview results indicated, however, that theme colors by themselves were not adequate. Three-fourths of the employees interviewed admitted they did not know the color theme of individual floors after working in the new building for over 6 months. When asked how they knew the number of the nursing floor that they were entering when coming off of the elevators, employees cited other visual cues but seldom mentioned color. A frequent response was "I watch for the number to light up in the elevator," or "I look for a resident or staff face that I know belongs on that floor," or "I look for a lot of plants, then I know it's the fifth floor." Observation and interview data indicated that residents, staff members, and visitors frequently got off elevators on the wrong floors.

Residents in high-rise buildings often suffer from the same inability to identify a particular floor. The problem can be especially frustrating to older residents. This situation was corrected, but only 9 months after the opening of the building, when large floor numbers were painted in the lounge areas across from the elevator lobby. The numbers met with immediate approval on the part of nursing residents, staff members, and visitors. People leaving the elevator could immediately confirm the number of the floor before exiting from the elevator.

Plants Located on the Fifth Floor Made it Easy to Recognize: In addition to design strategies such as color coding and the numbering of different floors, different sections of the building can be named. Another strategy involves "individualizing" floors with plants or artwork. It was found at Westside that residents, staff members, and visitors were more likely to recognize the fifth floor than the fourth, third, and second floors because a large number of potted plants were located there. These plants were clustered in a lounge space directly across from the elevators. The idea of individualizing each floor could give them a separate, distinct identity. For example, one floor could have sculpture opposite the elevators, another could have a large fish aquarium, and so on.

Designing for Increased Home Range

In addition to designing for better orientation and visual legibility, the designer should also use design to stimulate the activity level and behavior of residents. In a typical nursing home, residents rarely leave the building and often become extremely dependent on interior spaces for virtually all activities. Various social programs and architectural space relationships may lead to an increase or decrease in the activity level of residents. Before exploring the relationship of design to the resident activity level, it is useful to introduce the concept of "home range."

Home Range Tends to Decrease as Age Increases and Physical Mobility Becomes a Problem: "Home range" is defined as a composite of all the places where activities significant to the daily life of an individual take place. In a nursing environment, home range consists of the individual's trips to places outside his room. Increased age, reduced mobility, sensory losses, and a general decline in competence acting together often reduce home range. Most daily activities for elderly nursing home residents take place inside the building. Residents often depend on staff, friends, and relatives to determine how often and when they go places. A physical environment without spaces for various activities can lead to an isolated, withdrawn, and lonely life.

Spivak (1973) describes "archetypal" places for life-tasks, which he theorizes must be available to a person at all times. These places encompass the activities of shelter, sleeping, intimacy with spouse,

TABLE 16.1   Components of Home Range at Westside

On Individual Floors
  Walks in hallway
  Visits to hallway lounge
  Vist to T.V. lounge
  Visits to dining lounge
  Visits to nursing station
  Trips to meals in dining lounges
  Trips to bath or shower room
  Trips to other residents' rooms
  Visits from others to resident's room

Beyond the Individual Floors but Within the Building
  Visits to other three nursing resident floors (identical spaces on all four floors)
  Visits to roof garden/green house
  Visits to main floor (main dining room, chapel, receptionist, administration
    offices, medical clinic, gift shop, hair dresser-barber shop, library heritage
    room)
  Visits to lower level (large activity room with work alcoves, residents' kitchen)

Outside the Building
  Visits to drug store (within one block walk)
  Visits to grocery store (within one block walk)
  Planned trips with friends, relatives, or volunteers
  Visits to hospital or doctor's office

grooming, eating, bodily function, defending territory, playing, going places, meeting, and competition. Nursing home residents have few archetypal places, and those that they do possess often serve multiple functions. In fact, some individuals may spend the remainder of their lives within the walls of one room. A severe reduction in the accessibility of archetypal places or a reduction in home range can reduce opportunities for establishing and maintaining interpersonal relationships. As a nursing resident relinquishes control to staff and the immediate environment, it becomes increasingly difficult to maintain an extended home range.

A special feature of the new Westwide nursing wing was the number and type of places to go within the building. Table 16.1 lists the possible components of home range for the residents of Westside's new nursing wing.

The Home Range of Many Residents Increased in the New Building:
The home range of nursing residents before and after relocation to the new nursing wing was documented through nurse and aide interviews. The single most important change in home range for many of the residents involved mealtime activity. Table 16.2 illustrates that many residents who formerly took meals in their room now left their rooms regularly for meals in the dining-lounge area on each floor. These same floor dining rooms were used to serve residents two or more meals a day. In the old building, residents

TABLE 16.2 Where Nursing Residents Regularly Eat Their Meals

	Old Nursing Wing		New Nursing Wing	
In own rooms	83.6%	(N = 51)	40.3%	(N = 27)
Dining-Lounge area on nursing floor	N.A.		52.2%	(N = 35)
First floor dining area	16.4%	(N = 10)	7.5%	(N = 5)
	100.0%		100%	

had to choose between eating in their room or eating in the large first floor dining space. The new design allowed more residents to take meals in a communal setting. The staff of the home believed this promoted socialization among residents. Resident reaction to the change was found also to be generally favorable. Most residents enjoyed visiting a different place two or three times a day. In fact, many arrived in the dining area well ahead of mealtime.

In addition to dining rooms, lounges were also located on each floor. Floor lounges were thought to attract nursing residents out of their rooms and thus increase their mobility and home range.

Some individuals who had not left their rooms in the old wing were observed exploring more after the move. However, 6 months after the move the novelty of the floor lounges and social spaces had worn off for most people. Case No. 1, the story of Mrs. Noltry, is an example of novel behavior that followed the move.

Case No. 1: Mrs. Ida Noltry's Increase in Mobility Lasted 6 Months: In the old nursing home, Mrs. Noltry seldom left her room except to use the first floor dining area twice a day for meals. She was rarely seen in the hallways or lounge areas. Immediately following Mrs. Noltry's move to the new nursing floor, she began to take frequent walks in the hallways. Although her vision was poor, her arthritis severe, and her ambulation hindered, Mrs. Noltry embarked on several walks a day. Using a walker, she would stroll around the circular loop of connecting hallways. Sometimes she would continue for a second trip around the loop. As time progressed, Mrs. Noltry's trips became less regular. Six months after the move, she returned to her before-move pattern of behavior, leaving her room only for meals.

Case No. 2: Mrs. Mimi Sanders Walked More than Anyone Expected: While Ida Noltry's behavior following the move was typical of four or five individuals, Mrs. Sander's case was quite atypical. Mrs. Sanders was an active person on the old nursing floor. Although she could ambulate fully without aid, she often used a walker as an ad-hoc crutch. There were only a few places to go on the old nursing floor, and therefore Mrs. Sanders often sat in the hallway lounge watching the passing activity. Her walking consisted primarily of trips from her room to the hallway lounge and back again, a distance of approximately 10 feet. With the move to the new nursing floor, her activity level changed abruptly. She began exploring the entire nursing floor on a regular basis several times a day. She would often be out of her room for the entire day. One regular pattern was to walk around the loop, stopping at the dining lounge to rest. She would sit for a couple of minutes and then embark on another walk.

In the weeks following the move, Mrs. Sanders' walking increased to such an extent that the nurses became concerned about her health. She was often exhausted at the end of the day from walking. This walking behavior did not change in the following months. The nurses theorized her constant walking around the loop was related to memory problems. She would quickly forget she had just taken a walk and would proceed to take another.

Case No. 3: Mrs. Amy Attenberg Had a Reason to Leave the Floor Periodically: Mrs. Attenberg's behavior was atypical, but it serves to illustrate the case of a person whose home range suddenly increased. Mrs. Attenberg was one of a few nursing residents allowed to leave the nursing floor unattended. She was not considered a particularly alert resident. In fact, she was frequently confused and lost, sometimes forgetting her immediate destination. Mrs. Attenberg was a strong-willed person, however, and nurses and aides allowed her to come and go as she pleased. Because she was one of only three residents of the home who smoked, she frequently left the nursing floor regularly because, by law, smoking was not permitted there. In the old wing Mrs. Attenberg would go downstairs for meals twice a day and to smoke two or three times a day. She was off the resident nursing floor more often than any other resident. The old building limited her explorations because there were few places to visit. Following the move she quickly discovered many more places throughout the building where she could wander. Her activity level out of her room and off the floor remained high in the months that followed.

While Mrs. Sanders increased her activity level and home range on her own floor, Mrs. Attenberg increased her activity level and home range throughout the entire building. Both residents experienced increased activity because of their own initiative and the "draw" of the new environment. This kind of self-initiated increase in home range in the new environment was typical of only a few residents.

Case No. 4: Mr. James Barton Was Negatively Affected by the Change: Sometimes improvements in the overall environment can contribute to a decline in an individual's activity level or home range. The following example illustrates this point.

Mr. Barton, a nursing resident of advanced age, was limited by poor vision and hearing but still managed to ambulate with the aid of a walker along the old nursing floor. Mr. Barton was often seen pushing his walker along the tiled floors of the hallway. Mr. Barton's limited bladder control required that he frequently push his walker down the hallway to a nearby toilet room. Two architectural characteristics in the new nursing floor modified his behavior. The carpeting used throughout the new nursing floor made it impossible for him to slide his walker ahead of him as he had in the old wing. Nurses and aides tried in vain to teach him to overcome the surface resistance of the carpet by lifting his walker. Mr. Barton's movements were also affected by the location of the toilet in the new home, which was now adjacent to his room. These two architectural characteristics reduced Mr. Barton's home range because he now rarely left his room. Without participating in any activity he withdrew to his chair and his condition declined. Although his physical and mental decline might have occurred independently, the reduction in home range seemed to exacerbate the decline. Within 2 months of the move, Mr. Barton was dead.

There is no way of determining whether the sudden reduction in his walking activity related to Mr. Barton's decline and death; however, these problems could have been easily resolved. Aides could have brought Mr. Barton out of his room despite his adjoining toilet room and a modified walker (with wheels on the front two legs) could have been used to overcome the carpet's resistance. When an individual loses the ability to self-ambulate, nurses and aides should be encouraged to respond creatively to correct the situation.

The four preceding case studies illustrate the variety of adaptive responses that develop in a new environment. Although it is difficult to predict precisely how a new environment will affect residents, it can be said that an environment that includes a greater number of spaces for activities allows the resident reasons to explore and thus increase home range. The case studies also demonstrate the role management plays in helping residents adapt to a new setting.

Management Also Plays an Important Role in Increasing Home Range

Management increased the home range of residents by initiating trips to the dining lounge, beauty shop, bath or shower rooms, arts and crafts rooms, the horticultural therapy program, and exercise sessions. While the number of trips to the beauty shop and bath and shower rooms remained relatively constant before and after the move, trips to planned activities sharply increased after the move. Table 16.3 illustrates the greater number of nursing residents who participated in planned activities in the new wing. Two

TABLE 16.3   The Number of Activities Attended by Nursing Residents

	During the 1-Month Period Before the Relocation (Old Nursing Floor) (of 5 Activities Available) (N = 62)	During the First Month After Relocation (New Nursing Floor) (of 7 Activities Available) (N = 64)	During the Eighth Month *After* Relocation (of 30 Activities Available) (N = 42)
Number of residents who attended 0 activities	51.6% (N = 32)	59.4% (N = 38)	35.7 (N = 15)
Number of residents who attended 1–5 activities	48.4% (N = 30)	31.2% (N = 20)	35.7 (N = 15)
Number of residents who attended 6–10 activities	0 (N = 0)	9.4% (N = 6)	28.6 (N = 12)
Number of residents who attended 10 or more activities	0 (N = 0)	0 (N = 0)	0 (N = 0)

factors account for this increase: the new facility offered more places to hold planned activities, and a more active volunteer program and a newly employed crafts director solicited more and more nursing residents for activities after the move.

Resident self-initiated activities (such as walking trips) increased home range in the new environment for a few residents, while staff initiated activities (such as meals and planned activities) increased the home range of many others.

These changes, however, did not increase the home range of 15 nursing residents who did not want to or for health reasons could not participate. Some of these 15 residents may have participated in activities had they been brought to them.

The design program for Westside assumed that nursing residents would have access to all of the spaces within the new building wing. However, instead of having access to the total community of the building, most residents were allowed access to spaces only on their own floor. Nurses and aides felt it necessary to keep close track of residents' whereabouts, and this task was made too difficult if residents were allowed free movement off their nursing floor. Restrictions such as this limited social interaction and discouraged friendships between floors. With the only activity spaces on each nursing floor being lounge areas, residents had little to draw them out of their rooms. The idea of having free movement throughout the building was perhaps an unrealistic assumption.

The creation of a more supportive environment to facilitate extended home range does appear to be an appropriate goal in the design of dependent care settings. This goal can only be realized through the successful interface of design and management. Both are necessary.

DESIGN DIRECTIVES

DESIGN DIRECTIVE **ONE**	*A building environment should be organized to facilitate the identification of distinct parts within a cohesive whole.*

1. The careful placement of objects, such as plants or sculptures, can assist occupants in distinguishing similar parts of a building from one another.

2. Floor number indications on walls or posts can aid positive identification.

3. Distinctive wall and floor coverings can provide additional identification clues.

4. An effective strategy is to combine the identification methods throughout a building, thus making all parts of a building legible and easily identifiable.

DESIGN DIRECTIVE **TWO**	*Glare can be reduced through the use of low-reflective floor and wall surface materials and the judicious choice of natural and artificial lighting.*

1. Windows at the end of long corridors can increase glare and reflections on floors and walls.

2. Windows on side walls of long corridors provide more even lighting while reducing glare and reflections.

3. Balanced interior lighting can further reduce glare. It is far better to use three 100-watt lamps than one 300-watt lamp in a room.

DESIGN DIRECTIVE **THREE**	*Glare can be further reduced through the thoughtful choice of window control devices and room furnishings.*

1. Thin venetian blinds can be set at a desired angle to regulate the amount of light (and resulting glare) admitted to a room.

2. Combining window control devices such as venetian blinds, draperies, exterior overhangs, and shading devices provides for greater control of window glare.

3. Highly polished smooth surfaces on furniture such as tables, bed stands, and dressers should be avoided.

4. Shiny stainless steel tubing on apparatus such as bed rails, geri chairs, and lifting devices should be substituted where possible with nonreflective materials.

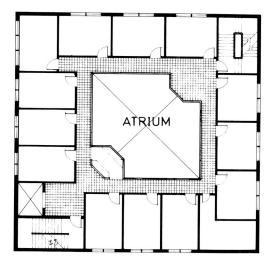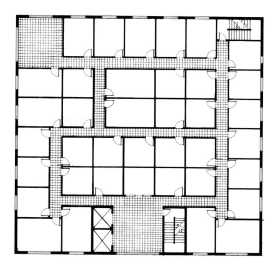

FIGURE 16.8 An atrium design can be used to simplify organization and clarify orientation.

Brighter than normal colors can be selected for carpeting, draperies, wall coverings, and room furnishings to facilitate the perception of colors for elderly occupants who have age-related vision losses.

DESIGN DIRECTIVE
FOUR

The corridor system within a building should be organized to aid occupants in knowing where they are within a building (orientation).

DESIGN DIRECTIVE
FIVE

1. A confusing arrangement of interior corridors can easily disorient building users. Unnecessary turns and complications should therefore be avoided.

2. Atriums or large central interior spaces can serve as places of visual reference; such spaces can be repeated on different floors or building wings (Fig. 16.8).

3. A simple orderly arrangement of corridors combined with an atrium will aid building users in orientation.

In addition to central points of reference, such as atriums, "nodes," or visual points of interest can be used to further facilitate orientation.

DESIGN DIRECTIVE
SIX

1. Nodes can assist building occupants in confirming where they are within a building (Fig. 16.9).

2. Nodes also provide opportunities for personalizing, sitting, reading, and socializing. Nodes can also help draw residents out of their rooms and increase the activity level of residents.

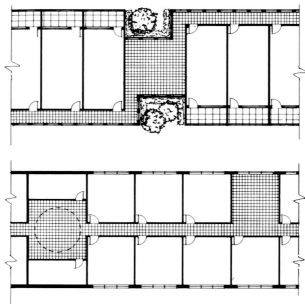

FIGURE 16.9 Changes in the hallway configuration can help to orient residents and visitors.

| DESIGN DIRECTIVE **SEVEN** | *Where individual parts of a building are repetitious in design, efforts should be made to make them distinct from one another.* |

1. Similar building parts can be made distinguishable through differing furniture types and arrangements, differing color schemes, naming and numbering, and personalization (Fig. 16.10).

FIGURE 16.10 Treating lounge spaces differently can add to their personalization and orientation.

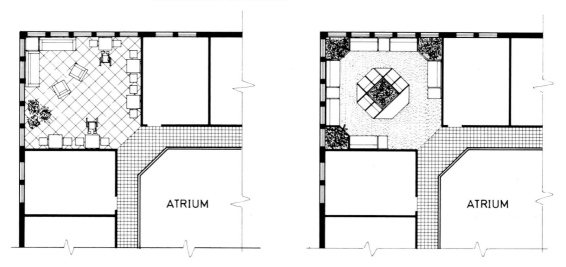

POLICY CONSIDERATIONS

Post-occupany evaluations should be used to improve planning and design.

Post-occupancy evaluations are useful in gaining an understanding of how a building performs and can be used to strengthen the basis for future planning and design decisions. Evaluations should incorporate a multimethod approach involving all users and should be thorough enough to provide an accurate, comprehensive picture of a building's performance. In this way planners, designers, and managers can recognize and avoid the mistakes of past projects as well as recognize and repeat successes.

POLICY CONSIDERATION
ONE

Retirement facilities should be planned and designed to ensure visual legibility.

An important program objective for the design of any retirement facility is to create a visually legible interior environment through the reduction of glare, the use of bright colors, and the use of balanced lighting. Sensory losses can be offset to a certain extent through the judicious use of carpeting, vinyl wall covering, and other materials, and the careful placement of windows to control glare. Bright colors can be used to cheer up residents and increase their visual responsiveness.

POLICY CONSIDERATION
TWO

Orientation should be a key principle in planning environments.

When designing a retirement home or nursing facility for elderly residents who often suffer from sensory losses and memory problems, it becomes extremely important to consider the effect of the environment on the orientation of residents. The basic organization of a facility can enhance the ability of residents and other building users to orient themselves to spaces within a building when certain design principles are followed. These principles, when properly employed in planning and design, allow users to understand and negotiate the building environment. Individuals involved in policy decisions regarding planning and design should be aware of these principles.

POLICY CONSIDERATION
THREE

Management should encourage residents to increase their home range.

By including many supporting activity spaces throughout the building, planners and designers can promote the independence of residents and create an active community. The success of this

POLICY CONSIDERATION
FOUR

strategy, however, can hinge to a great extent on management regulations. The separation of spaces on separate floors can reduce activity levels for some residents. Various strategies for increasing the activities of residents from floor to floor should be explored. A well-designed nursing home environment should include a wide variety of spaces within residents' access. The autonomy, or free movement, of residents should be encouraged by management to allow the home range of residents to increase.

If the free movement of nursing residents from floor to floor within a building is an unrealistic expectation, as seems to be the case at Westside, then perhaps a better strategy is to provide a greater number and variety of activity spaces on the individual floors within the building rather than centrally locating them on a floor that is separated from resident rooms.

17

EASING RELOCATION
An Environmental Learning Process

Michael E. Hunt and Leon A. Pastalan

R elocation is a stressful experience that involves leaving a familiar environment and accompanying social relationships as well as adapting to new physical and social environments. Relocation has been the subject of much concern in recent years because some studies have indicated that relatively frail older persons experience increases in morbidity and mortality rates following moves. So pronounced has been this phenomenon that it has received such ominous titles as "transfer trauma" and "transplantation shock."

Buildings Should be Designed So as to Facilitate Environmental Learning

Attempts to better understand how and why relocation affects older people have revealed the importance of familiarizing residents with the new facility prior to the move. This has implications for how people are prepared for relocation and for the design of buildings. The strategy used to familiarize older people with an unknown building needs to be based on how people learn the environment. This chapter focuses on the evaluation of an environmental learning strategy—simulated site visits. The simulation technique provides a means to familiarize people with an unknown building, and the evaluation provides information on how people "learn" buildings. The simulation technique helps to illuminate the importance of environmental learning in the process of preparing older people for relocation and sheds light on how buildings should be designed.

Related Research

There has been an abundance of research concerning the relocation of older people. However, the findings have been apparently contradictory. For example, Aldrich and Mendkoff (1963); Killian (1970); Lieberman (1961); Markus, Blenkner, Bloom and Downs (1972); and Pablo (1977) have found the manifestations of relocation to include increased mortality, depression, stress, and decreased life satisfaction. On the other hand, Carp (1968 and 1977); Lawton and Yaffe (1970); Lieberman, Tobin and Slover (1971); Miller and Lieberman (1965); and Wittels and Botwinick (1974) have not substantiated these debilitating effects of relocation on older people. These inconsistent results have fostered uncertainty in some circles as to the existence and/or degree of relocation trauma in various situations.

Prediction and Control Are Key Concepts in Relocation

In response to this dilemma, Schulz and Brenner (1977) have developed a framework that takes into consideration the various circumstances in which relocation may occur. This framework is based on the assumption that relocation is a stressful experience and that the mediation of this stress should occur as it does in laboratory research on stress. Such research on both animals and humans has revealed two factors that mediate responses to stress: controllability and predictability. "In general, the greater the perceived controllability or predictability of a stressor, the less aversive and harmful are its effects on the organism" (Schulz and Brenner, 1977, p. 324).

The concepts of controllability and predictability are readily applied to relocation. In this context, controllability refers to the degree of choice offered the person, and predictability refers to the degree of environmental change between the old and new sites.

In an effort to organize and explain the relocation literature, Schulz and Brenner (1977) have proposed a framework based on the concepts of controllability and predictability. One factor of the framework, the degree of choice, has two categories: involuntary and voluntary moves. The other factor, the degree of environmental change, is divided into three categories: home to home, home to institution, and institution to institution. The authors hypothesize that this model can predict how well people will respond to the stress caused by one type of move in relation to other types.

> . . . the model predicts that individuals moved involuntarily from home to an institution should show the greatest negative effects, with the outcomes being somewhat better for involuntary relocatees moved from institution to institution. The outcomes of individuals moving voluntarily from institution to institution and home to home should be the least negative compared to the other groups (1977, p. 325).

These predictions by the authors leave the voluntary home to institution and involuntary home to home moves in the midrange of negative effects on the person.

The Schulz and Brenner framework has been analyzed by comparing the voluntary and involuntary moves in each environmental change category (Pastalan, 1979; Bourestom and Pastalan, 1981). In each of the three categories, the involuntary move was shown to have a more negative impact of the person than a similar move made voluntarily.

The concept of environmental change has been investigated and expanded by Pastalan and Bourestom (1975). They divided a move from one institution to another into two types: a radical move that involved changes in the physical environment, staff, program, and patient population; and a moderate move that involved a change primarily in the physical environment. The results indicated that the radical move was associated with higher mortality rates than the moderate move. In addition, the survivors of the radical move were not able to adjust to the new environment as well as were the survivors of the moderate move.

To summarize, the existing literature seems to support the Schulz and Brenner hypothesis that controllability and predictability can mediate stress. Therefore, the degree of choice and the degree of environmental change involved in a given relocation situation are crucial factors to be addressed when relocating older people.

A Preparation Program Ensures That a Move Will Be Less Traumatic

A predictable environment does not necessarily have to be an environment that is similar to other environments experienced by the person in the past. Instead, a predictable environment could be a dissimilar environment with which the person has been familiarized prior to the actual move. This logic has led to the development of programs to prepare older people for relocation.

Pastalan and Bourestom (1975) have developed a program intended to prepare older patients for transfer between nursing homes. Their preparation program has three goals: to familiarize the person with the building, staff, and patients; to reduce the patient anxiety; and to ensure a network of support. Site visits are a major component of the preparation, as is apparent from the following program directive:

> Site visits will constitute the core of the preparation program for the resident. It is urgent that patients be thoroughly familiar with the spatial layout of important functional areas and with the social, medical and other supportive services offered at the new facility. Hence when the transfer is made, the patient will be adequately oriented

in locational terms, i.e., he will know where his room is in relation to other important spaces in the facility—he will have established his point of reference, he will know the staff, he will be familiar with the various therapy and recreation programs; in sum he will have a working knowledge of the facility by the time he moves in to stay (Pastalan, Davis, and Haberkorn, 1975, pp. 23–24).

This preparation program has been tested longitudinally during the forced relocation of older people from one long-term care facility to another in the State of Michigan (Pastalan and Bourestom, 1975). The group of patients who received the preparation program had a 73 percent survival rate during the first year following transfer, while the control group had only a 48 percent survival rate. Thus, it seems that the intervention of the preparation program into the relocation process can mitigate some of the negative effects of forced relocation. This finding is also consistent with the Schulz and Brenner hypothesis that the greater the perceived predictability of a stressor, the less aversive and harmful are its effects on the organism.

The Commonwealth of Pennsylvania has adopted the preparation program developed by Pastalan and Bourestom as a policy guideline concerning nursing home relocation. The Pennsylvania Relocation Program was evaluated by comparing mortality rates of the relocated patients to the nursing home population at large. Patients were followed for a period of 12 months after the move took place in order to measure survival and adjustment. The evaluation found the program to be quite successful in mitigating the negative effects of forced relocation.

> For 236 persons relocated between July 1975, and July 1976, the mortality rate is 11 percent as compared to 26.6 percent for the Commonwealth of Pennsylvania and 27.5 percent for the United States (Haberkorn, Davis, Pastalan, and Walker, 1977, p. 4).

Problems with Implementation Led to a Simulation Approach

Although the Pennsylvania experience has demonstrated the effectiveness of the preparation program, several implementation problems arose related to the site visits prior to relocation, an important program component. For example, site visits can take a great deal of time and be costly in terms of staff participation. In many cases, site visits have also often not been feasible because of the distance between old and new sites. In addition, it has been found that people over 80 years of age tend not to respond well to the visits. Finally, bed-bound and blind patients have been unable to take advantage of the visits.

In light of these problems with implementation of the site visit procedure, there was a need to develop an alternative method by which people might learn about buildings short of physically visiting them. This need fostered the idea of developing a simulation technique that could essentially bring the building to the residents instead of taking them to the building.

The Simulation Technique Was Based on the Type of Information Needed to Find One's Way Around the Environment

Although the literature contains inconsistent terminology, there seem to be two generally agreed upon types of environmental learning information: the ability to recognize landmarks and knowing where the place or object being sought is located in space.

There are several authors who lend credence to the establishment of these essential types of information for way-finding. Stephen Kaplan (1976) argues that way-finding is facilitated by visually distinctive landmarks and a comprehensible structure or path system. Allen et al. (1978) state that people acquire knowledge concerning landmarks and routes as they move through the environment. And finally, Golledge and Rayner (1973) contend it is essential to learn the location of places and the paths that connect them in order to learn about an environment. (For a more indepth examination of the way-finding literature, please refer to chapter 18 by Weisman in this volume.)

In light of these informational needs, the simulation technique was composed of a small-scale, schematic three-dimensional model of the building and a series of sequential photographic slides that moved the observer directionally through the building. The sequential slides provided identification information as well as the sequential experience of walking through the building. The model was used to provide an understanding of the spatial configuration of the building and to foster spatial orientation. It also allowed the viewer to physically trace the route of the slides through the model of the building.

Since the slides were to provide a sequential experience, it was important that they be cohesive and continuous. Therefore, a person was included in each slide who served as a guide. The guide signaled the direction and location of the following slide by turning or looking in the direction of the next slide while walking along the route. In this way, the viewer was essentially following the guide through the building. The inclusion of a guide in the slides not only served to improve the cohesiveness of the slides but also simplified the task of following the simulation route in the slides.

Although sequential slides have been shown to successfully provide identification and sequential information, the provision of spatial orientation information has proven to be difficult. Allen et al. (1978) found that sequential slides were unable to provide sufficient information concerning spatial orientation. Hence, the need for another component of the technique.

A Scale Model Simplifies a Building and Facilitates Its Perception

A scale model was chosen as the medium to provide spatial orientation information for several reasons. First, models help to streamline the process of developing spatial orientation information by making it possible to comprehend the entire building with a single glance. Ordinarily, a person constructs an understanding of spatial relationships over time by compiling information received from numerous exposures to the building. Second, Arnheim (1977) has written that since a model is quantitatively diminished, it seems qualitatively simplified. Thus, a model not only makes the spatial relationships readily apparent but also simplifies the building. Finally, a three-dimensional model was included in the simulation because models seem to be more readily understood than floor plans. In this regard, Appleyard has written that floor plans "are good for the comprehension of spatial relationships if the viewer is trained in the medium and if the project is relatively simple" (1977, p. 71).

The model was constructed as a three-dimensional plan in a "layer-cake" fashion that allowed one to remove the top floor to reveal the floor below. The only areas illustrated by the model were those selected for inclusion in the simulated visit and the major corridor system. All other areas were covered in the model. Extraneous detail was omitted to make the model more understandable by minimizing information overload and helping viewers order the information. Rachel Kaplan et al. (1974), Stephen Kaplan (1977), and Moore (1979) have written in support of the notion that a model designed to orient people to a building should be simple

FIGURE 17.1 Exterior model: The model is simplified by not illustrating facade details or landscaping.

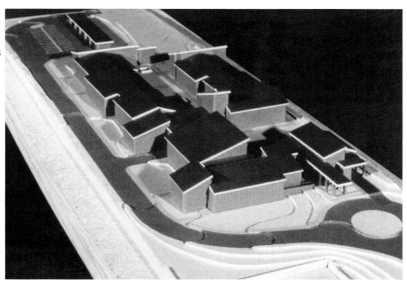

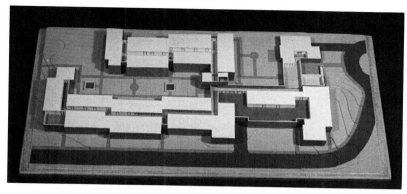

FIGURE 17.2 Interior model: To make the model more understandable, only areas included in the simulated visit and the major circulation system were included.

and contain little extraneous detail. Figures 17.1 and 17.2 illustrate the models constructed as part of this simulation technique. Figure 17.1 is a simplified model of the exterior of the building, and Figure 17.2 is a model of the building's interior.

The Simulation Presentation Involved Both the Model and Sequentially Presented Slides

Although the model and slides were designed to provide differing types of information, it was important for viewers to be able to assimilate the information into a single image of the building. Failure to do so might have resulted in diminished benefit from either or both of the media. Therefore, the model and slides were presented simultaneously. The slides were shown on a rear-projection screen so as to keep the projector away from viewers and to project an image uninterrupted by shadows from the viewers. The model was placed directly in front of the projection screen. This placement made it possible for the viewers to interrelate information gained from the two media. A photograph of the simulation as it was seen by the viewers is illustrated in Figure 17.3.

The presentation of the simulation consisted of two showings. The first contained only the most crucial settings, that is, those that would be essential for a person to carry out minimum daily activities. Examples of such settings are the main entrance to the building, dining room, elevator, one's apartment or room, and the nurses' station. The second showing added the remaining settings chosen for inclusion in the simulated visit. Thus, the second showing added to and reinforced the information presented in the first showing. The additional places in the second simulated visit to the nursing home included the chapel, library, laundry room, recreation room, and administrative offices. This two-staged presentation served to reduce the possibility of overloading the viewer with more information than could be handled at once.

FIGURE 17.3 Simulation presentation: This presentation technique allows the viewer to assimilate information from the model and slides into a single image of the building.

The Most Crucial Settings Were the First Presented

Golledge (1973) contends that environments contain a limited number of places that have a high probability of being defined as primary nodes by inhabitants. Golledge argues further that this set of nodes should provide the anchors for the mental image of inhabitants. Carr and Schissler (1969) confirm this contention by writing that meaningful elements of the environment seem to be anchored in one's image. Thus, it seems important to correctly establish the most crucial settings in one's image. Failure to do so could result not only in the misplacement of the crucial settings but in their subordinate settings as well.

Methodology and Data Analysis

The evaluation of the simulation technique was designed as a field experiment to determine the technique's effectiveness in providing a working knowledge of a previously unknown building (Hunt, 1981a and 1984). There were three experimental groups in the evaluation to which participants were randomly assigned: a simulation group, a site visit group, and a control group. The simulation group was shown (one person at a time) a simulated walk through the building but was not exposed to the actual building prior to testing. The site visit group was taken (one at a time) to the building and shown the same parts of the building in the same order as contained in the simulation. The control research group was not exposed to the building in any way prior to testing. This research design enabled people's knowledge of the building derived from the simulation to be compared and contrasted with people's knowledge derived from an actual site visit and no preparation at all.

The site of the evaluation was a retirement center located in Ann Arbor, Michigan. It offered a complete range of personal services including meals, health services, and creative activities. The population of the retirement center was 110 at the time of the study, and it contained 93 ambulatory rooms and 20 infirmary beds. It is important to note that although this building was used as the site of the evaluation, the residents of the facility did not participate in the study.

The sample of participants consisted of 51 older people (ages 57–79) who volunteered to participate in the study (17 per group). All participants were living independently in the Ann Arbor area and were ambulatory. No one was allowed to participate who had ever visited the building used in the evaluation. Even though the problem that the simulation technique was designed to address dealt with the forced relocation of older people, the sample did not consist of people who were actually being relocated. It would have been inappropriate and, in fact, unethical to provide an untested form of preparation for an actual relocation procedure, since the consequences of inadequate preparation could have been sickness or even death.

The Subjects' Working Knowledge of the Building Was Assessed

The measurement procedure utilized in the evaluation involved assessing a person's working knowledge of a building. This is a broad and multifaceted construct that is difficult, if not impossible, to define with a single operational definition. Three types of measures were used to tap the various dimensions of working knowledge: confidence in way-finding ability, mental image of the building, and way-finding ability in the building. The first two types of measures were administered after the appropriate exposure to the building had been completed but before the simulation and control groups had seen the building in person. In addition, the control group only participated in the evaluation of way-finding ability. It would have been impossible for the control group to participate in other measurement procedures because they had no previous information about the building.

The measurement of confidence in one's way-finding ability was considered a "mental" way-finding exercise in that it required participants to imagine how they would walk from one place to another. The measurement consisted of asking participants how confident they were in finding their way between eight pairs of locations in the building.

The second step of the measurement procedure involved an assessment of the mental image participants were able to derive of the building. The measurement of a mental image was based on the two types of information that are necessary to form an image: identification and spatial orientation. The measurement of spatial orientation was broken down into two components: sequential arrangements and knowledge of the spatial organization of the building.

Identification and sequential arrangement knowledge were assessed by using photographs. To measure identification knowledge, participants were asked to match photographs to cards with locations printed on them. One question dealt with views from the elevator on each of the three floors, another with the views out of five windows, and the last with views of five hallways. Sequential arrangement knowledge was measured by asking participants to arrange three or four photographs of places in the building in the order they would see them or walk by them if walking between two places.

The Participants' Understanding of the Organization or Configuration of the Building Was Measured

Spatial organization was too broad a construct to define with a single operational definition. Therefore, it was broken down into three categories: external shape of the building, vertical organization of the building, and horizontal organization of the building. An understanding of the external shape of the building was measured by asking each participant to identify the shape of the building (in plan view) from a group of four shapes. An understanding of the vertical organization of the building was measured by asking each participant to identify the floor on which each of a series of nine rooms was located. Finally, an understanding of the horizontal organization of the building was measured by asking each participant to locate nine rooms on a "hollow" plan of the building. The plan given to the participants for this exercise was composed of only the exterior walls of the building with no interior walls or division into separate floors. The quality of these maps was assessed by asking ten judges to independently rank-order the maps by their quality into five categories.

The final step of measurement assessed efficient mobility through the building itself. This was accomplished by taking each participant to the building and asking him or her to find the way to a series of nine places throughout the building. Evaluations of the participants' way-finding performance for each task were made by both the interviewer and the participants. Participants were asked how well they had been able to find their way. The interviewer assessed the mistakes and/or hesitations made by participants while way-finding.

Findings

Older Elderly Are Less Confident than Younger Elderly in Finding Their Way Through a Building

Analysis of the confidence data revealed that any differences between the scores of the simulation and site visit groups could be explained by controlling for the age of participants. Without controlling for age, there was a significant difference between the confidence of the simulation and site visit groups. However, after controlling for age the differences were found not to be significant in either age group. Thus, the older elderly appear to be less confident than the younger elderly in finding their way through a building even when both age groups receive the same information.

This finding has significance for the relocation of older people. Since the older elderly appear to be less confident than younger elderly people in finding their way through a building, steps need to be taken to raise the confidence of the older elderly. Such steps could include providing them with extra preparation for the move.

Simulation Subjects Noticed and Used Landmarks to Way-Find

As stated earlier, one's mental image of the building was measured by assessing knowledge in three areas: identification, sequential arrangement, and spatial organization. Analysis of identification knowledge revealed that the simulation group scored significantly better than the site visit group (Kruskal-Wallis, $p < 0.05$). The simulation group was better able to notice and use landmarks as clues to aid way-finding. It was also found that the color coding of floors or hallways was not effective unless users had been familiarized with the coding. Such training was part of the simulation procedure but not part of the site visit procedure. In addition, the assessment of identification knowledge provided insight into how views out windows were used. It seems they were used to help people locate where they were going rather than to establish their location.

The analysis of the sequential arrangement questions revealed that the simulation group generally scored better than the site visit group. However, there were no significant differences in three out of the four sets of pictures. Thus, it was concluded that the two groups had about equal knowledge of sequential arrangements in the building. By analyzing the errors that were made in the arrangement of the pictures, however, it was found that the simulation group was better able to notice and use the subtle differences in views of the building. This finding verifies that of the identification analysis.

The Simulation Group Acquired the Best Knowledge of Building Configuration and Spatial Relationships

The measure of spatial organization knowledge was divided into three categories: knowledge of the external shape of the building, knowledge of the vertical organization of the building, and knowledge of the building's horizontal organization. Analysis of these measures revealed that the simulation group had a significantly better understanding in all three categories than did the site visit group. Thus, it is concluded that the simulation technique was able to provide a better developed understanding of the configuration of the building and the spatial relationships within it than was an actual visit to the building.

To summarize the various mental image assessments, there were clear differences in the simulated and actual visit groups. The site visit group was able to understand the sequence in which objects or places were seen but not the spatial relationships of the places to each other. On the other hand, the simulation group was able to derive an understanding of these spatial relationships. This implies that the image provided by the site visit was relatively linear in nature, while the simulation provided a more fully developed understanding of the spatial relationships.

The Simulation Group Found Their Way Around the Building Better than the Site Visit and Control Groups

The final step of the analysis assessed way-finding performance. Statistical analysis was performed by calculating nonparametric t-tests (Mann-Whitney U) between all pairings of treatment groups for each task. This analysis revealed that the simulation group was able to find their way significantly better than the site visit group in four of the eight tasks and significantly better than the control group in seven tasks ($p < 0.05$). On the other hand, the site visit group was able to way-find significantly better than the control group on only five tasks ($p < 0.05$). In fact, the control group was actually able to way-find better than the site visit group on two tasks, although the differences were not statistically significant.

A more detailed analysis of way-finding performances revealed similarities with the mental image assessments. The simulation group was able to find places in the building without having to follow the same route shown in the simulation. Furthermore, they were able to find parts of the building not seen in the simulation by relating new areas to places already known. On the other hand, the way-finding ability of the site visit group faltered if the place being sought was not in the same direction or sequence as the route followed during the site visit. In addition, the image provided by the site visit essentially became ineffective when the person ventured into unknown areas of the building. Thus, the simulation was more useful than site visits in that it accomplished more than teaching one to follow a path. It also provided the tools that enabled the person to design his or her own route to a desired location.

Efficient Mobility Is Dependent Upon One's Mental Image of the Environment

The analysis further revealed that the measures of one's mental image were able to significantly predict way-finding performance (multiple regression, $p < 0.01$, $r^2 = 0.66$). The high level of variance accounted for by this model underscores the basic premise of this research—namely, the importance of the mental image in facilitating efficient mobility. Thus, the basic assumption underlying the development of the simulation technique was confirmed.

The findings also reflected the strengths and weaknesses of the two components of the simulation technique. The quality of the identification and sequential arrangement information provided by the sequential slides was comparable to that provided by an actual visit to the building. However, the model was shown to provide spatial orientation information more successfully than did an actual visit. This suggests that it was the model that was responsible for the provision of a more fully developed mental image by the simulation technique.

During the way-finding tasks, it was found that the floorplan way-finding aids were confusing to the control group. Seven out of the group of 17 or 41 percent, thought that the three stories of the building on the floor plan were actually three separate buildings. This would have required them to go outside to walk from one building, or floor, to another.

Landmarks Provided Important Orienting and Reassuring Information

Landmarks appeared to be very important to participants as they found their way through the building. They seemed to serve as both necessary input to the way-finding process and as a means of reassurance that the route being followed was indeed correct.

One example of landmark usage concerns the search for the elevator in the building. Since the elevator had to be approached from a lateral direction, it was difficult to see because it was recessed into the wall, as most elevator doors are. The only landmark to signal the location of the elevator was a wall-mounted ashtray next to the elevator door on each floor. Although the ashtrays were not pointed out in the simulated or actual visits, it was found that several participants had noticed the ashtrays and were using them to help find the elevator. The implication from this finding is that signs or other landmarks should not only be placed parallel to the object but perpendicular as well, so as to be seen from a lateral direction.

To summarize, the goal of the simulation technique was to provide one with a working knowledge of a previously unknown building. This study has shown that the working knowledge provided by a simulation technique was, in fact, better than that provided by actual visits to the building itself.

Conclusions

The Model Is Helpful in Orienting the Visually Impaired

Since the completion of this study, a pilot study implementing the simulation technique in an actual relocation procedure has been conducted (Hunt, 1981b). The simulation technique used in the pilot study was the same as that evaluated in this study. Perhaps the most exciting finding of the pilot study concerned the preparation of visually impaired patients. In the original sample design, these persons were excluded from the study because of the visual nature of the simulation technique. However, the nurse who presented the simulation to residents discovered that the model could be used to orient the visually impaired. This was done by guiding their hands along the major hallways and locating major rooms. The construction of the model made this possible because the areas not included in the simulated visit were covered. Thus, the hallways and rooms included in the simulation could be felt as voids in the model. With this preparation, the visually impaired residents were able to derive an understanding of the shape of the building, the configuration of the major hallway system, and the spatial relationship of the major rooms. This demonstrates that the simulation technique not only is visual in nature but can be tactile as well.

The Simulation Technique Is Capable of Providing a Mental Image that Fosters Way-Finding and May Lessen Relocation Trauma

These findings coupled with the technique's application to the preparation of the visually impaired suggest that the technique has the potential to lessen the stress that accompanies the relocation of older people. As has been demonstrated in the case of actual site visits, this may in turn serve to mitigate some of the negative effects of relocation such as the increased incidence of illness and even death. In addition, the evaluation of the simulation technique shed some light on how people learn unfamiliar buildings, which, in turn, provide guidance for the design of buildings intended to facilitate environmental learning.

Summary

In attempting to better understand how and why relocation affects older people, the relationship between people's well-being and their understanding of the environment has become clearer. Under certain conditions, the lack of environmental knowledge may be lethal for some people. Policy makers should therefore realize that relocation should be considered not merely a physical move from one place to another but rather a process that necessitates creating programs that prepare the person both emotionally and environmentally for the move. Similarly, designers should recognize the importance of creating "imageable" environments—not only for older people but for people of all ages.

DESIGN DIRECTIVES

The implications of this research extend beyond the relocation of older people. The finding that familiarizing a person with a new facility prior to relocation demonstrated the importance of designing buildings that are understandable or imageable. The following directives have been derived from these results and address the design of buildings and way-finding systems so as to make buildings easier to learn and navigate. It should be noted that the design directives reflect the types of information that facilitate environmental learning: namely, identification and spatial orientation.

DESIGN DIRECTIVE
ONE

The building should have a clear circulation system.

1. The circulation system can then become the organizational framework on which to base an understanding of spatial relationships.

2. A circulation system may be made clear by avoiding unnecessary complexity and maximizing predictability. Predictability may be enhanced by allowing visual access (both interior and exterior) so as to provide a preview of the route ahead.

DESIGN DIRECTIVE
TWO

Buildings should contain distinctive areas or elements that may serve as landmarks to aid way-finding.

1. Areas may be made distinctive with the use of color, texture, furnishings, and/or any other methods that combine to produce a unique area or element of the building.

DESIGN DIRECTIVE
THREE

To help reduce the complexity of buildings, important rooms or places should be prominent so as to serve as anchor or reference points in the building.

1. Overall design of the building, interior design, and signage systems can all help simplify understanding of the building.

2. Social spaces and elevator lobbies are especially strong anchor points in independent and congregate housing. In long-term care facilities, on the other hand, nursing stations are often focal points, while often specialized spaces that can serve as landmarks include gift shops, greenhouses, beauty shops, convenience stores, and chapels.

Windows should be located so as to allow visual access to other portions of the building and to make apparent the relationship of the building to the ground level.

1. Views to other portions of the building foster an understanding of spatial relationships within the building as well as an understanding of the building's overall configuration.

2. If a building is designed to "step-up" a sloping site, windows should be located to make apparent changes in the relationship between the inside of the building and the outside. Failure of one's inside/outside reference system may lead to vertical errors in way-finding.

Views from elevator doors on various floor levels should be distinctive.

1. Color, texture, numbering, or other graphic techniques can be used to distinguish floor levels.

2. Without such distinctions, people may accidentally exit on the wrong floor or not be able to recognize the correct floor.

Color coding of areas or floors of a building is potentially useful but not sufficient as a landmarking system. If the significance of color codes is not taught, such a landmarking system may go undeveloped in one's understanding of the building.

1. Colors should be used to create light-dark, contrasting relationships between elements such as floors and furniture or doors and frames. Both pastels and dark colors may be difficult to differentiate.

2. A color coding system can be supplemented with a color coded way-finding aid system such as a three-dimensional model of the building. Such a system can help one to better understand the significance of changes in color by establishing their spatial relationships.

Floor plan signs are potentially confusing. In order to ensure clarity, the following steps should be taken:

1. Depict only major rooms or areas.

2. Orient the plans correctly to the building.

3. Provide appropriate color coding.

4. Present vertical relationships of multistory buildings.

Schematic models can be placed in public areas of the building such as the entry lobby and elevator lobby to supplement signage.

1. The models should illustrate only the major rooms or areas of the buildings and the major corridor system.

2. Color coding should be included in the model to help establish the significance of the color coding.

3. These models should be located at key vision points within the environment.

POLICY CONSIDERATIONS

The following policy issues were derived from the relocation and environmental learning research reported in this chapter. As a whole, they reflect the importance of environmental learning in the process of preparing older people for relocation.

Older people need to be prepared for relocation.

Older people who are being relocated should be prepared for the move before it takes place. The degree of preparation needed depends upon the degree of choice and the degree of environmental change involved. The less choice and more environmental change, the more preparation is needed.

POLICY CONSIDERATION
ONE

Preparation should address emotional and environmental needs.

Preparation for the move should address both the emotional and environmental needs of the person. The emotional needs should be met with individual and group counseling. Environmental needs should be met by familiarizing the person with the new facility, the new staff, and the new patients or neighbors to the greatest extent possible. In the event of less radical environmental change, environmental preparation can concentrate on familiarizing the person with the new facility.

POLICY CONSIDERATION
TWO

Environmental learning should precede the move.

A working knowledge of the new facility (environmental learning) is necessary well before the move takes place, since negative effects of relocation may occur not only after the move but prior to it as well. It may be necessary to provide the older elderly with more intensive preparation than the younger elderly.

POLICY CONSIDERATION
THREE

Several learning components may be useful.

The technique to familiarize residents with the new facility should be based on the concepts of environmental learning—identification and spatial orientation are necessary in order to form a mental image. Whether the preparation is carried out through actual site visits, simulated visits, or a combination of both, identification and spatial orientation information needs to be provided.

POLICY CONSIDERATION
FOUR

FIVE

Models should be considered as an important element in the program.

A schematic model or models should be used to help a person gain spatial orientation information. Models can be effective even if site visits are used to orient people to the building. In addition, models should be permanently placed in public areas of the building—such as entry lobbies and elevator lobbies—to supplement signage.

SIX

Landmarks should be identified.

The provision of identification information occurs during the visit to the new facility (either actual or simulated). This process should be enhanced by the noting of important landmarks. If this is not done, the landmarks will surely be noticed but may go undeveloped in the person's mental image of the building—thus, possibly diminishing the effectiveness of such landmarks.

SEVEN

Limit the spatial extent of preparation.

The site visits (actual or simulated) should present only the places in the building of importance to most residents in their daily activities. In this way, the danger of overwhelming people with too much information is minimized.

EIGHT

Plan multiple visits.

Multiple visits (actual or simulated) are desirable to familiarize people with a new facility. The first visit should include only the most important rooms or areas used in daily activities—for example, main entrance, apartment or room, elevator, and dining room. The second or later visits should include the remaining areas chosen for inclusion in the visits.

NINE

Consider using schematic models for the visually impaired.

A schematic model can be used to orient the visually impaired to the new facility by guiding their hands along the model. The schematic construction technique of the model calls for the covering of areas not included in the visit. This construction allows the visually impaired to feel visited areas as voids. Thus, they are able to obtain an understanding of the exterior shape of the building, the configuration of the major hallway system, and the spatial relationships of the major rooms to one another.

18

IMPROVING WAY-FINDING AND ARCHITECTURAL LEGIBILITY IN HOUSING FOR THE ELDERLY

Gerald D. Weisman

T he past decade has seen a major effort directed toward the creation of barrier-free accessible environments. Such efforts reflect a commitment to better meeting the needs of those individuals—including large numbers of older persons—whose environmental mobility may be limited by a variety of disabilities (Steinfeld, 1976). The elimination of such barriers, while necessary, is not sufficient. Accessibility additionally demands that a building be "legible" to the people who use it; it must facilitate way-finding and orientation within the environment.

Legibility of settings is important because it can have significant behavioral and affective consequences for elderly users, impacting goal satisfaction, sense of control, stress, and safety. Thus Pastalan (1975), in considering how the elderly negotiate their environment, emphasizes the importance of "organized space as orientation," and Windley and Scheidt (1980) include legibility in their proposed taxonomy of environmental attributes. The existing evidence, albeit limited, unfortunately suggests that many environments for older persons are relatively illegible in character.

The inability to effectively move into, through, and out of a building may have serious consequences for older people at several levels. For example, Hiatt (1980) suggests that "disorientation may be a crippling cause of inactivity in old age." The inability to find one's way may divert attention from other more important features of a setting or other life events and may lead to a fear of public embarrassment.

A Confusing Building May Diminish Perceived Control Over the Environment

The inability to locate and utilize desired settings and services may also impact an older person's sense of perceived control. Research by Langer and Rodin (1976), Rodin and Langer (1977), and Schulz (1978) points to the powerful and positive impact of enhanced control and predictability for the well-being of institutionalized elderly. There is also considerable evidence that perceived freedom and perceived control should be used as central dimensions for evaluation of the built environment (Barnes, 1981). It might reasonably be hypothesized that the inability to find one's way to desired destinations within a building contributes to a decrease in perceived control.

Spatial disorientation has been related to short-term discomfort and stress among nonelderly populations (Best, 1970; Wener and Kamanoff, 1983). More anecdotal evidence (Berkeley, 1973; Dixon, 1968; McKean, 1972) highlights the anger, hostility, and indignation of users faced with illegible public buildings, and a national news service has immortalized the college professor who, upon becoming lost in the new Dallas–Fort Worth Airport, suddenly began gibbering mathematical equations and tearing off his clothes (Kilday, 1979). Zimring (1981) has extended this argument to include more long-term stress-related consequences for older persons; he notes the increases in morbidity and mortality which may accompany the relocation of the elderly to new and therefore unfamiliar settings (Pastalan and Bourestom, 1975; Schulz and Brenner, 1977).

Building Legibility Is Particularly Important in Emergency Situations

Finally, emergency situations—such as fires within institutional settings—may attach life or death significance to environmental legibility and way-finding performance. Nursing home fires have been the focus of considerable research (Haber, 1980; Lerup, Conrath, and Lu, 1980; Edelman, Hart, and Bickman, 1980); data from Wood (1980) support the intuitively reasonable hypothesis that the numbers of injuries in fire incidents were higher when people were less familiar with the building they were in and with means of escape.

Thus legibility appears to be an important attribute of environments for older persons, influencing the functional accessibility of such settings and the degree to which they are perceived as truly barrier-free. Furthermore, to the extent these buildings thwart effective way-finding behavior, they may contribute to a diminished sense of personal control and/or heightened stress levels on the part of their elderly users. Enhancing the legibility of facilities for older persons therefore represents an important objective for the clients, designers, and managers of such settings.

As a consequence of the generally limited research attention directed toward the environment-behavior interface, however, the empirical literature on way-finding and legibility upon which design and policy guidelines might build is still quite limited. Therefore this chapter will begin with a presentation of a theoretical model of the way-finding process. This theoretical perspective will serve as the framework for a broader view of way-finding than is typically taken. Two pilot studies will be presented that, along with the theoretical and empirical literature reviewed, provide a basis for the design directives and policy implications intended to help designers create more legible housing environments for the elderly.

Spatial Orientation and Way-Finding: A Theoretical Perspective

Because most of us only infrequently find ourselves lost in various settings, we often do not reflect on or endeavor to analyze the way-finding process. What precisely does it mean to say that the occupants of a building are spatially "oriented" and able to find their way within it? A wide range of authors from diverse disciplines (English and English, 1958; Kaplan, 1976; Lynch, 1960) all provide similar answers to this question. They emphasize the necessity of being able to identify one's present location, know where one is going relative to this present location, and know how to get to the desired destination. It is likewise emphasized that way-finding is typically not a one-step process; more often it requires identification of a succession of subgoals or "choice points" (Kaplan, 1976) and the ability to make the appropriate decision, at each of these points, about where to go next. Finally, it is recognized that there are a variety of alternative strategies potentially available in finding one's way. The strategies actually employed in a given situation reflect both individual preferences or capabilities and the forms of environmental information available in the setting.

Strategy One: Use a Landmark or Goal to Guide Your Trip: The simplest strategy one can utilize in way-finding involves looking for the desired destination. Such a strategy, however, can only be successful in environments of quite limited spatial extent where the destination is within one's visual field. More typical settings, which do not provide some measure of perceptual access from start

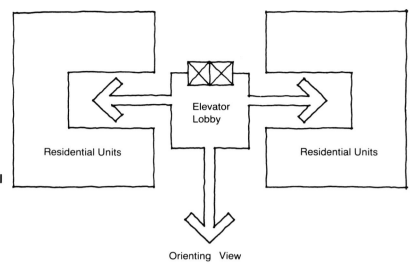

FIGURE 18.1 Perceptual access: Views to the exterior at key decision points can facilitate orientation and understanding of the building floor plan.

Elevator Lobby

Residential Units

Residential Units

Orienting View

to destination, require "a much higher and more complicated level of mobility" (Gibson, 1950). At the building scale, views through or out of a building—often provided by central courtyards or windows along corridors—may afford the way-finder such perceptual access (Fig. 18.1).

Strategy Two: Follow a Trail or Pathway that Leads to the Goal: In relatively more complex way-finding situations, the most direct strategy employed is known as "blind navigation," where one follows a road, a trail, or a leader (Griffin, 1973). Some facilities for the elderly endeavor to support this strategy through the provision of a system of colored lines running along corridor floors or walls. However, experience suggests that this seemingly simple approach to way-finding quickly grows in complexity and diminishes in effectiveness as it attempts to deal with branching paths, crossings, and changes in level.

Strategy Three: Signs and Landmarks Update Information and Clarify Choices Where Decisions Must Be Made: Two other indicators often provide clues that help guide a person towards a destination in complex environments—namely, signs and landmarks. Signs are the most common form of environmental information, although they provide somewhat less continuous guidance for way-finding than do approaches such as color coded systems. One must periodically locate the relevant signs, using them not only to identify the present location but also to direct oneself to the next path segment leading toward the destination. Visual or spatial features of the physical environment itself may also serve identification and directional functions. For example, some places are more readily recognized and remembered than are others. Places may achieve their "landmark" status in a variety of ways; they may possess unique visual characteristics; they may be distinctive relative to their larger context; or they may assume significant functional importance over time (Kaplan, 1976). Landmarks along with explicit or "manifest" signs can assist in the determination of both present location and the next subgoal or destination.

Strategy Four: Develop a Mental Image or Cognitive Map: As with blind navigation, exclusive reliance on signs or landmarks may impose some severe constraints upon the way-finding process; choice becomes limited, short cuts are impossible, and breaks in the system may leave a person lost and therefore unable to proceed to the desired destination. However, a person is likely to rely solely on visual cues such as lines or signs only in environments that are either novel or infrequently encountered. Ordinarily, the way-finding task requires less conscious attention. Both theory and empirical evidence suggest that the use of visual cues is coupled with some type of mental map of the environment to be negotiated.

> Even a simple path cannot be followed blindly without some idea of its spatial relationship to other objects. In practice following of a marked path is supplemented by some sort of *mental map* or schema. . . . In familiar surroundings people are usually quite unaware that they are using such a schema (Griffin, 1973, p. 297).

Thus, way-finding must be conceptualized as a cognitive as well as a perceptual task; it is contingent not only upon what one sees but also upon what one knows about the spatial disposition of elements within an environment and/or in comparable settings. And, much as some locations are more readily recognized and remembered as landmarks than are others, so some spatially extensive environments (such as buildings, neighborhoods, and cities) can be more easily represented in one's mental map; Lynch (1960) characterizes such settings as "imageable" in character.

Four Architectural Features Available to Assist Way-Finding

Recognition of the cognitive as well as perceptual demands of way-finding leads to a broadened view of both the potential strategies available to the way-finder and the forms of environmental information that designers can provide (Weisman, 1979, 1981). Using this framework, four classes of environmental variables have a potential impact upon orientation and way-finding, each of which can be used to design more legible housing environments for the elderly: signs, perceptual access, architectural differentiation, and plan configuration. For example, the use of signs can impact the legibility of a setting by providing identification and/or directional information. Orientation and way-finding can likewise be enhanced by some degree of perceptual access, providing views to

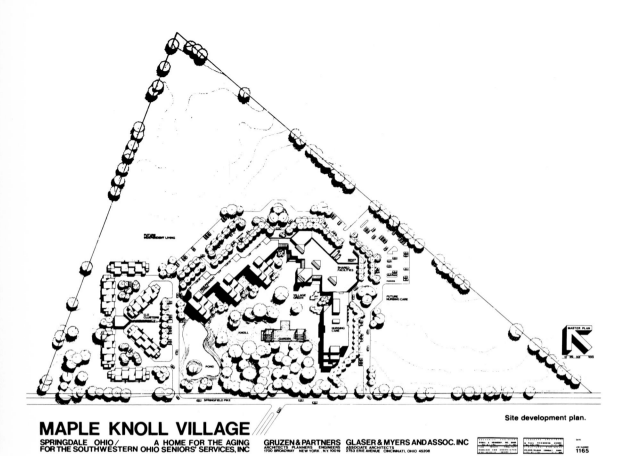

MAPLE KNOLL VILLAGE

SPRINGDALE OHIO / A HOME FOR THE AGING
FOR THE SOUTHWESTERN OHIO SENIORS' SERVICES, INC

GRUZEN & PARTNERS GLASER & MYERS AND ASSOC. INC
ARCHITECTS PLANNERS ENGINEERS ASSOCIATE ARCHITECTS
1700 BROADWAY NEW YORK, N.Y. 10019 2753 ERIE AVENUE CINCINNATI, OHIO 45208

Site development plan.

1165

**FIGURE 18.2   Maple Knoll Village, Springdale, Ohio: Spaces of functional
significance such as the gift shop, beauty shop, chapel, snack bar, and work-
shop provide landmarks along "main street."** *Source:* **The Gruzen Partner-
ship, New York, New York.**

familiar exterior landmarks and/or views to other locations within
the building (for example, a communal dining room on the far side
of a central atrium). The degree of architectural differentiation of
points or regions within a building, to the extent that it facilitates
recognition and recall, can also contribute to effective way-finding.
Finally, the overall plan configuration of a building—its shape or
layout—can influence the ease with which one can build a mental
map for use in way-finding within it (Fig. 18.2).

Related Research

Way-Finding and Disorientation are Problems for Some Older People

The research literature on way-finding behavior, although limited
in its extent, points to considerable problems in both independent

housing for the elderly and long-term care facilities and supports the necessity of enhancing the legibility of such settings.

Studies of housing for independent elderly conducted by Devlin (1980), Howell (1980), and Nahemow, Lawton, and Howell (1979) all uncovered problems in way-finding. Devlin presents data based upon interviews with 75 residents living in two high-rises and two garden apartment developments for the elderly. Getting off the elevator on the wrong floor, mistaking someone else's apartment for one's own, and even putting a key in someone else's door were "frequent and embarrassing" occurrences in one of the high-rise buildings and represented "a source of real discomfort for those people." Disorientation did not appear to the same degree in the second high-rise, where the presence of balconies served to differentiate alternate floors, and was significantly less in the garden apartments. Similarly, Nahemow, Lawton, and Howell (1977), in reporting data from a national study of housing for the elderly, point to similar way-finding confusion "brought about by lack of orienting codes and personalization of floors or doors." Residents in two of the three case study sites investigated by Howell (1980) likewise indicated an inability to differentiate floors and even individual apartments in their buildings.

Problems of disorientation appear to multiply among residents of long-term care facilities; such difficulties represent the interaction of several factors. For example, this population often has a reduced level of competence and cognitive functioning; it is estimated that "as many as 60 percent of nursing home residents are thought to be 'confused' " (Lawton, 1981). Nursing homes likewise represent new and unfamiliar settings for many of their recently relocated residents. Finally, as Lawton (1981) notes, both the physical and behavioral environments of such settings may be very impoverished in character.

Several Model Designs Have Attempted to Reduce Disorientation

The post-occupancy evaluation of a retirement/nursing home (Osterberg, 1981) assessed the efficacy of a range of design features purposefully incorporated in building renovations to facilitate way-finding among residents; these features included a simple and presumably more imageable loop corridor system on upper floors and a glassed-in, central atrium to enhance perceptual access in the setting (see Figure 16.4). Interviews with staff indicated that, except for the most confused residents, there was little disorientation on these four nursing floors. The lower levels of the facility, however, with a relatively complex plan configuration, were substantially less successful; "residents become visibly upset by the confusion of the spaces" and "by not knowing where they are." (For more information about this study, please refer to chapter 16 by Osterberg in this volume.)

Two design interventions at the Philadelphia Geriatric Center likewise explored the impact of enhanced perceptual access on resident behavior. In the first study (Lawton, Liebowitz, and Charon 1970), two large four-bed rooms were remodeled into six small single bedrooms plus a shared social space set off from the main corridor by a half-wall (see Fig. 18.3). Evaluation data indicated that residents' spatial range increased markedly with the number of times they were observed outside the bedroom increasing more than fivefold (from 7 to 38 percent). The author infers that "greater visual access to the space led to a greater desire and willingness to explore" (Lawton, 1978).

The Central Space Used for Programs and Therapy Is Directly Linked to the Patient's Room in the Weiss Institute: The second study focused on the Weiss Institute, a 40-bed treatment center for institutionalized older persons with organic brain syndrome that was designed through extensive collaboration between archi-

FIGURE 18.3
Philadelphia Geriatric Center: This renovation of two large four-bed wards into six smaller private rooms created an open social area that increased residents' spatial range.

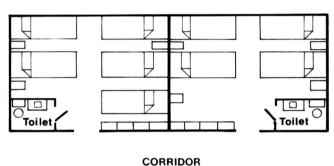

CORRIDOR

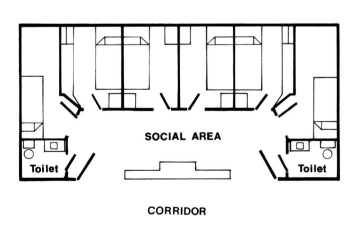

CORRIDOR

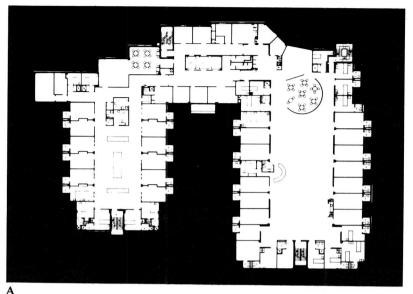

A

B

FIGURE 18.4 A and B Weiss Institute, Philadelphia Geriatric Center: The open central treatment area is designed to counter the effects of disorientation and memory loss.

tects, behavioral scientists, and service providers. Based upon the so-called Osmond plan, patient rooms are arrayed around three sides of a 40' by 100' central space (see Fig. 18.4 A and B). This open treatment area is intended to diminish the effects of disorientation and memory loss by giving residents an almost complete view of all areas from anywhere in the space (Liebowitz, Lawton, and Waldman, 1979). Evaluation of the setting suggests the occurrence of less pathological behavior, reduction in fixed staring, and a greater degree of interest on the part of residents in their surroundings. Additionally, both staff and residents' relatives expressed preference for a variety of features of the Weiss Institute, including the central treatment space (Lawton, 1980).

Graphic Identification Systems That Use Figures and Symbols Have Also Been Successful at Minimizing Disorientation: Weiner (1975) reports the results of a design intervention carried out in a contemporary nursing home of "modular" design, which resulted in a uniformity of appearance and the repetition of similar rooms, furniture, hallways, and colors in each wing and on every floor. As a consequence of the low level of architectural differentiation, residents as well as staff were found traveling down the wrong corridor. Approximately one-third of the residents of the study floor were unable to find their own room without the aid of a staff member. "Many stories of persons who were often found sleeping in the wrong room were related." Weiner's intervention involved development of a color code system, including large graphic symbols, to replace the previous cardinal direction designations on walls, directories, and equipment. The symbols were differentiated from one another in terms of subject matter (for example, bird versus clover), color, and shape. Weiner reports a positive response to the design changes, including use of the symbols in giving verbal directions, assumption of the symbol identity by residents in each area, and a substantial improvement in independent ambulation; "after a short time only a remaining few still had to be escorted to their rooms."

Wandering Behavior Can Be Made Less Anxiety Producing in Legible Environments: Hiatt (1979) presents an analysis of one type of way-finding dysfunction—wandering—which is characterized as relatively unique to geriatric facilities. Such behavior represents a potential source of harm to the wanderer, distress for relatives, legal liability for facility administration, and the cause of mobility restrictions for all residents. In one study by Snyder, Rupprecht, Pyrek, Brekhus, and Moss (1978), 19 percent of skilled care residents in a facility were characterized by nursing staff as wanderers; this group scored lower on a mental status questionnaire and was diagnosed as more likely to have organic brain syndrome, overall psychosocial problems, and memory impairment. While environmental design interventions may have relatively little impact on the habitual wanderer, in this study it is argued that enhanced legibility may be helpful to those residents who are otherwise alert but are experiencing difficulty in locating a specific room or route. This is significant since, as Liebowitz, Lawton, and Waldman (1979) point out, disorientation not only serves to set an individual off as deviant by social norms but also represents a source of great anxiety to the disoriented individual who is aware of his or her impairment.

In an especially significant study, Hunt (1981, 1984) endeavored to assess the impact of relocation to a new and unfamiliar setting upon environmental cognition and way-finding behavior; this research was precipitated by the previously cited findings of Pastalan and Bourestom (1975) regarding the increases in morbidity and mortality and marked decreases in home range, which followed the relocation of institutionalized elderly. One facet of Hunt's study assessed the way-finding performance of a sample of community-based elderly in an unfamiliar and relatively complex retirement home environment. The experimental task required finding eight target destinations within the building. The first group of participants had no familiarity at all with the facility prior to initiation of the way-finding task; the second group of participants (site-visitors) first received a 30-minute walking tour of the building. For the eight target destinations, mean way-finding performance for the control group ranged from roughly 2.0 to 3.5 on a five point scale (where 1 = very poor and 5 = very good); the mean score across all eight locations was 2.8. Performance of the site visit group was significantly better for five of the eight destinations, with a range of 2.0 to 4.6, and an overall mean of approximately 3.5. (For more information about this study please refer to chapter 17 by Hunt and Pastalan in this volume.)

Environmental Cognition Is Central to the Understanding of Way-Finding Within the Physical Environment: Effective way-finding is a consequence not only of the objective physical environment but also of the mental representation of that environment. The concept of the cognitive map has a rich if intermittent history in a variety of disciplines, including anthropology (Hallowell, 1955), environmental design (Lynch, 1960), geography (Wright, 1947; Golledge and Zanaras, 1973), and psychology (Tolman, 1948; Kaplan, 1973, 1976). More recently, issues of cognitive mapping have been extended and applied to the environment-and-aging field (Weisman, 1982; Walsh, Krauss, and Regnier, 1981).

One key issue, central to any consideration of environmental cognition and way-finding behavior among the elderly, concerns the relationship between basic spatial-cognitive abilities, as these are measured in the laboratory and/or with pencil-and-paper tests, and actual way-finding behavior in the large-scale environment. As Bruce and Hermon (1981) suggest:

> in order to negotiate the environment, the elderly individual . . . must maintain an adequate set of spatial abilities which allow him or her to find their way through familiar and unfamiliar environments (p. 1).

While research indicates age-related decrements in such spatial-cognitive abilities (Herman, 1981), as well as a relationship between spatial abilities and knowledge and use of the surrounding neighborhood environment (Walsh, Krauss, and Regnier, 1981), ties to actual way-finding behavior have yet to be empirically demonstrated. However, a small number of studies do shed additional light on the relationships between age, environmental knowledge, features of physical settings, and way-finding behavior at the architectural scale.

Visual Distinctiveness May Be More Powerful Than Familiarity in Some Settings: In a nursing home study conducted by Weber, Brown, and Weldon (1978), a sample of 20 alert and mobile residents was presented a series of 67 color slides of freely accessible areas within the facility. Respondents were first asked if they recognized each scene, and then asked in which section of the building it was located. Both recognition and location scores were found to vary greatly across areas of the home. Recognition ranged from 48 percent for one of the corridors to 97 percent for an exterior view, and location scores varied from 3.9 percent (for the same corridor) to a maximum of 60.5 percent for the dining room–living room. Testing of a comparison sample of university undergraduates, who received only a brief tour of the facility, indicated that "the student group acquired and/or retained more information . . . in five minutes per area than the patients had in an average stay of more than two years." While age was found to be negatively correlated to accuracy in identifying slide locations, location performance was not related to length of residency within the facility. The authors conclude that differential knowledge of areas within the home was a function of the varying levels of "visual distinctiveness" of spaces, rather than mere familiarity with them.

Research by Herman (1981) likewise addresses the relationships between age, spatial knowledge, and length of residence in institutional environments. A high functioning group of nursing home residents was asked to locate 12 color photos of important spaces within the home as accurately as possible on a "schematic" floor plan. As in the Weber et al. (1978) study, correlational analyses indicated a negative relationship between age and accuracy of location, but no relationship was found between accuracy of location and length of residency. Neither was there any evidence suggesting that walking residents have greater spatial knowledge than do those who are wheelchair bound. While this study did not explore the impact of differences in visual distinctiveness of the 12 areas on accuracy of location, more recent research by Bruce and Herman (1981) considers the impact of environmental "differentiation" on identification of scenes of business and residential districts.

Hunt's Research Underscores the Positive Influence of a Well-Developed Cognitive Map: The research of Hunt (1981, 1984), introduced in the preceding section, provides a more detailed analysis of cognition and way-finding behavior in housing environments for the elderly. In addition to the previously described performance measures, data were gathered on respondents' self-reported confidence in way-finding along with a wide variety of measures of their mental representations of the study setting.

A third group of study participants was presented with a slide model simulation of the study setting prior to being taken there for testing. The simulation was designed to determine if vicarious experience, as well as actual site visits, could provide useful environmental information prior to relocation of elderly retirement/nursing home residents.

Hunt's findings provide strong support for the central role of the cognitive map in effective way-finding behavior. Self-reports of confidence were not found to be significantly related to actual way-finding performance but were related to age; subjects over 70 years of age were less confident in their way-finding abilities, even when their performance was equal to that of younger elderly.

A final set of analyses, dealing with the relative efficacy of the site visit and slide-model simulation, found that the simulation group members were better able to find their way on all tasks than were the site visit and control groups. Furthermore, the simulation group was able to identify photos of the study setting at least as well as the site visit group and did better, but not significantly so, in most of the sequential ordering tasks. In understanding the external shape of the study setting as well as its spatial organization, the simulation group once again performed significantly better. Hunt (1981) concludes that "the working knowledge provided by the simulation technique was, in fact, better than that provided by actual visits to the building itself."

Methodology and Data Analysis

Building upon the theoretical perspective and existing research reviewed above, a pilot project was carried out in a nursing home environment to address three questions:

1. How well do elderly residents of differing levels of capability find their way within such an institution?
2. How do elderly find their way (for example, what cues and sources of environmental information do they utilize)?
3. Can a relatively simple simulation technique based on Hunt's methodology be utilized to improve both cognitive representation and resultant way-finding behavior of newly arrived residents?

Study Setting

Two pilot studies were carried out in a 125-bed, nonprofit, long-term care facility that offers both skilled and intermediate levels of care. The facility is housed in a three-story building, constructed in three stages over 40 years. The most recent addition to the facility, which was the focus of these pilot studies, incorporates a range of visually distinctive spaces and features, including a two-story lobby/lounge area with a large window wall. Other distinctive elements of the facility include a fireplace, organ, piano, paintings, and antiques. While considerable color variation is utilized in rooms and corridors, there is currently no overall color coding system. Signage is limited primarily to room labels, with relatively few directional signs to be found within the facility. The facility administration has a strong commitment to the maintenance of a "home-like" environment, and the presence of greater numbers of signs is perceived as running counter to this objective by creating a too-commercial atmosphere.

Study Participants

Eighteen individuals randomly selected from the home's 55 intermediate care level residents participated in Pilot Study I; all 18 were assessed by the staff as alert and capable of participation in staff-directed activities. Fifteen of the 18 were women; 10 were characterized by staff as "independent" (that is, capable of getting around on their own, even if a walker or cane was required), and 7 were characterized as "dependent" (that is, physically or cognitively reliant upon others for assistance in mobility).

Eight newly relocated residents (that is, with a length of residence of 3 months or less) participated in Pilot Study II; this group included five women and three men, and was evenly divided with respect to the independence variable. One independent woman in the control group was unable to complete the study.

Study Procedures

In Study I, two paths that connected significant locations through the facility were defined. One path moved from the first floor reception desk to the dining room, also located on the first floor, and then to the ground floor activity/recreation room. The second path began at this same activity/recreation room, proceeded to the second floor chapel, and terminated at participants' individual rooms, which were located throughout the facility.

Study participants were to lead staff members along one of these two paths, endeavoring to find their way to each successive destination.[1] During these trips, participants were asked a series of questions regarding specific elements within the environment that the resident utilized as cues or landmarks for way-finding; experience of any particular way-finding problems; and evaluation of

[1] Staff members kindly agreed to collect Study I data when an influenza epidemic and resultant quarantine closed the facility to the research team.

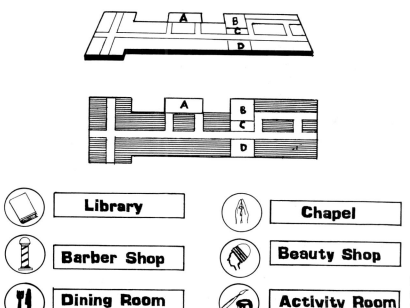

FIGURE 18.5 Aids to way-finding: Alternative floor plans and graphic symbols assessed in Study I.

existing orientation and directional aids. An additional set of questions, presented after completion of the path, assessed participants' comprehension of and preference for alternative way-finding aids, graphic symbols, and schematic floorplans (see Fig. 18.5).

Pilot Study II utilized a somewhat simplified version of the slide and model environmental simulation technique developed by Hunt (1981, 1983); the nursing home model was of relatively simple foam-core construction, and a conventional slide projector, rather than a rear projection system, was employed. The sample of eight residents was dichotomized into control and experimental groups, balanced with respect to mobility level. The initial way-finding performance of both groups was assessed through a slide identification task, observation, and interviews.

After completion of these initial tasks the experimental group was subsequently presented with an environmental simulation meant to increase their ability to identify and spatially relate locations within the building, thereby enhancing their way-finding capabilities. They were first presented with slides of five areas of the building, with these locations pointed out on the three-dimensional building model. Once participants seemed to recognize these areas and their locations, they were presented with a sequence of slides illustrating a walking tour through the home. While viewing the slides, participants were encouraged to follow the path taken by tracing their finger along the corridor of the model in front of them; they were likewise encouraged to keep looking from slides to model to better relate the forms of information and to ask questions of the experimenters regarding names of areas and floor levels. The amount of time spent with each participant, which ranged from 1 to 2 hours, was determined by his/her mental and emotional state at the time of testing. A comparable amount of time was spent socializing with each of the control group members.

Approximately 8 days later, all participants were tested, following the same pattern as the initial session. Participants were then asked to take the experimenters on a walking tour of the home, including all areas depicted in the slide presentation, albeit in any sequence of the respondent's choosing.[2]

Findings

In Study I, Latent Cues Were Important Aids in Way-Finding

The fact that the experimenters did not have direct access to the facility during Study I yielded less than complete but still useful data for way-finding performance on the two test paths. Data available for seven of the ten residents who traversed the first path indicate that 57 percent were able to successfully locate the dining room, and an equal percentage found the activity/recreation room. Only five of the residents assigned to the second path were sufficiently familiar with the chapel to even attempt to locate it; three of the five were able to successfully do so. Seven of the eight (87.5 percent) were able to find their way back to their own rooms. Mean length of residency was consistently higher for those residents able to find the target destinations, and mobility level (that is, dependent versus independent) likewise had a major impact upon orientation and way-finding.

Responses regarding cues utilized in way-finding indicate that signs are not the most salient source of environmental information. What might be characterized as "manifest" cues—signs or room numbers—represented only 18 percent of all cues mentioned by participants; "latent" cues—elements in the setting not explicitly intended for orientation and way-finding—comprised the remaining 82 percent of all cues mentioned. Among the elements reported as latent cues were (in descending order) elevators, doors, desks, tables and chairs, a clock, and plants. Color was reported as a latent cue for orientation or as a landmark for direction along a path by nearly 40 percent of respondents; however, fewer than 20 percent realized that at least some areas of the building had purposefully been painted in a way meant to aid way-finding.

[2] The author gratefully acknowledges the contributions of Linda Harper and Mark Davis, students in the Program in Man-Environment Relations at the Pennsylvania State University, who played a major role in the conceptualization and implementation of Study II.

For those 12 respondents for whom complete data are available, successfully finding the target destinations along the two walking tours of the building was found to be associated with the utilization of cues of the sort described above. Six of the seven individuals able to locate successfully both destinations reported using cues; four of the five individuals unable to locate both destinations made no mention of utilizing such cues.

Assessment of the potential value of additional signage in the building was found to be related to mobility level of respondent. Almost twice as many dependent as independent participants (67 percent versus 35 percent) indicated a desire for more signs. Considerable difficulty was reported in interpreting either of the two floor plans—plan or oblique views—that were presented (see Figure 18.5); no residents expressed a preference for plans as way-finding aids.

On the average, 30 percent of respondents were able to match the symbols or pictograms with their correct verbal label. The symbol utilized to represent the dining room—a knife and fork—was the most frequently identified (44 percent of respondents), followed by the striped pole for the barber shop (39 percent); the chapel, represented by hands folder in prayer, was correctly identified by only 17 percent of respondents (see Figure 18.5). More traditional signs with written labels were the most preferred way-finding aids for residents of both mobility levels.

Experimentals in Study II Who Had Experienced the Slide Show Simulation Were Able to Locate Significantly More Areas

Data gathered at the outset of Study II suggested that if a resident at all frequented a given area of the building, he/she was typically able to make a correct identification when shown a slide of it. However, when asked what floor it was on, what it was near, or how to get to it, respondents always commented that they did not know how to get to many places within the home since they hadn't lived there very long. Additionally, the majority reported being confused when they were not on the same floor as their room.

Thus four of the seven respondents indicated that, while they had looked down into the ground floor lobby area from a glassed-in overlook on the second floor, they did not know how to get from one location to the other. While the physical distance between these two areas is not great, it was perceived to be so, in large part because of difficulty and confusion in using the elevator.

Pre-test data indicate that in no case was a resident able to identify by slide or readily locate more than 4 of the 11 test areas. The mean number of locations correctly identified by the sample as a whole was 2; mean scores for the control and experimental groups were 2 and 3.25 respectively. Post-test data yield a strikingly different picture. The three residents in the control group were able to successfully locate an average of 1.67 test areas. The experimental group, after experiencing the slide-model simulation, was able to successfully locate 8.25 areas; analysis indicated this difference to be highly significant ($t = -6.82$, d.f. = 4, $p = 0.01$).

With respect to mobility level, dependent residents in the experimental group performed at roughly twice the level of independent residents in the control group. Finally, informal reports indicate that, between the first and second testing, three of the four experimental subjects had in fact gone off to explore the building by themselves, and one endeavored to provide "tours" for other new residents.

Conclusions

Given the exploratory character and small sample sizes of these two studies, the drawing of firm conclusions is clearly premature. Nevertheless, several issues of importance emerge with some degree of clarity.

First, Substantial Problems Exist in Way-Finding Among Elderly in Long Term Care Environments: Such problems were experienced by residents who, while limited in their mobility, were otherwise alert and capable. Indeed the ability to traverse a setting, and not just degree of cognitive functioning, may have much to do with successful way-finding performance.

Second, Latent Rather Than "Manifest" Way-Finding Cues Are the Most Effective Aids: "Latent" cues, such as elevators, furniture, or plants may also serve to provide a measure of "architectural differentiation" essential for effective way-finding. Cognitive mapping research at the urban scale (Appleyard, 1970) supports the importance of such latent cues; in housing developments without visually prominent landmarks, features as minor as curtains in an apartment window may be relied on for identification (DeJonge, 1962). In the design for an addition to the Motion Picture Country House in Woodland Hills, California, an alcove was created along the corridor that four units share. Each alcove will be decorated in a unique way adding to its ability to provide "latent cues" for orientation (Fig. 18.6 A and B). In Study I, utilization of such latent cues was positively associated with effective way-finding.

Third, Relatively Modest Training Efforts, If Appropriately Directed, May Substantially Improve the Way-Finding Capabilities of Older Persons: The slide and model simulation utilized in this study required only 1–2 hours per participant for presentation; the simulation procedure utilized by Hunt with a group of community-based elderly took an average of 1 hour to complete and could potentially be presented to several people simultaneously.

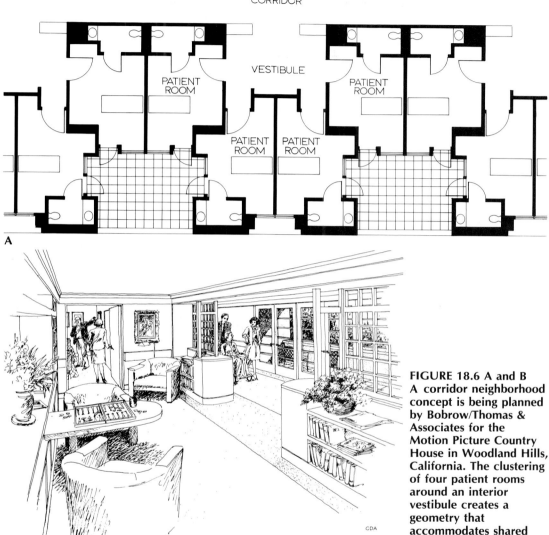

CORRIDOR

VESTIBULE

PATIENT ROOM

PATIENT ROOM

PATIENT ROOM

PATIENT ROOM

A

B

GDA

FIGURE 18.6 A and B A corridor neighborhood concept is being planned by Bobrow/Thomas & Associates for the Motion Picture Country House in Woodland Hills, California. The clustering of four patient rooms around an interior vestibule creates a geometry that accommodates shared balconies linked to each unit.

Fourth, Older Persons Can Effectively Utilize Cognitive Mapping as a Way-Finding Technique: As in the earlier work of Hunt, simulation was utilized to provide information about both significant locations and spatial relationships in the housing environment, and similarly the simulation had a positive and significant effect upon way-finding behavior. Such knowledge of locations and relationships, as characterized in the preceding theoretical discussion, constitutes the central components of a cognitive map.

DESIGN DIRECTIVES

Because of the limited research conducted in this field and the problems of generalizing from individual projects, design directions must be cautiously advanced. Furthermore, it should be noted that there is an inevitable interaction between design directives and policy implications. The environment, as people experience it, is a function of not only the physical setting but of people and organizations as well.

Thus, a signage and color coding system to enhance legibility will be maximally effective only if staff and management utilize this system in providing directions to residents. Similarly, no environmental aids to legibility are likely to succeed if users of a setting have no opportunity to explore it in as independent a fashion as possible. While design and policy implications will be treated independently for the sake of clarity, they remain interrelated. In some instances, where these relationships are particularly critical, cross-references between design directives and policy implications are provided.

As conceptualized in the earlier theoretical discussion, way-finding within the architectural environment is a cognitive and a perceptual task. A variety of forms of environmental information—beyond the normally considered lines, signs, and color—were hypothesized as impacting way-finding behavior and were grouped into four broad categories of variables: signs and numbers, perceptual access, architectural differentiation, and plan configuration. While the following directives are ordered in relation to these environmental variables, such distinctions are made for purposes of clarity. In real world settings, characteristics of one variable are often tied to others. For example, the most detailed signage is often found in buildings with complex plan configurations (Weisman, 1982).

| DESIGN DIRECTIVE ONE | *While signage and numbering systems can usefully serve as "supplemental direct information" (Green et al., 1975), they typically cannot overcome inherently illegible building characteristics.* |

1. Despite the more extensive and detailed signage systems often found in buildings of limited legibility (such as large settings of complex plan configuration), way-finding may remain more difficult in such settings.

Signage systems in housing environments for the elderly should be developed as a coherent system, wherein all signs are related to one another and to the building as a whole (Green et al., 1975).

1. Signs should be consistently located in terms of both building plan (at corridor intersections and other key decision points) and wall elevation (at a wheelchair eye level of 36″–52″) (Koncelik, 1979).

2. Size of signs should vary in relation to the importance of that which is being identified (dining room versus supply closet) (Berkeley, 1973; Green et al., 1975).

3. Signs should be high in contrast, with white characters on a dark background, and overly stylized type faces should be avoided (Green et al., 1975; Koncelik, 1978). It should be remembered that many residents of long-term care facilities cannot distinguish detail along a corridor at distances greater than 20 feet (Hiatt, 1978).

4. When utilized in conjunction with words, symbols can provide useful "redundant cueing" (see Figure 18.3). However, pictograms should only supplement and never supplant verbal information.

5. Room numbering systems must be coherent to building occupants as they traverse the setting. A numbering system may be quite clear when viewed in its entirety on a floor plan but difficult to interpret when experienced incrementally in the actual setting.

Recognize that a range of architectural and/or personal features (for example, elevators, plants, artwork) can and do serve as "latent" signs for way-finding.

1. Like explicit or "manifest" signs, such elements should be located at corridor interactions and other key decision points where identification and directional information are essential.

2. Elements such as artwork or distinctive furnishings can contribute significantly to both sensory enrichment (tactile as well as visual information) and personal meaning of spaces.

Enhanced perceptual access along major paths and at key decision points facilitates way-finding behavior.

1. Alternative organizational and design concepts such as the Osmond plan (see Figure 18.4), the "corridor neighborhood" (see Figure 18.6), or a central atrium (see Figure 16.4) can serve to enhance perceptual access in both new construction and renovation.

DESIGN DIRECTIVE	*Long, repetitive corridors are a disliked and often disorienting feature of*
FIVE	*many institutional environments (Alexander et al., 1968; Green et al., 1975). Thus they should be minimized and, to the extent possible, their visual and functional distinctiveness enhanced.*

1. Corridor segments should ideally not be more than 50'–75' in length; beyond these distances some means of differentiating segments should be introduced (Green et al., 1975).

2. Corridors should present the way-finder maximally distinct vistas in each direction.

3. Spaces of major functional significance (for example, chapel and gift shop) may be arrayed along a "main street" of heightened visual distinctiveness (see Figure 18.2).

DESIGN DIRECTIVE	*Since problems in way-finding often reflect a confusion of one floor or wing*
SIX	*with another (Best, 1970; Weiner, 1975), the differentiation of these "regions" should be maximized.*

1. If totally symmetrical or mirror-image floor plans cannot be avoided, efforts should be made to ensure that the wings on a given floor can be clearly differentiated from one another (Lawton, 1975).

2. Similar efforts should be made to assist residents, visitors, and staff in differentiating one floor from another. A coordinated system of color, symbols, and terminology (Weiner, 1975) is essential.

DESIGN DIRECTIVE	*The plan configuration of the building as a whole is likely to have consid-*
SEVEN	*erable influence on legibility (Weisman, 1981). It is therefore important to determine how, and how well, people conceptualize its floor plan.*

1. In existing facilities, relatively simple cognitive mapping exercises can be carried out to determine areas or features of the building that users cannot represent adequately or accurately.

2. Limited research evidence (Weisman, 1981) suggests that judgments of quite simple line drawings can assist in the assessment of legibility of as yet unbuilt facilities.

POLICY CONSIDERATIONS

Organizational policy, as well as properties of the physical setting, can contribute to effective way-finding behavior in housing environments for the elderly.

Staff can gather data on way-finding.

POLICY CONSIDERATION
ONE

In addition to simple cognitive mapping exercises, staff—working with residents and/or consultants—can gather other pertinent data that can be used to assess way-finding behavior of residents in a facility. Among the questions to be asked are the following:

> Based upon observed patterns of spatial usage, what are the most heavily trafficked routes within the facility?
>
> What aids, or obstacles, to orientation and way-finding occur along these routes?
>
> What area(s) of the facility do users—both staff and residents— know best and least?
>
> What terminology do users of the facility employ to describe particular spaces or regions?

Programs for initial environmental familiarization should be utilized.

POLICY CONSIDERATION
TWO

Such programs can take several forms and serve multiple audiences and functions. Site visits, where practical, provide important information to older persons who are considering or are about to relocate to a new housing environment. Simulations of the sort utilized by Hunt (1981, 1984) and in Pilot Study II can similarly fulfill both marketing and orientation purposes.

Ongoing orientation and way-finding training should be provided for residents.

POLICY CONSIDERATON
THREE

Beyond initial familiarization, the development of way-finding skills requires repeated experience with and practice in a setting. Staff and/or volunteers may work with residents as a part of a scheduled program in way-finding training; such programs may be a part of regular "reality therapy" (Hiatt, 1980) and/or emergency exiting instruction. Assistance should be provided for residents, particularly in long-term care facilities, in reduction of stress associated with way-finding—which may lead to further decrements in performance—and in utilization of alternative strategies that may best fit their way-finding "style" (Hiatt, 1980).

POLICY CONSIDERATION	*Common terminology should be used.*
FOUR	Staff, in presenting verbal instructions to residents and visitors, should endeavor to reinforce whatever orientation and way-finding aids are provided within the facility. Reference should be made to the specific signs, symbols, and terminology utilized to identify and differentiate specific areas (see Design Directive Two).

POLICY CONSIDERATION	*Additional aids should be included.*
FIVE	Brochures distributed to patients and visitors have successfully been utilized as way-finding aids within health care facilities; such publications should include floor plans, with appropriate explanation, and indicate key locations within the facility. In particularly complex and illegible settings, a "transportation corps," comprised of residents and/or volunteers, may provide needed way-finding assistance (Hiatt, 1980).

POLICY CONSIDERATION	*Independent ambulation should be stressed.*
SIX	There is often a tendency, particularly in long-term care settings, to move residents from location to location en masse. This sort of "herding" (Hiatt, 1980) typically reflects both a concern for regulation of wandering behavior on the part of some residents and a means of saving time on the part of over-burdened staff. However, problems in way-finding may in fact be a consequence of the lack of opportunity for independent ambulation and freedom to explore the housing environment. Administrative policy and design interventions, as opposed to simple physical constraint of residents, may contribute significantly to the reduction of wandering problems (Snyder, 1978).

POLICY CONSIDERATION	*Supports for way-finding should emphasize therapeutic approaches.*
SEVEN	Finally, following the lead of Lindsley (1964) and Lawton (1978), supports for way-finding behavior of residents in housing environments for the elderly should be more "therapeutic" than "prosthetic"; that is, therapeutic interventions are seen as leading to improved levels of performance while prosthetic interventions, which must be applied continuously, can only maintain behavior at existing levels. Throughout this chapter, it has been suggested that orientation and way-finding aids, to the extent that they contribute to the formation of a cognitive representation, are therapeutic in function. Conventional way-finding aids—signs and lines—are essentially prosthetic; they must be followed continuously to be effective. An adequate cognitive representation of an environment, once developed, is therapeutic in nature, leading to enhanced and independent way-finding behavior in housing environments for the elderly.

BIBLIOGRAPHY

Adams, J.R. (1973). "Review of defensible space." *Man environment systems*, 3(4), 267–268.

Aldrich, D. and Mendkoff, E. (1963). "Relocation of the aged and disabled: A mortality study." *Journal of American Geriatric Society*, 11, 185–194.

Alexander, C., Ishikawa, S., and Silverstein, M. (1968). *A pattern language which generates multi-service centers*. California: Center for Environmental Structure.

Allen, G.L., Siegel, A.W. and Rosinski, R.R. (1978). "The role of perceptual context in structuring spatial knowledge." *Journal of Experimental Psychology: Human Learning and Memory*, 4(6), 617–630.

Altman, I. (1975). *The environment and social behavior*. California: Brooks/ Cole.

American Foundation for the Blind (1972). *An introduction to working with the aging person who is visually handicapped*. New York: American Foundation for the Blind.

American Foundation for the Blind (1982). *Products for people with vision problems*. New York: American Foundation for the Blind.

American National Standards Institute (1980). *Specification for making buildings and facilities accessible to and usable by physically handicapped people, A117.1*. New York: American National Standards Institute.

American Telephone and Telegraph Co. (1975). *Universal public telephone height for handicapped and able-bodied users*. New York: Research Section/ Marketing Department, AT&T.

Anonymous (1981). *Elderly hearing impaired people.* Report of the mini-conference on elderly hearing impaired people prepared for the 1981 White House Conference on Aging. Washington, D.C.: U.S. Government Printing Office.

Appleyard, D. (1970). "Styles and methods of structuring a city." *Environment and Behavior, 2,* 100–117.

Appleyard, D. (1977). "Understanding professional media." In I. Altman and J.F. Wohlwill (eds.), *Human behavior and environment,* Vol. 2. New York: Plenum Press.

Aranyi, L. and Goldman, L.L. (1980). *Design of long-term care facilities.* New York: Van Nostrand Reinhold Company.

Archea, J. (1982). "Conceptual and methodological conflicts in applied interdisciplinary research on environment and aging." In M.P. Lawton, P. Windley and T. Byerts (eds.), *Aging and environment: Theoretical approaches.* New York: Springer.

Archea, J., Collins, B., and Stahl, F. (1979). "Guidelines for stair safety." *National Bureau of Standards, BSS 120,* Washington, D.C.

Arnheim, R. (1977). *The dynamics of architectural form.* New York: University of California Press.

Backett, E.M. (1965). *Domestic accidents.* Geneva, Switzerland: World Health Organization.

Baker, S. (1975). "Determinants of injury and opportunities for intervention." *American Journal of Epidemiology, 101,* 98.

Barnes, R.D. (1981). "Perceived freedom and control in the built environment." In J. Harvey (ed.), *Cognition, social behavior and the environment.* Hillsdale, N.J.: Lawrence Erlbaum Associates.

Battelle Columbus Laboratories (1977). *Study and evaluation of integrating the handicapped to HUD housing.* Washington, D.C.: U.S. Department of Housing and Urban Development.

Bechtel, R.B. (1976). "Perception of environmental quality: Some new wineskins for old wine." In K.H. Craik and E.H. Zube (eds.), *Perceiving environmental quality.* New York: Plenum Press.

Bell, W.G. (1973). "Community care for the elderly: An alternative to institutionalization." *The Gerontologist, 13*(3), 349–354.

Berkeley, E.P. (1973). "More than you may want to know about the Boston City Hall." *Architecture Plus, 1*(1), 72–77.

Berkowitz, M., Hiatt, L.G, de Toledo, P., Shapiro, J. and Lurie, M. (1979). *Reading with print limitations* (Vols. 2 and 3). New York: American Foundation for the Blind.

Best, G. (1970). "Direction finding in large buildings." In D. Canter (ed.), *Architectural psychology.* London: RIBA Publications.

Beyer, G.H. and Nierstrasz, F.H.J. (1967). *Housing the aged in western countries.* New York: Elsevier.

Beyer, G.H. and Woods, M.E. (1963). *Living and activity patterns of aged, research report no. 6.* New York: Cornell University Center for Housing and Environmental Studies.

Birren, J.E. (1964). *The psychology of aging.* Englewood Cliffs, N.J.: Prentice-Hall.

Blasch, B. and Hiatt, L.G. (1983). *Orientation and wayfinding.* Washington,

D.C.: U.S. Architectural and Transportation Barriers Compliance Board.

Blenkner, M. (1961). "Comments." In R.W. Kleemeier (ed.), *Aging and leisure.* New York: Oxford University Press.

Bley, N., Goodman, M., Dye, D. and Harel, B. (1972). "Characteristics of aged participants in an age-segregated leisure program." *The Gerontologist, 12*(4), 368–370.

Boldy, D. (1977). "Is sheltered housing a good thing?" *Some unresolved aspects of sheltered housing for the elderly and disabled.* Institute of Social Welfare, Nottingham, England, 7.

Boldy, D. (1976). "A study of the wardens of grouped dwellings for the elderly." *Social and Economic Administration, 10,* 59–67.

Boldy, D., Abel, P., and Carter, K. (1973). *The elderly in grouped dwellings: A profile.* Devon: University of Exeter, Institute of Biometry and Community Medicine.

Boyce, P. (1980). "The relationship between the performance of visual tasks and lighting conditions." In R. Greenhalgh (ed.), *Light for low vision.* Proceedings of a Symposium, University College, London, April, 1978. Hove: Sussex.

Bottenburg, R.A. and Ward, J.H., Jr. (1963). *Applied multiple linear regression* (Technical Documentary Report PRL-TDR-63-6,) 6570th Personnel Research Laboratory, Aerospace Medical Division, Air Force Systems Command, Lackland AFB, Texas, Project 7719, Task 771909.

Bourestom, N. and Pastalan, L. (1981). "The effects of relocation on the elderly." *The Gerontologist, 21*(1).

Brieff, R., Horwitz, J. and Hiatt, L. (1981). *Self-help and mutual aid for the elderly: A literature review. Grant Report.* New York: American Foundation for the Blind.

Brill, M. (1974). "Evaluating buildings on a performance basis." In J. Lang, C. Burnette, W. Moleski and D. Vachon (eds.), *Designing for human behavior.* Pennsylvania: Dowden, Hutchinson and Ross, Inc.

Brotman, H. (1973). *New facts about older Americans.* (Department of Health, Education and Welfare Publication No. SRS 73-2007). Washington, D.C.: U.S. Government Printing Office.

Brotman, H.B. (1977). "Population projections, Part 1: Tomorrow's older population (to 2000)." *The Gerontologist, 17,* 203–209.

Brotman, H. (1981). "Every ninth American." *Developments on Aging.* Report #96–55. Washington, D.C.: U.S. Government Printing Office.

Brown, A.S. (1974). "Satisfying relationships for the elderly and their patterns of disengagement." *The Gerontologist, 14,* 258–262.

Buffalo Organization for Social and Technological Innovation, Inc. (1982, December). *Accidents & Aging.* A Final Report prepared for the Administration on Aging, Grant #90AR0035, Buffalo, New York.

Bultena, G.L. and Wood, V. (1969). "The American retirement community: Bane or blessing?" *Journal of Gerontology, 24,* 209–217.

Butler, R.N. (1973). *Why survive? Being old in America.* New York: Harper and Row.

Butterfield, D., Anderson, J., Weidemann, S., O'Donnell, P., and Hoglund, D. (1981). *Being elderly in Longview Place.* Paper presented at the meeting of the Environmental Design Research Association.

Bytheway, B. and James, L. (1978). *The allocation of sheltered housing: A study of theory, practice and liaison.* University College of Swansea, Medical Sociology Research Centre.

Campbell, A., Converse, P.E., and Rodgers, W.L. (1976). *The quality of American life.* New York: Russell Sage.

Carp, F.M. (1966). *A future for the aged: The residents of Victoria Plaza.* Austin: University of Texas Press.

Carp, F. (1968). "Effects of improved housing on the lives of older people." In B. Neugarten (ed.), *Middle age and aging.* Chicago: University of Chicago Press.

Carp, F.M. (1968). "Person-situation congruence in engagement." *The Gerontologist, 8,* 184–188.

Carp, F.M. (1969). "Compound criteria in gerontological research." *Journal of Gerontology, 24*(3), 341–347.

Carp, F.M. (1969). *Some determinants of low application rate of Mexican-Americans of public housing for the elderly.* Hearings before the Special Committee on Aging, United State Senate, Ninety-first congress, First Session, Part IV. Washington, D.C.: US Government Printing Office.

Carp, F.M. (1970). "Communicating with elderly Mexican-Americans." *The Gerontologist, 10,* 126–134.

Carp, F.M. (1975a). Impact of improved housing on morale and life satisfaction. *The Gerontologist, 15,* 511–515.

Carp, F.M. (1975b). "Long-range satisfaction with housing." *The Gerontologist, 15,* 68–72.

Carp, F.M. (1976a). "Housing and living environments of older people." In R.H. Binstock and E. Shanas (eds.), *Handbook of Aging and the Social Sciences.* New York: Van Nostrand Reinhold.

Carp, F.M. (1976). "User evaluation of housing for the elderly." *The Gerontologist, 16*(2), 102–111.

Carp, F. (1977). "Impact of improved living environment on health and life expectancy." *The Gerontologist, 17,* 242–249.

Carp, F.M. (1978). "Effects of the living environment on activity and use of time." *International Journal of Aging and Human Development, 9,* 75–91.

Carp, F. and Carp, A. (1980). "Person-environment congruence and sociability." *Research on Aging, 2,* 395–415.

Carr, S. and Schissler, D. (1969). "The city as a trip." *Environment and Behavior, 1*(1), 7.

Cavan, R.S., Burgess, E.W., Havighurst, R.J., and Goldhamer, H. (1949). *Personal adjustment in old age.* Chicago: Science Research Associates, Inc.

Chippindale, A. (1978). "Society at work: A warden's day." *New Society, 45*(831), 508–509.

Christensen, D.L. (1984). *The residential environment and person/environment congruence for independent older women* (Unpublished doctoral dissertation). University of California, Berkeley.

Christensen, D. and Robinson, E. (1975). *Social activity and the housing environment of the elderly: Implications for design and planning.* California: University of California, Berkeley, Department of Architecture.

Clark, A. (1968). "Factors in fracture of the female femur." *Gerontological Clinica, 10,* 257–270.

Clemente, F. and Kleiman, M. (1976). "Fear of crime among the aged." *The Gerontologist, 16,* 207–210.

Cohen, G. (1979). "Language comprehension in old age." *Cognitive psychology, 11*(4), 412–429.

Cohen, S. (1981). "Sound effects on behavior." *Psychology Today, 15*(10), 38–42.

Comalli, P.E. (1967). "Perception and age." *The Gerontologist, 7*(2), 73–77.

Cooper, C. (1975). *Easter hill village.* New York: Free Press.

Corso, J.F. (1977). "Auditory perception and the aging." In J. Birren and K.W. Schaie (eds.), *Handbook of the psychology of aging.* New York: Van Nostrand.

Cranz, G. and Schumacher, T.L. (1977). "The impact of high-rise housing on older residents." In D. Conway (ed.), *Human response to tall buildings.* Pennsylvania: Dowden, Hutchinson and Ross.

Cranz, G., Christensen, D., and Dyer, D. (1977). *A user-oriented evaluation of San Francisco's public housing for the elderly.* Berkeley, California: University of California Berkeley, Center for Planning and Development Research.

Cranz, G. and DeVoe, D. (1977). *A proposal for a new social service in housing for the elderly.* Berkeley, California: University of California, Berkeley, Department of Architecture.

Cranz, G. and Schumacher, T.L. (1975). *Open space for housing for the elderly, working paper 19.* Princeton, New Jersey: Princeton University, Research Center for Urban and Environmental Planning, School of Architecture and Urban Planning.

Cullinan, T.R. (1980). "Low vision in elderly people." In R. Greenhalgh (ed.), *Light for low vision.* Proceedings of a symposium, University College, London, April, 1980. Hove: Sussex, 65–70.

Cumming, E., and Henry, W. (1961). *Growing old. The process of disengagement.* New York: Basic Books.

Curtin, R., Newman, S., and Chen, A. (1981). *Home repair services for the elderly: An evaluation of Baltimore's home maintenance program (Phase one).* Michigan: The University of Michigan, Institute for Social Research, Survey Research Center.

Cutler, N. (1983). "Age and political behavior." In D. Woodruff and J. Birren (eds.), *Aging: Scientific perspectives and social issues,* Monterey: Brooks/Cole.

David, T.G., Moos, R.H., and Kahn, J.R. (1981). "Community integration among elderly residents of sheltered care settings." *American Journal of Community Psychology, 9,* 513–526.

Davis, E. and Fine-Davis, M. (1981). "Predictors of satisfaction with housing and neighborhood: A nationwide study in the Republic of Ireland." *Social Indicators Research, 9,* 477–494.

Davis, M. (1979). "Stand-in call service provides relief for the warden." *Housing, 15*(8), 16–17.

Department of Health and Social Security (1979). *A happier old age.* London: Her Majesty Stationary Office.

DeJonge, D. (1962). "Images of urban areas: Their structure and psychological foundations." *Journal of the American Institute of Planners, 28,* 266–276.

Devlin, A. (1980). "Housing for the elderly: Cognitive considerations." *Environment and Behavior, 12*(4), 451–466.

Dickman, I. (1983). *Making life more livable.* New York: American Foundation for the Blind.

Dixon, J.M. (1968). "Campus city revisited." *Architectural Forum, 129*(2), 28–43.

Donahue, W. (1966). "Impact of living arrangement on ego development in the elderly." In F.M. Carp (ed.), *Patterns of living and housing of middle-aged and older people.* Washington, D.C.: U.S. Government Printing Office.

Droller, H. (1955). "Falls among elderly people living at home." *Geriatrics, 10,* 239–244.

Dudley, D.J. and Hillery, G.A. Jr. (1977). "Freedom and alienation in homes for the aged." *The Gerontologist, 17,* 140–145.

Edelman, P., Herz, E. and Bickman, L. (1980). "A model of behavior in fires applied to a nursing home fire." In D. Canter (ed.), *Fires and human behavior.* London: John Wiley and Sons.

Ellis, W.R. (1974). "Review of defensible space." *Journal of Architectural Education, 27*(1), 11–12.

Elmer, C.D. (1957). *A study to determine the specification of wheelchair ramps.* Ph.D. dissertation, University of Illinois.

English, H. and English, A. (1958). *A comprehensive dictionary of psychological and psychoanalytical terms.* New York: Longmans, Green and Company.

Faletti, M.V. (1981). *The normal elderly at home.* Paper prepared for the National Research Conference on Technology and Aging, Racine, Wisconsin.

Faletti, M.V. (1984). "Using technology to adapt environments." *Generations, 8,* 35–38.

Faye, E.E. and Hood, C.M. (1976). "Visual rehabilitation in the geriatric population." In E.E. Faye and C.M. Hood (eds.), *Clinical low vision.* Boston: Little Brown.

Finch, J. (1981). "Making things easier to see." *Retinitis Pigmentosa Foundation Newsletter, 8*(4), 2–4.

Flood, J.T. (1979). "Special problems of the aged deaf person." *Journal of Rehabilitation of the Deaf, 12*(4), 34–35.

Fozard, J.L. (1980). "The time for remembering." In L. Poon (ed.), *Aging in the 1980's.* Washington, D.C.: American Psychological Association.

Fozard, J.L. (1981). "Person-environment relationships in adulthood: Implications for human factors engineering." *Human Factors, 23*(1), 7–28.

Fozard, J.L. and Popkin, S.J. (1978). "Optimizing adult development: Ends and means of an applied psychology of aging." *American Psychologist, 33,* 975–989.

Fozard, J.L., Wolf, E., Bell, B., McFarland, R.A., and Podolsky, S. (1977). Visual perception and communication. In J.E. Birren and K.W. Schaie (eds.), *Handbook of the psychology of aging.* New York: Van Nostrand.

Francescato, G., Weidemann, S., Anderson, J., and Chenoweth, R. (1979).

Residents' satisfaction in HUD-assisted housing: Design and management factors. Washington, D.C.: U.S. Department of Housing and Urban Development.

Frieberger, H. (ed.) (1980). "Sensory aids in the VA RER&D service programs." *Bulletin of Prosthetics Research, 17*(2), 111–123.

Fried, M. and Gleicher, P. (1961). "Some sources of residential satisfaction in an urban slum." *Journal of the American Institute of Planners, 27,* 305–315.

Galster, G.C. and Hesser, G.W. (1981). "Residential satisfaction: Compositional contextual correlates." *Environment and Behavior, 13*(6), 735–758.

Galton, L. (1981). "Tintinnitus." *50-Plus, 21*(12), 24–25.

Gans, H.J. (1967). "Planning—and city planning—for mental health." In W. Eldredge (ed.), *Taming megalopolis, Vol. II.* New Jersey: Doubleday.

Gelwicks, L.E. and Newcomer, R.J. (1974). *Planning housing environments for the elderly.* Washington, D.C.: National Council on the Aging.

Genensky, S. (1980). "Architectural barriers to the partially sighted—and solutions." *Architectual Record, 167*(5), 65–67.

Genensky, S. (1980). "Data concerning the partially sighted and functionally blind." *Journal of Visual Impairment and Blindness, 72*(5), 177–180.

Gibson, J.J. (1950). *Perception of the visual world.* Massachusetts: Houghton-Mifflin.

Goering, J. (1980). *Housing in America: The characteristics and uses of the annual housing survey.* (Department of Housing and Urban Development, Annual Housing Survey Studies no. 6) Washington, D.C.: U.S. Government Printing Office.

Golledge, R.G. (1973). "Learning about urban environments." In R.G. Golledge and J.N. Rayner (eds.), *Cognitive Configurations of the City,* Vol. II, Columbus: Ohio State University Press, Department of Geography.

Golledge, R.G. and Rayner, J.N. (1973). "Spatial biases in cognitive configurations of a city and their influence on human spatial behavior." In R.G. Golledge and J.N. Rayner (eds.), *Cognitive configurations of the City,* Vol. II, Columbus: Ohio State University Press, Department of Geography.

Golledge, R. and Zannaras, G. (1973). "Cognitive approaches to the analysis of human spatial behavior." In W. Ittelson (ed.), *Environmental cognition.* New York: Seminar Press.

Gray, B. (1966). *Home accidents among older people.* London: Royal Society for the Prevention of Accidents.

Green, I., Fedewa, B.E., Johnston, C.A., Jackson, W.M., and Deardorff, H.L. (1975). *Housing for the elderly: The development and design process.* New York: Van Nostrand Reinhold Company.

Griffin, D.R. (1973). "Topological orientation." In R. Downs and D. Stea (eds.), *Image and environment.* Chicago: Aldine Press.

Griffin, J. and Dean, C. (1975). *Housing for the elderly: The size of grouped schemes,* London: Her Majesty Stationary Office, Department of the Environment.

Gryfe, C.I., Amies, A., and Ashley, M.J. (1977). "A longitudinal study of falls in an elderly population." *Age and Ageing, 6,* 202–210.

Gubrium, J.F. (1970). "Environmental effects on morale in old age and the resources of health and solvency." *The Gerontologist, 10*(4), 294–297.

Gutman, G. (1978). "Issues and findings relating to multilevel accommodation for seniors." *Journal of Gerontology, 33,* 592–600.

Gutman, R. and Westergaard, B. (1974). "Building evaluation, user satisfaction and design." In J. Lang, C. Burnette, W. Moleski, and D. Vachon (eds.), *Designing for human behavior.* Pennsylvania: Dowden, Hutchinson and Ross.

Haber, L.D. (1967). "Identifying the disabled: Concepts and methods in the measurement of disability." *Social Security Bulletin,* 17–34.

Haber, G.M. (1980). "Human behavior in fire in total institutions: A case study." In D. Canter (ed.), *Fires and human behavior.* London: John Wiley and Sons.

Haberkorn, S., Davis, L, Pastalan, L., and Walker, J. (1977). *The Pennsylvania nursing home relocation program: Process and impact.* Paper presented at the meeting of the Gerontological Society Conference, San Francisco.

Haddon, W. (1980). "Advances in epidemiology of injuries as a basis for public policy." *American Journal of Public Health, 95,* 411.

Hallowell, A.I. (1955). *Culture and experience.* Philadelphia: University of Pennsylvania Press.

Hamovitch, M.B. (1968). "Social and psychological factors in adjustment in a retirement village." In F.M. Carp (ed.), *The retirement process.* Washington, D.C.: U.S. Government Printing Office.

Hamovitch, M.B. and Peterson, J.E. (1969). "Housing needs and satisfactions of the elderly." *Journal of Gerontology, 35,* 232–240.

Hare, P.H. (1981a). "Carving up the American dream." *Planning, 47*(7), 14–17.

Hare, P.H. (1981b). "The empty nest as a golden egg: Using the unused space in single family neighborhoods." *Perspectives on Aging.*

Harel, Z. and Harel, B.B. (1978). "On-site coordinated services in age-segregated and age-integrated public housing." *The Gerontologist, 18*(2), 153–158.

Harris, C.S. (1978). *Fact book on aging: A profile of America's older population.* Washington, D.C.: National Council on the Aging.

Hartman, C. (1984). *The transformation of San Francisco.* Totowa, New Jersey: Rowan and Allanheld.

Hartman, C., Horovitz, J., and Herman, R. (1976). "Designing with the elderly." *The Gerontologist, 16*(4), 303–311.

Havighurst, R.J. (1963). "Successful aging." In R.H. Williams, C. Tibbits, and W. Donahue (eds.), *Process of aging,* Vol. 1, New York: Atherton Press.

Havighurst, R.J. (1969). "A report of a special committee of the gerontological society. Research and development goals in social gerontology." *The Gerontologist, 9,* Part 2.

Hempel, D.A. (1977). "Consumer satisfaction with the home buying process." In H. Deith Hunt (ed.), *Conceptualization and measurement of consumer satisfaction and dissatisfaction.* Proceedings of conference conducted by Marketing Science Institute.

Heumann, L.F. (1980). "Sheltered housing for the elderly: The role of the British warden." *The Gerontologist, 20,* 318–329.

Heumann, L.F. and Boldy, D. (1982). *Housing for the elderly: Policy formulation in Europe and North America.* London: St. Martins Press.

Hiatt, L. (1978). "Architecture for the aged. Design for living." *Inland Architect, 23,* 6–17.

Hiatt, L.G. (1979). "Environmental considerations in understanding and designing for mentally impaired older people." In H. McBride (ed.), *Mentally impaired aging: Bridging the gap.* Washington, D.C.: American Association of Homes for the Aging.

Hiatt, L.G. (1980a). "Disorientation is more than a state of mind." *Nursing Homes, 29*(4), 30–36.

Hiatt, L.G. (1980b). "Is poor light dimming the sight of nursing home patients? Implications for vision screening and care." *Nursing Homes, 29*(5), 32–41.

Hiatt, L. (1981a). "Aging and disability." In N. McClosky and E. Borgotta (eds.), *America's retirement population: Prospects, planning and policy.* CA: Sage.

Hiatt, L. (1981b). "Care and design: The color and use of color in environments for older people." *Nursing Homes, 30*(3), 18–22.

Hiatt, L. (1981c). "A self-administered checklist: Renovation for innovation." *Nursing Homes, 30*(1), 33–39.

Hiatt, L. (1981d). *Technology and chronically impaired elderly: Interpretations leading to performance demands and products in institutions and in community care systems.* Paper presented at the National Research Conference on Technology and Aging, a joint project of the Gerontological Society of America and the Western Gerontological Society, Racine, Wisconsin.

Hiatt, L. (1982). "Grouping older people of different abilities." In R.D. Chellis and J.F. Seagle, Jr. (eds.), *Congregate housing for older people: A new solution.* MA: Lexington Books.

Hiatt, L.G. (1983). "Environmental design and the frail older person at home." *Long Term Home Health Care, 2*(1), 13–22.

Hiatt, L. (1985). "Understanding the physical environment." *Pride Institute Journal on Long-Term Home Health Care, 4*(2), 12–22.

Hiatt, L. (1985). "The significance of the physical environment and of products to visually impaired and blind older people." In S. Timmerman and R. Kaarlela (eds.), *Handbook on Aging and Vision.* New York: American Foundation for the Blind.

Hillier, W. (1973). "In defense of space." *RIBA Journal, 80*(11), 539–544.

Hoglund, D. (1986). *The intangible qualities of housing.* New York: Van Nostrand.

Hogue, C.C. (1981). "Injury in later life, part 1: Epidemiology." *Journal of the American Geriatrics Society, 30*(3), 183–190.

Holahan, C.J. (1982). *Environmental Psychology.* New York: Random House.

Hochschild, A.R. (1973). *The unexpected community.* New Jersey: Prentice-Hall.

Howell, S. (1977). "The aged as user group: Aging as a process in design education." *Journal of Architectural Education, 31*(1), 26–29.

Howell, S. (1980a). *Designing for aging: Patterns of use.* Cambridge: MIT Press.

Howell, S. (1980b). "Environments and aging." In C. Eisdorfer (ed.), *Annual Review of Gerontology and Geriatrics, 1,* 237–260.

Hughes, P.C. and Neer, R.M. (1980). "Lighting for the elderly: A psychobiological approach to lighting." *Human Factors, 23*(1), 65–86.

Hull, R.H. and Traynor, R.M. (1977). "Hearing impairment among aging persons in the health care facility: Their diagnosis and treatment." *American Health Care Association Journal, 3*(1), 14–18.

Hunt, M.E. (1981a). *Simulated site visits: An environmental learning strategy for older people.* Unpublished doctoral dissertation, University of Michigan, Michigan.

Hunt, M.E. (1981b). *Simulated site visits: Preparation for relocation.* Final report to the U.S. Department of Health and Human Services. Michigan: University of Michigan Press, Institute of Gerontology.

Hunt, M.E. (1984). "Environmental learning without being there." *Environment and Behavior, 16*(3), 257–258.

J.G. Furniture Systems (1980). *G.P.F. Geriatric Personal Furnishings Planning Manual.* Quakertown, Pennsylvania.

Jacobs, B. (ed.). (1976). *Working with the impaired elderly.* Washington, D.C.: National Council on the Aging.

Jacobs, J. (1961). *The life and death of great American cities.* New York: Random House.

Jirovec, R., Jirovec, M.M., and Bosse, R. (1985). "Environmental determinants of neighborhood satisfaction among urban elderly men." *The Gerontologist, 2*(1), 21–32.

Jolicoeur, R.M. (1970). *Caring for the visually impaired older person: A practical guide for long-term care facilities and related agencies.* Minnesota: Minneapolis Society for the Blind.

Jordan, J.J. (1979). *Senior center design: An architect's discussion of facility planning.* Washington, D.C.: National Council on the Aging.

Kahana, E. (1973). "The humane treatment of old people in institutions." *The Gerontologist, 13,* 282–289.

Kaplan, R. (1973). "Predictors of environmental preference: Designers and clients." *Environmental Design Research, 1,* Pennsylvania: Dowden, Hutchinson and Ross.

Kaplan, R., Kaplan, S., and Deardorff, H.L. (1974). "The perception and evaluation of a simulated environment." *Man-Environment Systems, 4*(3), Michigan: University of Michigan Press, Psychological Laboratories.

Kaplan, S. (1973). "Cognitive maps in perception and thought." In G. Moore and R. Golledge (eds.), *Environmental knowing: Theories, research and methods.* Pennsylvania: Dowden, Hutchinson and Ross.

Kaplan, S. (1977). "Participation in the design process: A cognitive approach." In D. Stokols (ed.), *Perspectives on environment and behavior: Theory, research and applications.* New York: Plenum Press.

Kastenbaum, R. and Candy, S. (1973). "The 4% fallacy." *International Journal of Aging and Human Development, 4,* 15–21.

Katz, S.H. (1978). "Anthropological perspectives on aging." In M.E. Wolfgang, R.D. Lambert and A.W. Heston (eds.), *The Annals of the American Academy of Political and Social Science, 438.*

Kilday, P. (1977, July 8). "Travellers go crazy in big Dallas-Forth Worth airport." *Associated Press News Service.*

Killian, E. (1970). "Effects of geriatric transfers on mortality rates." *Social Work, 15,* 19–26.

Kira, A. (1966). *The bathroom: Criteria for design.* New York: Cornell University Press.

Kirchner, C. and Lowman, C. (1978). "Sources of variation in the estimated prevalence of visual loss." *Journal of Visual Impairment and Blindness, 72*(8), 329–333.

Kirchner, C. and Peterson, R. (1980). "Multiple impairments among non-institutionalized blind and visually impaired persons." *Journal of Visual Impairment and Blindness, 74,* 42–44.

Kistin, H. and Morris, R. (1972). "Alternatives to institutional care for the elderly and disabled." *The Gerontologist, 12*(2), 139–142.

Knapp, M.R.J. (1976). "Predicting services in the context of the housing environment." *The Gerontologist, 9*(1), 15–19.

Koncelik, J.A. (1976). *Designing the open nursing home.* Pennsylvania: Dowden, Hutchinson and Ross.

Koncelik, J.A. (1979). "Human factors and environmental design for the aging: Physiological change and sensory loss as design criteria." In T.O. Byerts, S.C. Howell, and L.A. Pastalan (eds.), *Environmental context of aging.* New York: Garland.

Koncelik, J.A. (1982). *Aging and the product environment.* New York: Hutchinson Ross Publishing.

Koncelik, J.A. and Bonner, D. (1974). *Environmental survey: First community village.* Columbus: Ohio State University, Department of Industrial Design.

Koncelik, J.A. and Kropet, R. (1981). *Product survey, aging and the product environment.* Final Report to the National Endowment for the Arts, Ohio.

Koncelik, J.A., Ostrander, E. and Snyder, L. (1972). *The new nursing home: Conference proceedings,* New York: Cornell University, College of Human Ecology.

Kozmo, A. and Stones, M.J. (1983). "Predictors of happiness." *Journal of Gerontology, 38*(5), 626–628.

Lake, W.S. (1962). "Housing preferences and social patterns." In C. Tibbits and W. Donahue (eds.), *Social and psychological aspects of aging.* New York: Columbia University Press.

Lane, T.S. and Feins, J.D. (1985). "Are the elderly overhoused? Definitions of space utilization and policy implication." *The Gerontologist, 25*(3), 243–251.

Langer, E. and Rodin, J. (1976). "The effects of choice and enhanced personal responsibility for the aged: A field experiment in an institutional setting." *Journal of Personality and Social Psychology, 34,* 191–198.

Laventhol and Horwath. (1983). *Lifecare industry, 1983.* Philadelphia: Laventhol and Horwath.

Lawton, M.P. (1969). "Supportive services in the context of the housing environment." *The Gerontologist, 9*(1), 15–19.

Lawton, M.P. (1970). "Ecology and aging." In L.A. Pastalan and D.H. Carson (eds.), *Spacial behavior of older people.* Michigan: University of Michigan Press.

Lawton, M.P. (1975). *Planning and managing housing for the elderly.* New York: John Wiley and Sons.

Lawton, M.P. (1976). "The relative impact of congregate and traditional housing on elderly tenants." *The Gerontologist, 16,* 237–242.

Lawton, M.P. (1977). "Evaluation research in fluid systems." In J.E. O'Brien and G.F. Streib (eds.), *Evaluative research on social programs for the elderly*. (OHD Publication No. 77-20120.) Washington, D.C.: U.S. Government Printing Office.

Lawton, M.P. (1977). "The impact of environment on aging and behavior." In J.E. Birren, and K.W. Schaie (eds.), *Handbook of the psychology of aging*. New York: Van Nostrand Reinhold Company.

Lawton, M.P. (1979). "A background for the environmental study of aging." In T.O. Byerts, S.C. Howell and L.A. Pastalan (eds.), *Environmental context of aging: Life-styles, environmental quality and living arrangements*. New York: Garland.

Lawton, M.P. (1980a). *Environment and aging*. CA: Brooks/Cole Publishing Co.

Lawton, M.P. (1980b). "Housing the elderly, residential quality and residential satisfaction." *Research on Aging, 3*, 217–233.

Lawton, M.P. (1981). "Sensory deprivation and the effect of the environment on management of the patient with senile dementia." In N.E. Miller & G.D. Cohen (eds.), *Clinical aspects of Alzheimer's disease and Senile Dementia*. New York: Raven.

Lawton, M.P. (1983). "Environment and other determinants of well-being in older people." *The Gerontologist, 23*(4), 349–357.

Lawton, M.P., Brody E. and Turner-Massey, P. (1978). "The relationship of environmental factors to changes in well-being." *The Gerontologist, 18*, 133–137.

Lawton, M.P. and Cohen, J. (1974). "Environment and the well-being of inner city residents." *Environment & Behavior, 6*(2), 194–211.

Lawton, M.P. and Cohen, J. (1974). "The generality of housing impact on well-being of older people." *Journal of Gerontology, 29*, 194–204.

Lawton, M.P., Greenbaum, M. and Liebowitz, B. (1980). "The lifespan of housing environments for the aging." *The Gerontologist, 20*(1), 56–64.

Lawton, M.P. and Hoover, S. (1981). *Community housing and choices for older Americans*. New York: Springer.

Lawton, M.P., Liebowitz, B. and Charon, H. (1970). "Physical structure and the behavior of senile patients following ward remodeling." *Aging and Human Development, 1*, 231–239.

Lawton, M.P., Moss, M. and Grimes, M. (1985). "The changing services needs of older tenants in planned housing." *The Gerontologist, 25*(3), 258–265.

Lawton, M.P. and Nahemow, L. (1973). "Ecology and the aging process." In C. Eisdorfer and M.P. Lawton (eds.), *Psychology of adult development and aging*. Washington, D.C.: American Psychological Association.

Lawton, M.P. and Nahemow, L. (1979). "Social science methods for evaluation the quality of housing for the elderly." *Journal of Architectural Research, 7*(1), 5–11.

Lawton, M.P., Nahemow, L. and Teaff, J. (1975). "Housing characteristics and the well-being of elderly tenants in federally assisted housing." *Journal of Gerontology, 30*(5), 601–607.

Lawton, M.P., Nahemow, L. and Yeh, T. (1980). "Neighborhood environment and the well-being of older tenants in planned housing." *International Journal of Aging & Human Development, 11*(3), 211–227.

Lawton, M., Newcomer, R.J. and Byerts, T.O. (1976). *Community planning for an aging society*. Stroudsburg: Dowden, Hutchinson and Ross.

Lawton, M. and Yaffe, S. (1970). "Mortality, morbidity and voluntary change of residence by older people." *Journal of American Geriatric Society, 18*, 823–831.

Lefitt, J. (1980). "Lighting for the elderly: An optician's view." In R. Greenhalgh (ed.), *Light for low vision. Proceedings of a Symposium*, University College, London, April, 1978. Hove: Sussex, 55–61.

Lemke, S. & Moos, R. (1980). "Assessing the institutional policies of sheltered care settings." *Journal of Gerontology, 35*, 96–107.

Lemke, S. & Moos, R. (1983). *Coping with an intra-institutional relocation: Behavioral change as a function of residents' personal resources*. Palo Alto: VA and Stanford University Medical Center, Journal of Environmental Psychology, 1984, Vol. 4, pp 137–151.

Lerup, L., Cronrath, D. and Lu, J. (1980). "Fires in nursing facilities." In D. Cantor (ed.), *Fires and human behavior*. London: John Wiley and Sons Ltd.

Lieberman, M.A. (1961). "Relationship of mortality rates to entrance to a home for the aged." *Geriatrics, 16*, 515–519.

Lieberman, M.A. (1974). "Relocation research and social policy." *The Gerontologist, 14*, 494–501.

Lieberman, M., Tobin, S. and Slover, D. (1971). *The effects of relocation on long-term geriatric patients*. Chicago: University of Chicago Press. IL Department of Health and Committee on Human Development.

Liebowitz, B., Lawton, M.P. and Waldman, A. (1979). "Evaluation: Designing for confused elderly people." *American Institute of Architects Journal, 68*, 59–61.

Lindsley, O.R. (1964). "Geriatric behavioral prosthesis." In R. Kastenbaum (ed.), *New thoughts on old age*. New York: Springer.

Linn, M.W., Gurel, L. and Linn, B.S. (1977). "Patient outcome as a measure of quality of nursing home care." *American Journal of Public Health, 67*, 337–344.

Lipman, A. (1968). "Services for the aged." In O.B. Thompson (ed.), *Potentialities for later living*. Gainesville: University of Florida Press.

Lipman, A. (1968). "Public housing and attitudinal adjustment in old age: A comparative study." *Journal of Geriatric Psychology, 2*, 88–101.

Lowenthal, M.F. and Bolar, D. (1965). "Voluntary vs. involuntary social withdrawal." *Journal of Gerontology, 20*, 363–371.

Lucht, U. (1971). "A prospective study of accidental falls and resulting injuries in the home among elderly people." *Journal of Socio-Medica Scandinavia, 2*, 105–120.

Lynch, K. (1960). *Image of the city*. Massachusetts: MIT Press.

Maddox, G.L. (1964). "Disengagement theory: A critical evaluation." *The Gerontologist, 4*, 80–82.

Marans, R.W. (1976). "Perceived quality of residential environments." In K.H. Craik and E.H. Zube (eds.), *Perceiving environmental quality*. New York: Plenum Press.

Marans, R. and Wellman, J. (1978). *The quality of nonmetropolitan living evaluations: Behaviors and expectations of Northern Michigan residents*. Ann Arbor: University of Michigan: Institute for Social Research.

Markus, E., Blenkner, M., Bloom, M. and Downs, T. (1972). "Some factors and their association with post-relocation mortality among institutionalized aged persons." *Journal of Gerontology, 27,* 376–382.

Marsh, G.R. (1980). "Perceptual changes with age." In E.W. Busse and D.G. Blazer (eds.), *Handbook of geriatric psychiatry.* New York: Van Nostrand.

Maurer, J.F. (1976). "Auditory impairment and aging." In B. Jacobs (ed.), *Working with the impaired elderly.* Washington, D.C.: National Council on the Aging.

Mayer, N. and Lee, O. (1980). *The effectiveness of federal home repair and improvement programs in meeting elderly homeowner needs.* Washington, D.C.: The Urban Institute.

McCartney, J. and Nadler, G. (1979). "How to help your patient cope with hearing loss." *Geriatrics,* 69–76.

McCullough, H.E. and Farnhan, M.B. (1960). "Space and design requirements for wheelchair kitchens." *Bulletin No. 661.* Urbana, Illinois: College of Agriculture Extension Service.

McCullough, H.E. and Farnham, M.B. (1961). "Kitchens for women in wheelchairs." *Circular 841.* Urbana, Illinois: College of Agriculture Extension Service.

McGillivray, R. (ed.) (1984). "Aids for elderly persons with impaired vision." *Aids and Appliances Review, 13,* Massachusetts: Carroll Center for the Blind.

McGuire, M. (1971). "Preventive measures to minimize accidents among the elderly." *Occupational Health Nursing, 19,* 13–16.

McGuire, M.C. (1972). *Design of housing for the elderly: A checklist.* Washington, D.C.: National Association of Housing & Redevelopment Officials.

McKean, J. (1972). "University of Essex: Case study." *Architects Journal, 156,* 645–667.

McNemar, Q. (1962). *Psychological statistics,* (3rd ed.). New York: John Wiley.

Mellow, M. (1981). *Aids for the 80s: What they are and what they do.* New York: American Foundation for the Blind.

Messer, M. (1967). "The possibility of an age concentrated environment becoming a normative system." *Gerontologist, 7*(4), 247–251.

Miller, D. and Lieberman, M. (1965). "The relationships of affect state and adaptive capacity to reactions to stress." *Journal of Gerontology, 20,* 492–497.

Ministry of Housing and Local Government (1962). *Grouped flatlets for old people: A sociological study, Design Bulletin 2,* London: Her Majesty Stationary Office.

Ministry of Housing and Local Government (1969). *Housing standards and costs: Accommodation specially for old people, Circular 82/69,* Her Majesty Stationary Office: London.

Moen, E. (1978). "The reluctance of the elderly to seek help." *Social Problems, 25*(3), 293–303.

Moore, G.T. (1979). "Knowing about environmental knowing." *Environment and Behavior, 11*(1).

Moos, R. (1976). *The human context: Environmental determinants of behavior.* New York: Wiley.

Moos, R. (1980). "Specialized living environments for older people: A conceptual framework for evaluation." *Journal of Social Issues, 36,* 75–94.

Moos, R. (1981). "Environmental choice and control in community care settings for older people." *Journal of Applied Social Psychology, 11,* 23–43.

Moos, R., David, T.G., Lemke, S. and Postle, E. (in press). "Coping with an intra-institution relocation: Changes in resident and staff behavior patterns." *The Gerontologist.*

Moos, R. and Igra, A. (1980). "Determinants of the social environments of sheltered care settings." *Journal of Health and Social Behavior, 21,* 88–98.

Moos, R. and Lemke, S. (1980). "Assessing the physical and architectural features of sheltered care settings." *Journal of Gerontology, 35,* 571–583.

Moos, R. and Lemke, S. (1984). *Multiphasic Environmental Assessment Procedure (MEAP): Manual.* Palo Alto: Stanford University and VA Medical Center, Social Ecology Laboratory.

Moos, R. and Lemke, S. (1985). "Evaluating specialized living environments for older people." In J.E. Birren and K.W. Schaie (eds.), *Handbook of the psychology of aging,* 2nd Edition. New York: Van Nostrand Reinhold.

Morris, W. (ed.) (1973). *The American heritage dictionary.* New York: Dell Publishing Co.

Mulvihill, R. (1977). "The relative importance of elements of low-rise housing estates." *Planning division working paper 1.* Ireland: An Foras Forbartha.

Musson, N. and Heusinkveld, H. (1963). *Buildings for the elderly.* New York: Reinhold Publishing Co.

Nagi, S.Z. (1975). *An epidemiology of adulthood disability in the United States.* Ohio State University, Mershon Center.

Nahemow, L., Lawton, M.P., and Howell, S. (1977). "Elderly people in tall buildings: A nationwide survey." In D.J. Conway (ed.), *Human response to tall buildings.* Pennsylvania: Dowden, Hutchinson, and Ross.

National Burn Information Exchange (1983). *National Institute for Burn Medicine, 2.*

National Center for Health Statistics (1971). "Chronic conditions and limitations of activity and mobility." *Vital and Health Statistics, 10*(51), Washington, D.C.: U.S. Government Printing Office.

National Commission on Architectural Barriers to Rehabilitation of the Handicapped (1968). *Design for all Americans.* Washington, D.C.: U.S. Government Printing Office.

National Council on the Aging (1975). *The myth and reality of aging in America.* Washington, D.C.: National Council on the Aging.

National Council on the Aging (1981). *Aging in the eighties: American in transition.* Washington, D.C.: National Council on the Aging.

National Council on the Aging (1984). *Older consumers home safety program. Final report of project activities.* Washington, D.C.: Prepared under contract to the United States Consumer Product Safety Commission.

National Council on the Aging. (1985). *The sixth sense* (film). Washington, D.C.: National Council on the Aging.

National Institute of Mental Health (1979). *Healthy people: The Surgeon General's report on health promotion and disease prevention.* (USDHEW No. 79–55071). Washington, D.C.: U.S. Government Printing Office.

National Safety Council (1980 Edition). *Accident facts.* Chicago: National Safety Council.

Neugarten, B.L., Havighurst, R.J., and Robin, S.S. (1961). "The measurement of life satisfaction." *Journal of Gerontology, 16*(2), 134–143.

Newman, O. (1972). *Defensible space: Crime prevention through urban design.* New York: Macmillan.

Newman, O. (1976). *Design guidelines for creating defensible space.* Washington, D.C.: LEAA, National Institute of Law Enforcement and Criminal Justice.

Noam, E. (1975). *Homes for the aged: Supervision and standards.* (United States Department of Health Education and Welfare) Washington, D.C.: National Clearinghouse on Aging.

Noam, E. and Donahue, W. (1976). *Assisted independent living in group housing for older people: A report on the situation in European countries.* Washington, D.C.: International Center for Social Gerontology.

Ohta, R.J., Carlin, M.F. and Harmon, B.M. (1981). "Auditory acuity and performance on the mental status questionnaire in the elderly." *American Geriatric Society, 29*(10), 476–478.

Osterberg, A.E. (1980). *A post construction evaluation of westside retirement home: The impact of design and the physical environment on building users.* Michigan: University Microfilms.

Osterberg, A.E. (1981). "Post occupancy evaluation of a retirement home." In A.E. Osterberg, C.T. Tiernan, and R.A. Findlay (eds.), *Design research interactions.* Indiana: The Environmental Design Research Association.

Overstall, P.W. (1978). "Falls in the elderly: Epidemiology, aetiology and management." In B. Isaacs (ed.), *Recent advances in geriatric medicine.* London: Churchill Livingstone.

Pablo, R. (1977). "Intra-institutional relocation: Its impact on long-term care patients." *Gerontologist, 17,* 426–435.

Parsons, H.M. (1981). "Residential design for the aging." *Human Factors, 23,* 39–58.

Pastalan, L.A. (1970). "Privacy as an expression of human territoriality." In L.A. Pastalan and D.H. Carson (eds.), *Spacial behavior of older people.* Michigan: University of Michigan Press.

Pastalan, L.A. (1976). *Age-related vision and hearing changes—An empathic approach* (slides). Michigan: Print and Audiovisual Resources from the Institute of Gerontology at the University of Michigan.

Pastalan, L.A. (1977b). "The empathic model. A methodological bridge between research and design." *Journal of Architecture Education, 31*(1), 14–15.

Pastalan, L. (1979). "Relocation: A state of the art." Unpublished manuscript, University of Michigan, Institute of Gerontology.

Pastalan, L.A. (1979). "Sensory changes and environmental behavior." In T.O. Byerts, S.C. Howell, and L.A. Pastalan (eds.), *Environmental context of aging.* New York: Garland.

Pastalan, L. and Bourestom, N. (1975). *Forced relocation: Setting, staff, and patient effects*. Final Report to National Institute of Mental Health. Michigan: University of Michigan Press.

Pastalan, L.A., Davis, L.F. and Haberkorn, S.B. (1975). *Pennsylvania nursing home relocation program*. Michigan: University of Michigan Press, Institute of Gerontology.

Pastalan, L., Maritz, R. and Merrill, J. (1973). "The simulation of age related sensory losses: A new approach to the study of environmental barriers." In W. Preiser (ed.), *Environmental design research*, Kansas: The Environmental Design Research Association.

Pastalan, L., Merrill, J. and Pormerantz, B. (1975). *Street and Highway Environments and the Older Driver*. Michigan: Wayne State University and the University of Michigan, Institute of Gerontology.

Peterson, R. and Kirchner, C. (1980). "Prevalence of blindness and visual impairment among institutional residents." *Journal of Visual Impairment and Blindness*, 74(8), 323–336.

Philips, R.H. and Salmen, J.P.S. (1983). "Building for accessibility: Design and product specification." *The construction specifier*, 20–34.

President's Commission on Housing (1982). *Report of the President's Commission on Housing*. Washington, D.C.

Proceedings of the United Nations (1968, October). *Housing for the elderly*, New York.

Proshansky, H., Ittelson, W. and Rivlin, L. (1976). *Environmental psychology: People and their physical settings*, 2nd Edition. New York: Holt, Rinehart & Winston.

Pynoos, J. (1985). "Continuum of care retirement communities: Option for mid-upper-income elders." *Generations*, 31–33.

Pynoos, J. (1984). "Setting the elderly housing agenda." *Policy Studies Journal*, 13(1), 173–184.

Pynoos, J., Regnier, V. and O'Brien, T. (1983). *Continuum of care retirement communities: Final report*. University of Southern California, Andrus Gerontology Center: Los Angeles.

Pynoos, J. and Salend E. (1982). "The delivery of long term care services to the elderly: Services to people or people to services." In *Aging households, long term care and environments for the elderly*, Occasional Papers no. 20. Vancouver: University of British Columbia, Center for Human Settlements, 3–21.

Pynoos, J., Schafer, R. and Hartman, C. (eds.) (1980). *Housing urban America*. New York: Aldine.

Raschko, B. (1982). *Housing interiors for the disabled and elderly*. New York: Van Nostrand.

Ralph, J.R. (1982). "Guidelines for print published materials for our aging population." *Journal of the American Optometric Association*, 53.

Regnier, V. (ed.) (1979). *Planning for the elderly: Alternative community analysis techniques*. Los Angeles: University of California Press.

Regnier, V. (1982). "The neighborhood as a support system for the urban elderly." In J. McRae (ed.), *Issues of the 80's enriching lifestyles for the elderly*, University of Florida, Gainseville.

Regnier, V. (1983). "Urban neighborhood cognition." In G. Rowles and

R. Ohta (eds.), *Aging and milieu: Environmental perspectives on growing old*. New York: Academic Press.

Regnier, V. (1985a). "Congregate housing for the elderly: An integrative and participatory planning model." In T. Vonier (ed.), *Proceedings of the Research and Design '85 Conference*. Washington, D.C.: American Institute of Architects.

Regnier, V. (1985b). "Design criteria for outdoor space surrounding housing the elderly." In T. Vonier (ed.), *Proceedings of the Research and Design '85 Conference*. Washington, D.C.: American Institute of Architects.

Regnier, V. and Byerts, T. (1983). "Applying research findings to the planning and design of housing for the elderly." In F. Spink (ed.), *Housing for a maturing population*. Washington: Urban Land Institute.

Regnier, V. and Gelwicks, L. (1981). "Preferred supportive services for middle to higher income retirement housing." *The Gerontologist, 20*(1).

Remnet, V.L. (1976). "The home assessment: A therapeutic tool to assess the needs of the elderly." In I.M. Burnside (ed.), *Nursing and the aged*. New York: McGraw Hill.

Rodin, J. (1980). "Managing the stress of aging: The role of control and coping." In S. Levine & H. Ursin (eds.), *Coping and Health*. New York: Plenum.

Rodin, J. and Langer, E.J. (1977). "Long-term effects of a controlled relevant intervention with the institutionalized aged." *Journal of Personality and Social Psychology, 35*, 897–902.

Rosenbloom, A.A. (1982). "Innovation and advancement in low vision services." *Journal of Visual Impairment and Blindness, 76*, 12–23.

Rosow, I. (1967). *Social Integration of Aged*. New York: Free Press.

Ross, M.A. (1984). *Fitness for the aging adult with visual impairment: An exercise and resource manual*. New York: American Foundation for the Blind.

Rubenstein, L. (1983). "Falls in the elderly: A clinical approach." *The Western Journal of Medicine, 138*(2), 273–275.

San Francisco Housing Authority (Undated). *Planning and design criteria*. San Francisco: SFHA Planning Department.

Sayre, J.M. (1980). *Handbook for the hearing-impaired older adult*. Illinois: Interstate Printers and Publishers.

Sayre, J.M. (1980). *Helping the older adult with an acquired hearing loss*. Illinois: Interstate Printers and Publishers.

Schroeder, S. and Steinfeld, E. (1978). *The estimated cost of accessible buildings*. Washington, D.C.: U.S. Government Printing Office.

Schulz, R. (1976). "The effects of control and predictability on the psychological and physical well-being of the institutionalized aged." *Journal of Personality and Social Psychology, 33*, 563–573.

Schulz, R. and Brenner, G. (1977). "Relocation of the aged: A review and theoretical analysis." *Journal of Gerontology, 32*, 323–333.

Schulz, R. and Hanusa, B.H. (1979). "Environmental influences on the effectiveness of control and competence enhancing interventions." In L.C. Perlmutter and R.A. Monty (eds.), *Choice and Perceived Control*. New York: Erlbaum.

Schumacher, T.L. and Cranz, G. (1975). *The built environment for the elderly: A planning and design study, focusing on independent living for elderly ten-*

ants. Unpublished manuscript. New Jersey: Princeton University, School of Architecture and Urban Planning.

Schwartz, A.N. (1975). "Planning micro-environments for the aged." In D.S. Woodruff and J.E. Birren (eds.), *Scientific prospectives and social issues.* New York: Van Nostrand Publishing.

Sekular, R. and Blake, R. (1985). *Perception.* New York: Knopf.

Sheldon, J.H. (1960). "On the natural history of falls in old age." *British Medical Journal, 2,* 1685–1690.

Sherman, S.R. (1972). "Satisfaction with retirement housing: Attitudes, recommendations and moves." *Aging & Human Development, 3*(49), 339–366.

Sherman, S.R. (1973). *Housing environments for the well-elderly: Scope and impact.* Albany: New York State Department of Mental Health.

Sherman, S.R. (1974). "Leisure activities in retirement housing." *Journal of Gerontology, 29,* 325–335.

Sherman, S.R. (1975a). "Provision of on-site services in retirement housing." *International Journal of Aging and Human Development, 6,* 229–247.

Sherman, S.R. (1975b). "Patterns of contacts for residents of age-segregated and age-integrated housing." *Journal of Gerontology, 30*(2), 103–107.

Sherwood, S., Greer, D.S., Morris, J.N. and Mor, V. (1981). *An alternative to institutionalization: The highland heights experiment.* MA: Ballinger.

Sicurella, V. (1977). "Color contrast as an aid for visually impaired persons." *Journal of Visual Impairment and Blindness, 71,* 252–257.

Silver, J.H., Gould, E.S., Irvine, D. and Cullinan, T.R. (1978). "Visual acuity at home and in eye clinics." *Transactions of the Opthalmological Societies of the United Kingdom, 98*(part 2), 252–257.

Snyder, L. (1978). "Environmental changes for socialization." *Journal of Nursing Administration, 8,* 44–50.

Snyder, L., Rupprecht, P., Pyrek, J. and Smith, K. (1978). "Wandering." *The Gerontologist, 18,* 272–280.

Snyder, L., Hiatt, L. and Bowersox, J.L. (1976). "Report of four case studies of federally sponsored housing for the elderly and disabled." In T.O. Byerts (ed.), *Residential environments for the functionally disabled.* Washington, D.C.: Gerontological Society, 159–212.

Snyder, L., Hiatt, L., Ostrander, E. and Koncelik, J. (1973). *The new nursing home: A response to the behavior and life style of the aging.* Proceedings of a conference for Nursing Home Administrators. New York: Cornell University.

Snyder, L., Pyrek, J. and Smith, K. (1976). "Vision and mental function." *The Gerontologist, 16*(3), 491–495.

Sommer, R. (1970). "Small group ecology in institutions for the elderly." In L.A. Pastalan and D.H. Carson (eds.), *Spacial behavior of older people.* Michigan: University of Michigan Press.

Sommer, R. (1972). *Design awareness.* San Francisco: Rinehart Press.

Spivack, M. (1973). "Archetypal places." In Preiser (ed.), *Environmental design research.* Kansas: The Environmental Design Research Association.

Steinfeld, E. (1975). *Barrier free design for the elderly and the disabled.* New York: Syracuse University, All University Gerontology Center.

Steinfeld, E. (1979). *Access to the built environment: A review of literature.* Washington, D.C.: U.S. Government Printing Office.

Steinfeld, E., Duncan, J. and Cardell, P. (1977). "Towards a responsive environment: The psychosocial effects of inaccessibility." In M. Bednar (ed.), *Barrier-free environments.* Pennsylvania: Dowden, Hutchinson, and Ross.

Steinfeld, E., Schroeder, S. and Bishop, M. (1979). *Accessible buildings for people with walking and reaching limitations.* Washington, D.C.: U.S. Department of Housing and Urban Development.

Streib, G.F. (1980). *Alternative living arrangements for the elderly: A research study.* Florida: University of Florida, Center for Gerontological Studies and Department of Sociology.

Struyk, R.J. (1980). *The demand for specially adapted housing for elderly-headed households.* No. 3014–01, Washington, D.C.: Urban Institute Press.

Struyk, R. (1982). *The demand for specially adapted housing by elderly-headed households.* (The Urban Institute, Project Report No. 3014–10). Washington, D.C.: U.S. Government Printing Office.

Struyk, R. (1986). "Future housing assistance policy for the elderly." In R.J. Newcomer, M.P. Lawton and T.O. Byerts (eds.), *Housing an aging society.*

Struyk, R. and Soldo, B. (1980). *Improving the elderly's housing: A key to preserving the nations' housing stock and neighborhood.* MA: Ballinger Publishing Company.

Struyk, R. and Zais, I. (1982). *Providing special dwelling features for the elderly with health and mobility problems.* Washington, D.C.: The Urban Institute.

Swedish Planning and Rehabilitation Institute (SPRI) (1978, June). Interview with the Office of Planning and Organization SPRI of Health and Social Services: Stockholm.

Teaff, J.D., Lawton, M.P., Nahemow, L. and Carlson, D. (1978). "Impact of age integration on the well-being of elderly tenants in public housing." *Journal of Gerontology, 33*(1), 126–133.

Toseland, R. and Rasch, J. (1978). "Factors contributing to older persons' satisfaction with their communities." *The Gerontologist, 18,* 395–402.

Tolman, E. (1948). "Cognitive maps in rats and men." *Psychological Review, 55,* 189–208.

Treas, J. (1977). "Family support systems for the aged: Some social and demographic considerations." *The Gerontologist, 17,* 486–491.

Uhlenberg, P. (1977). "Changing structure of the older population of the United States of America during the twentieth century." *The Gerontologist, 17,* 197–202.

United Nations Economic Commission for Europe, Belgium and the Netherlands. Committee on Housing, Building, and Planning (1968 October). *Housing for the elderly.* Proceedings of the Colloquium organized by the Committee on Housing, Building and Planning.

United States Bureau of the Census (1976). "Demographic aspects of aging and the older population in the United States." *Current population report* (Series PC-23, No. 59). Washington, D.C.: U.S. Government Printing Office.

United States Department of Commerce (1970). *Block Statistics.* Memphis Urbanized Area, Tennessee, Bureau of Census.

United States Department of Education Office of Special Education and Rehabilitative Services, Improving the deaf person's environment. (1980). *American Rehabilitation, 5*(5), 12–13.

United States Department of Health and Human Services (1981). Working papers on long-term care of the task force on long-term care. (DHHS Publication No. 341-155/144.) Washington, D.C.: U.S. Government Printing Office.

United States Department of Health Education and Welfare. (1979). *Health people: The surgeon general's report on health promotion and disease prevention.* USDHEW Publication No. 79–55071. Washington, D.C.: U.S. Government Printing Office.

United States Department of Housing and Urban Development (1967). *Minimum property standards.* Washington, D.C.: U.S. Department of Housing and Urban Development.

United States Department of Housing and Urban Development (1973). *Minimum property standards, multifamily housing, Vol. 2.* Washington, D.C.: U.S. Department of Housing and Urban Development.

United States Department of Housing and Urban Development (1976). *Federally-assisted congregate housing development for the elderly.* Washington, D.C.: Department of Housing and Urban Development.

United States Department of Housing and Urban Development (1979). *Annual housing survey: 1973, housing characteristics of older Americans in the United States* (HUD Publication No. 501-1-PDR). Washington, D.C.: U.S. Department of Housing and Urban Development, Office of Policy Development and Research.

United States Department of Housing and Urban Development (1979). *Barrier free design.* Washington, D.C.: U.S. Government Printing Office.

United States Public Health Service (1980). *Health, United States with prevention profile.* (DHHS Publication No. PHS 81–1232). Hyattsville, MD: U.S. Department of Health and Human Services.

United States Senate, Special Committee on Aging, 98th Congress, 2nd Session (1984). *Section 202 housing for the elderly and handicapped: A national survey.* Washington, D.C.: U.S. Government Printing Office.

Urban Institute (1975). *Report of the comprehensive service needs study.* Washington, D.C.: The Urban Institute.

Urban Land Institute (1983). *Housing for a maturing population.* Washington, D.C.: ULI.

Urban Systems Research and Engineering (1976). *Evaluation of the Effectiveness of congregate housing for the elderly.* Washington, D.C.: United States Department of Housing and Urban Development.

Vygotsky, L.S. (1978). *Mind in society.* Massachusetts: Harvard University Press.

Walsh, D., Krauss, I. and Regnier, V. (1981). "Spatial ability, environmental knowledge and environmental use: The elderly." In L. Liben, A. Patterson and N. Newcombe (eds.), *Spatial representation and behavior across the life span.* New York: Academic Press.

Walter, F. (1971). *Four architectural movement studies for the wheelchair and ambulant disabled.* London: Disabled Living Foundation.

Wardell, K.T. (1980). "Environmental modifications." In R.W. Welsh and B.B. Blasch (eds.), *Foundations of orientation and mobility.* New York: American Foundation for the Blind.

Weale, R. (1963). *The aging eye.* New York: Harper and Row.

Weber, R., Brown, L. and Weldon, J. (1978). "Cognitive maps of environmental knowledge and preference in nursing home patients." *Environmental Aging Research, 4,* 157–174.

Weidemann, S. and Anderson, J.R. (1980). September. *Post-occupancy evaluation: Multifamily housing.* Paper presented at the American Psychological Association Annual convention, Montreal, Canada.

Weidemann, S., Anderson, J., O'Donnell, P. and Butterfield, D. (1981). *Resident safety: Research and recommendations for Longview Place anti-crime program.* Illinois: Housing Research and Development Program.

Weiner, B. (1975). "Industrial designers response to corridor disorientation and the geriatric walker." In M. Bednar et al. (eds.), *Environment and aging: Concepts and issues.* Washington, D.C.: Gerontological Society.

Weisman, G. (1979). "Way-finding in the built environment: A study in architectural legibility." (Unpublished doctoral dissertation, University of Michigan, 1979).

Weisman, G. (1981). "Evaluating architectural legibility: Wayfinding in the built environment." *Environment and Behavior, 13,* 189–204.

Weisman, G. (1982a). "Developing man-environment models." In M.P. Lawton, P. Windley and T. Byerts (eds.), *Aging and the environment: Theoretical approaches.* New York: Springer.

Weisman, G. (1982b). "Modeling environment-behavior systems: A brief note." *Journal of Man Environment Relations, 1,* 32–41.

Weiss, A.D. (1976). "Auditory perception in relation to age." In J.E. Birren, R.N. Butler, S.W. Greenhouse, L. Sokoloff, and M.R. Yarrow (eds.), *Human aging I.: A biological and behavioral study.* Washington, D.C.: National Institute of Mental Health.

Weissert, W.G. (1981). *Long-term care: Current policy and directions for the 80's.* Paper presented at the 1981 White House Conference on Aging. Washington, D.C.: The Urban Institute.

Welch, P., Parker, V. and Zeisel, J. (1984). *Independence through Interdependence.* Boston: Building Diagnostics.

Welsh, R.L. and Blasch, B.B. (eds.) (1980). *Foundations of orientation and mobility.* New York: American Foundation for the Blind.

Wener, R. (1983). *Selis Manor: A post occupancy evaluation of an apartment house for the blind.* New York: Brooklyn Polytechnic Institute.

Wener, R. and Kaminoff, R. (1979). "Environmental clarity and perceived crowding." In A. Seidel and S. Danford (eds.), *Environmental design: Research, theory and application.* Washington, D.C.: Environmental Design Research Association.

White House Conference on Aging, 3rd, Washington, D.C., 1981. Mini-Conference on Vision and Aging (1981). *Vision and aging.* Washington, D.C.: U.S. Government Printing Office.

Whyte, W. (1980). *Social life of small urban spaces.* New York: Conservation Foundation.

Wilcocks, A. (1972). *A Critical review: Role of the warden in grouped housing.* London: Report of a Working Party, Age Concern.

Willems, E.P. (1977). "Behavioral ecology." In D. Stokols (ed.), *Perspectives on environment and behavior: Theory, research and applications.* New York: Plenum.

Windley, P. and Scheidt, R. (1980). "Person-environment dialectics: Implications for competent functioning in old age." In L. Poon (ed.), *Aging in the 1980's: Psychological issues*. Washington, D.C.: American Psychological Association.

Winer, M. (1978). "A course on resources for the newly blind." *Journal of Visual Impairment and Blindness, 72*(8), 311–315.

Wittels, I. and Botwinick, J. (1974). "Survival in relocation." *Journal of Gerontology, 29*, 440–443.

Wood, P. (1980). "A survey of behavior in fires." In D. Canter (ed.), *Fires and human behavior*. London: John Wiley and Sons Ltd.

Woodruff, D. and Birren, J. (1975). *Aging: Scientific perspectives and social issues*. New York: Van Nostrand Co.

Wright, J. (1947). "Terrae incognitae: The place of imagination in geography." *Annals of the Association of American Geographers, 37*, 1–15.

Yeadon, A. and Grayson, D. (1979). *Living with impaired vision: An introduction*. New York: American Foundation for the Blind.

Zais, I., Struyk, P. and Thibodew, T. (1982). *Housing assistance for older Americans*. Washington, D.C.: Urban Institute.

Zeisel, J. (1975). *Sociology and architectural design*. New York: Russell Sage Foundation.

Zeisel, J. (1981). *Inquiry by design. Tools for environment-behavior research*. CA: Brooks/Cole.

Zeisel, J., Epp, G. and Demos, S. (1977). *Low-rise housing for older people: Behavioral criteria for design* (HUD Publication No. 483). Washington, D.C.: U.S. Government Printing Office.

Zeisel, J. and Griffin, M. (1975). *Charlesview housing: A diagnostic evaluation*. Massachusetts: Harvard University Press, Architectural Research Office.

Zeisel, J., Welch, P., Epp, G. and Demos, S. (1983). *Mid-rise elevator housing for older people*. Boston, MA: Building Diagnostics.

Zimbardo, P.G. and Andersen, S.M. (1981). "Induced hearing deficit generates experimental paranoia." *Science, 212*(26), 1529–1531.

Zimring, C. (1981). "Stress and the designed environment." *Journal of Social Issues, 37*, 145–171.

INDEX

Page numbers followed by *f* indicate figures; page numbers followed by *t* indicate tables.

Human needs, designing for, 373
Hyperthermia, 22
Hypothermia, 22

I

Inactivity. *See also* Mobility, limited
    spatial disorientation and, 441–442
Insulation, 148
Interpretation, of environmental information, 379–
    380, 380f
Inventory, environmental, 355

J

J.G. Furniture Company, Geriatric Personal
    Furnishings System, 386–393
Journal of Housing for the Elderly, The, 105

K

Kitchen
    as accident site, 280
    design, 100
        cabinet height, 114, 130
        in congregate housing, 217, 218t, 219f, 381–382
        counter heights, 323–325, 324f, 327, 329
        disabled-accessible, 309, 323–325, 324f, 327,
            328, 329, 331f, 332–334
        in private homes, 264t
        in public housing, 64–65, 66f, 100, 114, 130
        design adaptations, 290–291t, 292f, 297, 309, 323–
            325, 324f, 327, 328, 329, 331f, 332–334
        design problems, 375
        wheelchair access, 325, 327, 332–333
Kneeling ability, of disabled, 322
Kuhn, Maggie, 18

L

Lamps, 345f
    halogen, 357
    touch-on, 357
Landing, 7, 7f
Landmark recognition, in way-finding, 425, 431–
    432, 433–434, 436, 437, 443–445, 444f
    by color coding, 437
    visual distinctiveness and, 452
Landscaping. *See also* Outdoor areas
    of public housing sites, 92, 111, 129
    as way-finding aid, 147
Laundry facilities
    in public housing, 63, 110f, 113–114, 129
    in residential housing, 192t, 193
Lay-warden concept, 258
    neighborhood-type, 250–251
    resident-type, 237, 244–249, 252–253
    role, 231, 237, 244–249, 252–253
    support services and, 252–253
    training, 246, 247–249
    in United Kingdom, 231, 237, 244–249, 252–253
    in United States, 249–251
Lever door handle, 11, 11f

Libraries
    in congregate housing, 214, 214t
    in public housing facilities, 68
    public housing tenants' use of, 116, 117
    in residential housing, 189t, 190
Life satisfaction, of public housing residents, 28,
    50–51
Lifting ability, of disabled, 322
Light switch adaptations, 264t
Lighting
    as accident cause, 279, 280, 289
    design directives, 362–363
    Geriatric Personal Furnishings System, 389, 390
    glare, 343f, 344, 345
        control, 9, 11, 345f, 347f, 355f, 363–364, 365,
            396, 416
        in nursing homes, 403, 404f, 405f, 406f
    for kitchens, 100
    lamps, 345f, 357
    outdoor, 144, 150, 189t
    requirements of elderly, 362t
    on staircases, 279, 280
    technological advances, 357
    for visually impaired, 9–11, 10f, 343f, 344, 345,
        347f, 355f, 357, 362–364
        research needs regarding, 370
Limousine service, 214, 214t
Living room
    as accident site, 280, 289
    design adaptations, 290–291t, 292
Lobby, 124, 124f, 125
    design directives, 171–172
    glare control, 403, 406f
    lack of privacy, 67, 172
    "lobby sitter" problem, 67
    management policy regarding, 84
    in residential housing, 189t, 190
Loneliness, 54
Longevity, of public housing residents, 28, 56–57
Long-term care, 36–39, 37f. *See also* Nursing homes
Lounge, 412
    underutilization, 7–8
Low vision services, 348
Low-rise buildings, for public housing, 108f, 109f
    residents' satisfaction with, 112, 129, 136

M

Mail delivery, 63, 89
Mailbox, 326
Maintenance
    housing satisfaction and, 5, 6, 142–144, 149
    pathways, 111
Management. *See also* Policy considerations
    design intention understanding of, 8, 9
    policy considerations, 151–152
    of public housing, 84–85, 125–126
    resident satisfaction and, 5, 6, 8–9, 8f, 33–34, 33f,
        133–134, 142
Management-tenant relationship, 84
Meal service. *See also* Dining
    in congregate housing, 210, 214, 214t
    at public housing facilities, 72, 74
    in residential housing, 192, 192t, 197, 197f

Medical services
    in congregate housing, 210, 214, 214t, 216, 218t,
        220t, 221, 223, 225
    in public housing, 31f, 68, 72–73, 97, 126–127, 132
        design directives, 76
    in residential housing, 192, 192t, 196
Mental function, environmental effects on, 342
Microenvironment, 377–382
Mid-rise buildings, for public housing, 108f, 110f
Mirrors, 191
Mobility, limited
    barrier-free environment and, 380, 381f
    health problems and, 261–264, 262t, 264t, 267
    housing adaptations and, 259–275
    percentage of elderly, 331
    of sensory-impaired elderly, 342, 345, 346, 349t
Moderately impaired elderly
    number of households, 262t, 263
    percentage of total population, 260
    supportive housing
        congregate housing, 207–226
        housing adaptations, 259–303
        residential housing, 179–205
        sheltered housing, 227–258
Monitors, for security, 96f
Morale, of public housing residents, 28, 50–51
Mortality rate
    accident-related, 278, 280
    relocation-related, 421, 422, 424, 451
    in residential housing, 197
Mortgage, annuity, 36
Multiphasic Environmental Assessment Procedure
        (MEAP), 180–197
    daily activities assistance, 192–193, 192t, 196–197
    orientational aids, 189t, 190, 196, 197
    Physical and Architectural Features Checklist,
        182, 182f, 184, 188, 204
    Policy and Program Information Form, 182–184,
        183f, 184, 188, 204
    preference measurement development, 187–188
    prosthetic aids, 188, 189t, 190, 196, 197
    recreational activities, 189t, 190–191, 192t, 193,
        196, 197
    resident control, 193–195, 193t, 201
    safety features, 188, 189t, 190, 196, 197, 198
    social environment, 190–191, 190t, 196–197
Music, background, 395

N

National Council on Aging, 353
National Health Interview Survey, 284
Negotiation, of movement, 380, 381f
Neighborhood
    deterioration, 93–94
    importance, 30
    quality, 8
    resident satisfaction and, 135
    supportive services, 21
    surrounding public housing, 77
        residents' lack of adjustment, 69–70
Neighborhood Housing Services, 34
Noise, recreational activity-related, 68

Noise control, 11, 357, 358, 358f, 361f, 389
    design directives, 366–367, 394
    insulation for, 148
Nurses, as sheltered housing wardens, 248
Nursing homes
    congregate housing on-site, 214, 214t
    design directives, 394–397, 416–418, 417f, 418f
    design innovation evaluation, 399–420
        atrium, 405, 406f
        corridors, 405, 406f, 407, 408, 417
        glare control, 403, 404f, 405f, 406f
        home range increase, 410–415, 411t, 419–420
        mealtime activities, 411–412, 412t
        nurses' station, 405f
        recreational areas, 407, 407f
        related research, 401
        for way-finding, 403–410
    fires in, 442
    furniture design, 378, 382–398
        Geriatric Personal Furnishings System, 386–393
    microenvironmental design, 377–398
    percentage of elderly population in, 342
    policy considerations, 419–420
    residents' personal control in, 381–382
    sensory-impaired elderly in, 342–343

O

Orientational aids. *See* Way-finding, aids
Osmond Plan, 449
Outdoor activities
    accidents related to, 282
    at public housing facilities, 111
Outdoor areas. *See also* Gardens
    aesthetics of, 134, 142–144, 145–147, 149
    future design research regarding, 22
    as home-like environment, 145–146, 146f
    lighting, 144, 150
    personalization, 146–147, 146f
    privacy and, 142, 145
    at public housing facilities, 61–62, 62f, 111
        outdoor seating, 117, 118–119f, 120–121, 120f
        private, 88, 89f
        public, 89–94, 89f, 91f, 93f, 94f, 101
    in sheltered housing, 247f
Oven, 281f, 325, 327, 334
    counter-top, 291t, 292, 297

P

Paralysis, 262t, 263
Parking facilities
    for handicapped, 189t, 190
    resident satisfaction with, 143, 149
    for residential housing, 189t
Parks, 116, 117
Pathways
    dual, 364
    indiscriminate, 145
    maintenance cost, 111
    privacy and, 145–146, 148
    way-finding function, 425, 444, 445
        simulated site visits, 454–456
Patios, 88, 101